Enhancing adult basic learning

Enhancing adult basic learning

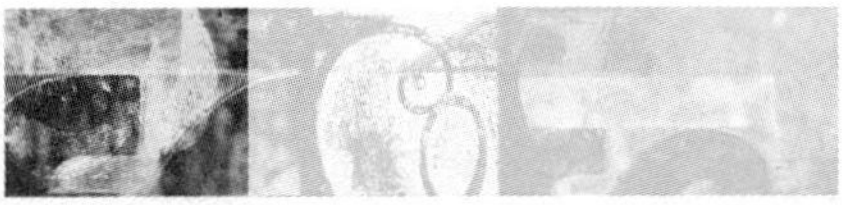

Training educators and unlocking the potential of distance and open learning

Edited by Madhu Singh and Veronica McKay

Adult Basic Education and Training
University of South Africa

UNESCO

UNESCO Institute for Education

UNISA PRESS
University of South Africa Press

University of South Africa, Pretoria

First edition, first impression

ISBN 92-820-1135-6

Published by UNESCO Institute for Education
Feldbrunnenstr 58, 20148, Hamburg, Germany
and
Unisa Press, University of South Africa
PO Box 392, Unisa 0003

ABC Press, Epping
Cover and layout design: Doris Hyman, Unisa Press

CONTENTS

Preface ix
Abbreviations and acronyms x
Acknowledgements xiii
List of contributors xv

Introduction 1

1 Improving the quality of adult basic learning and training adult educators 1
Madhu Singh and Veronica McKay

SECTION I

Country studies 29

2 Approaches to training grassroots level workers in literacy and adult basic education: The Indian scenario 31
S Y Shah

3 Training initiatives in the field of adult basic education in Tanzania: Exploring the potential of open and distance learning . . . 69
Nderikyo Elizabeth Ligate

4 Methods of distance education for training adult educators in South Africa 108
Veronica McKay

5 How are training policies responding to training needs in Nigeria . . 139
Gidado Tahir

6 An NGO perspective on training grassroots facilitators in literacy and adult basic education in Bangladesh 163
Harun ur Rashid and ANS Habibur Rahman

SECTION II

The relevance of training in the framework of international development goals 189

7 Can open, distance and flexible learning assist with adult basic education? Pursuing the concept of quality in the context of education for all . . . 191
Christopher Yates

8 Open learning in basic education for adults and the contribution of international co-operation . . . 223
Wim Hoppers

SECTION III

Diversity in institutional arrangements and partnerships for effective delivery of training programs 239

9 The solidarity in literacy programme: A strategy for literacy training for the youths and adults of Brazil . . . 241
Regina Célia Vasconcelos Esteves

10 Open and distance learning: Training and support for adult educators in the field . . . 261
Tony Dodds

11 The certificate in education for development: A direct response to the training needs of adult literacy promoters, agricultural extension and community development workers . . . 273
Frances J Mensah

12 Adult educators' training in Egypt . . . 283
Mohsen Kamal Abu Seif

13 Training of local government councillors in Tanzania mainland: A case study . . . 287
Nderikyo Elizabeth Ligate

14 Partnerships in distance education for youth and adult educators . . . 298
F Benito Fernández

15 Networking among organisations involved in training adult education specialists . . . 304
Wolfgang Leumer

SECTION IV

Implications of technology for literacy, open learning and information networking 323

16 The use of communication technology for literacy . . . 325
Anita Dighe

17 ICTs and open and distance learning for training trainers in the context of the labour market and lifelong learning in Central America . . . 336
Peter Gerasch

18 Professional backup to adult educators through networking resources using technology and media . . . 352
Vitalicy Chifwepa

SECTION V

Some reflections on adult basic learning from South Africa 363

19 Unisa and how it has pioneered distance education . . . 365
M S Makhanya

20 Monitoring for quality in a mass literacy programme . . . 379
Elijah Sekgobela

Index . . . 385

Preface

With increasing numbers of adults and young people needing basic education, it is apparent that traditional or conventional modes of education have been unable to satisfy learning needs – both explicit and implicit. It is in this context that basic educational programmes need to embrace open and distance learning among its repertoire for meeting mass educational demands. This book makes a significant intervention: international in scope, and drawing upon real cases from different social contexts, the volume outlines different endeavours to reach the cross-sectoral learning demands made on the educational sector. The book highlights models of distance and open learning capable of satisfying individual and collective learning aspirations. It draws attention to the way in which open and distance learning may, and has been used as a vehicle for breaching the gap left where conventional modes of education failed to provide basic quality education for all the world's citizens. The book has a wide variety of applications. It should be of value to governments and policy makers in the formulation of strategies, and to academics and educational managers in the field of distance and/or basic education who will undoubtedly find that the book makes a valuable contribution. The authors are to be applauded for documenting their experiences in basic learning for adults and young people – an area of education which is often overlooked as deserving rigorous academic attention. This book thus takes us all one step closer to realising our vision of providing quality education for all. Moreover, the project has demonstrated the close and productive co-operation between the UNESCO Institute for Education, Hamburg and the UNISA Institute for Adult Basic Education and Training.

Dr Adama Ouane
Director
UNESCO Institute
for Education

Prof Barney Pityana
Principal and Vice Chancellor
University of South Africa

Abbreviations and acronyms

ABE	Adult Basic Education
ABET	Adult Basic Education and Training
ADB	Asian Development Bank
ALAT	Local Authorities of Tanzania
ANC	African National Congress
AMREF	Adapted Africa Medical Research foundation
APPEAL	Asia Pacific Programme of Education for All
BARD	Bangladesh Academy for Rural Development
BEMP	Basic Education Master Plan
BGVS	*Bharat Gyan Vigyan Samithi* (Indian Education and Science Organisation)
BRAC	Bangladesh Rural Advancement Committee
CAMPE	Campaign for Popular Education
CBO	Community-based organisation
CCDB	Christian Commission for Development in Bangladesh
CC-DFE	Co-operative College, Moshi, Directorate of Field Education
CEDHA	Centre for Education Development in Health
CFTC	Commonwealth Fund for Technical Support
CHOGM	Commonwealth Heads of Government Meeting
CLGF	Commonwealth Local Government Forum
COMSEC	Commonwealth Secretariat
CEC	Co-operative Education Centre
CONFITEA	International Conference on Adult Education
COSATU	Congress of South African Trade Unions
DAM	Dhaka Ahsania Mission
DE	Distance Education
DFID	Department for International Development
DNFE	Directorate of Non-Formal Education
DoE	Department of Education (South Africa)
EDF	Economic Development Fund
EFA	Education for All
EMAU	Elimu ya Malezi ya Ujana (Youth Education Programme)
ETDP	Education Training Development Practice (or Practititoners)
EU	European Union
FED	Field Extension Department
FIVDB	Friends in Village Development, Bangladesh
GCE	General Certificate of Education

GER	Growth Enrolment Rate
HESAWA	Health Through Sanitation and Water
HRD	Human Resource Development
IAE	Institute of Adult Education
IEC	International Extension College
IFTZ	INADES – Formation Tanzania
IGNOU	Indira Gandhi National Open University came into existence on September 20, 1985 in New Delhi. It offers 240 courses ranging from PhD to certificates.
IIZ/DVV	Institute for International Co-operation of The German Adult Education Association
INADES	French Acronym for The African Institute for Economic and Social Development. (Institut Africain le Development Economique et Social)
INFEP	Integrated Non-Formal Education Programme
JSS	*Shikshan Sansthan* (Institute of People Education), India
KRP	Key resource persons.
LGM	Learner Generated Materials
MEP	Mass Education Programme
MCHA	Maternal Child Health Aid
MLY & SD	Ministry of Labour Youth and Sports Development
MNRT	Ministry of National Resources and Tourism
MS	*Mahila Samakhya*, India
MT	Master trainers train voluntary instructors. They are at the level of headmasters, supervisors and school inspectors.
MOEC	Ministry of Education and Culture
NCI	National Correspondence Institution
NECTA	National Examinations Council of Tanzania
NEPI	National Education Policy Investigation, South Africa
NGO	Non Governmental Organisation
NOS	National Open School.
NQF	National Qualifications Framework
OUT	Open University of Tanzania
PAC	Pan African Congress
PMO	Prime Minister's Office
RLM	Real Literacy Materials
RP	Resource persons, India They are generally lecturers or programme officers.
RTD	Radio Tanzania Dar es Salaam
SA	South Africa
SACCOS	Savings and Credit Co-operative Societies
SAEU	Southern African Extension Unit

SANLI	South African National Literacy Initiative
SAQA	South African Qualifications Authority
SETA	Sector Education and Training Authority
SRC	State Resource Centres.
TAMWA	Tanzania Media Women Association
TGNP	Tanzania Gender Network Programme
TLM	Total Literacy Movement
TNA	Training Needs Assessment
TOT	Training of Trainers
TRC	Teachers Resource Centre
ToR	Terms of Reference
TV	Television
UEWs	Universal Education Workers
UIE	UNESCO Institute of Education
UMATI	Uzazi na Malezi Bora Tanzania (Family Planning Services)
UNESCO	United Nations Education and Scientific Cultural Organisation
UNHCR	United Nations High Commissioner for Refugees
UPE	Universal Primary Education
URT	United Republic of Tanzania
V-AID	Village Agricultural and Industrial Development
VERC	Village Education Resource Centre
VIPP	Visualised in Participatory Planning
ZSS	*Zilla Saksharta Samithi* District Literacy Committee, India

Acknowledgements

We acknowledge the work of the various authors whose work in the field of adult and basic education and the areas of distance education have made such a book possible. We are indebted to Yvonne Kemp of UNISA for her editorial assistance, and to Barbara Payne of DFID (SA) for supporting the project.

And finally, we wish to dedicate this book to our children Anja Singh and Patrick and John McKay who, as always, have been a constant source of support to us.

Madhu Singh and Veronica McKay

List of Contributors

Mr Vitalicy Chifwepa is a Senior Lecturer in Information and Library Studies, University of Zambia, Lusaka, Zambia.

Prof Anita Dighe is the Director, Campus of Open Learning, University of Delhi, India.

Prof Tony Dodds (UK) is a consultant in France.

Mrs Regina Célia Vasconcelos Esteves is the Executive Superintendent of the Association for the Support of Solidarity in Literacy, Brasília, Brazil.

Mr F Benito Fernández is a representative of the Institute for International Co-operation of the German Adult Education Association (DVV/IIZ), Bolivia.

Mr Peter Gerasch is Director and sector Co-ordinator, Economic Development and Employment Promotion of the German International Co-operation, Managua, Nicaragua.

Dr Wim Hoppers is at the Royal Netherlands Embassy, Pretoria and the University of the Witwatersrand, Johannesburg, South Africa.

Mr Wolfgang Leumer is the Project Director at the The Institute for International Co-operation of the German Adult Education Association (DVV/IIZ) Cape Town, South Africa.

Ms Nderikyo Elizabeth Ligate is the Executive Director, Southern Africa Extention Unit, Dar-es-Salaam, Tanzania.

Prof Mandla Makhanya is Dean of the Faculty of Humanities, University of South Africa and Chair of the UNESCO Commission, South Africa.

Prof Veronica McKay is Director, Adult Basic Education and Training, University of South Africa, Pretoria, South Africa.

Mr Sekgobela is currently a senior lecturer at the Institute for Adult Basic Education and Training, University of South Africa, in Pretoria, South Africa.

Dr Frances J Mensah is the Director, Namibian College of Open Learning, Windhoek, Namibia.

Mr Harun ur Rashid is the Head, Universal Education Programme and Deputy Director PROSHIKA, Dhaka, Bangladesh.

Mr A N S Habibur Rahman is the Head Development Cell and Deputy Director, PROSHIKA, Dhaka, Bangladesh.

Mr Mohsen Kamal Abu Seif is the Director, Office of Civil Society Strengthening and promotion (OCSSP). NGO service Centre, Cairo, Egypt.

Prof S Y Shah is the Director, Group of Adult Education, School of Social Sciences, Jawaharlal Nehru University, New Delhi, India.

Dr Ms Madhu Singh is a Senior Research Specialist, UNESCO Institute for Education, Hamburg, Germany.

Prof Gidado Tahir is the National Co-ordinator of the Universal Basic Education Programme, Abuja, Nigeria.

Dr Chris Yates is Education Co-ordinator, International Extension College, Cambridge, United Kingdom.

1

Introduction

Improving the quality of adult basic learning and training adult educators

Madhu Singh and Veronica McKay

This book is a collective contribution by its writers towards improving the quality of adult basic learning and literacy by focusing on the training of adult educators and grassroots workers. The book has evolved through a participatory process. In order to gain an understanding of the current state of training for adult educators and grassroots workers, the UNESCO Institute for Education conducted a five-country study in Bangladesh, Nigeria, India, Tanzania and South Africa. This was discussed at a meeting held in Pretoria from 7 to 9 January 2003 by a group of practitioners who, either wholly or partially, use distance and open learning as a vehicle for the professional development of adult educators. The studies and the expert meeting examined factors that influence quality adult learning and educator training, such as policies, institutional contexts, delivery methods, training methodologies and curriculum, networking, research and evaluation as well as the role of media and new information technologies.

The aim of this introduction is to provide a background to the context of adult basic learning. It points to developments at the international level that have promoted a vision of basic education as a lifelong, multisectoral and diverse process capable of enhancing the personal and social life worlds of citizens whose critical thinking abilities will have been engaged by the process. Literacy is fundamental to this process. An important stance emerging from the papers in this volume is that open and distance learning can play a powerful role in energising this process.

The context

The World Education Forum held in Dakar in April 2000 committed itself to halving adult illiteracy levels, which stood at 860 million in 2000 (UNESCO 2002), by 2015 (UNESCO 2000 par 7). While some progress has been made, absolute figures still remain very high. The Asian region has 614 million illiterate adolescents and adults. In South Asia alone there are 429 million adults who are categorised as 'illiterates'. In Africa the absolute number of illiterate people stands at 182 million (aged 15 years and over) (UNESCO 2002) and in the sub-Saharan region there are 137 million illiterates (above 15 years). According to the latest statistics on the Arab States, there are about 70 million illiterate Arab people with women representing two-thirds of this figure. There is an alarming drop-out from basic education in these countries, resulting in 10 million Arab children not registered in formal basic education.

In the Latin American and Caribbean region, while literacy and basic education are close to universal, important gaps still remain, especially in reaching and educating marginalised groups. The parents of 80 per cent of urban youths fall short of the basic educational threshold required to access well-being levels (ECLAC 2000:101). A large majority of the gainfully employed population is not sufficiently educated to move beyond the income levels associated with the lower occupational categories (ECLAC 2000).

There are estimated to be 140 million youth in the world (86 million females) regarded as illiterate in 2000. It is estimated that the youth illiteracy situation (15-24 years) will be 107 million by 2015, of whom 67 million will be female, at the current rate of access to basic education (UNESCO 2002: 66).

Adult learning is more than literacy

While statistics on levels of literacy abound, the complexities surrounding these arise from the varying yardsticks used to measure and define literacy. Adults may be defined as being illiterate in the national language, but seldom do national surveys consider communicative practices of adults who do not speak the increasingly narrow range of official languages, as Yates points out in his contribution to this book. Street (cited in Prinsloo & Breier 1996) indicates in this regard that the standards employed are cultural artefacts defined by the West, which should not be regarded as universally given. He argues that it is uncertain how many so-called literates can actually be assumed to be functionally literate and are able to participate effectively in their communities. The most recent literacy studies of the social uses of literacy point to the view of many educators and policymakers who see literacy as a neutral skill – that literacy is the same everywhere. These studies stress that people need different literacies in differing contexts and that there is no standard measure that can be used to establish whether or not a person is literate. It is therefore argued that educational and policy decisions have to be based on prior judgements regarding which literacy to impart and why.

Adult basic learning is not just literacy. Adult literacy projects aim to enable adults to improve the skills and knowledge of people so that they can fully and effectively function in their daily lives and in their social contexts. They strive to engender human values of tolerance, gender justice and interculturality and to serve a range of social, economic and developmental roles. A fundamental aim of such projects is to build the dignity and self-esteem of the learner.

Youngman (1999:2) urges theorists in the field of adult education to ask questions about the role of adult education vis-à-vis our developmental expectations. He argues that it is assumed, for example, that an agricultural extension programme can improve agricultural production and food security and thereby reduce malnutrition; that skills training can strengthen income generating projects and help to eradicate poverty; and that literacy classes can increase women's involvement in public affairs and extend democratic participation. The expectation is, he says, that adult education programmes can therefore contribute to the economic, political and social dimensions of development in these ways. He warns, however, that we need to consider the extent to which adult education in the South is in fact capable of meeting these expectations. Research into the field of adult education consists mainly of descriptive accounts of adult educational activities and reports of evaluations. Youngman stresses the need for educationists and policymakers to be more theoretically rigorous and to clarify the historical structural constraints that limit our choices about adult education policies and programmes. He suggests, as an alternative to the atheoretical empiricism which prevails, that adult educators use the political economy approach to move the focus of analysis from individualised humanistic considerations towards the historical and structural context within which individual action takes place. It is necessary to highlight the constraints on human agency. In this regard, he argues that it is an important task for adult educators to analyse the determining factors in their situations so that their choices are well understood.

While Youngman (1999) rightly states that our analysis of the social context needs to be more theoretically rigorous, it is argued here that the debate as to what adult education 'is' or 'ought to be' cannot be rectified by the application of a rigorous definition or by positing that a specific analysis should be employed. McKay and Romm (1992:iv), in their endeavour to analyse adult and popular education in the nineties, also state that educators need to be more theoretically rigorous. However, they contend that all conceptions of education are either knowingly or unwittingly theoretical and tend to fall within the realms of either a *structuralist* or a *non-structuralist* paradigm. McKay (1990; 1994) and McKay and Romm (1992) propose that it is essential that educational discussions be located firmly within a non-structuralist paradigm which emphasises the capacity of human beings to reconceptualise the world around them. The non-structuralist position is based on the belief that to effect true liberation, it is necessary to offer a way to democratise the production of knowledge. It is therefore necessary to explore the link between knowledge and power and to explore and elaborate on an epistemological position that portrays knowledge as a world-construction activity. In this regard they propose a fusion of morality of the *non-realist,* critical Marxist tradition with the humanist's view of a symbolic ontology and voluntarist anthropology. This fusion gives rise to their label of *critical humanism.* They argue that the emancipatory potential of a model based on critical humanism is not accommodated in the educational models of economic or cultural reproduction.

What is needed is an alternative social analysis which breaks with the pessimistic view that it is with education that the social reproduction of class structure becomes inevitable. Such analyses, do not allow for the possibility of human participation in modelling social relationships and offer little scope for emancipation in the true sense. The meaning of production in terms of structural models tends to become commodified or reified as people forget the constructed and symbolic character of social reality, and this weakens the discursive character of society.

In emphasising the importance of human participation, McKay and Romm (1992) follow Gouldner (1980) who states that critical Marxism at its best is humanism. At its best it affirms human emancipation as its goal but does not pretend to have accomplished this emancipation. It is aware that it contains a repressive potential insofar as it poses as a source of moral authority and offers a fixed vision of what emancipation would entail. Gouldner (1980:70) indicates in this regard that 'the [critical Marxist] critique, therefore, aims at making human potency manifest; it is grounded in a humanism optimistically convinced that humanity can make and remake the world'.

Following Gouldner (1980), McKay and Romm (1992) argue that critical Marxism at its best links to a humanistic culture which recognises that contestation can occur and choices can be made on any level of society; it does not restrict discourse to class analysis and avoids positing a predefined vision of any societal arrangement. It does not, however, exclude the possibility of a class analysis but cautions against approaches being limited to all forms of domination in society – including the domination by experts who fail to allow for popular participation at the point of defining what society is and can be. Liberation is aimed at fostering a society where domination in the form of the suppression of discourse is averted and possibilities are not decided in advance by the theoreticians. Stressing the humanist component of the humanism/critical Marxism fusion highlights the symbolic ontology, thus allowing theorists and educationists to participate in debates about what adult education 'is' and what it 'ought to be'.

In agreement with Youngman (1999), McKay and Romm (1992) emphasise the importance of educators being theoretically literate in order to analyse the social contexts of their work. This of necessity requires a deeper understanding of the ontological and epistemological assumptions that inform policies and practices. This understanding will not be obtained by chance, it is a competency which needs to be factored into the professional training of adult educators.

Relevance of adult learning and educator training in the framework of international development goals

Several important initiatives, which directly affect educator training, have been taken in the international policy arena. One major such initiative has been UNESCO's promotion, in alliance with other partners, of adult learning and its provision of support to improve practices and methodologies. To understand the issues and stimulate dialogue, UNESCO has convened a number of international conferences. *The 5th International Conference on Adult Education (CONFINTEA V)* was particularly significant in that it took place within the context of an intensifying process of globalisation. CONFINTEA V proposed a vision of adult learning which cut across a variety of sectors and was firmly rooted in a framework of human development and social justice comprising elements such as democracy, critical citizenship, cultural diversity, social inclusion, human rights, peace and gender equality. The final outcome of the conference, expressed in the *Hamburg Declaration* and the *Agenda for the Future*, was a strong commitment to promoting the right of education and learning and the creation of a learning society. CONFINTEA V re-established the importance of adult education as an essential part of the education system and stressed the centrality of the adult learner and of learning as a lifelong process.

While the problems of adult education are complex and varied, the conference identified, within a range of quality indicators, the availability of competent personnel to develop, organise, promote, teach and evaluate modes of learning for adults as being fundamental to the successful implementation of adult education policies and programmes (UNESCO 1997). It stressed the importance of quality training that would enable adult educators to acquire the theoretical understanding, practical abilities and personal qualities needed to execute their roles.

Training adult educators is a neglected theme in deliberations on education in general and, more specifically, in educational policy. Governments and policies have tended to marginalise adult learning and the training of adult educators and the number of illiterates therefore increases on a daily basis, often without the legislative will for redress. In most developing countries there are huge numbers of literacy and basic education workers who need training, but due to the paucity of resources and limited expertise at the local level, only a small percentage of field practitioners get trained. The training is sometimes reduced to knowledge transmission guided by the instructor and not conceived of as multi-dimensional, interactive, participative and learner-centred. Since some of the countries adopt the top-down training approach based on the trickle-down theory, considerable transmission loss occurs. Often training programmes are conducted in an ad hoc and superficial manner, and literacy workers and educators of adults remain ill equipped to meet their challenges and professional commitments. There is a real need to improve the quality of literacy and non-formal education for adults and young people and it is important for policymakers to think of new approaches to training adult educators and literacy workers.

An overview of international experience shows there is general agreement that quality training of teaching personnel is a neglected aspect of adult basic education programmes and that it has not been integral to the planning of adult education. The UNESCO Institute for Education, reviewing training activities in a number of developing countries, describes many of the training programmes for adult educators as a mere ritual and their contribution to the professional growth of personnel involved as minimal (NEPI 1992).

The role of adult and non-formal education in achieving basic education for all

The second major initiative at the international level is the agreement on a number of key goals for education systems and policy laid down by the *Dakar Framework for Action* (UNESCO 2000). Among the six goals set up in Dakar, two address priority themes and areas of adult learning. These are: Goal 3 – ensuring that the learning needs of all young people and adults are met through equitable access to appropriate learning and life-skills programmes; and Goal 4 – achieving a 50 per cent improvement in levels of adult literacy by 2015, especially for women, and equitable access to basic and continuing education for all.

CONFINTEA V is gaining new relevance in the context of the commitments and resolves made in Dakar by the states and community of nations in favour of basic education as a foundation to learning throughout life. It is important for adult education to engage with the Dakar goals, because investing in quality education for children cannot be achieved without investing in quality education for adults and vice versa. Furthermore, as Hoppers in his contribution to this book maintains, with its integrative perspective on learning opportunities, adult education can be a major force in opening up the mainstream and working towards an integrated and more diverse yet in principle equitable system of basic education. The big challenge therefore is to articulate adult basic learning with the Education for All national plans.

Adult learning in the context of lifelong learning

A third major policy initiative is placing the work on the common objectives for education and training systems more clearly within the context of lifelong learning as an overarching principle. This means that learning should not be limited to a specific sector. If one looks at the various phases of learning throughout life, one sees that certain of these have tended to be undervalued and under-resourced. Adult education is one of these. Yet adult learning is absolutely vital if our commitment to lifelong learning is to be more than mere rhetoric. The idea of lifelong learning is to create multiple opportunities for adults to learn throughout life. It involves crossing the current boundaries of formal, non-formal and informal learning and integrating basic education as the foundational part of lifelong learning. In order to be innovative and inclusive, learning and education strategies must move beyond conventional education frameworks to comprehend all the places where learning is taking place – at work, in small enterprises, in the community, in trade unions and in social movements. By recognising and benefiting from the multiplicity of learning contexts, modalities, experiences and competencies – including multiple literacies – it will be possible to prevent social exclusion, as this approach respects and values people in their diversity, gives meaning to their backgrounds and experiences and empowers them to act.

Even the content of these multiple opportunities needs to be changed. In relation to lifelong learning we need to think of lifewide learning, which implies that other sectors and ministries than education (in health, agriculture, labour, social welfare), will also get involved in adult and lifelong learning programmes.

In the context of the *Millennium Development Goals* (United Nations 2000)adult learning provides a critical way of making local poverty reduction and economic development efforts – whether in agriculture, natural resource management, small enterprise or credit mediation – more participant driven, cost effective and locally self-managed and therefore more sustainable. The development of civil society and progressive democratisation of social institutions all require the means for imparting new skills and broader knowledge to leaders and constituents alike. Adult learning is central to this process. Similarly, public health promotion and, in particular, the effort to overcome the HIV/AIDs pandemic are arenas where necessary knowledge and skills and the active participation of adults in eradication efforts are absolutely essential.

Potential role of open and distance learning in adult learning and educator training

Through CONFINTEA V adult education has placed itself within the paradigm of the learning society and lifelong learning as an overarching principle of education and training systems. The *Hamburg Declaration* puts much emphasis on the basic principles of open learning, focusing on creativity, flexibility, diversity and responsiveness to diverse needs in the social, economic and cultural sphere. It is in this context that the authors of this volume examine the potential of open and distance learning in adult basic learning and educator training. Hoppers argues that open and distance learning implies not merely the use of media and ICTs. It is, he maintains, an approach to education. It not only removes constraints of time and space; it is also the means whereby teaching and learning are a response to the learning needs and circumstances of the learners, and actual choices are context specific.

Similarly, for Yates the concept of *open learning* could be more relevant than that of distance education. It may, he contends, be much more important to understand how forms of openness and flexibility are achieved and how the many and varied barriers to learning are reduced than to overcome spatial distance by learning how to transfer mass-produced texts. For Dodds, too, the addition of 'open' is essential. Any adult education programme must stress the opening up of education opportunities to all. It must use flexible delivery systems, including face-to-face communication and contact, and must have an organised learning structure. Dodds therefore sees open and distance learning as permitting expanded provision and improved quality, rather than as just a training approach or a delivery system.

The limited evidence that is available suggests that open and distance learning (ODL) can be very effective in creating a new system of non-formal education which complements what is done in the formal system. Coombs (1985:22) parallels the increasing use of open and distance learning with the interest in non-formal basic education that arose in the 1970s, when the formal educational systems of many developing countries, particularly in Africa, were crippled by economic recession and growing debt burdens. It became clear that a wide variety of non-formal learning activities using alternative modes would be required, especially to serve out-of-school youth and adults.

This view resonated at the 1990 *World Conference on Education for All* held in Jomtien, Thailand, which not only highlighted the importance of non-formal education but also provided global strategies for strengthening it. Article 5 of the *World Declaration on Education for All* calls for broadening the means and scope of basic education in order to address the stagnation and deterioration in educational provision. It states that the 'diversity, complexity and changing nature of basic learning needs of children, youth and adults necessitates broadening and constantly refining the scope of basic education' (WCEFA 1990:45). According to Perraton (2001), while the needs of adults were given renewed emphasis at Dakar, little work is reported 'either of education directly targeting the *adult audience* or the *extension agents* and *health workers* who work with large rural publics'. He suggests that more reporting needs to be done among adult educators who are involved as health workers or educators of adults in the area of HIV/AIDS, and in areas of non-formal education carried out by non-governmental organisations and Ministries other than the Ministry of Education.

Siaciwena (2000:16) and Dodds (1996:56) lament the gap in our knowledge and understanding of the use of open and distance education in literacy, non-formal and basic education programmes. They indicate that a considerable amount of non-formal education is being carried out around the world using distance teaching methods, but that these programmes are neither adequately documented nor analysed. This book is intended as one contribution towards remedying this lacuna. It provides a suite of case studies that document the extent to which distance education has been employed as a vehicle for, particularly, large-scale training of adult educators.

The method of open and distance learning

Current literature leaves little doubt as to the need to extend the reach of education and utilise ways of engaging in learning processes that stretch beyond present institutional settings, especially in the context of burgeoning technological advances.

In response to such needs, distance education and open learning are increasingly being included in the array of strategic educational solutions. Present-day distance education has its roots in early university correspondence and extension programmes designed to educate via text-based processes. In 1947, the University of South Africa pioneered its application of correspondence teaching for students at a distance (see Makhanya's chapter in this book). The British Open University followed suit in 1969 and one distance university was established about every two years thereafter. As Willis (1992:7) points out, media and communications technology – radio, TV and other emerging technologies – were rapidly incorporated to enhance these methods. McKay, in her chapter on the use of distance education to take adult educator training to scale in South Africa, states that given the lack of infrastructure and electrification in most rural areas, the Unisa ABET Institute had to resort to 'low tech' methods for training educators. While material was text led, local radio and audio cassettes were also used to supplement the teaching package. However, she argues that the face-to-face component provided by the tutors contributed significantly to the success of the teacher programmes since this allowed for customisation at a local level and for the establishment of tutorial groups and development brigades in even the most remote areas.

Distance learning in a developing world

Learning at a distance is becoming increasingly common in many countries and the increased use of distance education in the developing world has received much attention. In this regard, Perraton (1992:16) points out that distance education has been taken more seriously in the South than in the North.

Thus Tanzania has used a distance education radio campaign in adult education to teach people about political issues, health and the environment. Kenya has used distance education to provide the training required by 3 000 educators in its adult basic education programme. The Namibian College for Open Learning has trained almost 500 adult education facilitators using a mixed mode of educator training, and the University of South Africa has trained in excess of 37 000 adult basic education and training educators by using the methods of distance education. As Perraton (1992:16) observes, distance has been used in a number of countries in Africa on a scale that is proportionally far greater than in Europe and in America. On the other hand, Yates maintains, in his chapter, that adult basic learning using ODL methods has often failed to go to scale or achieve sustainable quality because the product-focused approach to distance education has not always proved successful in the developing country context, particularly when it is used as a 'go-alone' method. He argues for an approach that integrates mass media and smaller-scale group-based methods.

Distance education has many advantages over contact teaching, the most salient of which is that fewer teachers are able to reach large numbers of learners. Another characteristic to which Dodds refers in this publication is that learners can learn while they are employed and do not need to be removed from their productive activities while they study. Dodds points out, as well, that infrastructure costs are drastically reduced since distance education does not require building infrastructure such as schools or classrooms: learning takes place at a site chosen by the learner or in existing buildings. It is generally accepted that high costs are accrued at the outset but Dodds maintains that once courses are established the benefits of the economies of scale make it a relatively economical mode of education.

However, what makes distance education meaningful in the context of developing countries is not the method but its use. Dodds examines this question in his contribution and offers a number of recommendations to ensure that the method is used to best advantage. The chapter by Esteves shows that when distance learning is used as a pedagogical resource, as has been demonstrated in the Brazilian *Programa de Afabetización*, it can improve and reinforce the learning content. This ensures continuous training and expands the knowledge of literacy teachers on specific themes linked to regional popular culture and literature. Digital literacy and new informational technologies can be used to reduce exclusion by making literacy teachers and training providers familiar with resources offered by technology.

Chifwepa's chapter also examines the use of ICTs in developing countries. He maintains that it is by and large the simpler technologies, such as print and radio, that dominate and that print materials are still the most important medium in literacy and distance education. According to Chifwepa, the use of print materials should not be arbitrarily discarded in favour of the more advanced technologies, because print media will remain the most reliable tool for learner support.

Current state of adult educator's training: UIE country studies and expert meeting in Pretoria

The UIE studies on the training of adult educators examine a variety of factors that influence training. They examine the policies, the enabling and hindering factors in policy implementation and delivery, and the institutional contexts and processes that allow training to occur across sector. They deal with the outcomes of training curricula and the extent to which these are informed by local needs and promoted in the framework of sustainable development. The country studies also seek information about existing training capacity, the use of various media, and the application of distance and open learning and new information technologies in training interventions.

There are a variety of terms used to describe adult learning in the different countries – basic literacy, adult literacy, basic education, adult basic education and training, non-formal education, and so on. These variations accord with the various countries' policies. We have not, therefore, attempted to impose a standardised terminology in this volume, and have also retained specific authors' usage of the different terms used to designate those who do the teaching: adult educators, facilitators, literacy teachers, grassroots workers or extension workers.

Policy context

The country studies reflect varying degrees of commitment to adult learning at the policy level. Often, as is discussed in the South African case study presented here by McKay, commitment at even the most sophisticated policy level is insufficient in itself for actual implementation, which may be hindered by inadequate dissemination of the policy to educators and delivery agents 'on the ground'.

The cases refer to three main reasons for this: firstly, bureaucratic bottlenecks which tend to hamper the diffusion of policy at the level of implementation; secondly, the lack of capacity to translate policy into practice; and thirdly, obstacles to delivery which arise from class, gender and ethnic divisions within the social structure

While all the case studies refer to adult education as cutting across a variety of sectors, and indeed McKay's case study outlines attempts to integrate education, training and development, the Nigerian case study presented by Tahir refers to the problems associated with the split between these dimensions. This case study refers to the often narrow conception of the meaning and scope of adult education practice in Nigeria and shows how National Policy on Education (1998 revised edition) seems to contribute to this by unwittingly upholding a narrow, traditional meaning of adult education. Consequently, many adult educators involved in health, agriculture or social welfare departments do not see themselves as providing adult basic education even when they are involved in public enlightenment, social mobilisation, diffusion of innovation and so on. Nevertheless, in spite of policies that often seem inadequate to the overwhelming need, the countries referred to in this book do reveal a commitment to a multisectoral approach and an awareness of the relationship between adult education and other interventions such as community-based rural development. The various contributions highlight themes such as HIV/AIDS, income generation and sustainable development. A few of the studies, for example Rashid and Rahman's Bangladesh case study, highlight the role of government in providing an environment conducive to intersectoral delivery for adult education. Important policy changes have occurred here, made possible by the shift to a more decentralised, district-run approach, in which there is a broader emphasis on post-literacy and continuing education instead of the more narrow focus on literacy alone. NGOs are playing a significant role in the training of personnel for post-literacy and continuing education initiatives that go beyond literacy to deal with multisectoral concerns.

Institutional context

In most developing countries only a very small or residual component of the formal institutional structure, both public and private, is connected to the needs and demands of out-of-school young people and adults, not least the training needs of adult educators. For Nigeria, Tahir points out that generally both national and state training institutes lack adequate infrastructure and facilities. Training takes place through formal curricula and is neither regular nor based on a systematic analysis of training needs. In the Central American context it has been pointed out that National Training Institutions are not only lacking in funds and well-trained staff, but that their courses are primarily administrative in content. When we examine the source of institutional structure of support for the new areas of ODL and ICTs, created by the state and the private sector over the years, the relevance of this is again limited to a small section of the adult population with higher educational levels. The majority of the adults at the lower end who are without literacy and basic education, as well as workers in the survival or subsistence informal economy, lack access to these institutions.

Instances of how youth and adult education are being institutionalised through *partnerships* between civil society and non-governmental organisations and government have been highlighted in this volume. In the Bolivian *Proyecto Formación de Educadores de Jóvenes y Adultos a Distancia (FEJAD),* training of facilitators and teachers by distance education was made possible by co-operation between the state, civil society, universities and international agencies, all having different roles: financial support being provided by state and international agencies, pedagogical support by civil society and the universities. The Brazilian *Programa de Alfabetización Solidaria* started in 1997 in municipalities with high illiteracy rates and promotes national mobilisation and alliances among many social sectors. The case studies show that partnerships tend to be stronger if the partners' functions are quite different. While the Brazilian Ministry of Education finances the didactic and support material and 50 per cent of the monthly cost of the studies, the municipal administration provides the entire local infrastructure. The project on *Technology Based Literacy Centres* in India, reported in this volume by Dighe, highlights the importance of seeking partnerships with institutions that emphasise the centrality of the adult learning and believe in and practise bottom-up and participatory approaches, rather than with those, such as the state resource centres, which normally adopt the top-down approach to training adult educators.

Where there is insufficient government funding and the national training institutions lack the necessary competencies, the role of *multilateral and bilateral* agencies (such as the GTZ, DFID and DVV/IIZ) in the institutionalisation of education and training for adults has been highlighted. An important element of this process of institutionalisation is the emphasis on long-term sustainability, continuity of training opportunities and proposals for successive transferring responsibilities to national institutions. Decentralisation as well as strong identification and involvement of stakeholders and interested institutions right at the planning phase are key strategies in this process.

However, whatever is to be achieved has to be in partnership with the state education systems, because it is the government/state that has the main responsibility for providing basic education of good quality to its citizens. In any case, government has the responsibility for providing a facilitatory national framework. It also plays a role in setting up national bodies that are crucial for managing and sustaining relationships with partners and in overseeing problems regarding the issue of role definitions, agreements, communication and co-ordination.

NGOs are important role-players in the institutional process involved in raising the educational or literacy levels of adults and young people, which is seen to determine their mobility. However, given the transitory nature of the operation of NGOs and other groups, and since these groups operate and are driven by the funding pattern of public and private agencies, they can be seen as relevant only in the short or medium term. McKay points out that in South Africa the NGO sector has been declining as a result of lack of regular funding from donors. Institutions like the *NGO Service Centre* in Egypt described by Mohsen in this volume are, however, crucial in strengthening the capacity of civil society organisations and offering training and technical assistance services to NGOs.

The scope of training for adult educators

Just as the definition of adult education is broad and contested, so too is the definition of who in fact might be considered an adult educator. Many people who work in the field of adult education do not perceive themselves as educators. An agricultural demonstrator, for example, will identify herself or himself as an agricultural extension worker rather than as an adult educator, and a health educator might regard himself or herself as a health worker. It is clear, however, from the studies in this book that a definition of 'who might be considered to be an adult educator' embraces all those whose job function includes helping adults to learn and that the function can comprise different roles, such as teacher, community organiser, administrator, materials designer and so on (Youngman 1999).

Also, as reflected in the papers in this volume, the technical content taught by adult educators can be very varied across the variety of sectors. McKay points out that the educators working in the South African literacy programme are expected to do far more than teach literacy and basic numeracy. They are required to promote the ideals of democracy and human rights, to enable learners to eke out a living for themselves in some kind of informal employment activity, and to work in the context of strategies that focus on poverty eradication and improved livelihood.

In view of the wide diversity of skills required by adult educators it is inevitable that more professional training is necessary.

To address this gap, provision has been made in some countries for specialists and local expert trainers to amplify and help apply the functional information introduced by instructors/facilitators. This is the case in the Nigerian Interactive *Radio for Adult Education among pastoral Nomads* project described by Tahir. It is the extension workers who have the knowledge of animal husbandry and rural development, whereas the volunteers are those who lead the radio listening and discussion sessions. Yates mentions that specialists have also been used to ensure programmes are accurate. The case studies point out the importance of close working relationships between specialists and the generalist instructors and generally recommend that adult education programmes and educator training should take place in the context of alliances between educational and specialist agencies.

Adult educator competencies

An important issue addressed in the papers in this volume are the key dimensions that provide the basis for identifying the essential competencies that all adult educators require if adult education is to be centred in the development of the person and oriented to the everyday world of adult education practice. Three sets of competencies are important. The first is the rich variety of *content specialisation,* such as how to teach literacy for entrepreneurial or agricultural expertise. The second set of skills is the *generic,* cross-curricular or psychosocial skills. In South Africa, these skills are referred to as critical crossfield outcomes which are deemed necessary regardless of the educational level or discipline. These include competencies such as critical thinking, creativity, the ability to organise, social and communication skills, adaptability, problem-solving skills and the ability to co-operate on a democratic basis. In the training of adult educators, specific consideration needs to be given to key themes emerging internationally as central concerns, including the importance of *values* and *attitudes*. The case studies almost all refer to the importance of democratic values and attitudes including participatory methodologies, and a commitment to the values of social justice, human rights and democracy. McKay points out that human rights and democracy are taught to provide a cross-cutting competency for all trainee educators at the Unisa ABET Institute. She also refers to the partnership between Unisa ABET, the Human Rights Commission and the Independent Electoral Commission in South Africa to enhance the teaching of democracy and human rights to hundreds of thousands of learners. This mode of partnership opens up windows of possibilities for learners.

Tahir's empirical study of training needs indicates that supervisors who are government officials were more likely to be motivated to join training courses for certification, career development and instructional inputs than for personal development. In responding to educator training, we might therefore also have to address the fundamental tension between the need for vocational preparation of the adult educator and needs that are related to personal development, cultural and human values, active citizenship and democracy. In the training of adult educators a balance needs to be sought between training in instructional techniques and other professional matters, and learning critical values such as citizenship, democratic participation and gender justice. To achieve this it is perhaps necessary to provide general education to all educators and practitioners.

Tahir argues that curricula should also allow for the appropriate combination of the theoretical and practical, guided by concepts such as praxis and the critically reflective practitioner, enquiry-based learning, communication skills, academic writing, critical thinking, co-operative learning, learner assessment, materials development and selection, as well as awareness of best practices and policies of adult educators. These are some of the recommendations for the training of adult educators based on the experiences of practitioners in India, Bangladesh, Nigeria, Tanzania and South Africa.

Can open, distance and flexible learning assist with adult basic learning and educators' training? Looking for alternatives

In view of the above, the question for policymakers concerned with the provision of literacy and basic education for adults is: 'What can open and distance learning contribute to meeting the challenge?'

Whereas Tahir's discussion of Nigeria's distance learning programmes tends to focus on formally certified conventional training, Shah considers some of the main approaches to the training of grassroots functionaries in India to tackle the backlog of 300 million adults in need of basic literacy. Shah points out that although the participatory approach has been used effectively by NGOs, it has been difficult to use it on a large scale. He examines the use of open and distance learning in the implementation of adult education programmes and argues that achievements with this method of delivery far exceed those of programmes using other approaches to training. However, he comments that its use was limited. So far only one state resource centre has used ODL for training instructors. The main weakness Shah identifies is the inadequate personal contact programme.

Rashid and Rahman maintain that the minimal outreach literacy and basic educational programmes available in Bangladesh could be expanded if ODL methods were employed and they conclude their discussion with a proposed structure for large-scale delivery and a proposed training curriculum for educators.

McKay examines the training of grassroots facilitators in South Africa using the methods of distance education. She focuses on a case study of the training of adult educators by the University of South Africa's ABET Institute. Modes and methods of delivery are discussed as well as the competencies required. The chapter ends with a discussion of how the ABET Institute has extended the use of its network of tutors and graduate students to assist the national Department of Education with the South African Literacy Campaign, reaching a targeted 307 000 learners in two years.

The importance of ensuring quality in mass programmes is addressed by Sekgobela, who outlines the methods and instruments used for assessing the quality of literacy classes by the University of South Africa, which is spearheading the South African Literacy Campaign. He stresses that the instruments employed merely set standards for quality that are then discussed and customised for application at more than 6 000 learning sites across South Africa. He indicates that this is necessary given the variety of sites – from churches to prisons, to classes on the river bank or under a tree.

Based on the results of the study on Tanzania administered with the help of structured and unstructured interviews, Ligate presents possible strategies for improving training programmes in adult basic education. According to Ligate, the current education and training policy in Tanzania does not clearly address issues related to open and distance learning. Nevertheless Ligate reports on the various training initiatives provided by the government and NGOs in the country, which combine ODL with other methods such as traditional training and participatory seminars. Ligate concludes by saying that the main problem is that NGOs and associations lack co-ordination and there is duplication of work among them. She offers suggestions on how such duplication could be avoided. Finally Ligate gives an outline of a module in distance education for adult education fieldworkers. She proposes that government and policymakers should examine the possibilities offered by open and distance learning as a reliable option for the training of adult educators

All the case studies point out that distance education is only one element in a mixed mode delivery model of quality teaching for adult educators and development practitioners.

Quality issues in professional support to adult educators

Ultimately the role distance learning might play in the process remains problematic unless the more positive changes relating to quality emerging from research and practice are integrated into adult basic learning programmes. Some of these issues are examined below.

Pedagogical issues

Until now literacy has been viewed as the acquisition of decontexualised skills. Yet research has shown (see Yates in this volume) that literacy is embedded in and dependent on the immediate environment. Further, literacy is a tool of empowerment for groups and communities seeking to eliminate injustices and social inequalities through cultural and political transformation. The new literacies imply the development of literacy materials which are authentic and which emerge from intercultural dialogue with beneficiaries.

The academic discussion of literacies is an integral part of the pedagogical issues that influence literacy teachers in their actions as reported by several authors in this volume. In the context of the Brazilian *Programa Alfabetizacao Solidária*, literacy is understood broadly as more than just mastering the graphic elements of reading and writing. Rather, literacy education aims to educate individuals to exercise citizenship. It is the development of a critical and contextual understanding of reality for the conscious transformation of reality, and a reflection on a community's culture to develop reading and writing skills. The new understanding of literacy implies that teachers are expected to use materials that are relevant to the contexts of their students' lives. Students and teachers adapt and construct knowledge by interacting with the communities they live in.

Similarly, in the *Proyecto Formación de Educodores de Jóvenes y Adultos a Distancia (FEJAD)* in Bolivia, an important component of educator training is the enrichment and improvement of pedagogical theory and practice among educators. This includes promoting the techniques of self learning and learning the situation in the country. There is also considerable emphasis on grassroots education and community development approaches.

Research and practice have shown that literacy teaching, when integrated into development plans and action points of poor adults, is more likely to have success than when literacy precedes concerns relating to the daily lives of poor adults. Leumer examines five pilot projects that apply the 'literacy second' approach in South Africa. IDASA, FAIR SHARE, Women for Peace, Kruger to Canyon and Learning for Development, all deal with introducing literacy and numeracy into already existing local initiatives ranging from local budgeting, domestic violence, handicraft production and urban agriculture projects to benefiting from resource streams generated by tourism. It is important to stress the importance of introducing literacies into existing programmes since the 'ready-made' nature of the groups is an important point for interventions. However, it must be stressed that adult education cannot only rely on already formed groups. Educators might need to intervene to organise learners into groups which might tackle development initiatives which they identify.

Central to *The Building Literacy with SOLO Press Project (BLSP)* described in Yates's article is the emphasis on the practice and use of literacy as a response to the learning needs of newly literate refugees and internally displaced people in Sudan. It deals with peace, war and marriage customs and it enables adult learners to apply the technical skills of literacy to texts and publications that are reflective of their lives. *Women in Fishing Industry Project (WIFIP)* is another case study cited by Yates that offers non-formal education via radio and audio to fisherwomen in Kenya, in response to their expressed need for information on health and AIDS and for improving their business skills. Radio programmes use drama story lines that provide a sense of reality and familiarity to the listeners.

Cultural and language diversity

The homogenisation of language and culture has been at the heart of the debate on educational quality and will be a challenge for adult educator training. Despite the increased opportunities for exchange, encounter and political dialogue between heterogeneous cultural backgrounds made possible by globalisation, there is growing pressure for cultural and linguistic uniformity. The threat of the loss of cultural diversity and the ongoing extinction of a great number of the world's languages are significant not only for culture itself but also for human development. The existing unequal access to the means for cultural expression seriously affects a number of individuals and communities, since access determines whether they are part of – or excluded from – the learning society and the creation and sharing of knowledge. The lack of exchange of self-expression and the subsequent withdrawal of many entails the risk of cultural tension and conflict.

Many programmes described in this volume place emphasis on the promotion of local languages, because it is only in one's own language that a person can truly understand and read the written word. Esteve's examination in this volume of the Brazilian National Literacy Programme, the *Programa Alfabetizacao Solidária,* shows that literacy teachers are encouraged to plan and develop their pedagogical project giving priority to the Portuguese language. Intensive educator training therefore involves promoting the relationship between education and culture accompanied by seminars, which are linked to reading and writing. Continuous training takes place through studies, workshops, analysis and reflection on the literacy teachers' practices. As Esteves indicates, the success of the Brazilian programme relies on the continued support of the higher education institution co-ordinators for these training efforts.

Elsewhere in the volume concern is expressed about the dominance of the English language in the use of materials developed on and made available through the use of modern technologies such as the Internet. These technologies are often acknowledged as having a great potential for information exchange and networking, but are also, on the other hand, regarded as restrictive because the language does not relate to or is not relevant to the local cultural context (see Chifwepa's contribution). This may not be a problem for adult educators in formal employment, but it certainly is a problem for those who are not formally employed, such as traditional trainers and volunteer literacy instructors who teach young mothers and young adults traditional and cultural values and practices. On the other hand, in the Central American context it has been shown how ICTs can be used in the preparation and development of bilingual or multilingual instructional material. Translation facilities are an important instrument in the Internet-based information network for entrepreneurs and training providers in Central America described by Gerasch.

Curriculum design and production of authentic materials

Educators need to be trained to develop curriculum content derived from local experiences and to apply this to what is learned. However it is not enough to establish linkages between learning and action points of the learning. While learner-generated texts are extremely valuable in all adult education settings, information transfer from outside is still necessary, but it should be matched to the defined needs and experiences of the recipient users themselves. It will still be necessary to introduce new ideas through externally generated material, but the texts must be relevant to the learning context and appropriate to the needs of the learners. While Yates suggests that externally produced texts are often best 'used to support and supplement learning', McKay and Esteves indicate that in a mass campaign, with hundreds of thousands or even millions of learners, it is necessary to supply learning support material based on a common core of content, and to supplement and contextualise this with teacher and learner-generated support materials.

Similarly, Leumer refers to a textbook series on *African perspectives in adult learning,* which is a package aimed at mass distribution. This proposed package is similar to the package referred to by McKay in that it is wholly African and is used as a core for the professional training of practitioners in the SADC region. Leumer argues that professional training textbooks should reflect African social realities and theoretical modes of practice rather than dominant western realities. The aim is to promote recognition of distinctive African perspectives on adult learning and to build the capacities and commitment of African writers on the subject of adult learning. This is not to say that African educators are to be restricted only to what is considered to be African. Their studies and reading references will nevertheless embrace texts which are also considered to be 'western'.

Facilitating learning: Creating a learning environment and empowering people

An important lesson learnt from the experience of using technology in adult basic learning is the emphasis it places on quality issues, content, the learning processes and the development of skills rather than simply on how technology should be used as a tool or medium for training literacy workers.

In examining the technology-based Community Learning Centres in India and Zambia, Dighe argues that technology has been used to facilitate adult learning and create a learning environment. Access to computers and to training in basic computer literacy has been a motivating factor for young adults, who recognise the market value of such skills. Over and above the literacy and non-formal adult education, technology has made informal learning opportunities available to adults. It has also opened channels of communication and provided access to important resources for marginalised individuals, thus supporting a learning process that is transformative and empowering.

Promoting networking of adult educators

Leumer, writing on networking activities in adult basic learning in South Africa, laments the inability of adult educators and institutions to come together to identify the commonality of their interests at the national level. He elaborates on the role of his organisation, DVV/IZZ, in attempting to rejuvenate the adult learning sector in South Africa by assisting in the development of textbooks in adult learning, training of volunteers in AIDS, and promoting advocacy learning events. McKay, too, laments the lack of national networks. She states that her university department has consistently been compelled to act as trade union to the 37 000 trained UNISA alumni of educators. She says that in the absence of any organised structure, the university has had to be involved in 'bread and butter' matters, ensuring career-pathing for educators and lobbying for salaries which are commensurate with their qualifications.

Networks are the best way of communicating in terms of transfer of information. They permit nodal communication, are without hierarchy and generate links of solidarity among its members. The aim of networking should be to exchange information on current programmes and projects with a view to systematising practices and sharing experiences. At the regional level, networks could be instrumental in defining and financing proposals for action, exchanging research results, following up on programmes and designing teacher training strategies. This is not to say that networks should or could take on the roles of gatekeepers or that they should be allowed to stifle debate on what adult education is by enforcing one definition in a hierarchical fashion. In fact, the open nature of networks is necessary to avert monolithic definitions of adult education assuming a legitimacy and being canonised as a 'given' definition.

Strengthening information networks

Professional support to adult educators can also be given in the form of information resources or materials, and forums for the exchange of information and experience. With Internet use growing rapidly in Africa, India and Central and South America, it is becoming possible not only to produce materials in more flexible formats but also to make materials and information more rapidly available.

Chifwepa explores programmes like the *Commonwealth of Learning Literacy Project* (COLLIT), which have made literacy materials available for training literacy workers and learners, and the *Community-based non-formal Education for Rural People* (CERP) model in Zambia, which uses culturally useful materials that incorporate local practices appropriate to the target communities. In the process of producing such materials, new methodologies for sharing knowledge are also developed. These include study groups, models for testing outcomes, skills development in the production of educational material and sustainable networks of exchange.

In the different contexts of five central American countries, Gerasch presents the *Toolbox Network for Development and Training of MSMEs* (Micro-Small-Medium Enterprises) for training providers and entrepreneurs. This is an Internet-based information and data system that provides information to small and micro entrepreneurs who already have practical knowledge. Decision-making requires more than practical knowledge. It also requires knowledge of business consultancy, trade agreements and so on. Gerasch shows that these can be had virtually through the tool box, which is flexible in terms of themes and level of co-ordination, offers an efficient means of delivering materials, and has the potential for considerable interactivity through the establishment of exchange and feedback forums.

In-service and continuing education

Training is not just a one-shot affair. It is an ongoing and continuing process. While traditional training adopted the top-down and cascade approach and was directed towards control and regulation, alternative in-service and continuing education programmes are adapted to local knowledge, and courses offer career development and motivation to learn by offering certification.

Many of the papers published here examine the importance of in-service training and continuing education. The operative models of professional support described in this collection of papers have highlighted a number of elements: 1) the possibility of establishing certificates; 2) the opportunity for modular curricula that emphasise local context and incorporate non-formal educational themes; 3) in-service training alternating with practice and reflecting on practice; 4) a broad understanding of adult educators' training as including electronic media, simple printed materials and face-to-face contact through mentoring and tutoring, study groups, rural forums or reading circles; 5) integration of a variety of technologies including print, radio and internet; 6) opportunities for self learning for facilitators in remote and scattered areas; 7) study groups with materials on set themes in practice and theory.

Dodds examines some programmes using the methods of ODL for adult educators' training and support. One is the *Network for Advanced Professional Development in Open Learning for Southern Africa* (NAPRODOLSA). Its purposes include sharing local expertise in the region and using existing materials adapted to the regional environment. The other is the University of Namibia pre-graduate

Diploma in Adult Education and Community Development through ODL methods. A particular advantage of offering such a programme at a distance, according to Dodds, is the potential for relating the course directly to the educators' own experiences in the field.

Training methodologies which articulate with the political and ethical dimensions in the national context are examined in several papers. Mensah describes the *Certificate in Education for Development Programme* designed and implemented by the Namibian College of Open Learning (NAMCOL), in conjunction with the Adult Basic Education and Training Institute (ABET) of the University of South Africa. These programmes go beyond training literacy teachers to include multisectoral actors such as extension agents and community development workers who need expertise in promoting democracy and community development. Ligate examines the *Local Government Councillors Distance education Project,* a training programme used to train local government councillors in Tanzania after the first multiparty civic elections held in October 1994. She indicates that great care was taken to ensure that materials included a history of local government in Tanzania, as well as the knowledge and skills needed to fulfil responsibilities in a multiparty system.

The lessons learnt: Successes and difficulties

This review of the articles presented in this volume singles out a number of lessons identified by the authors with regard to instructor training and the role played by instructors.

Adult educator training using open and distance learning basically requires the following ingredients for success: well-designed learning materials, student support services, theory, content and instructional practice. These must be integrated into the courses, while theory needs to be related to practice. Plentiful feedback on students' progress should be given, and a mentoring system should be put in place. Finally, some form of recognised accreditation or qualification which will contribute to career development should be offered.

Another important element of success is the importance attached to content issues such as the development of an overarching and expanded vision of literacy and learning as lifelong, multisectoral and diverse. The diversity of learning and training needs must also be taken into account. It seems that the most successful approaches to educator training using distance education have achieved quality outcomes by combining a mass-based industrialised model of material production with participatory and face-to-face approaches.

Some disappointments are also examined. One of these is that too few countries use distance education as a vehicle for going to scale and for penetrating large parts of their rural community. Educator training needs to be delivered on a large scale so that adult learners can acquire stable skills. Countries should engage in adult learning from a lifelong learning perspective, and this calls for a long-term commitment. Training providers such as NGOs need intensive training and supervision, in order that they reach beneficiaries in specific local areas effectively. NGOs do not always possess expertise in instructional delivery.

Challenges and the way forward

A number of issues still need to be addressed and noted if quality in adult learning is to be achieved.

Policy framework. Governments need to allocate more funds to adult basic learning and literacy and to move away from the current focus on universal primary education. Clear official policies on the integration of open and distance learning in adult and non-formal education are also required. National frameworks need to be constructed for ensuring stakeholder co-ordination and for overseeing that NGOs work within this framework rather than in a fragmented way.

Money is not always the issue. What is important is to develop clear strategies for training adult educators. In addition, a single model is regarded as insufficiently flexible to achieve mass delivery while simultaneously dealing with local needs and issues. The value of collaboration and of forging partnerships across sectors and between stakeholders and educators is also strongly emphasised.

A need to improve working conditions. Ministries in areas other than education seem insufficiently aware of the importance of field practitioners' contribution to adult and basic education. The establishment of national bodies can strengthen the identity of adult educators. There is a need for the system to lobby for its recognition. This will shift the delivery from appearing voluntary to mandating and compelling government to provide for adult learners.

Quality of learning environment. Content and curriculum design must be based on documented good practices to ensure the quality and sustainability of training programmes. There needs to be a balance between curricula developed externally through experts and those developed in a .participatory way. Programmes need to recognise – and provide for – multiple literacies and should give importance to pedagogical and learning issues. It is important that quality frameworks accommodate diversity and that trainees be introduced to issues of quality and its measurement before they begin practising.

Research. Support for policy formulation and clear statistical reflection for interested parties as well as conceptual developments in diversifying methods and cultural content, and the promotion of an expanded vision of adult learning will be the acid test of good research. However, more funds are needed from donors and stakeholders to enable researchers to undertake needs analyses in the field. Research should also be undertaken to measure the impact of training, to document the inputs, processes and outputs of training and to highlight its effectiveness and cost efficiency. Research should be qualitative, participatory and collaborative. It is important to see research more broadly, since action research at grassroots level is as valuable as large-scale research and evaluation projects. Universities need to find ways of promoting and including adult basic learning and literacy in their research agendas. At the international level, it is essential to develop a framework for the classification of appropriate indicators and measures which need to take into account the various socio-cultural environments and national contexts in which adult basic education takes place.

The need for establishing central depositories that facilitate access to global collections of research and practice reports on adult basic learning needs to be emphasised.

A clear purpose for applying new technologies. While on the one hand the number of people who want ABE and literacy education will not be served unless we harness ICTs and distance education methods, the question, on the other hand, is how to harness them for the purposes of adult basic education and educator training. The challenges have to do with lack of skills to use the technology and the sustainability of adult basic learning using new technologies. Stakeholders must be sensitised in order for governments to understand the importance of ICTs in adult basic learning. New approaches such as internet toolkit approaches need to be developed to support, resources and information to adult educators and learners. The application of ICTs needs to be viewed differently according to whether they are used for teaching/learning processes or for management and administrative tasks. Also, ICTs may be more appropriate to use at intermediary levels for tutors, teachers and facilitators rather than for beneficiaries at the grassroots level.

Adult educators seldom use ICTs in a professional way and tend to expect that the medium will do magic. The standardising and casting of content into a curriculum (industrial product) should be taken up seriously in the training of adult educators. Adult learning protagonists should learn more about the potential use of different ICT modes, including video-conferencing. ICTs should also be explored in more depth for networking purposes and for training of intermediary personnel. However, the issue of user-friendliness needs to be taken into account and the technology must be demystified.

Conclusion

The papers in this volume show that the conventional system of training won't do any longer. Adult educators require new and flexible provisions for learning and training. Only then will it be possible to meet the undiminished demand for basic education for adults; take non-formal and basic education to rural and marginalised parts of our countries; promote greater participation among women; provide training and education for millions of out-of-school youths; and make flexible learning opportunities available for grassroots workers, health workers and agricultural workers.

The major challenge remains the moral, professional and economic recognition of youth and adult educators by government and by the society as a whole. Adult educators are crucial to the success and quality of literacy and non-formal education for adults as they can provide both the intellectual and operational leadership for implementing its vision.

References

Brookfield, S. (ed). 1988. *Training educators of adults.* London: Routledge.

Dodds, T. 1996. *The use of distance learning in non-formal education.* Vancouver: Commonwealth of Learning; Cambridge: International Extension College.

ECLAC. 2000. *Equidad, desarrollo y ciudadania.*

Gouldner, A 1980. *The Two Marxisms*. London: MacMillan.

Hawop, S & Woodcock, J. 1992. Issues in the construction of a modular curriculum for university professional adult education courses. *Studies in the education of adults,* 24(1):86-94.

Jacinto, C & Gallart, MA. 1998. *Por una segunda oportunidad: la formacion para el trabajo de jóvenes vulnerable.* Montevideo: Cinterfor/RET

McKay, VI. 1990. An exploration of people's education in South Africa. D Litt et Phil thesis. Pretoria: Unisa.

McKay, VI. 1994. Theories of education, in *Sociology of educating*, edited by VI McKay. Johannesburg: Lexicon Heinemann Publishers.

McKay, VI & Romm, N. 1992. *People's education in theoretical perspective: towards the development of a critical humanist approach.* Cape Town: Maskew, Miller, Longman.

National Education Policy Investigation. 1992. *Report of the adult basic education research group: a project of the National Education Co-ordinating Committee.* Cape Town: Oxford University Press.

Nyirenda, JE, Indabawa, SA & Avoseh, MBM. 1999. *Developing professional adult education programmes in Namibia.* Windhoek: Department of Adult and Non-Formal Education, University of Namibia.

Nzoma, J & Osman, A. 2000. *Making alternatives count.* Report of the sub-regional workshop on development of statistical information systems for non-formal education. Nairobi: Commonwealth Secretariat.

Oduaran, A. 1986. The development of curriculum in adult education: a case study of the University of Benin. *Benin Journal of Educational Studies,* 5(1& 2):173-187.

Perraton, H. 2000. *Open and distance learning in the developing world.* London: Routeledge.

Peters, JM & Kreitlow, BW. 1991. Growth and future of graduate programmes, in *Adult education: evolution and achievements in a developing field of study,* edited by JM Peters, P Jarvis & Associates. San Francisco: Jossey Bass, 145-153.

Prinsloo, M & Breier, M. (eds). 1996. *The social uses of literacy.* Cape Town: SACHED.

Siaciwena, R. (ed). 2000. *Case studies of non-formal education by distance and open learning.* Vancouver: The Commonwealth of Learning.

Singh, M. (ed). 2002 *Institutionalising lifelong learning: creating conducive environments for adult learning in the Asian context.* Hamburg: UNESCO Institute for Education.

UNESCO. 1997. *Agenda for the future.* Hamburg: UNESCO Institute for Education.

UNESCO. 1998. Series of 29 booklets documenting the 5th International Conference on Adult Education. Hamburg: UNESCO Institute for Education.

UNESCO. 1999. *Statistical yearbook.* Paris: UNESCO Publishing and Bernan Press.

UNESCO. 2001. *Distance education in the E-9 Countries: the development and future of distance education programmes in the nine high-population countries.* Paris: UNESCO.

UNESCO. 2002a. EFA Global Monitoring Report. Education for All. Is the World on Track? Paris: UNESCO.

UNESCO. 2002b. *The challenge of achieving gender parity in basic education: a statistical review 1990-1998.* Paris: UNESCO.

United Nations (2000) *Millennium Declaration,* New York, United Nations.

World Conference on Education for All (WCEFA). (1990) *World Declaration on Education for All. Meeting Basic Lerning Needs.* Jomtien, Thailand.

Youngman, F. 1999. *The political economy of adult education and development.* London: Zed Books.

Youngman, F. 1999. *Training the post-CONFINTEA adult educator.* Paper presented at the UNESCO CONFINTEA International Forum. Manila, September 25-27.

Youngman, F. 2000. Training the post-CONFINTEA adult educator. *Adult Education and Development,* 54: 285-299.

Section I

Country studies

2

Approaches to training grassroots level workers in literacy and adult basic education: The Indian scenario

SY Shah

This article examines some of the main approaches to the training of grassroots functionaries in India in order to tackle the backlog of 300 million adults in need of basic literacy. It considers the use of open and distance learning in the implementation of adult education programmes and it is argued that this method of delivery far exceeds the achievements of programmes using other approaches to training.

Introduction

A series of national and international developments during the last two decades has given a tremendous push to Adult Basic Education (ABE) and Open and Distance Learning (ODL) in India. The policies and plans of the federal government have not only given due importance to these two areas but have also recognised ODL as a powerful instrument for democratising education and promoting it as a lifelong learning process (see, for example, Government of India 2000:102; 1992:8). However, in spite of the tremendous expansion of ABE, and an increase in the literacy rate from 43.57% to 65.38% between 1981 and 2001, there is still a massive backlog of 300 million non-literates in India (Premchand 2001:5). This may be partly because adult education programmes have been ineffective and because of the failure to universalise primary education. During the period 1988 to 2000, while the target was to impart literacy to 133 million people, the actual achievement was 64.85 million (or 48.76% of the number targeted) (National Literacy Mission 2001:8-9).

One of the reasons for the dismal performance of adult education, as has been observed by several review committees and evaluation and research studies, may be traced back to the poor quality of training of grassroots level functionaries (National Literacy Mission 1995:19). How to devise an effective strategy for improving the training of ABE practitioners so that they, in turn, can train the massive numbers of illiterates in a short period and in a cost-effective manner is one of the challenges facing adult educators in India. With the wide variety of ODL opportunities available in the country, can we afford not to use them for training such a cadre? To answer this question we must first examine the experience of using ODL for the promotion of adult education in India.

A review of programmes offered by different national and state level adult education organisations bears testimony to the limited use of ODL in the training of grassroots level functionaries in the field of adult education in India. Why has this been so? Is it because specialists in ODL are biased against ABE? Can it be because of their preoccupation with formal higher education? Or is it due to the inhibition of adult educators to utilise ODL for the training of functionaries? What are the potentialities and problems of using ODL for the training of adult education functionaries? By critically reviewing the training scenario in adult education and analysing some of the training packages used by government agencies, NGOs and universities, this article argues that adult education and training in India may have to rely much more on ODL in future not only because of its cost-effectiveness and wide reach but also because of the tremendous expansion of communication and information technology and the inherent limitations of the more traditional approaches to training.

This study is organised into four sections: Section one, *Adult education training in context,* examines the concept of adult education in India, identifies significant training institutions and studies their role in training. Some of the select training packages designed and applied by government agencies, non-governmental organisations (NGOs) and universities are critically analysed in the second section, *Approaches to training*. The use of ODL in the applicatation of adult education programmes and specifically in imparting training to grassroots level functionaries is reviewed in the third section, *Role of open and distance learning in adult education*. The last section, *Training of Preraks,* provides a sample module for organising a training programme for grassroots functionaries in ABE through ODL.

Adult education training in context

India is the second most populous country in the world with a population of 1027 million (*Census of India* 2001:34). It has a GDP of US$447.3 billion and ranks 128 out of 174 countries on the Human Development Index (UNDP 2001). Although the country has achieved a literacy rate of 65.38% it still has 300 million non-literates. This high number means that the major thrust of adult education in India continues to be towards achieving basic literacy. However, the scope of adult education policy and programmes in India are not limited to literacy, but include achieving self-reliance in literacy and numeracy; examining the reasons for (non-literates') educational deprivation; moving towards enabling them to participate in development processes; acquiring the skills to improve their economic status and wellbeing; acquiring the civic values of national integration, environmental conservation, women's equality, observance of the small family norm and so on (Government of India 1988:14).

In pursuance of the above, a number of adult education programmes have been put into practice by official agencies, NGOs and academic institutions. Examples of these programmes are the Rural Functional Literacy Project, National Adult Education Programme, Total Literacy Campaigns (TLCs), Mass Programme of Functional Literacy, *Mahila Samakhya* and Continuing Education (for details of these programmes, see Shah 1999). Depending upon the nature and duration of each programme, different types of training packages have been developed in India.

In addition to formulating training policy, the federal government also develops training curricula through a series of national level consultations and workshops in which administrators, academics and activists participate and discuss and decide on content areas and training methodology. The federal government also takes the initiative in organising all-India programmes to orient key personnel from different states. However, with the emergence of the TLCs during the 1990s, there was a marked shift towards decentralising training strategies and programmes, and each district started developing district-specific training packages. Most of the federal government training programmes are designed in keeping with the job specifications of field functionaries as specified in the programme manual. Although the different training agencies at state level have the freedom to modify the suggested model of the National Literacy Mission (NLM), or to develop local specific training designs, in practice most of them do not undertake such exercises mainly because there is too little time. For the same reason, specific needs assessment surveys of field functionaries are also not undertaken.

The training of adult education functionaries in India is organised by a number of organisations at national, state and district levels (see Table 1). Apart from 27 State Resource Centres which primarily train state level functionaries, there are 85 *Jan Shikshan Sansthans* (Institutes of People's Education) that present vocational training at district level. District Resource Units (DRUs) of the District Institute of Education and Training (DIET) are also involved in training voluntary instructors. In addition, there are several national level institutions, such as Directorate of Adult Education; National Institute of Educational Planning and Administration; National Institute of Rural Development; NGOs, namely *Bharat Gyan Vigyan Samithi*, *Pria*, *Astha*, *Nirantar* and Indian Adult Education

Association. All of these are actively involved in planning and managing training programmes for adult education functionaries. In addition, the adult education university departments in India all have a mandate to design and present training programmes.

Some of the institutions of open learning, especially Indira Gandhi National Open University (IGNOU), BR Ambedkar Open University and the National Open School (NOS), also offer innovative courses for grassroots level functionaries in the development sector. To a limited extent, international organisations such as WHO, UNESCO, UNDP, Action Aid, World Literacy of Canada and Asian South Pacific Bureau of Adult Education have also been organising training programmes for fieldworkers and programme managers associated with HIV/AIDS, environment, population, health, rural development, women and child development. Most of the national training institutions are located in New Delhi, the capital city of India (see Table 1) More than 80% of the State Resource Centres are also situated in the state capitals. Though some NGOs operate at district level, there is a dearth of training institutions in the districts, which is a great handicap in imparting training to grassroots level functionaries. This can, however, be effectively overcome by using ODL methods.

Table 1 Typology of key training institutions in adult education in India

Category	Level		
	National level	State level	District level
Government organisa-tions	Directorate Of Adult Education (New Delhi) National Institute of Adult Education (New Delhi) National Institute of Educational Planning & Administration (New Delhi) National Institute of Public Corporation and Child Development (New Delhi) National Institute of Rural Development (Hyderabad) National Literacy Resource Centre (Mussorie)		District Institute of Education and Training (451) (District Resource Units)

NGOs	Bharat Gyan Vigyan Samithi (New Delhi)Indian Adult Education Association (New Delhi)PRIA (New Delhi)Nirantar (New Delhi)ACORD (New Delhi)Literacy House (Lucknow)YMCAs and YWCAs	State Resource Centres (22)Seva Mandir (Udaipur)Astha (Udaipur) Jagori (New Delhi) SPARC (Bombay)	Jan Shikshan Sansthan (85)
Universities and other academic institutions	Indira Gandhi National Open University (New Delhi) National Open School (New Delhi) University Grants CommissionInstitute of Rural Management (Anand) Madras Institute Of Development Studies (Madras) Institute of Social And Economic Change (Bangalore) Institute of Development Studies (Jaipur) Tata Institute of Social Sciences (Mumbai)	State Resource Centres (5)University Departments of Adult Education (103)State Open Universities (9) State Open Schools (9)Academic Staff Colleges (45)	Colleges of Home Science and Social work (168)

Category	Level		
	National level	State level	
Private (business) organisations	NIITAPTEC EGurucool.com	——	——
International organisations	UNESCO (New Delhi)UNDP (New Delhi) UNFPA (New Delhi)ASPBAE (Mumbai) ACTION AID (Bangalore) World Literacy Canada (Varanasi) World Education (New Delhi)	——	——

Source: Compiled from Shah 2000; Government of India 2000.

Approaches to training

India uses four main approaches for training adult education functionaries: cascade (or pyramid) approach; direct approach; participatory approach; ODL approach. The *cascade approach* was extensively adopted during the TLCs (1989-1996) and continues to be used in the Continuing Education Programme that started in 1999. The state (in the shape of the National Literacy Mission) prepared a training kit for continuing education, comprising four publications, viz. *Manual for Training of Preraks; A Handbook for Preraks; Manual for Training of Key Resource Persons* and *Handbook on Training Methods*. It was, however, Bharat Gyan Vigyan Samithi, a national level NGO, which developed detailed training guidelines and curricula for the TLCs in two comprehensive volumes.

The *direct approach* to training was devised by the University Grants Commission and developed by the university system in India during the 1980s. Its aim was to give direct training to student volunteers and non-student animators involved in adult education programmes such as the Mass Programme of Functional Literacy and Centre Based Adult Education Programmes put into practice during the 1980s. The main emphasis was on acquainting participants with the conceptual and operational aspects of adult education programmes. The initial training was to be followed by a refresher course of ten hours after six months. As is shown below, the achievements of universities in imparting training to adult education functionaries were far below expectation.

The *participatory approach* has been very effectively used by several NGOs. The Society for Participatory Research in India (PRIA), a prominent NGO, has played a key role in promoting this approach by organising workshops and developing a series of publications, especially *A manual for participatory training methodology in development,* which has been widely acclaimed by trainers and gone into a fifth edition.

A few organisations, such as the National Institute of Public Co-operation and Child Development, the MP State Resource Centre in Adult Education and the Asian Centre for Organisation Research and Development, have used an *ODL approach* on a very limited scale for training grassroots level functionaries in adult education. The open learning institutions, especially the National Open School (NOS) and the Indira Gandhi National Open University (IGNOU), started developing innovative training courses only during the late 1990s. (These are more fully discussed in Section 3.)

The comparison below of the different approaches reveals considerable variation in terms of training content, methodology, materials and duration.

Cascade approach

Total Literacy Campaigns. The cascade approach of the TLCs envisaged a three-tier system of training comprising key resources persons (KRPs), resource persons (RPs), master trainers (MTs) and voluntary instructors (VIs). The organisers of the training programme – Zilla Sakharta Samithi (District Literacy Committee) – identified a limited number of KRPs (five to ten) with rich experience and expertise and entrusted them with the responsibility of designing the training curricula and training RPs. The RPs in turn trained MTs who were then responsible for training VIs. Figure 1 shows the ratio between KRPs, RPs, MTs, VIs and learners.

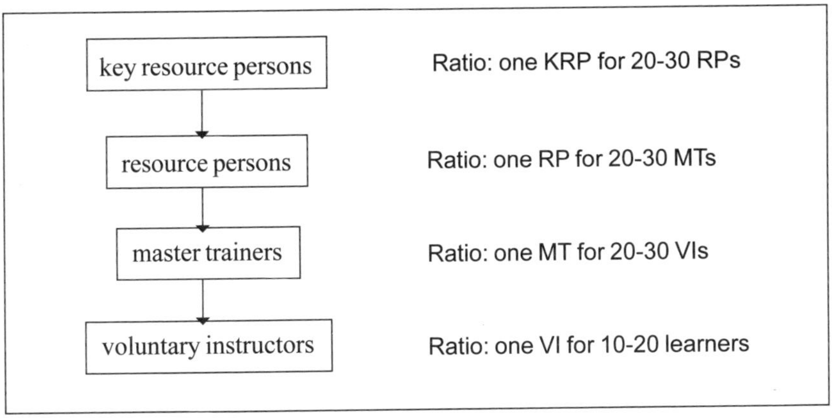

Figure 1 Cascade approach to training

The ratio of KRP to RPs, of RPs to MTs and of MTs to VIs has varied from district to district; but generally it has been found to be in the range indicated in Figure 1 According to the training guidelines, the initial round of four to five days (24 hours) of training for VIs was to be followed by three 'booster rounds' of training for MTs and VIs. While the training curriculum (see Table 2) rightly gives 50% weight to the primer and primer-based training, there is very little emphasis on adult psychology, adult teaching strategies and learning styles, which are crucial for the effective mediation of the curriculum.

Table 2 Cascade approach: training curriculum for volunteer instructors of the TLC

Sr no	Content area	Methodology	Time (hours)
1.	Why literacy?	Group discussion	2-3
2.	Why a people's movement for literacy?	Group discussion, lecture, discussions	2
3.	How to approach adult learners	Lecture, discussion, role-play.	1.5
4.	Introducing the primers	Lecture, group reading, group exercise	3
5.	Primer-based training reading and writing numeracy	Role-play, model class, brief lecture and discussion	9
6.	Functionality and awareness	Group discussion, lecture, role-play	2
7.	Monitoring and problem management at centre level	Lecture, discussion, practical work, case studies	2
8.	Organisational aspects of a centre	Self introduction, group activities	1
9.	Evaluation	Group discussion	1

Source: Bharat Gyan Vigyan Samithi nd:5.

Several evaluation and research studies on training have identified a number of weaknesses in this approach. A review of the experiences of training in ten TLCs conducted in different districts in India showed that the training strategies adopted in various campaigns do not always clearly integrate objectives, structure and training inputs (Society for Participatory Research in Asia 1993:243-246). The review observed that the pedagogy of training was not geared to meet the needs of adolescents and women learners, who constituted the bulk of the learners (249). Mainly due to what the reviewer called 'the perfunctory attitude to training' and the short duration of the campaign, follow-up training was rarely organised.

Another review indicated that there was considerable training loss due to the time gap between the training of RPs and MTs, and a lack of motivation among MTs and VIs who had neither genuine interest in nor any aptitude for teaching adults (State Resource Centre for Non-formal Training 1998:29-30).

Based on the extensive fieldwork conducted in Udaipur District in Rajasthan, Yagi (2001:237) notes that due to the practical difficulty of spending a few days continuously on training, about 20% of VIs in sample villages remained 'untrained'. According to her, one of the basic reasons for the poor quality of training of instructors lay in the 'superficial training' of Master Trainers, who perceived training as 'official compliance', and attended it mainly as an 'official duty'. Most of them were unable to grasp the skills required for training VIs and mostly received inadequate resource materials and insufficient knowledge.

An evaluation study of a training programme for 63 RPs, 84 MTs and 140 VIs from seven districts of Madhya Pradesh showed that only 58.6% of MTs received teaching-learning materials. While 40% received three days of training, 6.4% received only one day of training in place of five. The study also revealed that 27% of the MTs did not conduct any training of VIs and that the training lost much of its tone and tenor as it progressed from resource persons to grassroots level.

It was concluded that while the cascade approach was useful for involving more people in literacy work, the availability of resources – in terms of training contents, materials, duration, funds and technical imputs – gradually diminished and reached its minimum at the level of VIs, whose training therefore remained weak (State Resource Centre in Adult Education nd: 8-9; see also Supekar, Bajpayee & Gokhale nd). Figure 2 shows the availability of resources at three levels. While maximum resources were available for MTs, only minimal resources were available for VIs.

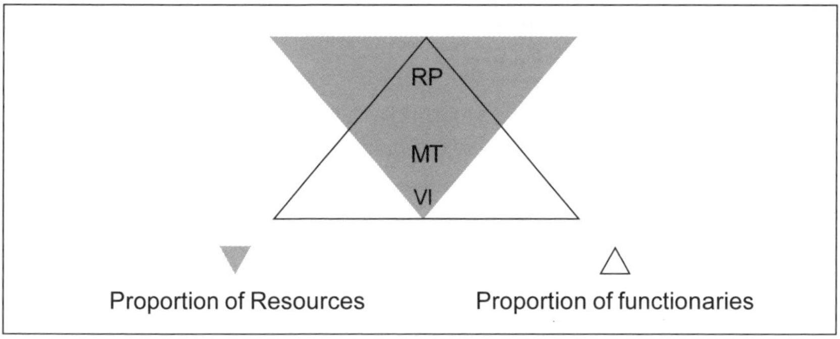

Figure 2 Utilisation of resources for training

An evaluation study conducted in Bihar state showed that the interest of VIs declined during the course of the training and that the quality of training suffered due to the negligible use of audiovisual equipment, the large number of trainees and the inadequate and untimely supply of training materials (Lal Das & Singh 2000:25; Krishna Reddy, Subba Reddy & Ramakrishna 1996:12).

The success of training of VIs being dependent on the effectiveness of the training of MTs, a study was conducted to ascertain the views of 30 MTs who attended a training programme at the State Resource Centre, Indore (Shah 1998:19-23). A short questionnaire comprising ten items was administered to the group. The main results are depicted in Figure 3 below.

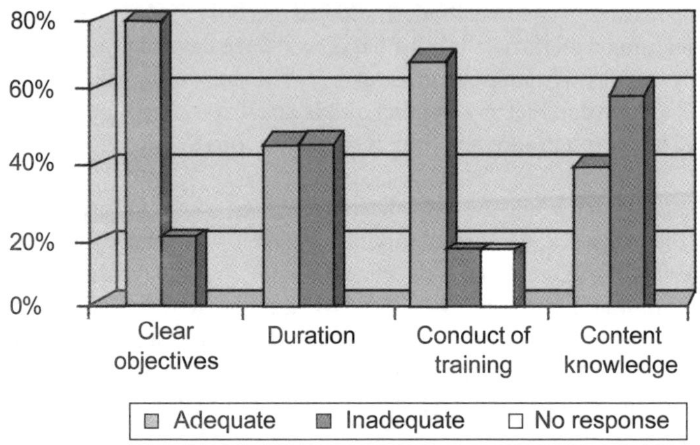

Figure 3 Evaluation of Indore state resource centre training programme

As may be seen from Figure 3, 80% strongly agreed that the training course had clearly defined objectives but only 50% felt that the duration of the course was adequate to cover the objectives. While 70% strongly agreed that the resource persons conducted the training in the best possible manner, 15% disagreed and the rest did not express any views. Since only 40% of the respondents felt that the content knowledge provided during training was adequate to conduct the VI training effectively, it is not surprising that the quality of training of VIs remained poor. Unless the training of MTs is strengthened and streamlined, it may be difficult to organise an effective training programme for grassroots level functionaries using the cascade approach.

Continuing education scheme. After the conclusion of the TLCs, the Government of India launched a Continuing Education Scheme which introduced a new category of grassroots level functionaries, known as *Preraks* (facilitators) and Assistant *Preraks,* whose job is to set up and manage Continuing Education (CE) Centres and organise a series of CE Programmes for local communities. Unlike the TLC instructors, who worked on a purely voluntary basis, the *Preraks* are paid workers with twelve specific job responsibilities, ranging from surveying the needs of the local community to organising CE Programmes (for details see National Literacy Mission 2000:29-45). The Continuing Education Scheme envisages one CE centre for population units of 2 000 to 2 500 each, which includes 500 to 1 000 neo-literates (National Literacy Mission 2001:9). Each centre is expected to be managed by two functionaries – a *Prerak* and an Assistant *Prerak.* The training of the *Preraks* also follows the cascade approach but was conceived as a two-tier (not a three-tier) programme. The main organiser of the training programme (*Zila Saksharta Samithi or* State Resource Centre) identifies and trains key resource persons who in turn train the *Preraks*. The basic purposes of training are to equip *Preraks* with the knowledge and skills needed for setting up and managing CE centres and organising CE courses for local communities.

The training is planned in two phases. The first phase of training of eleven days (71.5 hours) is to be followed by a second phase consisting of a three-day refresher course after a gap of six months (National Literacy Mission 2001:85-90). An analysis of the content of the training programme *vis-à-vis* the job specifications for *Preraks* reveals several lacunae (see Table 3). The time allocated for different content areas seems inadequate to equip the *Preraks* with the necessary skills and knowledge to perform their duties. One of the significant tasks of the *Preraks* is to organise a series of need-based CE courses. For this, the *Preraks* have to be thoroughly oriented in curriculum design and transaction, but these are totally absent from the training design. The acquisition and classification of books and the management of a library are highly technical and time-consuming tasks which cannot be effectively undertaken by *Preraks* who have had only seven hours of training. Although the training methodology includes role-plays, discussions, practical demonstrations and field visits spread over eleven days, in practice the average duration of the training is no more than seven days and the lecture continues to be the main methodology.

During field visits the author noted that in several places the training of *Preraks* had not been conducted prior to the setting up of the CE centres, but often only three to six months later, which defeats the purpose of the training. In one of the training programmes, it was observed that several *Preraks* could not follow the lectures (delivered in English by resource persons) and could therefore not participate in discussions.[1] Unless the organisers make special efforts to offer some form of translation or invite resource persons who can conduct the sessions in the local language, the training may not yield the required results. It is also not uncommon for organisers to arrange training sessions at very short notice and as a result *Preraks* are often unable to attend.[2]

Table 3 Cascade approach: training design for *Preraks* of CE programme

Sr no	Content area	Methodology	Time (hours)
7.	Understanding needs of local community, selecting and conducting activities	Presentation and discussion, resource mapping	3
8.	Management of information window	Practical demonstration	4
9.	Organisation of literacy classes; introduction of IPCL method and methodology of teaching primers	Practical demonstration, exercises	7
10.	Mock literacy class session, procedures for monitoring and evaluating and financial management	Presentation, role-play	7
11.	*Preraks* 'training needs: cognitive competencies	Presentation, group discussion, role-play	2
12.	Roles and functions of *Preraks* and nodal *Preraks*	Presentation, group discussion, role-play	5
13.	Participatory rural appraisal	Demonstration, fieldwork with community	7
14.	Establishment and management of library at CE centre	Presentation, group discussion	3.5
15.	Organisation of lectures/ discussions/sports and cultural activities	Presentation, group discussion	3.5
16.	Convergence and networking, and community support	Brainstorming, role-play	3
17.	Record maintenance	Brainstorming, role-play	4
18.	Methods of forming self-help groups	Presentation and discussion	4
19.	Functioning of the development department and process of implementation of various schemes.	Field visit	3
20.	Concept and methods of monitoring the programme.	Presentation, group work	3
21.	Preparation of progress report , feedback on training	Presentation, group work	1.5

Source: National Literacy Mission 2001:85-90.

Direct approach

The direct approach to training developed by the university system in India during the 1980s targeted student volunteers and non-student animators involved in the Mass Programme of Functional Literacy and the Centre Based Adult Education Programme (University Grants Commission 1985:20-23). While the duration of training was ten hours for student volunteers (see Table 4), it was seventy hours for non-student volunteers (see Table 5). The thrust of the training programme was to acquaint participants with the conceptual and operational aspects of adult education programmes. In terms of the programme guidelines, the initial training was to be followed by a refresher course of ten hours after six months. The course content revolved around information and its dissemination. The methodology made no provision for developing group dynamics and there was little scope for sharing experiences or building on participants' strengths and weaknesses. As observed in the *Report of the Review Committee of University Grants Commission* (University Grants Commission 1987), the training of functionaries was a weak link in the programme and in overall terms its quality was not satisfactory. In fact, the achievements of universities in imparting training to adult education functionaries were 'far below expectation' (University Grant Commission 1987:38).

Table 4 Direct approach to training student instructors

Sr no	Content area	Methodology	Time (hours)
1.	Initial pro forma giving details about the learner (name, address, occupation, time of teaching)	Practice in completing the pro forma	0.30
2.	Monthly report on progress made by instructor and the learner in form of learning activities covered	Practice in filling in form and feedback on teaching problems	0.30
3.	Mid-term assessment (after two months)	Use of test and analysis of test results	1
4.	Skills in using the primer and other learning activities	Practice teaching, group work	8

Source: University Grants Commission 1985.

Table 5 Direct approach to training instructors of UGC-sponsored adult education programme

Sr no	Content area	Methodology	Time (hours)
1.	Concept of adult and continu-ing/extension education	Lecture/discussion/film/slides	2
2.	Exposure to 20 point program-me with emphasis on population education, national integration, co-operatives, health and environment, science for masses	Charts, slides, films followed by lecture and discussion	2
3.	Introduction to developmental and welfare programmes like PRYSEM, NREP, IRDP, etc (adult education and development)	Case study, presentation and discussion	2
4.	Planning/programming for areas/ communities for adult education work	Discussion on the basis of surveys and group work	2
5.	Preparation of learners' profile	Discussion on conducting surveys, fieldwork	6
6.	Characteristics of the learner group (age group 15 to 35)	Lecture and discussion on some cases	1
7.	Motivational aspects	Role-play, slide show, followed by discussion	2
8.	Role and functions of an instructor and relationship with other functionaries	A checklist, pamphlet and charts followed by discussion	2
9.	Organising and conducting an adult education centre	Panel presentation/slide show/with discussion. Visit to an AEC followed by discussion	6
10.	Communication skills and types of communication	Introduction, role-play, games followed by discussion	2
11.	Methods of adult education: Literacy methods Conducting discussions Developing skills in learners	Note on guidelines on planning and presentation of a lesson, followed by discussion Demonstrations of different approaches; Practice lessons by participants (under supervision and guidance)	2 4 6

Sr no	Content area	Methodology	Time (hours)
12.	Importance of recreation and entertainment role of different media, both traditional and modern.	Lecture cum demonstrations (visual aids, slide show, puppet plays, songs, improvi-sations, radio/ television/video/films, tape recorders, among other things)	4
13.	Introduction to available teaching/ learning materials such as literacy cards, primers, workbooks, folders, charts, practice books, visual aids etc	Lectures cum display (exhibition)	3
14.	Preparation and use of simple low-cost teaching/learning aids, like literacy cards, flash cards, charts, folders, etc	Demonstration, followed by workshop/group work	2
15.	Supporting programmes to be organised for the centre	Lecture, list of items and program-mes followed by discussion	2
16.	Monitoring and evaluation	Lecture, charts, interview schedules, guidelines for evalua tion, demonstration on conducting interviews and administering schedules, practical exercises, interpretation of data, etc	4
17.	Financial and administrative arrangements	Lecture note followed by discussion	6
18.	Maintaining records such as attendance register, visitors' book, register for teaching learning material and equipment, different forms, pro forma, correspondence, daily diary etc	Demonstration and practical exercises	4
19.	Preparation of initial report and monthly report	Demonstration and practical exercises	2
20.	Planning for post-literacy, follow-up and CE programmes	Project work in group followed by discussion	4

Source: University Grants Commission 1985.

Participatory approach

Several NGOs that are actively involved in social development programmes have adopted *participatory training* methods. Here the focus is on experiential learning and on people's participation in building their own future. Participatory training emphasises not only knowledge but also awareness, skill and building the internal competencies of development workers. A review by Acharya and Varma (1996:357-371) of a training design adopted in Gujarat during 1993 lists the modules below: The need for training; The role of training in social change; Developing insights into how disadvantaged people learn; Group behaviour; Self-development of trainers; Understanding the effective use of training methods; Training design; and Facilitation skills.

These modules were put into practice in three phases (see Table 6). The first and third phases were residential programmes each lasting eight days. During the second phase, which extended to four months between the first and third phases, participants were expected to practise what they had learnt during the first phase. Reviews of experience, analysis, action and reflection were built in to all three phases. A variety of methods, such as analysis of participants' experiences, selected case studies and simulated experiences, were used (Acharya & Varma 1996:357-371). This methodology, which helped in designing a people-centred, locally relevant training programme, was spread over a long period and depended on the total commitment of trainers and trainees.

While this methodology may be very effective for training a small group, it may be difficult to use when training large numbers.

Table 6 Participatory training design (adopted during 1993 for Gujarat-based NGOs)

Days	Phase	Methods
	Phase I	
1.	Setting the context of the training Introduction of participants Re-articulation of learning needs Spelling out the objective of training Understanding training and participatory training	Dyads Group discussion Group discussion
2.	Understanding participatory training (continued)	Group work; self-study; consolidation

Days	Phase	Methods
3.	Articulation of participatory training principles Role of trainer Small group dynamics and processes	Group work; consolidation; group discussion; simulation; role-play
4.	Small group process (continued) Inter-group process Mid-term review	Video review Exercise Open verbal
5.	Trainers' capacities Trust, respect, gender	Exercise
6.	Self-awareness and development	Reflection
7.	Training design Training methods and analysis	Case analysis Demonstrations
8.	Planning	Group work; questions

All the learning themes above were dealt with using a variety of methods, such as analysis of participants' experiences, analysis of cases and analysis of simulated experiences, with adequate input to sharpen the theoretical base.

Table 6 (continued)

Phase II	
Participants practise training at their work place and review their performance. Help the participants during the training.	
Phase III	
Phase	**Methods**
Analysis of training experience	Group work
Training design preparation	Group work
Training design preparation	Case work
Use of training methods	Practice in group, video review
Facilitation	Group work, video review, lecture
Training evaluation, follow up, report	Case study
Insight into gender issues, trainer authority, team work, participation	Guided group work; group work
Self-development of trainer	Discussion, lecture
Participatory training philosophy	Group discussion
Follow-up planning	Group work
Evaluation	Group work
Closure	Open

Source: Acharya & Verma 1996.

The open and distance learning (ODL) approach

Since ODL emerged as an effective tool of education and training only during the 1990s, and its main focus was formal education, there is hardly any experience of using ODL in the training of grassroots level functionaries in the non-formal sector. Although prime facie it may be possible to argue that the adoption of ODL would have improved implementation, there is hardly any research evidence to support this argument. Systematic studies need to be initiated to examine the impact of ODL on training. However there have been some significant cases where educational technologies have been used in the non-formal education of learners and have played an important role in promoting lifelong learning.

Radio

Radio has been particularly useful in supplementing literacy learning because of its wide coverage, relatively low cost and diversity of programmes, and because learning groups may be readily organised.

Farm forums and radio rural. All India Radio (AIR) has been actively promoting farm forums since 1949 with the aim of enabling listeners to put the information broadcast to them to good use and of encouraging post-broadcast discussions. By 1950 there were 150 farm forums in Delhi, Bombay, Madras and Uttar Pradesh, but it was only after the launching of the Community Development Project in 1952 that more systematic attempts were made to strengthen the farm forums (Mathur & Kapur n.d.). Based on the Canadian experience of Radio Rural forums, India started a pilot project in 1956 in 145 villages near Pune in Western India. The aim was to enable farmers to listen, discuss and act. A typical Radio Rural forum was a club of about 15 to 20 farmers who wished to listen, in an organised way, to selected radio programmes covering agriculture, health and education and to conduct discussions among themselves, increase their knowledge and information and take appropriate actions. A radio programme was typically 30 to 35 minutes long and started with answers to questions sent in by forum members and reports on action projects undertaken by members. This was followed by the presentation of the main topic of the day. The presentation took various forms: dramatisation, interviews, talks, discussions among farmers or with experts.

During the pilot phase 20 programmes (each of half an hour) were broadcast twice a week for 20 weeks, covering agriculture, health, home management, education and community development. With the implementation of the Farmers' Training and Functional Literacy Project in 1967, when farm broadcasting became an integral part of this project, AIR started an intensive Farm and Home Radio Broadcast with the twofold purpose of providing a package of technical and service information on crops of particular importance to each area and informing and educating women about their role in the process of change from traditional to more modern forms of agriculture. By 1987, 73 AIR stations were broadcasting Farm and Home Radio Programmes.

ICDS radio forums. In 1975, Integrated Child Development Services (ICDS) started an experimental media orientation project modelled on the radio forums and focusing on the theme of mother and child health. The target audience was rural women, particularly pregnant and lactating mothers. The project established no fewer than 14 000 ICDS radio forums (Chen 1989:13). The project evaluation showed that literates started and finished with more knowledge than non-literates, but that in amount of knowledge gained non-literates did just as well as literates, indicating that the forum was an effective means of teaching non-literates. It also fostered decision-making in the villages in which the broadcasts were received, thereby serving as an important instrument of village democracy (Diaz Bordenave 1971:36-42).

Project radio education for adult literacy. One of the world's largest radio-based literacy projects, Project Radio Education for Adult Literacy (PREAL), was put into practice in India during 1990 and 1991 by the National Literacy Mission in collaboration with AIR in sixteen districts of four states (Madhya Pradesh, Rajasthan, Uttar Preadesh and Bihar). A set of special radio lessons (Akashwani Pathmalas) was developed based on the language and culture of the target group. The main target group was women learners, and the project duration was six months. PREAL broadcasts contained enrichment, entertainment and didactic programmes on literacy. The taped radio lessons and a primer were provided to learners to improve their pace of learning. Two-in-one radio-cum-audio-cassette players were distributed free of charge by the government to 3 500 adult education centres and approximately 10 000 women listened to the radio lessons broadcast by eight radio stations. In this experiment radio was used primarily to reinforce the reading skills initially acquired by learners at local literacy centres.

The project evaluation showed that while the younger age groups took greater advantage of the lessons, the benefits of literacy were not perceived by many. Training of instructors and monitoring of programmes were weak. Due to linguistic difficulties, learners could not understand the lessons, which were couched in complex language, nor could they enjoy drama. PREAL was, moreover, undertaken at a most inappropriate time of social tension caused by *Mandir-Masjid* (Temple/Mosque) agitation which had rocked the four states, and people's attention could not be engaged by the programme to the desired extent. For the same reason the ground work went awry. The evaluation also showed that PREAL was not suitable for those who live in extreme poverty and in an underdeveloped society (Sivaswami 1997:16-17). Though well researched, the project did not continue beyond the pilot phase mainly due to a shift in government policy, the emergence of the campaign approach and the introduction of a new pedagogy of 'improved pace and content of learning' (IPCL).[3]

Impact of the campaign approach. While both national and regional AIR stations continued to broadcast a number of knowledge-based and life enrichment programmes, especially on and around International Literacy Day, a special radio programme on literacy titled *'Aao Ek Deep Jalayen'* ('Come, light a lamp') was broadcast in Delhi Times FM every Thursday from 14:00 to 15:00 from 1996 to 1998 (Government of India 2001:26). In order to make the programme more interesting and attractive, listeners were given prizes for the right answers to questions asked in the programme. Since the launching, in different parts of the country, of the TLCs in 1990, radio and television have started playing a key role in motivating and mobilising the masses through jingles and literacy songs and plays.

Television

Television has been effectively deployed to disseminate information, create awareness, motivate and educate the masses by several agencies in India, notably the Central Health Education Bureau, ICDS, Directorate of Agricultural Extension Co-operative Education, Workers Education and the National Literacy Mission. Different agencies have had different target groups and the content of the programmes has also varied.

Satellite instructional television experiment. In 1975 India became the first country in the world to broadcast mass television from space when it launched a Satellite Instructional Television Experiment (SITE) using the American Satellite ATS-6. During 1975 and 1976, instructional TV programmes especially designed for young and adult viewers were beamed to 2 400 villages spread over the states of Bihar, Madhya Pradesh, Orissa, Rajasthan, Karnataka and Andhra Pradesh. Two-and-a-half hour evening transmissions for adults covered themes related to agriculture, animal husbandry, health and family planning. The evaluation of the experiment showed that lecture formats used for health and hygiene programmes were not very effective and that instructional telecast needs to be location-specific in terms of language, idiom, dress and culture (Satellite Instructional *Television Experiment* 1976:6-7).

Madras University's literacy through television experiment. During the 1980s Madras University launched an experimental project on literacy through television ('life education') with a view to teaching illiterate adults and communicating effectively with them. It reached 1 500 adults in the three districts of Chingalpet, South Arcot and North Arcot in South India. It was designed to transmit knowledge and skills to create opportunities for self-fulfilment. The project had three components – awareness, vocational skills and literacy (including numeracy). Each component was designed on the basis of a survey undertaken in 169 villages of the three selected districts. The state government provided community television sets to 200 villages located in the selected districts. Feedback was collected by animators through weekly letters which revealed the utility of the programme in enabling villagers to open bank accounts and apply for loans (Jayagopal 1985:98-102).

The INSAT programme. These experiences helped in planning and launching the INSAT programme. Whereas in SITE, transmission could be viewed only on specially made direct reception sets (DRS), with INSAT a combination of both DRS and very high frequency (VHR) sets was introduced. The Indian Space Research Organisation took the lead by configuring a two-year project on Development Communication and implementing it at Jhabua in Madhya Pradesh in 1996. Development programmes in the areas of health, agriculture, watershed management, local governance *(Panchayati Raj)* education, general information and entertainment were transmitted and viewed using 150 DRS. One of the aims of the project was to promote literacy through the daily transmission of literacy support materials. Satellite talk-back terminals were provided to all the 12 neighbourhoods (blocks) in the town of Jhabua in Madhya Pradesh, and an interactive programme, with a one-way video and two-way audio teleconferencing network, was utilised for effective communication among viewers and experts.

Altogether 100 half-hour programmes were produced. Twenty of these were based on awareness building, 60 on the three literacy primers and 20 on post-literacy. These programmes basically served as support materials for voluntary instructors. A typical one-hour programme started with thirty minutes of face-to-face literacy teaching, twenty minutes of telecast by learners and ten minutes of recapitulation and reinforcement of learning. The programme was telecast five days a week in the evening. Its success depended on the educational level and extent of training received by the instructors (Ghosh 2000:24).

Joint national literacy mission and ET&T project. The National Literacy Mission, in collaboration with ET&T Corporation, in launched a project in 25 villages in four states Rajasthan, Uttar Pradesh, Madhya Pradesh and Bihar to promote literacy among the rural masses through electronic media, to give them vocational guidance to help them improve the quality of their lives and to make them aware of the importance of health, hygiene, nutrition and rural development. Each village (Adult Education Centre or *Jan Shikshan Nilayam*) was given a *Sangamitra* set consisting of a colour television, a video cassette player in a special cabinet as well as software already available from several government departments. Screening of the software was followed by discussions led by the centre's *Preraks*. Some of these programmes motivated a number of learners to open bank accounts and take an active part in development programmes *(Report on Vivek Darpan* 1990).

Film

During the last decade, the National Literacy Mission produced about 300 motivational, educational, recreational and training films in adult education (Shah 1997:301-324). The films on the training of voluntary instructors (*Dhai Akar*) and literacy based films (*Chauraha, Khilt Kaliyan*) were well received by learners. However, these films were not widely used by adult education organisations in the country mainly due to the lack of infrastructure facilities and the large number of trainees that had to be catered for at each screening.[4]

Training through ODL

Several organisations in India are involved in training adult education functionaries at national and state levels, but it was only during the 1990s that they started exploring the potential of ODL for training. An overview of ODL utilisation shows that of the 27 State Resource Centres in the country, which are key training institutions in adult education, only one State Resource Centre in Indore (Madhya Pradesh) has made use of ODL for training grassroots level functionaries. At national level, Indira Gandhi National Open University (IGNOU) and the National Council of Educational Research Training are taking a keen interest in ODL for training teachers of formal schools (Phalachandra nd; Menon 2001:114-127). In the non-formal sector, the National Institute of Public Co-operation and Child Development (NIPCCD) has adopted ODL for orienting functionaries of ICDS and women *Panchayat* (Village) Members (*A Report on National Consultation* 1996:31). Of the 262 universities in India, 103 have Departments of Adult Education, but only one, Shivaji University, Kolhapur in Maharashtra, offers a postgraduate Diploma in Adult Education through distance mode (*All India Directory* 2001:87).[5] Of the ten Open Universities, two IGNOU and BR Ambedkar have designed a number of certificate courses targeting grassroots level functionaries. Of the ten Open Schools in India, the National Open School (NOS) has been enthusiastic about adult education and has designed a course entitled Open Basic Education, with a view to providing a learning continuum for neo-literates and to make secondary level education accessible to them through a three-stage curriculum equivalent to standards 3,5 and 8 of the formal school (Sangal 2001; n.d.; see also *The school that made the difference*, NOS publicity brochure). NOS also offers a number of vocational and life enrichment courses which may be of immense use to grassroots level functionaries.

Training of Preraks in Madhya Pradesh: a case study

Madhya Pradesh (MP) is one of the biggest states in India and has been implementing a number of innovative programmes in the field of adult and basic education. In response to the policy guidelines of the National Literacy Mission of the Government of India, a decision was taken by the MP government in 1988 to set up *Jan Shikshan Nilayams* (JSNs) to provide post-literacy and CE programmes for neo-literates. Each JSN was expected to cater for the needs of 5 000 people, and was managed by a *Prerak* (facilitator) who organised a range of educational and developmental activities for the local community. During 1991 and 1992, the MP government recruited 1 928 *Preraks* to be posted in 45 districts. In line with the National Literacy Mission guidelines, the *Preraks* were to be given an initial training of 21 days.

Training a large number of Preraks who were geographically scattered through the traditional face-to-face method being a time-consuming, costly and tedious process, it was decided to adopt a distance training approach. The project was planned, executed and evaluated by the State Resource Centre, Indore, which is managed by a reputed non-governmental organisation, *Bhartiya Grameen Mahila Sangh (Report on Training of Preraks* n.d.). The main characteristics of the programme included:utilisation of multimedia and a team approach in the preparation of course materials; provision for a contact programme through interdepartmental collaboration; adoption of a modular approach to learning; assessment and institutionalising continuous assessment.

The curriculum, preparation of audio programmes and evaluation strategies were evolved through workshops. The key institutions, viz. the District Institutes of Education and Training, and the District Adult Education Offices, were identified as supportive and monitoring units. The State Resource Centre gave faculty members of these institutions adequate orientation in the distance training mode. The course materials were divided into 13 areas: Introduction to adult education; Concept of Jan Shikshan Nilayam; Role and functions of a *Prerak*; People's participation; Effective communication; Evening classes; Setting up libraries and reading rooms; Study circles; Training programmes; Sports, cultural and entertainment programmes; Information and communication centres; Population education; Final evaluation.

The materials for each area were despatched as learning kits comprising the main topic; a response sheet; an audio-cassette; a file containing pad and pen; reference materials, viz. *Prerak Margdarshika* (guidelines for *Prerak*), *Sandharba Pustika* (contextual material); a diary; a serial publication of SRC *Akshar ki Chauh; and* folders on people's co-operation, role-play and report writing.

The learning kits were mailed to the District Adult Education Offices for onward distribution to the *Preraks*. After every third dispatch a personal contact programme was arranged. During the year, four personal contact programmes were held at the district level, which gave the *Preraks* the opportunity to discuss problems or seek clarification.

The evaluation of the programme revealed that while 22% (390) of the *Preraks* dropped out at various stages, 78% were regular in sending back responses sheets. Trainees' performance and the quality of training were analysed from the response sheets. The *Preraks* were given certain field assignments to assess their ability to organise field activities and undertake practical work. These assignments related to a number of areas, such as surveying the reading interest of neo-literates, organising sports, study circles, population education and so on. It was observed that only 6% to 24% completed between one and six assignments. The project was also evaluated in terms of the number of assignments completed by the *Preraks*. This showed that 48% received an 'A' grade, 46% 'B' and 6% a 'C' grade in their final assessment. It was noted that the distance mode of training did not succeed in encouraging the self-learning habit among *Preraks*.

The programme was put into practice over a period of about twelve months after a preliminary three-month period of preparatory work. Although the State Resource Centre succeeded in covering 90% of the target group, the main weakness was the inadequate personal contact programme and orientation of project administrators. Media support was also extremely limited and confined to an audio programme. Since tape recorders were available only at district headquarters and many *Preraks* did not have tape recorders or had no access to them in their homes, the audio support was not fully utilised. Monitoring of the programme was also found to be weak.

As the country's first attempt at imparting training through distance mode to adult education field functionaries, the project provided a model which could have been refined and further tried out. This did not, however, happen. As mentioned by the Director of SRC, Indore, the project was not sufficiently publicised to draw the attention of adult educators (Supekar 2001). It is surprising that the National Literacy Mission, which sponsored the project, did not show an interest in replicating it in other states.

Were the *Preraks* trained through ODL any better than those who were trained by traditional methods? Since the main focus of the organisers was to cover large number of geographically scattered trainees within a limited time, there was no research agenda to compare training through ODL with traditional approaches. Besides, the National Literacy Mission stopped funding JSNs during 1992 and 1993 and there were thus no resources for undertaking any studies. An informal interaction with two ODL-trained *Preraks* revealed that, unlike the 'one-shot training' of seven to ten days, the ODL training provided more time and space to absorb the relevant knowledge and skills. Strongly endorsing the training through ODL, these *Preraks* suggested there was a need to improve the media support through video conferencing, television and radio.

Training through open schools

There are nine state Open Schools and one National Open School in India, which offer education programmes through distance mode at school level. They cater to the educational needs of out-of-school children, unemployed or working adults, physically and mentally disabled people and neo-literates. In addition to formal courses, these schools offer life enrichment, vocational courses and open basic education through 731 accredited institutions and 141 vocational institutions spread over the country. Programmes are offered through printed self-learning materials, audio-video and personal contacts (Government of India 2001:6-7; Profile of NOS 1999). Some of these courses, such as *Jan Swasthya* (Community Health) *Paripurva Mahila* (An Aware and Empowered Woman) are sought after by development functionaries and are considered as being on a par with other well-designed training programmes. Apart from these life enrichment courses, NOS also offers a number of vocational training courses (National Open School 2001:7).

Paripurna Mahila Course: a case study

The Paripurna Mahila course was developed by an NGO, the Asian Centre for Organisation Research and Development (ACORD), in 1992 and approved and accredited by NOS. This brief overview throws light on the course content, methodology and the socio-economic background of learners. The course is currently offered in the Hindi Gujarati, Telugu and Oriya languages.

This one-year course consists of nine modules and aims at raising critical awareness of both men and women of gender issues and at reaching out to women at grassroots level particularly fieldworkers who are associated with NGOs working in rural areas and urban slums. In addition the course provides educational inputs with a view to raising women's self-esteem and self-confidence and making them realise that they themselves are not responsible for their low status in society. Since education and knowledge systems are patriarchal, they have often domesticated and marginalised women instead of empowering them. A number of NGOs, government departments and universities involved in women's development programmes are not clear about the concept of empowerment. There is therefore a growing awareness of the need to establish gender issues as a priority concern in developmental initiatives. In fact, the main objective of the course is to change attitudes and sensitise both men and women regarding women's contribution to society as equal partners in development. The course also equips development workers with modern and effective communication techniques so that they can impart this knowledge to the community in an effective way.

When the course began in 1993, nine modules were provided to learners as printed booklets in Hindi: Communication; Indian history and status of women in different religions; Women of today; Women and family; Woman as a person; Women's contribution to the economy; The Indian political system and women's NGOs; Women and the law; Women and government organisations, including the role of women in Panchayati Raj (village government).

In addition to the printed materials, two sets of flashcards and an audio cassette (containing songs and a play on gender issues) were provided to each candidate. The methodology of the course included participation in workshops, self study of printed materials and examination. The course was administered through distance mode and the modules were sent to the candidates by mail. Enrolled candidates were invited to attend a three-day introductory workshop at which they filled in a questionnaire on their perceptions about women's status in and contribution to society. The workshop introduced the course materials, provided training in the effective use of communication materials (flashcards and audiotapes) and gave input on filling up the answer sheets attached to the module. Trainees attended a second workshop at the end of the course, where the same questionnaire was administered to ascertain to what extent their perceptions and views had changed as a result of their exposure to the course. These workshops facilitated face-to-face interaction among candidates and faculty and gave them an opportunity to share their experiences.

The evaluation of the course showed that it had played a significant role in giving women access to information they generally do not have. During the first two years, ACORD enrolled about 500 candidates employed in 12 non-governmental organisations located in Delhi, Rajasthan, Uttar Pradesh, Bihar, Jammu and Kashmir and Haryana. The course not only empowered women but also enabled male candidates to examine their own stereotypes about women and brought about attitudinal and behavioural changes in the long run (Dighe 1994; see also ACORD, Course Brochure on 'Gender Sensitization' and 'Jan Swasthya').

Training through the open universities: Empowering women through self-help groups

There are ten Open Universities in India which offer 288 formal and non-formal education programmes at certificate, diploma, degree and postgraduate levels (Distance Education Council 2001:36). Some of the courses, particularly 'Empowering women through self-help groups', 'Youth and development', 'Rural development' and 'Participatory project planning', are highly sought after by grassroots level workers in the development sector. Broadly, they aim at imparting training in supervisory, organisational and employable skills, upgrading professional competence and providing technical and vocational training in diverse fields, among them health, nutrition, environment, human rights, agriculture, microcredit, participatory planning, rural development and women's empowerment. Most programmes are offered at certificate level and their duration varies from 6 to 9 months. Fees are designed to attract low-income field functionaries and unemployed youth.

Self-help groups (SHGs) have emerged as one of the major strategies in group formation in various government developmental schemes in India, including the CE programme of the National Literacy Mission. Currently India has about 700 000 government-supported women's groups, 230 000 facilitators and 11 600 supervisory level functionaries. Several research studies have shown that strong women's groups contribute substantially to the development and convergence of services and activities, besides developing self-confidence among women. However, the sustainability of SHGs has been a major problem due to the poor quality of training. To strengthen the SHGs through well-structured training, INGOU has designed a certificate course on 'Empowering women through self-help groups'. (Certificate Programme 2000: 9-10)

The course is a joint venture of IGNOU, the Department of Women and Child Welfare and the Indian Satellite Research Organisation. Although the minimum duration of the course is six months, learners have the freedom to take up to two years to complete it. The course is open to all those above 18 years with an educational level of class VIII. The target group includes supervisory level practitioners, trainers and other field functionaries of various women's development programmes, ICDS, NGOs and those interested in women issues. The course aims at helping learners acquire the necessary knowledge, attitude and skills to train others in similar areas of work and assess the effectiveness of the satellite-based direct broadcasting-cum-interactive-communication network. In the process it is hoped that the course will help evolve an effective and sustainable training network in the country. (Brochure on Certificate Programme 2000)

The 16-credit certificate programme consists of four courses of four credits each. Assessment consists of course-based assignments (50% weight) and an end of term examination (50% weight). Instruction is through multimedia, which include self-instructional print materials, non-print (audio-video) materials and personal contact including teleconferencing and radio counselling (see Figure 5). It is estimated that the course will require a total of 480 hours of learning spread as follows (see also Figure 4): study of print materials (168 hours); viewing TV programmes (96 hours); listening to radio broadcasts (96 hours); preparing assignments (48 hours); attending personal contact programmes (72 hours). (See Programme Guide on Certificate Programme 2000: 38-39)

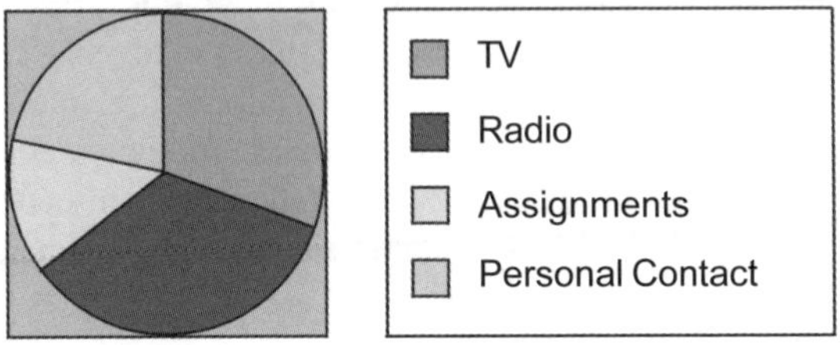

Figure 4 Spread of learning

The IGNOU audio-video programmes are regularly broadcast and telecast through the national AIR network and on national television. Learners can also participate in radio counselling and teleconferencing conducted at IGNOU study centres.

Table 7 Course outline

Course no	Name of course	Main content areas
1.	Women's empower-ment perspectives and approaches	Introduction; Historical background; Feminism; Patriarchy ; Environment for advancement of status of women; Dynamics of women's empowerment
2.	Self-help groups	Nature of group Process of forming self-help groups Self-help group operation
3.	Development through self-help groups	Understanding micro enterprises and micro credit Organising for micro enterprise
4.	Towards sustenance of self-help groups	Management of self-help groups Group sustenance
	Supplementary reading materials	Learners' journal Understand and interpret laws What is a boy and what is a girl?

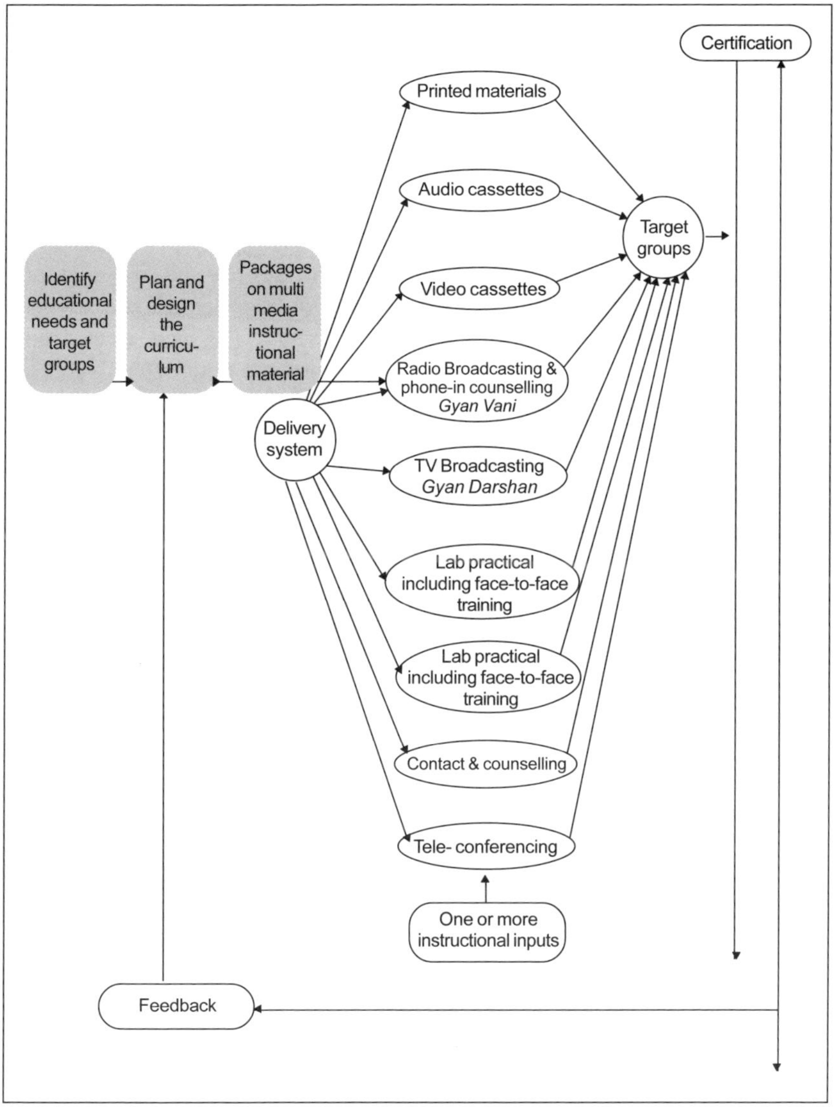

Figure 5 Teaching-learning system of Open University

Source: Distance Education Council, Open Universities in India, 2001, New Delhi: IGNOU, 2001, p.3.

The course is delivered through a satellite-based direct broadcasting-cum-interactive-communication network. It provides two-way audio and one-way video communication support at all levels. Teaching by counselling discussion and pre-recorded audio-video programmes is conveyed by television signals through a workstation (teaching end) and via satellite transponder and received at the training-cum-classroom locations (receiving end) through a Direct Reception System (DRS). The system enables recipients at the learning end to ask questions using STD phone facilities that are networked and heard live by all the locations. The programme was launched in 2001 to coincide with the Year of Women's Empowerment, with 150 DRS sites with receiving terminals and TV facilities and 250 new telephone connections.

Panchayat ODL training programme. ODL strategies have also been successfully used to impart mass training to different categories of clientele such as school teachers, Anganwadi (preschool teachers) and *Panchayat* members (elected representatives at the village level). While NCERT took the initiative in organising mass teacher orientation programmes through the distance mode, IGNOU, in collaboration with the Ministry of Rural Development, launched an innovative mass training programme to make the elected representatives of *Panchayats* (the lowest level of local self-government in India) aware of their roles and responsibilities. Since many of the more than 3 million members elected to various levels of local self-government after the 73rd amendment of the Constitution in 1972 were non-literates and had little idea of the concepts and practices of self-governance and practically no expertise in formulating and implementing developmental projects, it was crucial to educate them so that they could initiate the socio-economic transformation of their communities. Because the task was so great and so urgent, and given the limitations of conventional training, IGNOU designed a multimedia approach consisting of 23 booklets of self-learning print materials with extensive illustrations, six videos and twelve audio programmes, and a contact programme. An innovative feature was the use of a mobile reception system located at weekly markets which disseminated information through an audio-video package with an interactive element. The introduction of self-learning print materials and AV packages was followed up by contact sessions of intensive counselling by trained counsellors in every village.

The evaluation of the programme put into practice in four districts (among 58 000 elected members) of Madhya Pradesh revealed that the materials had generated a great deal of discussion and created more awareness among participants. Due to demand from other states, not only were the print materials translated into several language but the audio-video package was also dubbed into regional languages (Aslam 2000:309-315).

ODL courses in the development sector. Today several ODL courses are available to grassroots level functionaries in the development sector in India. These are designed by professionals and follow well-defined curriculum and evaluation procedures. They are offered through state accredited institutions, and are rated highly by employment agencies. They test both theoretical knowledge and practical skills through written examinations, field-based assignments and practicums conducted at accredited institutions. The courses are regularly and thoroughly evaluated by external consultants/agencies using extensive data generated through interviews, questionnaires and studies of academic records and course materials. The effective performance of the field functionaries bears testimony to their successful acquisition and transfer of skills. The increasing demand for the course materials and their translation into regional languages is also an indicator of their effectiveness.

Conclusion

Since the 1980s significant changes have taken place in the training of adult education functionaries in India. Apart from the increasing trend towards decentralisation, there has been a growing interest in Open and Distance Learning for evolving innovative training programmes. Over the years, India has experimented with radio, television, satellite telecast and teleconferencing for the promotion of basic education. However, a recent study entitled 'Current use of distance education mode in basic education' reveals that the use of electronic media has been 'not very encouraging and weak mainly due to the financial and other constraints' (Ambasht & Sharma 2000:4; *Reaching the Unreached*). Though a number of training and open learning institutions in the country offer a variety of training programmes, they target senior and middle level professionals working in the area of health, human resource development, agriculture, management, information technology and school education.[6] The large number of functionaries (see Table 8) working at grassroots level in the developmental sector rely heavily on traditional methods of training. A survey of 200 NGOs in Delhi that are actively involved in training field functionaries revealed that only one NGO ACORD has adopted the distance mode (*Development Alternatives Information Networks* 1998).

Table 8 Profile of grassroots level workers in ABE in India

SI. no	Name of programme	Designation of worker	Minimum educational qualifications	Remuneration/ honorarium per month (Rs)
1.	Continuing education	Prerak, Assistant Prerak	XII X	700 500
2.	Mahila Samakhya	Sahayogini	VIII	1500
3.	Total Literacy Campaign	Voluntary instructors	VIII	Voluntary work
4.	Rural Functional Literacy Project	Literacy instructor	V or VIII	200

SI. no	Name of programme	Designation of worker	Minimum educational qualifications	Remuneration/ honorarium per month (Rs)
5.	Developmental programmes: health, education, agriculture extension, women's development programme, rural development etc	Extension/health worker	X	As per government scale
6.	School education	Primary school teacher	X & JBT	As per government scale
7.	Non-formal education	Non-formal education instructor	VII	500

Source: Annual Report of Ministry of Human Resource Development, Government of India, for the year 1999-2000. New Delhi: Government of India Press, 2001.

In view of the limited attempts made by NGOs like the ACORD (New Delhi), *Bharatiya Grameen Mahila Sangh* (Indore), and IGNOU in training select categories of grassroots level functionaries through ODL, will it be prudent to develop ODL as a key mode of training? Are there adequate expertise and infrastructure in the country? The NASSCOM (National Association of Software Services Companies) in India conducted a Survey in 2000 which shows that India has witnessed unprecedented growth in communication and convergence services in recent times (see Table 9.). With the institutional infrastructure developed in different parts of the country by open learning institutions both public and private the availability of exclusive educational channels (*Gyan Darshan* and *Gyan Vani*) and a wide variety of audio-video programmes, it may now be easier to explore the possibilities[6] of using ODL for the training of grassroots level functionaries in adult education. The excellent teaching learning systems devised by IGNOU and NOS can be effectively adopted for training. However, for ODL to be successfully deployed, the[7] policymakers and programme administrators in adult education need to be familiarised with ODL strategies and structures. In addition, the specialists in open learning also need to be oriented in the teaching-learning styles of adults and their psychology. Such an attempt seems to be timely and relevant in view of the increasing number of *Preraks* (of CE Centres) who need to be trained. According to the Scheme of Continuing Education launched in 1999, the Government of India proposes to set up one CE centre for every population unit of 2 000 to 2 500. Since each centre will employ two people, a *Prerak* and an assistant *Prerak,* their number will be enormous and they can be effectively trained through ODL cost-effectively and quickly.

An outline of a training course developed in consultation with a group of selected *Prerak* is given in the next section of this article.

Table 9 Status of communication and convergence services in India

NASSCOM Survey	Level on March 31 2000 (millions)	Target for 2008 (millions)
Total number of personal computers	4.3	20
Internet subscribers	.77	35
Internet users	3.3	100
Fixed phones	26	125
Cable TV subscribers	37	70
Television set	75	225

Source: NASSCOM 2000)

Box 1

Outline of a sample course for Training of Preraks	
Aim	To enhance the capabilities of participants to set up and manage community-based Continuing Education (CE Centres
Specific	To enable the grassroots level functionaries (Preraks) to acquire a basic **objectives** knowledge and understanding of adult and continuing education the skills to organise and manage a CE programme expertise in studying the needs and resources of the local community
Content Areas	**Module 1** 1. Concept of adult education and development national and international perspective 2. Literacy scenario world, Asia, developing countries (with special reference to India) 3. Links between adult education and development 4. Current policy and programmes of adult education in India 5. Philosophy and programme of CE in India
	Module 2 1. Broad features of CE centres in India 2. Understanding the perceptions, needs, interests of members of local community 3. Technique of participatory rural appraisal

	7. Mapping local resources and networking with local institutions and experts 8. Organising skill development programmes[7] 9. Using electronic equipment and computers
Methodology	Self-learning print materials, audio-video materials, personal contact programmes, teleconferencing
Duration	3 months (study hours: 240)
Credits	8
Evaluation	Field-based diary, observation of a CE centre by examiner and end of term examination

References

Acharya, B & Varma, S. 1996. Participatory training for promotion of social development. *Adult Education and Development*, 47:357-371.

ACORD, Course Brochure on 'Gender Sensitization' and 'Jan Swasthya'.

All India directory of correspondence and distance education courses. 2001. New Delhi: Student Aid Publication.

Ambasht NK & Sharma, HL. 2000. *Current use of distance education mode in basic education*. New Delhi: National Open School.

Annual Report of Ministry of Human Resource Development, Government of India, for the year 1999-2000. New Delhi: Government of India Press, 2001.

Aslam, M. 2000. Education and training for millions: pedagogical challenges for distance education. *Open Learning* 15(3):309-315.

Bharat Gyan Vigyan Samithi. N.d.a. *Total Literacy Campaign training curriculum*. New Delhi: BGVS.

Bharat Gyan Vigyan Samithi. N.d.b. *Total Literacy Campaign: training strategy.* New Delhi: BGVS.

Census of India. 2001. Provisional Population Totals Series I, New Delhi: Controller of Publications.

Certificate Programme (2000).

Brochure on Certificate Programme (2000).

Programme Guide on Certificate Programme (2000).

Chen, P. 1989. Choice of media for adult education campaigns. *Jeevan Shiksha*,3(3):13.

Development Alternatives Information Networks. 1998. *DAINET NGO Directory Delhi* Vol 1. New Delhi: Development Alternatives.

Diaz Bordenave, JE. 1971. *Communication and rural development.* Paris: UNESCO.

Dighe, A. 1994. *Paripurna Mahila: an assessment report.*,New Delhi: ACORD.

Distance Education Council. 2001. *Open universities in India 2001: brief information.* New Delhi: IGNOU.

Ghosh, A. 2000. *Role of media in education for all.* New Delhi: NIEPA.

Ghosh, V. 2002. Personal communication, 4 January. Based on the telephonic interview with Mr. Avik Ghosh, Senior Fellow of National Institute of Adult Education, New Delhi, held on 4th January 2002.

Government of India. 1988. *National Literacy Mission.* New Delhi: Ministry of Human Resource Development.

Government of India. 1992. *National policy of education 1986* (as modified in 1992). New Delhi: Department of Education.

Government of India, Ministry of Human Resource Development. 2001. *Distance education and NICTs for basic education reaching the unreached: Country Paper, India.* New Delhi: National Open School.

Government of India, Prime Ministers' Council on Trade and Industry. 2000. *A policy framework for reforms in education.* New Delhi (Mimeograph).

IGNOU. 2000a. *Certificate programme: empowering women through self-help groups.* Programme guide. New Delhi: IGNOU.

IGNOU. 2001. New Delhi: IGNOU.

IGNOU. 2000b. *Certificate programme: empowering women through self-help groups.* Course brochure. New Delhi: IGNOU.

Jayagopal, R. 1985. *Adult learning: a psycho-social analysis in the Indian context.* Madras: University of Madras.

Kejarwal, S. 1997. Use of radio in tribal literacy programme. Paper presented at National Seminar held in Niepa, 17-19 March:16-17.

Krishna Reddy, B, Subba Reddy, PV & Ramakrishna, S. 1996. *An evaluative study of training programmes for volunteers of Total Literacy Campaign in Andhra Pradesh.* Hyderabad: State Resource Centre.

Lal Das, Y & Nand Singh, S. 2000. *Improving the training of literacy personnel and their social status in the context of literacy work.* Patna: State Resource Centre for Adult Education.

Mathur, JC & Kapur, CL. Nd. Radio in rural adult education and schools in India. (Mimeograph)

Menon, MB. 2001. Primary teacher training through distance mode. In *Studies in distance education*, edited by J Mohanty, New Delhi: Deep Publication, 114-127.

NASSCOM 2000.

National Literacy Mission. 1995. *Evaluation of Literacy Campaign in India: report of Expert group.* New Delhi: Directorate of Adult Education.

National Literacy Mission. 2000. *A handbook for Preraks.* New Delhi: Directorate of Adult Education.

National Literacy Mission. 2001. *Literacy campaign in India Annual Report,* 1999-2000. New Delhi: Directorate of Adult Education.

National Literacy Mission. 2001a. *Manual for training of Preraks*. New Delhi.

National Literacy Mission. 2001b. *Scheme of continuing education for neoliterates.* (Mimeograph)

National Open School. 2000. Prospectus: vocational courses 2000-2001.

National Open School (n.d.) *The school that made the difference*. Publicity Brochure.

Phalachandra, B. Nd. *Report on primary teachers' training through interactive video technology: Tel-SOPT Programme (Madhya Pradesh Karnataka).* New Delhi: NCERT

Premchand 2001. *Statistical database for literacy 2001.* New Delhi: Indian Adult Education Association.

Profile of NOS. 1999.

Reaching the Unreached: Report of the National Workshop of Reading the Unreached: Current use of Distance Education mode in Basic Education.

Report on national consultation of innovative approaches to ICDS training. 1996. Bangalore, 10-12 September.

Report on training of *Preraks* through distance learning approach. Nd. Indore: State Resource Centre.

Report on Vivek Darpan. 1990. New Delhi: Directorate of Adult Education. (Mimeograph)

Sangal, SS. 2001. Telephonic interview 4 October.

Sangal, SS. Nd. *Open basic education equivalency programme of NOS a part of continuing education.* (Mimeograph).

Satellite Instructional Television Experiment. 1976. Ahmedabad: Space Applications Centre.

Shah, SY. 1998. *An evaluation study of State Resource Centre for Adult Education in Madhya Pradesh*. New Delhi: Jawaharlal Nehru University.

Shah, SY. 1999. *An Encyclopedia of Indian adult education*. New Delhi: National Literacy Mission.

Sivaswami, G. 1997. PREAL world's largest radio-based literacy experiment. *Literacy Mission*, Nov:18-20.

Society for Participatory Research in Asia. 1993. *Learning for literacy: experiences under Total Literacy Campaign in India*. New Delhi: PRIA.

State Resource Centre for Non-formal Education. 1998. *Study of training loss.* Pune: Indian Institute of Education.

State Resource Centre in Adult Education. Nd. *Our research studies*. Indore: SRC.

Supekar, K, Bajpayee, A & Gokhale, M. Nd. *The pyramidal training structure in TLCs of Madhya Pradesh an impact study.* (Mimeograph paper)

Telephonic interview with Smt. Kunda Supekar, Director, SRC, M.P held on 18 September 2001.

UNDP. 2001. *Human development report 2000*. New Delhi: Oxford University Press.

University Grant Commission. 1985. *Training manual for adult education functionaries under point no. 16 of the New 20 Point Programme.* New Delhi: UGC.

University Grant Commission. 1987. *University system and extension as the third dimension: report of the Review Committee appointed by the UGC.* New Delhi: UGC.

Yagi, R. 2001. Process analysis of a Total Literacy Campaign in India: a case study of Udaipur District, Rajasthan. DPhil thesis, Oxford University.

Notes

1 Based on an interview with a participant (OP Swamy) in a training programme organised by State Resource Centre, New Delhi, in August 2001.

2 This observation is based on an interview with Ms Sonia Varma, a Prerak and one of those invited to attend the above training programme.

3 Based on a telephone interview with Mr Avik Ghosh, Senior Fellow of National Institute of Adult Education, New Delhi, held on 4th January 2002.

4 In a telephonic interview on 4 October 2001, Dr Mohan Kumar, Additional Director of Directorate of Adult Education, explained that audio-video cassettes are mailed free of charge to different organisations in the country. Since the cassettes can be used only for a limited number of screenings, there should have been repeated requests for fresh cassettes if they were in regular use. Since there was no such demand, he feels that their use was minimal.

5 Recently (in January 2002), the University of Kerala launched a one-year postgraduate Diploma in Continuing Education through its Institute of Distance Education, to train graduates in Programme Management of Continuing Education and Extension.

6 For example, Indian Society for Training and Development, New Delhi has been offering an 18-month Diploma in Training and Development for graduates since 1979. In addition the National Institute of Health and Family Welfare, New Delhi and the Indian Institute of Technology in Kharagpur, the Birla Institute of Technology, Pilani and a host of institutions of higher learning also offer several courses in the areas of health, technology, agriculture, management etc.

7 Grateful acknowledgements are due to the following institutions and individuals:The UNESCO Institute of Education, Hamburg for assigning me the study and Dr Madhu Singh, Senior Programme Specialist of UIE for encouraging me to undertake it; Prof Anita Dighe, Prabha Chawla, Mohammed Aslam, Savita Jain and MM Ansari of the Indira Gandhi National Open University, New Delhi; Prof NK Ambasht and Dr SS Sangal of the National Open School, New Delhi; Drs Mohan Kumar and Rajashekar of the Directorate of Adult Education, New Delhi; Ms Nishat Farooq, State Resource Centre, New Delhi; Prof KM Gupta, National Council of Educational Research and Training, New Delhi; Dr Kiran Wadhera, Asian Centre for Organisation Research and Development, New Delhi; Mr KC Choudhary, Indian Adult Education Association, New Delhi; Mr

Avik Ghosh, National Institute of Adult Education, New Delhi; Dr Anita Rampal, National Literacy Resource Centre, Mussorie; Ms Jaya Sharma of Nirantar, New Delhi; Ms Kunda Supekar, State Resource Centre, Indore; all for providing me with relevant materials and discussing different aspects of their work related to this project; also Ms Kamala Bahukhandi; Mr A Sundara Rajan, Mr Varun Mehra, Mr OP Swamy and Ms Sonia Varma for providing able research assistance.

3

Training initiatives in the field of adult basic education in Tanzania: Exploring the potential of open and distance learning

Nderikyo Elizabeth Ligate

The study presents suitable strategies for improving training programmes in Adult Basic Education (ABE) in Tanzania, based on the results of a study administered with the help of a structured questionnaire and unstructured interviews to collect the required data and information.

Adult education programmes have been conducted in Tanzania for some years since independence in 1961, but without proper training of its grassroots level workers and no comprehensive policy for conducting distance and open education. Each institution has its own, unique training policy, reflecting the variety of content offered but not showing clearly the strategies, approaches and training modalities used.

Distance and open education programmes rely heavily on print materials, sometimes supplemented by radio or audio cassette programmes. Face-to-face tutorials are avoided in most institutions due to financial constraints. Gender imbalance is a feature of the programmes in almost all institutions.

There are a number of innovative cases in the training of grassroots level workers through distance learning provided by various institutions, NGOs, associations and government ministries. Some of the initiatives are interesting, some are success stories, while some have aimed at upgrading and re-orienting the existing traditional system through distance education. In some instances, the training needs of employers at various institutions and ministries require a focus on professional and vocational training needs, whereas the beneficiaries' needs are for career enhancement and personal development. Nevertheless, some of the training interventions have resulted in both direct and indirect impacts.

This paper highlights three important outcomes that result from the study: an outline of a module in distance education for adult education fieldworkers; a set of criteria, action tools, methodologies and a framework for policy formation in the area of training local literacy workers; a list of six essential elements for replicable and sustainable initiatives. It is also proposed that Governments and policymakers should again examine the possibilities offered by open and distance learning as a reliable option for the training of grassroots functionaries in the field of ABE.

Background

ABE and adult literacy are recognised as important programmes in the drive for Education for All. Its success depends, however, on a set of quality criteria and indicators reflected in a facilitative, interactive learning environment, motivating learning programmes and activities, trained, innovative facilitators and relevant, challenging curriculum material. The motivation, training and performance of fieldworkers are decisive for quality and success of ABE and literacy learning programmes. In most developing countries there are a massive number of literacy and ABE workers who need training. Due to the paucity of resources and limited expertise at local level, only a small percentage of workers get trained. Where training is available, it is sometimes reduced to knowledge transmission guided by the instructor and not conceived of as part of a multi-dimensional, interactive, participative and learner-centred approach. Since some developing countries adopt a top-down, hierarchical approach to training based on the trickle-down theory, considerable transmission loss occurs, which dilutes the quality of training. Training programmes are often conducted in an ad hoc and superficial manner and hence literacy workers and adult basic educators remain ill-equipped to meet the challenges of their work and their professional commitments. In fact a number of research studies have attributed the ineffectiveness of ABE and literacy programmes to the poor quality of training. A strong, renewed approach to training will be inevitable for the success of ABE and literacy programmes.

Distance education can avert the top-down, hierarchical approaches to training to avoid loss of transmission of knowledge and diluted training. This is possible because distance education: (a) Uses specially designed, reader-friendly, interactive materials which are different from textbooks. They include: study objectives, which explain to students what they can expect to learn; self-assessment questions which enable students to check the extent to which they have mastered the objectives; assignments to be sent to tutors for marking and comment; study guidance; conversational, friendly and personal style to keep the interest high – for example, by writing in a lively and clear manner and relating new concepts to the students' experience (Lewis 1981, cited in Ramakrishna & Mouli 1997). (b) Uses tutors/supervisors/counsellors at study centres to provide face-to-face help in case students are unable to understand the material (to give tutorial support). (c) Uses multimedia approaches, correspondence, radio, audio, video, computer and other media. (d) Democratises access to education and training so as to reach everyone down to the lowest level of the community, therefore more people can be trained. (e) Learners can retain what they are learning since they learn it at their own pace, in their own spare time, without having to leave their homes or workplaces for too long. (f) Is a more cost-effective method of education provision in that a single tutor can teach a large number of students. ((g) The poor training given in developing countries results in: rote learning for examination purposes, which is the norm in many schools in the developing world, and is copied by ABE trainers and trainees unless they are properly trained. There is a lack of trained teachers in many underdeveloped countries. There is a lack of resources, such as books and teaching materials, to be given to trainees. Training given in seminars is much diluted because of lack of teaching equipment and materials and trainees forget what they have learnt the moment they leave the seminar room). (h) Distance education methods can prevent the dilution because a few teachers can reach many learners and still get two-way communication and feedback from learners through the various media adopted.

The terms of reference for the study

The study included a discussion of training needs and policies in adult education; examination of training packages; preparation of two case studies of effective training programmes; and an examination of the potential of ODL for training literacy workers in the field of ABE. The objectives of the study were to: evolve suitable strategies for improving training programmes in ABE and adult literacy for grassroots fieldworkers; enlarge access to information or selected training policies and programmes for policymakers, educational planners and curriculum developers in the field of ABE and literacy; improve co-operation between different stakeholders in the training of local ABE and literacy field; improve content and quality through the development of culture and gender-sensitive approaches; develop indicators pertaining to quality training through ODL

Scope of work and tasks

The study concentrates on training needs for grassroots level workers in both urban and rural areas, focusing on forward-looking training strategies and identifying skills which would improve the effectiveness of ongoing ODL practice.

The area of study included Dar es Salaam city, Kibaha District in the coastal region and the towns of Morogoro and Moshi in Tanzania. While Kibaha district represented rural areas, Dar es Salaam, Morogoro and Moshi represented urban areas. Due to time and financial constraints the consultant could not cover a wider area. However, the findings represent the situation in Tanzania.

The methodology

A three-pronged approach was used to collect the required data: literature review, structured questionnaire and unstructured interviews. Some of the existing literature on the subject of ABE and ODL reviewed dealt with policy, earlier findings, experiences and recommendations resulting from previous training initiatives; models of distance education and modules for distance education.

Administration of structured questionnaires

Seven sets of structured questionnaires were designed. The first set was for the grassroots level workers. The second set was for NGOs and CBOs that conduct ODL programmes. The third questionnaire was for the Institute of Adult Education which is responsible for ABE in Tanzania. The fourth questionnaire was for the Co-operative College Moshi, one of the reputed institutions that conduct distance education (DE) in the country. The fifth questionnaire was a case study questionnaire completed by the IAE, Co-operative College, Moshi, ABE and DE experts. The sixth questionnaire was for government ministries with grassroots level workers. The last questionnaire was for education experts in ABE and DE.

The questionnaires were distributed to 10 NGOs, 7 Ministries, 10 Education Experts, 60 grassroots level workers, the Moshi Co-operative College and the IAE.

The questionnaires focused on the following issues, derived mainly from the terms of reference: assessment of training needs for grassroots level workers; categories of grassroots level workers; assessment of training approaches; determination of successful training initiatives; effectiveness of policy in enhancing successful training initiatives; potential of DE for training adult literacy workers; policies in adult education and DE, and training packages.

While administering the questionnaires, the consultant carried out unstructured interviews for the following purposes: to define the terminology used in the questionnaire; to clarify some of the questions in the questionnaire; to elicit any relevant information not covered by the questionnaire.

Addressing the terms of reference

Existing secondary data and studies on the subject

Tanzania, one of the three East African countries, achieved its independence from the British in 1961. At that time it was considered necessary to restructure the western-oriented education systems to respond to growing pressure from the general public for more education, to meet human resource requirements and to ad-

dress the need to build an egalitarian society based on the principles of socialism and self-reliance (Chale 1979, cited in Mushi 1999).
There was a rapid expansion in primary school enrolment in the late sixties and seventies as part of the drive for Universal Primary Education (UPE) declared in 1974. However, there has been a decline in the gross enrolment rate (GER) from a high of 98% (1981) to 74.77% (1995). The current enrolment rate is estimated to be around 55% (URT 1997).

ABE, which in Tanzania involves functional literacy and post-literacy non-formal education, expanded considerably in the seventies and eighties, especially after the then President of Tanzania, the late Mwalimu Julius K Nyerere, proclaimed 1970 as the Year for Adult Education. However, enrolments in functional literacy dropped from 2 191 315 in 1984 (MOEC 1989) to 1 689 712 in 1997 (MOEC 1997). The decline in enrolments in adult classes and the lapse into illiteracy of the newly literate for lack of reading materials does not indicate that there has been an achievement in reducing the number of illiterates. Further, the fact that a number of school-age children pass the age limit for primary school without being enrolled indicates that the number of illiterates is growing rather than dropping. It is estimated that only 32% of 7 to 9 year olds and 82% of the 10 to14 year olds are enrolled in school (URT 1997).

Besides this group of children who are not enrolled and will therefore need to learn the three 'Rs' (Arithmetic, Reading and Writing), we also have the children who drop out from primary education due to a number of resource constraints. These require some basic skills which would enable them to adjust socially and economically in their localities in both urban and rural areas.

It is, therefore, important to look for strategies for providing education to adults. In Tanzania there are adult education teachers who teach adults the three Rs. These teachers are divided into two groups: the volunteer teachers who have received no pedagogical training for teaching adults; and primary school teachers who are also not necessarily trained to teach adults.

ABE and training

For more than three decades, Tanzania has been conducting adult education programmes without offering proper co-ordinated training to its grassroots level workers. For all this time, the facilitators have been primary school teachers, other extension fieldworkers in the community and volunteers. This was established from a study carried out by Bwatwa (1989: 83), who states: 'Most of the primary school teachers and the voluntary teachers did not have the requisite training and experience in adult education work.' Although the IAE offered certificate, diploma and advanced diploma courses in adult education, the successful trainees became adult education co-ordinators at the regional, district and ward levels (URT 1995) instead of participating in the actual teaching of adults.

With regard to adult education facilitators, Mpogolo (1985) observes that the process and failure of literacy classes depends to a great extent on the personality of the teachers. The personality of a teacher refers not only to his or her exterior self but also to the interior self which requires him or her to demonstrate the expected competence on what he or she is performing. Similarly, Bwatwa (1989) asserts that it is difficult for untrained adult education teachers to create the participative learning environment recommended by the designers of the programme.

However, in terms of the Education and Training Policy (MOEC 1995) the ministry responsible for teacher education was commissioned to provide for the training of a specific cadre of adult education teachers and tutors. Thus in the Basic Education Master Plan (BEMP) (URT 1997), the government of Tanzania included an Adult Education/Literacy Expansion programme for the training of district co-ordinators/facilitators and literacy teachers in order to provide equitable access to adult literacy and post-literacy training for disadvantaged groups.

This three-phase programme started with a sample literacy survey in 1997 as phase one; completion of a project design by the end of 1997 as phase two; and literacy service delivery as phase three. The programme is managed by the IAE, local government authorities alongside local and international NGOs (URT 1997).

According to MOEC (1998), Tanzania has a population of 109 936 primary school teachers who have received training in how to teach children under 14 years of age. They are not trained to handle adults. Moreover, the other extension workers and volunteer teachers who assist in teaching adult learners have no initial training at all in teaching. It is of this group that Mpogolo (1985:13) states: 'This group needs much more training on both the content and methods of literacy teaching than the professional teachers'.

Policies

Tanzania has an education and training policy (1995) which covers the training of ABE workers. Article 9.6.9 of this policy states: 'The existing stock of functional literacy teachers, most of whom are primary school teachers, are not adequately trained to handle adult classes. Therefore, the Ministry responsible for teacher education shall provide for the training of a specific cadre of Adult Education teachers and tutors'. (MOEC 1995: 89)

Despite this provision, implementation of the policy is difficult because of the huge number of teachers involved. According to the adult education statistics (URT 1998), the number of teaching staff was 59 362 in 1997, which is 55.3% less than the expected number.

Training such a huge number of teachers requires considerable resources, taking into consideration also the vastness of the country. The only viable alternative is to provide the training through ODL methods. Hall and Dodds (1974), evaluating the radio study campaigns conducted in Tanzania in the early 1970s, observe that radio, as one of the media used in DE, has proved effective in reaching large numbers of people in rural areas who have previously not been reached by either formal or traditional adult education approaches. According to these authors, radio offers a practical alternative to the traditional teacher-student relationship. However, Tanzania's education and training policy does not articulate a clear ODL policy. MOEC (1995: 86) article 9.6.4 states that it is continuing education that is to be an integral part of the education system and does not refer to open/distance learning. It is this situation that prompts Chale (1996: 28) to comment: 'Practically, a number of institutions, public and private have and are carrying out Open Distance Education programmes and courses without being guided by a policy direction in the system.'

So, while we have a clearly stated adult education policy (MOEC 1995, articles 9.6.1, 9.6.2 and 9.6.4), we lack a clearly stated policy for conducting open/distance education in the country.

Mushi (1999: 88) argues: 'The current Education and Training Policy (1995) does not address issues relating to Distance Education as an important component of non-formal education in the country. Thus there is a need to have a comprehensive Policy, a broad framework that will guide the provision of Distance Education at all levels of education, and which should be aligned to the government's policy on education.'

Open/distance education as a strategy

Open/Distance Education methods started being used in the country in the early 1960s to provide education and professional training in various fields (Mushi 1999), as is clearly shown in the following examples.

a) Co-operative College Moshi: In 1964 the Co-operative Education Centre (CEC) Moshi was established with the intention of educating members of the primary co-operatives on their duties. CEC conducted courses in Elementary Bookkeeping, Duties of the Committee, Basic Economics, Principles of Agricultural production,

Savings and Credit Societies, Commercial Arithmetic, Principles of Management as well as Leadership and Supervision. These courses were conducted through correspondence, radio study circles and women's education units meant to encourage women's participation in co-operative societies (Manyanya 1979, cited in Mushi 1999).

A study conducted by Manyanya (1991) revealed that CEC managed to reach more than 40 000 students by the late 1980s, but that the students could not follow the study materials due to poor literacy skills. Similarly, their teachers lacked the requisite academic and professional skills to perform institutional activities.

(b) National Correspondence Institution (NCI): The NCI was established in 1970 as a division of the IAE to develop distance training programmes for standard 7 leavers, as well as professional courses, basing their activities on the experience generated by the CEC initiative (Mushi 1991). It was the NCI that was later required to develop training programmes for the newly recruited teachers for Universal Primary Education. These were primary school leavers with no initial training in teacher education. According to a study by Worf (1997), NCI had already trained 37 998 grade C teachers (95% of the total population of grade C teachers) by mid 1980.

Although NCI managed to provide training to such a large number of students, Mushi (1999) points out that NCI suffered as a result of competition for resources with other departments, and that the available resources were not sufficient to replace and sustain its facilities.

(c) Open University of Tanzania: The Open University of Tanzania (OUT) was set up by Act No 17 of 1992 and became operational in 1993 (Mmari 1996). It was established to provide greater access to higher level education for qualifying candidates who were unable to get access to university education despite their qualifications (Mushi 1999). This means that the OUT gives training mostly to workers. OUT enrolled about 3 811 students between 1994 and 1997, of whom only 400 (or 10.49%) were female (Mushi 1999). Besides the questions of equity and access, OUT has experienced problems in finance due to scaled-down budgets (OUT 1997).

(d) INADES – Formation Tanzania: INADES–Formation Tanzania (IFTZ) is part of an African NGO with a network of 11 national offices in East, Central and West Africa. It was founded in 1962 at Abidjan in Cote de Ivoire. Its Tanzanian office was opened at Dodoma in 1989 as a branch of INADES Kenya before becoming a full national office in 1992 and gaining recognition from the Tanzanian Government as a legal NGO in 1994.

IFTZ provides correspondence courses to rural people (farmers) all over the country and, through training workshops and visits to the field, to farmers in Dodoma, Singida and Morogoro Regions. The organisation also visits people in Babati, Shinyanga and Iringa Districts.

The major objective of IFTZ is to increase the ability and power of farmers and other rural people to manage their natural resources effectively, both in groups and individually. The training strategies are mainly correspondence or face-to-face. For correspondence courses, the trainees contribute to the purchase of the books while the face-to-face workshops are participatory. In 2000 IFTZ enrolled 501 trainees in agriculture correspondence courses; of these 111 were women. A further 109 trainees were enrolled in management correspondence courses; here, only 17 were women. IFTZ has developed 34 correspondence manuals in Livestock, Agriculture and Environment Development.

IFTZ collaborates mainly with NGOs which deal with farmers in the field of agriculture and the environment. Accordingly, one of its collaborators is the Co-operative College, Moshi – Directorate of Field Education (CC-DFE) – Dodoma branch.

(f) Other Organisations: Some NGOs have established units to provide education and training through distance/open education. The SAEU is one such organisation. SAEU was established by the Commonwealth Secretariat in 1984 to provide distance education and training to South African refugees. SAEU has now diversified its activities to cover Community Services, Election Sensitisation, Guidance and Counselling, Course Development and Consultancy Services (SAEU 2001).

The Health through Sanitation and Water (HESAWA) project has a DE Unit, which was set up in 1986 in the Lake regions to disseminate printed educational packages on the promotion of public health through the use of safe and clean water (Mushi 1999).

The Centre for Educational Development in Health (CEDHA) has been involved in the production of adapted African Medical and Research Foundation (AMREF) and other courses for use at a distance in the Ministry of Health's Continuing Education Unit. These courses are intended to assist primary health and medical personnel to keep abreast of current knowledge and practices in their respective fields and to improve performance (Ligate 1994).

(g) DE Methodology: DE can be provided through various media. However, in Tanzania it has mostly relied on printed materials, which are supplemented by other media such as radio programmes, audio cassette programmes and face-to-face tutorials (Mushi 1999). The NCI in the IAE has failed to conduct face-to-face sessions or radio programmes because of financial constraints. The OUT conducts face-to-face sessions only twice a year, for the same reasons. These sessions last at least one hour for a particular course and are, in any event, too short to make any impact on the learners.

Chambo (2001) states that the print materials used for DE in Tanzania are not learner centred or action oriented. They are fit for general knowledge and lesser skills. To him the instructional perspective assumes a classroom environment rather than self-support and action guided material. As he points out, there are two solutions to these problems. One is to improve the print materials so that they include more self-support and are more learner centred and action oriented. The other is to diversify the media by means of which DE is provided. Wherever possible, other methods like face-to-face tutorials, group discussions, audio programmes and the electronic media should be employed.

Accessibility and equity of DE: Similar to conventional education, DE is faced with the problem of gender imbalance. As Mushi (1999) points out (see 3.1.4 (c) above), gender imbalance is more prevalent in higher learning institutions. Mushi therefore proposes that efforts should be made to ascertain the causal factors for the low enrolment among female students and to work out strategies that will attract them in order to raise their representation rate to 50% in higher learning institutions and in DE programmes. He argues that such measures should be spelled out in the national policy on DE. He cites the measures taken by the University of Dar es Salaam, which include female cut-off points and pre-entry programmes for unqualified female candidates, as worth considering.

The Minister for Education and Culture, His Excellency J Mungai, in his budget speech for the year 2001/2002, said the IAE (through NCI) ran correspondence courses for 5 000 primary school teachers in 2000/2001, of whom 980 were women. Another study (Ligate 1994) revealed that NCI had offered training through DE to more than 69 000 students in other fields. According to Mushi (1999) only 11 313 or 16.5% were female. This further reveals the imbalance in gender, which needs to be addressed.

(h) Sustainability in DE: Sustainability has been affected mainly by two issues, namely policy and finance. Chale (1996) observes that the sustainability problems that are found in a number of institutions, programmes and projects are the product of a lack of policy to guide and direct them. He cites the NCI, which functions under the auspices of the IAE, and the Correspondence Education Centre (CEC) (or Field Extension Department [FED], as it is now known) of the Co-operative College, Moshi as institutions which have been operating without defined policies and without any constitutional status. He says that the lack of legal status tends to keep the DE department on a lower level in such organisations. Such departments are subject to greater financial constraints than other departments in the same institutions, which therefore puts them in a difficult position when it comes to sustaining their activities.

Chambo (2001) sees lack of financial sustainability as the major cause of the failure of ODL in Tanzania. He feels that although the 1995 education and training policy has solved the problem of policy, it does not indicate how ODL will be funded and what role the community will play in financing this kind of education. This again calls for a clearly stated and defined policy in order for DE to become sustainable in both finance and resources.

(i) Management of DE and ABE: ABE in Tanzania falls directly under the Institute of Adult Education in the department of Adult Education in the Ministry of Education and Culture (MOEC). However, there is one director for the Institute and another (separate) director for the Department. There is the National Correspondence Institution (NCI), which runs correspondence courses under the IAE. The NCI was required to offer courses for standard VII leavers, secondary school level courses and professional courses such as Bookkeeping, Management and Administration (Mushi 1999).

While there is a structured administration in ABE from the national to the grassroots level, DE has remained a concern for NCI and other support institutions that offer ODL. According to Chambo (2001), apart from government and co-operative-based distance learning adult education structures, there are fifteen other support institutions in the country including those found in extension ministries (Agriculture, Community Development, Health, Natural Resources and Tourism), as well as private institutions and NGOs. However, with all these delivery organs, Chambo sees no co-ordination at all and criticises them for duplicating efforts, for poor outreach systems and for lack of a consistent methodology. He cites the radio broadcast of Federation of Co-operatives as one example of an initiative that could well be integrated with the Co-operative College radio systems without much harm. To Chambo, a well-co-ordinated educational system would be more effective and would make the work of ABE through ODL more cost effective.

Chale (1996), on the other hand, tackles the question of DE management from another perspective. He sees DE as a practice in both formal and non-formal education and therefore compares the management of bimodal/dual mode institutions, affiliated college models/semi-autonomous models with those of the autonomous institutions. He also discusses the question of leadership, infrastructure, resources, communication technology, time management and coping with technology advances as principal management areas in ODL. For him, DE management will be greatly enhanced if these factors are taken into account.

Policies governing provision of training to grassroots level workers

Ministries, institutions, associations and NGOs were required by the consultant to list the policies that govern training of grassroots level workers in their respective areas. The findings are:

Table 1 Policies that govern training

No.	Institute/Ministry/ NGO Association	Training Policies
1. 2.	Institute of Adult Education Ministry of Labour, Youth and Sports	Education and Training Policy 1995 ◆ Youth Development Policy ◆ National Deployment Policy ◆ Child and Family Welfare Service Policy
3.	Ministry of Natural Resources and Tourism	Ministry of Natural Resources training Policy
4.	Ministry of Education and Culture	Education and Training Policy 1995
5.	HESAWA	◆ Rural Water Development Policy ◆ Health Policy ◆ Community Development Policy
6.	TAMWA	The Association Constitution of 1987 – creation of awareness of human rights
7.	SAEU	To reach as many people as possible through Distance Education in collaboration with other organisations. (1999 Organisation Constitution)
8.	Open University of Tanzania	Its policy for providing degree courses for those who missed access to the current universities emanates from Act No. 17 of 1992; also delivers certificate course which caters well for the needs of ABE
9.	Co-operative College, Moshi	Sustainable distance education and training policy emphasising cost sharing, knowledge and skill development, training tailored to needs of clients

It was observed that for each ministry, institution, association or NGO, there is a unique policy or variety of policies for the provision of training. The various policies reflect the variety of content offered by the institutions rather than the strategies and approaches used.

Two problems were observed to be associated with the wide range of policies:

(1) Lack of a central control mechanism, which may affect implementation in terms of evaluation, effectiveness, impact, outreach, gender and cultural context.

(2) Duplication of work as a result of two or three different NGOs or government undertaking similar training initiatives in the same locality.

Specific policies for ABE and distance and open Learning

The education experts were asked whether there were specific policies for ABE. Four experts said that there were specific policies on ABE, two said there were none and four did not respond.

However, the education experts in the country are divided on the question of whether or not there is a policy for distance/open learning in the country – two responded in the positive and two responded in the negative. One said there was no clear policy and two did not respond.

Training needs of fieldworkers

Views of ministries, NGOs and associations

Ministries, NGOs and associations were asked to list the training needs of their fieldworkers.

Table 2 Views of ministries, NGOs and associations

Ministry/NGO/Institution	Training Needs
MNRT	◆ Job-related training ◆ Career enhancing training ◆ Personal development training ◆ Experience sharing training
Institute of Adult Education	◆ Adult education methods ◆ Adult psychology ◆ Guidance and counselling ◆ Training in management and administration of education ◆ Special needs education ◆ Gender sensitisation
HESAWA	◆ Repair and maintenance of water facilities ◆ Bookkeeping ◆ Health education

	• Sanitation • Life skills • Hygiene
Ministry of Labour Youth and Sports Development	• Computer • Typing • Management skills • Community-based initiative projects
Co-operative College, Moshi	• Bookkeeping • Co-operation, leadership and supervision • The work of the committee • Principles of management • SACCOS management – life skills
SAEU	• Awareness • Gender sensitisation • Democracy • Human rights • Management and community mobilisation • Good governance

Each ministry or organisation has specific training needs for their grassroots level workers, depending on their professional and vocational needs. The employers do not give life skills training to their workers but tend to give them skills training designed to improve quality of work and productivity.

Views of grassroots workers

Some of the training needs identified by the grassroots level workers are listed below:

Table 3 Views of Grassroots Workers

Type of Worker	Training Needs
Teachers (Primary School teachers)	• Diploma in teaching/adult education • Library keeping • Book writing • Special education • Administration in education • Agriculture • Aids campaign education • Refresher courses in science and mathematics • Store keeping • Proper skills in reading books

	◆ Environmental keeping ◆ 'A' level education
Nurses and MCHA	◆ Personal development ◆ Job-related training ◆ Health education ◆ Laboratory technician training
Agriculture/Livestock Field Extension Officers	◆ Proper animal husbandry and treating ◆ Integrating the family in promoting economy ◆ Long and short term courses ◆ Seminars and workshops
Registry Assistants	◆ Office management course ◆ Personnel management course ◆ Manpower management course

The training needs identified by the grassroots level workers are job related and the worker needs the training to improve her or his work efficiency. However, other training needs are for personal development; that is, an individual would like to climb from one level of education to the other or enhance her or his career through undertaking various training programmes. Although these training needs differ from those cited by employers, they must be taken into account in any training programme.

The consultant also observed that DE can assist in the provision of training to the fieldworkers through correspondence courses, radio programmes, self-tuition modules and cassettes and face-to-face sessions. This could be achieved by identifying the training needs of the workers, and identifying the strategies for proper effectiveness and preparation of course programmes. With distance learning the course programme will reach more workers at lower costs and using fewer resources. Long-term courses are those which take more than three months while short-term courses take less than three months. Just as we have long and short-term conventional courses, distance learning courses may also be short or long-term. Seminars and workshops are short-term courses.

Innovative cases in training through the ODL mode

The consultant selected a few innovative cases in training through the ODL mode among the training initiatives and analysed them as follows:

Table 4 Innovative cases

No.	Innovative Case	Training Package	Beneficiaries	Strategies/Methods	Provider
1.	Basic English Programme for Burundi Refugees	English language Elementary to ordinary level	Burundi refugees ◆ Audio cassettes ◆ Face-to-face session	◆ Print materials	SAEU
2.	Distance Education Teacher Education (Grade 'B/C' to 'O' level	◆ Ordinary level education involving six subjects ◆ Professional development	Tanzanian Grade B and C teachers intending to improve their quality of education - Radio programmes	◆ Print materials ◆ Face-to-face sessions in teacher resource centres (TRCs)	MOEC Teacher Education Department
3.	Primary Societies, Secretaries' Training	Capacity building Co-operative Societies (SACCOS) Secretaries	Savings and Credit training ◆ Correspondence courses follow-up ◆ Radio programme ◆ Group discussion	◆ Participatory classroom	Co-operative College, Moshi
4.	Man is HealthRadio Study Campaigns	Health and hygiene practices	Adult groups of Education learners CEC and IAE	◆ Radio programme ◆ Group discussion	Inter Ministerial co-ordinated by

A number of innovative cases of training programmes are provided by the government or NGOs. The experience obtained from running these can be used to develop new training initiatives using ODL strategies. All these training initiatives are ABE and DE programmes.

Table 5 Initiatives and training packages provided by government and NGOs

Initiative	Govt./NGO	Training Package	Activities/Methods	Beneficiaries	Effectiveness
1. Primary Societies Secretaries' Training	Co-operative College, Moshi	Capacity building	Participatory classroom training and correspondence courses follow-up	Secretaries of co-operatives	Could keep records and run meetings
2. Committee training on Roles and Responsibility	Co-operative College,Moshi	Capacity building	Participatory classroom training and correspondence courses follow-up	Committee members	Capacity to question Union accounts
3. Savings and Credit Co-operative Societies (SACCOS)	Co-operative College,Moshi	Capacity building	Participatory classroom training and correspondence courses follow-up	Co-operative leaders	Capable of running meetings and writing up books of account
4. Repair and Maintenance of Water Facilities Training	HESAWA	Skills for maintaining water facilities	Participatory	Village leaders and village community development assistants	Could maintain their water facilities
5. Local Government Training Programme for Local Government Councillors	SAEU	Professional development for the Councillors	Training manuals, cassette programmes, face-to-face tuition, learners' guide	Local Government Councillors	◆ Tolerance in a multiparty democracy ◆ Effective revenue collection ◆ Proper management of meetings

Initiative	Govt./NGO	Training Package	Activities/Methods	Beneficiaries	Effectiveness
6. Paramilitary Training on Wildlife Protection	MNRT	Skills for protection of wildlife – career enhancing	Face-to-face and participatory in field practical and instructions	Game assistants	◆ Reduction in poaching ◆ Proper management of meetings
7. Seminars on Illegal Harvesting of Natural Resources	MNRT	Skills for protection and conservation of natural resources	Face-to-face supported with field practicals, radio, posters	Forest assistants	Increased royalties on revenue from forest products
8. Ordinary Secondary Education for those who did not get it	Institute of Adult Education and MOEC	Academic development 'O' level syllabus	Face-to-face and correspondence courses	All adults and workers	Most of them pass and continue to higher levels of education
9. Basic English for Burundi Refugees	SAEU	Basic English through elementary to ordinary level to orient the refugees to a new system of education	Manuals supported with face-to-face and audio cassettes	Burundi refugees	Most of them have successfully joined the Tanzanian system of education

Various training initiatives are provided by the government and NGOs in the country. Some of these training initiatives are provided through ODL methods and others through traditional training and participatory seminars.

The role of NGOs and local associations in training provision

NGOs and associations included in the study had the following roles

Table 6 Roles

Name of NGO	Roles
TAMWA	◆ Support services ◆ Creation of awareness in the community in rural and urban areas through the use of fliers, posters, other media and seminars. ◆ Counselling people who are faced with problems, for example divorcees ◆ Giving training to workers and the community on issues related to their specific areas, like genital mutilation ◆ Reminding workers and the community on their rights and raising gender awareness ◆ Sensitising people on the essence of group formation as a means of overcoming their economic problems
HESAWA	◆ Support services – creation of awareness in the community on all issues related to health, hygiene and sanitation ◆ Training of workers within the community who will help people to confront these issues
SAEU	◆ Offer Distant/Open Education to the community e.g. refugees and local government councillors ◆ Carry out training and create awareness in the community by giving human rights and civic education through the use of fliers, posters, face-to-face, radio and booklets.

NGOs and associations lack co-ordination and there is duplication of work among them. For instance, SAEU and TAMWA both deal with human rights and the consultant found no evidence that the two organisations follow an agreed training curriculum. It was also observed that they give support services which include face-to-face tuition, counselling and guidance, monitoring, evaluation and record keeping.

ABE should include literacy, post-literacy, functional literacy. Functional literacy includes knowledge and skills that affect everyday life of rural people e.g. health, nutrition, gardening, child care, home repairs, road repair, construction and family planning (Chambo 2001).

How to avoid duplication by NGOs

NGOs can avoid duplication and overlapping of efforts by: creating partnerships for rural ODL distribution because not all institutions and NGOs can reach the rural areas; producing generic training materials; opening common focal knowledge centres in districts or villages; training local operators of DE programmes together; sharing subject matter specialists and experts in rural settings; and funding and operating projects on a central basis.

Interesting cases of training

Ministries and institutions documented cases of training initiatives for field level workers in terms of relevance, outreach, impact, effectiveness, sustainability, equity and gender aspects. Below are interesting cases of training documented by the various ministries and training institutions.

There are various interesting cases of training for fieldworkers. The aspect of equity is difficult to realise since gender imbalance is still reflected in the labour market in Tanzania.

Table 7 Interesting cases

No.	Training Initiative	Relevance	Outreach	Impact	Effectiveness	Sustainability	Equity	Gender
1.	Primary Societies Secretaries' Training (by CEC)	Fulfils the needs of the trainees	Nationwide	Created a change in behaviour, attitudes and knowledge on the part of learners	It was adversely affected by social political and economic changes taking place in the country	The objectives of training were achieved	Not realised	Both female and male
2.	Committee Training on Roles and Responsibilities (by CEC)	"	"	"	"	"	"	"
3.	Savings and Credit Co-operative Societies Managers' Training (by CEC)	"	"	"	"	"	"	"
4.	Local Government Training Programme for Local Government Councillors (by SAEU)	"	"	"	Effective, it is being reviewed for the new batch of Councillors	Ministry concerned is providing funding for it to continue	"	"

Success stories in training of fieldworkers

Table 8 Success in training fieldworkers

No.	Success Story	Enabling Conditions	Quality Criteria in Curriculum	Status after Training	Provider
1.	Primary Credit Societies, Secretaries, Leaders and Members	◆ Vibrant co-operatives between 1984 – 1997 ◆ Government withdrawal to provide subsidised inputs ◆ Savings culture arising out of lack of loans affordable by small farmers	◆ Undertook TNA first before developing course ◆ Use of andragogically designed syllabi ◆ Procedures of production using external and internal auditors ◆ Pre testing of new course ◆ Feedback questionnaire	◆ Capable of writing books of account ◆ Capable of running meetings ◆ Transparency in running associative business ◆ Participants became leaders and active members ◆ Capable of writing up union accounts ◆ Participants become more confident in their work	Co-operative College, Moshi (CEC)
2.	OUT Foundation Courses for workers intending to pursue degree courses	◆ Applicants lacking entry qualifications to degree programmes	Foundation courses in preparation for higher learning in five subjects ◆ English Language I & II ◆ Kiswahili ◆ Basic Maths ◆ Humanities and Social Sciences ◆ Science and Technology	◆ Most of the participants who were successful in this programme entered degree programmes of the OUT ◆ They got certificates in foundation courses	Open University of Tanzania

No.	Success Story	Enabling Conditions	Quality Criteria in Curriculum	Status after Training	Provider
3.	Universal Primary Education on the Job Teacher Training 1976 – 1984	◆ Need for more teachers during implementation of Universal Primary Education ◆ Increased enrolment	◆ 'O' Level syllabus for Secondary Education ◆ Grade C teachers Education Syllabus	◆ Certification by NECTA ◆ Employment in Primary Schools as Grade C teachers	MOEC & IAE
4.	Local Government Councillors training – Tanzania Mainland 1996 – 1998	◆ Political will ◆ Donor funding ◆ Government willingness to collaborate ◆ ALAT supported the project ◆ Beneficiaries were involved and contributed to curriculum formulation and financing	◆ Clear objectives ◆ Learner centred ◆ Tested content ◆ Pre-tested course	◆ Recognition as having knowledge on local government ◆ Ability to understand duties and responsibilities and perform them ◆ Status of a knowledgeable councillor	SAEU

No.	Success Story	Enabling Conditions	Quality Criteria in Curriculum	Status after Training	Provider
5.	South African Basic Education in English Mathematics and Agriculture 1984 – 1996	◆ The SA exiles moved the hearts of the nations and therefore enough money was available to support the programme ◆ Support services were good, e.g. face-to-face & audio programmes, record keeping and follow-up of progress were continuous.	◆ Clear objectives ◆ Learner centred ◆ Tested content ◆ Pre-tested course - promotion in jobs - scholarship - higher education	◆ Ability to do their work with confidence ◆ Improvement in their status and personal development, e.g.	SAEU

There are various success stories in training grassroots level workers. However, some of the success stories documented no longer exist due to unavailability of funding. While the South African exile programme came to an end when they returned home, training Universal Primary Education teachers from 1976 to 1984 was a temporary measure and when the needs were fulfilled the initiative ended.

Below are details of two success stories in ABE and DE

Box 1

Case Study I

South African exiles basic education in English, Mathematics and Agriculture: 1984 - 1996

1. *Training Initiative:*
   The South African Exiles Basic Education in English, Mathematics and Agriculture 1984 – 1996

2. *Provider of Training:*
   The South African Extension Unit (Now Southern Africa Extension Unit (SAEU), P.O Box 7004, Dạr es Salaam, Tanzania.

3. *Aims of the Training Initiative:*
   - To give opportunities to South African exiles in Southern Africa to acquire/upgrade their basic education and advance to secondary/vocational/educational qualifications through the distance learning approach as a way of broadening their career prospects.

4. *Enabling Conditions for the Programme*
   - The South African exiles moved the hearts of the nations and therefore there was enough funding available to support the programme.
   - Support services were established such that each country in which the South African exiles resided, i.e. Tanzania, Zambia, Zimbabwe, Angola, Botswana and Uganda, had a co-ordinator for each Liberation Movement. This co-ordinator was responsible for one or two study centres. The co-ordinators were supported by a skeleton staff and tutors drawn from both the South African refugee population and the local community of that particular country. Most of the tutoring was done by part-time tutors. Study centres were usually housed in rented venues mainly at educational

establishments. Students would read their interactive materials on their own but would meet with their tutors at face-to-face sessions to clarify the more difficult parts of the subject matter. The tutors would also mark and comment on the students' exercises. The co-ordinator would register students for examinations, mainly General Certificate of Education (GCE) 'O' and 'A' levels. Although the exiles were quite nomadic in that they frequently moved about from one country to the other within the group of countries mentioned above, they were always able to continue their studies as soon as they settled down. SAEU monitored and evaluated the programme globally through visits and letters, and kept easily retrievable records. The support services may therefore be said to have been good.

5. *Training of Trainers*

Training of trainers was conducted at two levels. The first level was at the global centre, the Southern Africa Extension Unit headquarters, where country co-ordinators from all the countries that accommodated South African exiles attended a workshop on co-ordination and monitoring skills, studying the modules and acquiring the skills to deliver the subject matter through the distance mode. One country could have a number of country co-ordinators, depending on the number of Liberation Movements (PAC, ANC or UNHCR) present in that country. For instance while Tanzania had three co-ordinators, Zambia had two, one for the ANC and the other for the UNHCR.

The second level of training was conducted in the target country. SAEU staff in collaboration with the country's co-ordinator conducted training to camp co-ordinators and tutors.

Evaluation was done by the SAEU through visits, reports, telephones and letters.

6. *Implementation Stages*

- The 1983 Commonwealth heads of government meeting (CHOGM) in New Delhi, India decided to set up SAEU.
- SAEU was launched in Tanzania in November 1984 under a Memorandum of Understanding signed by the COMSEC – UNHCR and Government of Tanzania.
- SAEU organised course writers' workshops for basic education subjects but from 1985 bought DE study materials for GCE 'O' and 'A' Levels from the UK's Open Learning College and Wolsley Hall.

- Initial learners were recruited in 1985 and offered basic education courses (prepared by the SAEU in collaboration with the exiles themselves) in Mathematics, English and Agriculture.
- By the end of 1987, SAEU began to recruit learners and to organise and manage study centres extending beyond Tanzania (Angola, Zambia, Zimbabwe, Botswana and Uganda).
- SAEU trained co-ordinators of study centres who were appointed by their respective organisations, i.e. African National Congress (ANC) and Pan African Congress of Azania (PAC).
- In 1991 SAEU introduced short, full-time vocational skills programmes to equip learners who were going to be repatriated with skills which they needed to obtain gainful employment in South Africa.
- In 1992, the Commonwealth Fund for Technical Co-operation (CFTC), through a consultancy team from the International Extension College (IEC), advised SAEU to phase out the exile programme and establish SAEU inside South Africa so as to continue serving its former students and others.
- In May/June 1994, 43 learners (returnees) registered to do the London GCE examination.

7. *Quality Criteria in Curriculum*
   - The initiative used clearly stated objectives which were prepared in collaboration with learners.
   - The objectives were learner centred, that is they fulfilled the needs of learners.
   - The content used was relevant to the learners and suitable for each level.
   - The course was tested to see if it would yield the expected results or make the required impact on the learners.

8. *Status after Training*
   - Most of the South African refugees were able to do their GCE 'O' and 'A' level examinations and were therefore capable of going for further education.
   - The exiles could do their work with confidence, especially in matters related to agriculture. This helped them to increase their income.
   - Some of the exiles got promotions after completing the SAEU course and when they went back to South Africa an unspecified number managed to get jobs or promotions, especially in the Armed Forces.

Box 2

Case Study II

Training of local government councillors in Tanzania mainland implemented by Southern Africa extension unit

1. The Local Government Councillors' Training Project was put into practice by the SAEU in 1996/7 under the overall project management of the Commonwealth Local Government Forum (CLGF). Funding for this project was provided by the European Union (EU), the Irish Government and the Royal Netherlands Embassy. It targeted over 3 000 councillors elected in 1994, who required basic training both in order to ensure the effective operation of local democracy and to facilitate a smooth transition to multi-party democracy at national level which was launched in November 1995.

   1.1 Following the local elections, consultations were held with stakeholders, namely the government of Tanzania, Prime Minister's Office (PMO), the Association of Local Authorities of Tanzania (ALAT), the councillors themselves and the SAEU, to determine the sort of induction training the newly elected local councillors would require in order to fulfil their new tasks within a multi-party democracy.

2. The project objectives were to:
   - (i) develop and operationalise a training programme for local government councillors throughout Tanzania
   - (ii) provide local government councillors with the skills to operate smoothly within the local government machinery under the conditions of multi-party democracy
   - (iii) prepare teaching modules which could also be used for the training of senior local government officers (elected and employed)

3. Based on knowledge of the felt needs, councillors' levels of education and stakeholders' inputs, the following activities were carried out:
   - Course design of printed and audio materials was done in a workshop of experts on local government issues.
   - Writing of printed and audio materials was also done in a workshop of experts but the task was completed by individual consultants.
   - Editing and reviewing of course materials were done in workshops of experts with the final touches done by individual consultants.

- Course materials were produced for a pilot exercise which was conducted in five selected councils. Pilot inputs were subsequently included in the materials.
- Finalised materials were applied to all the local councils in Mainland Tanzania except Dar es Salaam, which did not have councillors due to dissolution of the city council.

3.1 Course materials produced included a study guide and three course modules as follows:
(iv) Study guide
(v) Brief History of the Local Government in Tanzania
(vi) Roles of the Councillor in a Multi-Party Democracy system in Tanzania
(vii) Finance, Planning and Management and Local Government.

All the materials were produced in Kiswahili, which is the lingua franca of Tanzania, each module being supported by an audio (radio and cassette) programme and face-to-face tuition.

3.2 After the materials had been developed, student support systems were set up, and regional and district co-ordinators and tutors recruited. The SAEU trained the regional co-ordinators, in other words the SAEU conducted a training of trainers (TOT) programme for regional co-ordinators. The regional co-ordinators in turn trained the district co-ordinators in their regions, who in turn trained the tutors. The TOT was thus operationalised at three levels, namely national, regional and district. The TOT was conducted in the form of workshops which covered two aspects: studying the modules, and acquiring the skills to deliver the subject matter of the modules by distance mode in the case of the tutors. The co-ordinators had, additionally, to be acquainted with co-ordination skills. SAEU monitored and evaluated the project through visits, telephones and letters and kept records for the purposes of evaluating the project and certification.

4. External evaluation of the councillor training programme was carried out by Carl Bro Management, a firm of consultants contracted by the EU under Evaluation of EDF Support to Human Resource Development in Tanzania 1990 – 1997. Their report shows that the councillor training programme had the following qualities. It was relevant, in terms of project idea and project design. It was efficient in terms of costs, organisation and management, intervention methods,

monitoring and evaluation. It was also effective in terms of reaction and learning behaviour changes. Further, it had an impact, in particular that the councillors were able to educate members of their constituency (ward) on the purpose and authority of the council and the work to be carried out by it. Furthermore, it was sustainable and could be replicated in terms of policy support measures, economic and financial sustainability, socio-cultural embedding – gender issues. The consultants noted also that appropriate technology was used and that SAEU's institutional and management capacity were assessed as being adequate.

> The summary given by the evaluators on the aspect of sustainability and replicability reads as follows:
>
> While it would be possible to sustain the training provision in future with local funding only, it is likely that the quality would be improved through foreign financial assistance. The concept as well as the actual project lends itself perfectly to replication.

Initiatives to upgrade and re-orient the existing traditional system of education through distance learning

Education experts described initiatives which aim at upgrading the traditional system of education through the ODL mode. The findings given by the experts are:

1. cookery and other home economic classes by radio or TV (multimedia);
2. mathematics and other subjects for school programmes by local tabloids and TV;
3. establishment of the OUT with centres and libraries all over the country;
4. establishment of the Publicity Unit in the Ministry of Natural Resources and Tourism (MNRT).

The consultant observed that there are various training initiatives which can re-orient the traditional systems of learning, but they have yet to be fully exploited.

Direct and indirect impact of training intervention

The direct and indirect impact of training interventions on literacy and ABE programmes showed that many people are now equipped with the basic skills, knowledge and attitudes.

There have been changes of attitude and behaviour among the trainees who have undergone such training. People who undergo such training are capable of solving their day-to-day, work-related problems. There is increased participation in development issues or projects in areas where training has been implemented. There is an improvement in the health, hygiene, sanitation and environmental wellbeing of areas where training has been implemented. People are more aware of their problems and thus more confident in tackling them.

For each training initiative undertaken there is a direct or indirect impact on the learner or the society.

Various forms of training modalities

Various modalities are used by various institutions and NGOs that deal with open distance learning. Below are the training modalities as developed by the author on the basis of the existing training programmes.

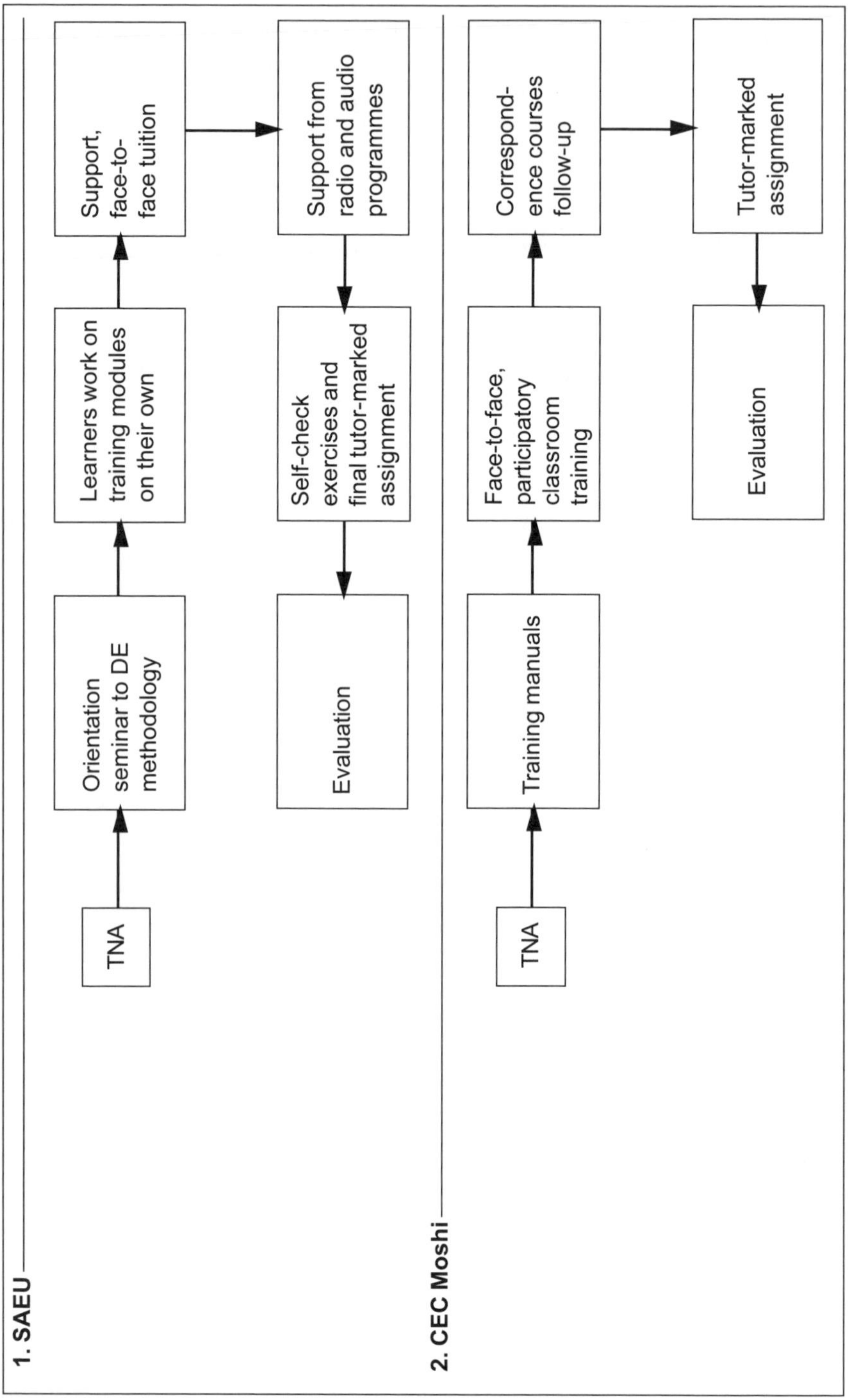
1. SAEU
TNA
Orientation seminar to DE methodology
Learners work on training modules on their own
Support, face-to-face tuition
Support from radio and audio programmes
Self-check exercises and final tutor-marked assignment
Evaluation
2. CEC Moshi
TNA
Training manuals
Face-to-face, participatory classroom training
Correspond-ence courses follow-up
Tutor-marked assignment
Evaluation

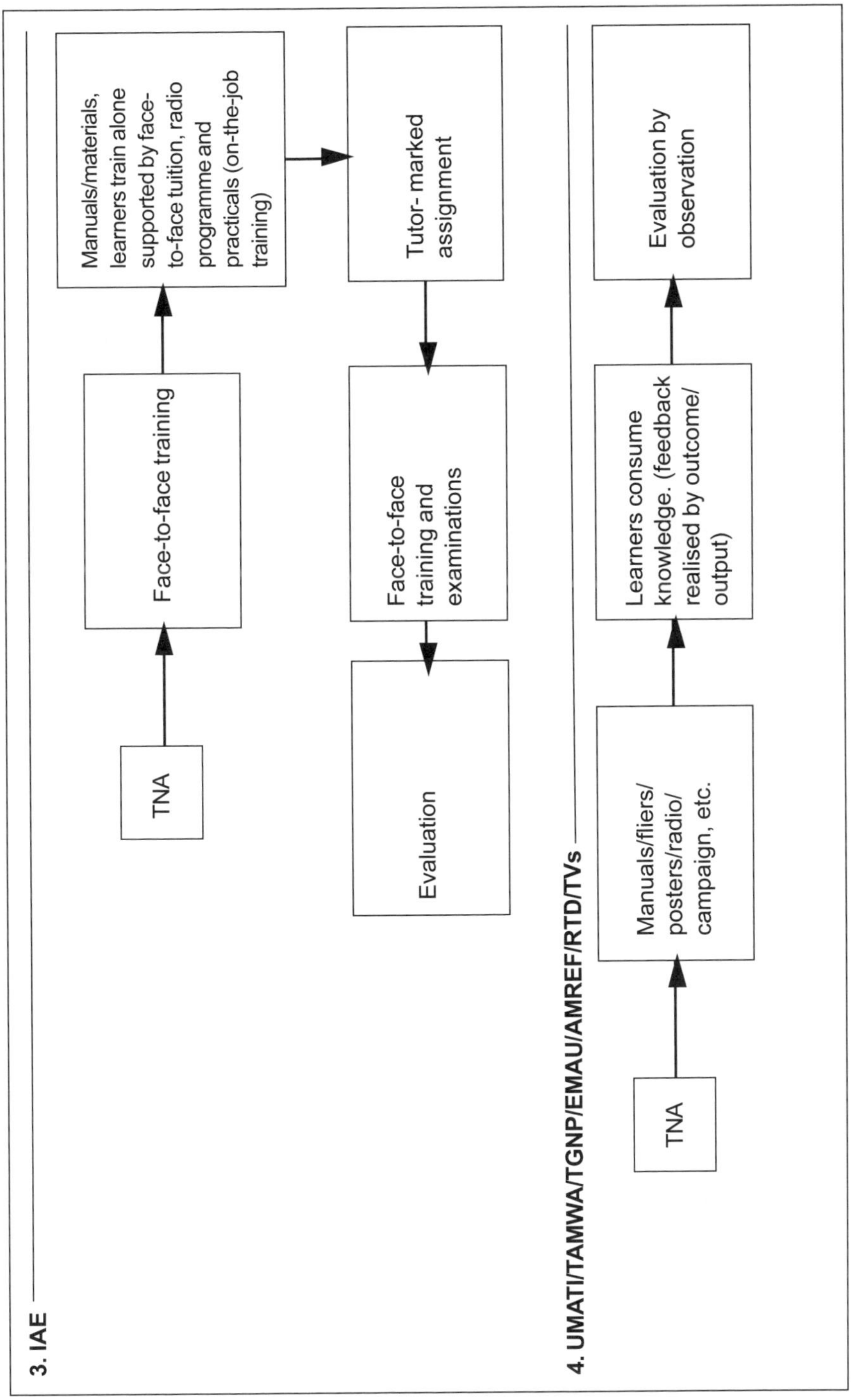
3. IAE
TNA
Face-to-face training
Manuals/materials, learners train alone supported by face-to-face tuition, radio programme and practicals (on-the-job training)
Tutor- marked assignment
Face-to-face training and examinations
Evaluation
4. UMATI/TAMWA/TGNP/EMAU/AMREF/RTD/TVs
TNA
Manuals/fliers/posters/radio/campaign, etc.
Learners consume knowledge. (feedback realised by outcome/output)
Evaluation by observation

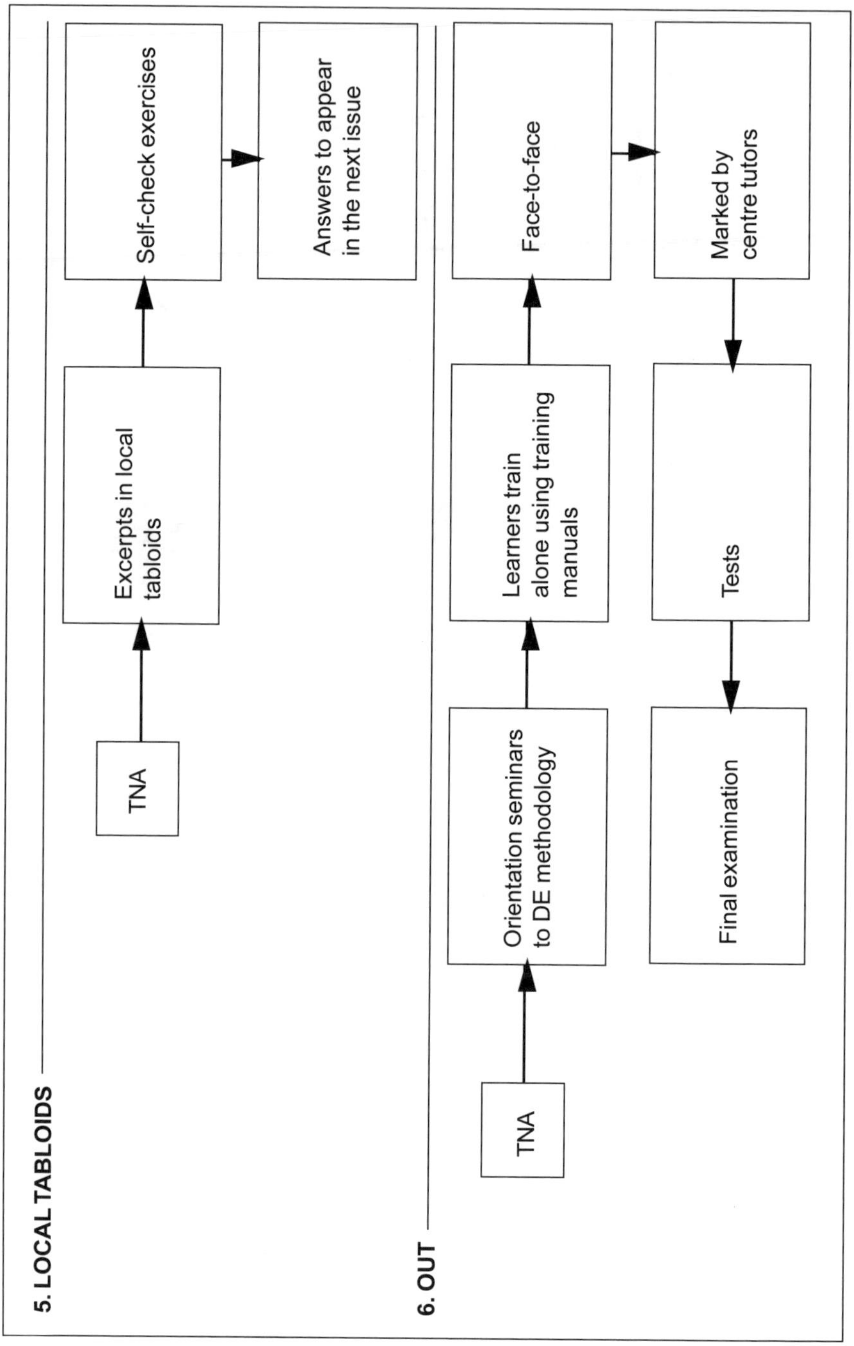

Figure 1 Training modalities

Institutions, organisations and government use a variety of modalities in the provision of ODL. With regard to gender, there have been massive sensitisation programmes to address the gender issue.

Principles for replicability and sustainability

The education experts suggested the following as the principles for replicability and sustainability: (i) An initiative must have clearly stated objectives; (ii) it must have long-term strategies (materials and methods). (iii) it must be well financed. (iv) it must have qualified facilitators. (v) It must involve the grassroots workers as stakeholders in designing the curriculum so as to build a sense of ownership – ownership will also ensure sustainability; (vi) the beneficiaries must contribute to the project financially to ensure sustainability.

The principles given by the experts reflect what various studies and papers point out about replicability and sustainability of training initiatives. The principles are based on the following: Training initiatives must deliver the expected results according to the objectives. Policies have clearly delineated priorities, specific objectives indicating the means for implementation and evaluation.They must fulfil the needs of learners and society. The quality of a programme depends on the qualities of resources, i.e. materials and facilitators. Finance is a key resource for all projects. In order to avoid donor dependence, beneficiaries should contribute towards initiatives.

An outline of a module in DE for adult education fieldworkers

An outline of a module in DE for adult education fieldworkers, based on the needs identified in the study is presented below. The objectives of the course are to: expose ABE fieldworkers to principles of adult psychology so that they may be able to understand how to deal with adults who have various ambitions and needs; expose ABE fieldworkers to adult education teaching methods so that they may improve their teaching techniques; expose ABE fieldworkers to guidance and counselling techniques so that they may apply them in teaching adults who are faced with various problems; introduce ABE fieldworkers to special needs education so that they may apply its principles when needed; train ABE fieldworkers regarding their roles and duties as adult education fieldworkers, and regarding their relationships with the other stakeholders in the education system; equip ABE fieldworkers with basic subject skills to deal with functional and literacy modules used in teaching adults; sensitise ABE fieldworkers to gender and minority group issues and to how these may affect their teaching of adult learners.

The objectives were selected in order to: increase the ability and power of ABE fieldworkers to handle literacy classes, and increase their knowledge of methods of teaching adults, guidance and counselling and minority group issues; create mastery of ABE field techniques; create respect, self-responsibility, recognition and confidence on the part of fieldworkers; enable ABE fieldworkers to increase and determine their own personal development; increase efficiency, especially in the teaching of literacy classes; improve acquisition of the expected product or outcome of the programme (impact)

In order to realise these objectives the consultant proposed that a set of six self-instructional modules, written in Kiswahili, the national language, be prepared: (i) Adult education teaching methods and subject teaching methodologies; (ii) Adult psychology; (iii) Guidance and counselling techniques; (iv) ABE management and administration; (v) Special needs education; (vi) Gender and other minority group issues.

It is proposed that the self-instructional material should be written to conform to the following outline: Each module should contain a table of contents; an introduction to the course; an introduction to the subject and its objectives; topics covered under each subject, which will be named as chapters; an introduction to every chapter; Objectives of each chapter; subtopics under each topic; a self-check exercise at the end of every topic or subtopic as needed; symbols to guide the learners; tutor-marked assignment at the end of the module.

The outline includes self-check exercises which will act as a continuous self-assessment for the learners, while the tutor-marked assignment will act as a final assessment for the whole module. Answers to the self-check exercises should be provided at the end of the module so that the learner can check the correctness of the answers, while the tutor-marked assignments should be sent to the tutors for marking and comment.

It is also proposed that selected experts in the field of ABE and ODL should be involved in the writing of the modules. The drafts for the modules should be edited in a workshop involving various stakeholders in the field of ABE. The modules approved by the review workshop should then be piloted in a number of districts (not fewer than five) representing both urban and rural areas, taking into account the geographical spread of the country. Gender balance must be ensured as well.

The modules should be supported by radio programmes, which could be aired once or twice a week as there are several radio stations in the country. Other electronic media could also be used in future.

Conclusions and recommendations

The current education and training policy (MOEC 1995) does not clearly address issues related to ODL. The government and other organisations use unique policies to implement ODL programmes. However, there is no co-ordination among organisations and government in implementing ODL programmes, hence duplication of work occurs.

The sustainability of training initiatives is mostly affected by a lack of clearly stated policies and insufficient finance. Grassroots level workers have their own training needs, which sometimes differ from those of their employers. These include the desire to enhance their careers and to achieve promotion. Training needs for grassroots level workers proposed by employers are related to improved quality of their work and greater productivity.

There are a number of successful training initiatives targeting grassroots level workers, which have been implemented in the country through ODL. Training initiatives have a direct or indirect impact on their beneficiaries as individuals and on society at large. There are various forms of training modalities used in the country for the provision of ODL. ODL rather than the traditional system of education can be used as a mode of bringing about social change. An finally, there is gender imbalance at all levels of education except in the lower primary school level.

A set of criteria, action tools, methodologies and framework for policy formulation in the area of training of local literacy workers

Based on the experience gained from the study, the consultant recommended the following items to guide the formulation of policy for the training of local literacy workers. The policy should meet the following criteria: (1) The short and long-term objectives of beneficiaries and society should be taken into account. (2) Literacy education should be a responsibility of the whole nation and not the responsibility of the IAE and MOEC only. (3) The ministry responsible for ABE should give guidelines on the training of grassroots level workers. The guidelines should be mandatory for all NGOs and other institutions. (5) For the training to be cost effective, it should be conducted by means of DE methods. (6) Literacy education facilitators passing through the programme should be certified and if already employed should receive a salary increment as well. (7) A cadre of adult education facilitators should be established. (8) The existing TRCs currently under MOEC should be knowledge distribution centres. They should accommodate the ABE programmes and train grassroots level workers through DE. (9) Government should set aside a budget for conducting this programme as well as soliciting outside donors to fund it. (10) Beneficiaries of programmes should be expected to contribute towards the programmes. (11) Women should be given more opportunities to participate in the training; measures and strategies to attract them to participate should therefore be identified and devised. (12) A time frame for the training of literacy workers should be set by the ministry and agencies responsible for adult education. (14) The means of distributing materials and the dissemination of information should be determined by the policy. (16) Evaluation of impact, effectiveness and gender balance should be carried out by a different agency from the one that carries out the training. (17) Continuous assessment of the training programme should be done by the agency responsible for training, while final examinations should be provided by the National Examinations Council of Tanzania (NECTA).

References

Bwatwa, Y. 1989. *Adult Education (The Tanzanian Experience)*. Nairobi: Oxford University Press.

Chale, 1996. Policies, planning and management of distance education institutions in Tanzania. *HURIA Journal of the Open University of Tanzania* 1(1).

Chambo, SA. 2001. Open distance learning and community initiatives. Paper presented to the Open University of Tanzania Convocation Annual General Meeting Conference.

Hall, BL. & Dodds, T. 1974. Voices for development: the Tanzanian National Radio Study Campaigns (International Extension College). *Broadsheets on Distance Learning* 6.

Ligate, NE. 1994. Distance education in Tanzania: state of art and some recommendations in addressing future national and sub regional needs.

Paper presented at the UNESCO Sub-Regional Seminar on Distance Education held in Dar es Salaam, November.

Manyanya, M. 1991. *Adult education: the Tanzania experience*. Nairobi: Oxford University Press.

Ministry of Education and Culture. 1995. *Tanzania education and training policy.* Dar es Salaam: URT.

Ministry of Education and Culture. 1998. Basic statistics in education 1997: regional data. Dar es Salaam: URT.

Ministry of Education and Culture. 2001. Budget speech for 2001/2002 by His Excellency Hon JJ Mungai (MP) to the National Assembly. Dodoma: URT.

Mmari, G. 1996. An idea takes shape: the Open University of Tanzania, early days. *HURIA Journal of the Open University of Tanzania* 1(1) Sept.

Mmari, G. 1997. Distance education in Tanzania towards the 21st century: problems and prospects. Paper presented at the National Forum on Distance Education held at the Institute of Finance Management, July.

Mpogolo, ZJ. 1985. *Methods of functional literacy.* Dar es Salaam: Premier Publishers.

Mushi, PAK. 1991. Origins and development of adult education innovations in Tanzania. *International Review of Education* 37(3).

Mushi, PAK. 1999. Distance education in Tanzania: emerging issues and implications for reforms. Journal of the Faculty of Education, University of Dar es Salaam, November.

Open University of Tanzania. 1997. Prospectus OUT. Dar es Salaam.

Ramakrishna, P. & Mouli, C. 1997. Readability of distance education materials. *HURIA Journal of the Open University Tanzania* 1(2) Sept.

SAEU. 2001. Newsletter Issue 6, January.

URT. 1997. Basic Education Master Plan (BEMP), Medium Term Strategic and Programme Framework: 1997 – 2002. Dar es Salaam

Wort, MA. 1997. Distance education and the training of primary school teachers in Tanzania. Unpublished PhD Thesis, University of UPPSALA.

4

Methods of distance education for training adult educators in South Africa

Veronica McKay

This chapter examines the training of grassroots facilitators in South Africa by using the methods of distance education. In order to contextualise the need for adult basic education in South Africa, this paper begins with a brief background to the South African context. It highlights the need for adult basic education in South Africa and considers the policies which inform its delivery in South Africa. The chapter then focuses on a case study of the training of adult educators by the University of South Africa's ABET Institute. Modes and methods of distance education delivery are discussed. Finally, the chapter ends with a discussion of how the ABET Institute has utilised its network of tutors and graduate students to assist the National Department of Education with its rollout of the South African Literacy Campaign.

Background to the South African context

The Republic of South Africa is situated at the southernmost point of the African continent, bordering Namibia, Botswana, Zimbabwe, Mozambique and the Kingdoms of Swaziland and Lesotho. Its total land area is 1 219 090 sq km, and according to the National Census of 1998[1] its population is approximately 40.1 million. Slightly more than a third of the population is younger than 15 years of age, a statistic that indicates the youthful nature of the population and highlights the implications for population growth and the need for education.[2] Currently South Africa has a large number of children out-of-school – this suggesting the long-term need for adult basic education. South Africa also has high levels of unemployment – contributing to high levels of poverty. In 1999 about 34%[3] of the South African labour force was unemployed – a phenomenon which would have increased by 2002.

Poverty and unemployment in rural areas are higher than in urban areas. One of the reasons for this may be the poor social and economic conditions in rural areas, the lack of basic infrastructure such as electricity and transport, and the lack of employment opportunities. Women in general are poorer than men – a fact that can be explained by their disadvantaged position in the labour market. The table below shows the percentage of men and women living in poverty by area.

Table 1 Rural/urban poverty distribution by gender

Location	Women	Men
Rural	63.2%	57.4%
Urban	31.6%	28.1%
Total for South Africa	48.3%	43.5%

Source: Whiteford, Posel & Kelatwang (1995).

The impact of South African history on the literacy crisis

The social-political and economic situation in South Africa cannot be seen independently of the apartheid policies that were in place prior to democratisation in 1994. The implications of apartheid were far-reaching, and entrenched inequalities and poverty along racial lines. These inequalities penetrated the delivery of services such as water and sanitation and also the system of education. As a result, a significant proportion (19.3%) of the South African population aged 20 years and older have never been to school. The prevalence of no schooling and poverty is highest in the rural areas.

Since 1994 South Africa has seen the emergence of a variety of government policies and legislative frameworks that inform and support adult basic education and affirm its role in the process of social change and development. These include: the South African Qualifications Act (1995); National Education Policy Act (1996); Education White Paper No 4; Policy for Adult Basic Education and Training; 1998 national multi-year implementation plan for adult education and training in the Department of Education; South African Constitution, which enshrines the rights of adults to a basic education. A consideration of the legislative framework for ABET is crucial in providing a backdrop to ABET thinking and practice. For this reason, this chapter begins with a brief overview of relevant legislation, which also serves the purpose of providing a context for the subsequent discussion on training adult educators by way of distance education. It is necessary to draw attention to the gap between legislation and implementation – a gap which exists because of problems such as bureaucratic bottlenecks, lack of capacity, inadequate resources for the sector and general disagreements within the sector.

The integration of education and training

Already in this chapter I have referred several times to the concept of ABET. This is an acronym used in South Africa to refer to Adult Basic Education and Training. The acronym attempts to highlight the integration between *education* and *training* – a marriage which was arranged by the wide range of post-apartheid legislation and which is grounded in the National Qualifications Framework (NQF) via the

SAQA Act of 1995. As will be indicated in the discussion of the SAQA Act, the NQF allows for the recognition and accreditation of learning achievements on the part of even basic level learners. It permits portability, accessibility and transferability of skills, knowledge and abilities.

In order to fully understand the implications of the integration of education and training, this relationship must be considered in terms of a developmental context: Adult basic *education* refers to the educational base which individuals require to improve their life chances; Adult basic *training* refers to the foundational, income-generating or occupational skills which individuals require for improving their living conditions. Putting the two together, Adult Basic Education and Training (ABET) implies the foundational knowledge, skills, understanding and abilities that are required for improved social and economic life. In bringing education and training together, individuals are enabled to integrate the full range of knowledge, skills, understanding and abilities at this level, providing them with a platform for further learning, should they so choose, and with the capacity to bring these integrated understandings to bear upon the improvement and development of their own lives and the lives of those around them. It must be noted that the 'T' in ABET refers to more than technical or employment skills. This would constitute a narrow and restrictive interpretation of training. Rather, the 'T' refers to a wide range of skills and expertise that includes technical skills such as plumbing, dress-making, beadwork and crafts, together with specialised skills such as conflict management and negotiation and including creative skills such as dance and praise poetry. In addition to these, ABET also provides the skills needed for further learning to adults who have been unable to gain, or have been denied access to, basic education. It therefore provides a foundation of fundamental skills, knowledge and understanding which give people a basis from which they can progress along a chosen career path. (Department of National Education: October 1997)

It is clear from the above that ABET implies more than just literacy: it is intended to serve a range of social, economic and developmental roles and it is also viewed as fundamental to building the dignity and self-esteem of the learner.

Constitution of South Africa: The Bill of Rights

The South African Constitution draws attention to adult basic education as a basic human right and highlights the state's obligation to provide adult basic education. Clause 29 1(a) of the Constitution enshrines the right to basic education, including ABET, and states: 'everyone has the right to a basic education including adult basic education and to further education which the state through reasonable measures must make available ... all forms of organised education and training that meet the basic learning needs of adults, including literacy and numeracy, as well as the general knowledge, skills and values and attitudes that they require to survive, develop their capacities, live and work in dignity, improve the quality of their lives, make informed decisions, and continue learning'.

National Education Policy Act (No 27 of 1996)

This Act, too, is concerned with the protection of the right to basic education – in particular 'the right of every person to basic education and equal access to education institutions'; The right to a basic education implies, by extension, the right to good quality learning programmes with good quality learner support materials, good quality teaching practices and appropriate learning sites.[4]

White paper on education and training

The White Paper on Education and Training emphasises the growing need for ABET. It observes that, as a result of the high attrition rates in schools, millions of adult South Africans are functionally illiterate. In the large, poorly-resourced sectors that cater for the majority of the population, a majority of students drop out prematurely (Government Gazette, No. 16085 of 1994:7). The policy thus stresses the need for targeting out-of-school youth for basic education. The Multi-year Implementation Plan (referred to below) also stresses the importance of other categories of learners.

While the policy is aimed at all adults who 'would like to participate' in ABET programmes, the following target groups are singled out as needing special attention and special motivation: women, especially those from the rural areas; out-of-school youth; the unemployed; prisoners and ex-prisoners; adults with disabilities that prevented them from obtaining a basic education.

ABET policy and the multi-year implementation ilan

The multi-year plan outlines the proposed model for delivery and spells out the criteria and norms for quality ABET delivery. It also draws attention to the multiple roles of the ABET practitioner. These roles are reflected in the proposed models for Education, Training and Development Practitioners, which define the roles and functions of the ABET practitioner. These are discussed in more detail below.

Employment of Educators' Act

Until recently, adult educators were excluded from the Educators' Employment Act. They were not included within the definition of an 'educator', a category that was reserved for those who taught in schools and in the institutions of further education. However, following amendments to the Act, the definition of 'educator' now encompasses adult practitioners. This implies that ABET practitioners employed by the state now fall within the parameters of the legal framework governing their practice, conditions of service and remuneration in accordance with adult practitioner qualifications. However, this Act applies only to adult practitioners in the state sector. Practitioner bodies would therefore need to ensure that adult educators employed in other government sectors that do not fall under the auspices of this Act actively lobby for recognition.

Skills Development Act

The National Skills Development strategy must be seen as part of the government's commitment to overall human resource development, which includes education reform. In this regard, the Act stipulates that for South Africans to participate meaningfully in the country's economic and social development, as well as for their own advancement, they must have general capabilities such as the ability to read, write, communicate effectively and solve problems in their homes, communities and workplaces.

South African Qualifications Act (No 58 of 1995)

The South African Qualifications Authority (SAQA) was established in 1995. One of its key functions was to develop and put into practice the National Qualifications Framework (NQF), which would create an integrated national framework for learning achievements. It would also facilitate access to, and mobility and progression within, education, training and career paths; enhance the quality of education and training; accelerate the redress of past unfair discrimination in education, training and employment opportunities, and thereby contribute to the full personal development of each learner and the social development of the nation at large. The central function of the NQF is to accredit unit standards which culminate in qualifications. This Act has particular significance for educators of adults and for ABET learners.

The table below illustrates the various levels, sites for learning and bands of accreditation. Basic education is accommodated in levels 4 and below and teacher's qualifications are located from level 4 upwards.

Table 3 The national qualifications framework

NQF LEVEL	BAND	QUALIFICATION TYPE	
Higher Education & Training (HET)			
8 7	HET	• Doctorates • Master's degrees • Professional qualifications • Honours degrees	
6	HET	• National first degrees • Higher diplomas	
5	HET	• National diplomas • Higher certificates	
Further Education & Training Certificate (FETC)			
4 3 2	FET	National certificates	Obtained in schools, colleges, NGOs
General Education & Training Certificate (GETC)			
1	GET	Senior phase	ABET 4 (grade 9)
		Intermediate phase	ABET 3 (grade 7)
		Foundation phase	ABET 2 (grade 5)
		Pre-school	ABET 1 (grade 3)

The SAQA Act makes provision for the development of unit standards which guide the delivery of courses and programmes. In practice, this means that what is taught in formal ABET programmes to learners attending basic education classes and what is taught to trainee adult educators is guided and informed by the unit standards, which are communally developed.

The Adult Basic Education and Training Act

The ABET Act of 2000 applies to the establishment and delivery of state adult centres. In terms of this Act a public centre may only employ an educator in a post if the educator is registered with the South African Council for Educators (SACE) and employed in accordance with the terms of the Employment of Educators Act.

Language policy and ABET

The issue of language underlies much of the educational debate in South Africa. The country has 11 official languages (English, Afrikaans, Sepedi, Sesotho, Setswana, siSwati, Tshivenda, Xitsonga, isiNdebele, isiXhosa and isiZulu). Under the apartheid government only two languages (English and Afrikaans) were considered 'official' while the other 9 languages were diminished both in terms of official use and status. Recognising the historically diminished use and status of the indigenous languages, the 1994 South African Constitution requires the state to take positive measures to elevate the status and advance the use of these languages.

There are various ways in which this is put into practice. The national and provincial governments may use any particular official language for the purpose of governance, taking into account practicality, expense, regional circumstances and the needs and preferences of the population as a whole or in the province concerned. Government must monitor the use of official languages to ensure that all official languages enjoy parity of esteem and are treated equitably.

The Pan African Language Board was established and charged with promoting multilingualism by creating conditions for the development and equal use of all official languages, fostering respect for other languages and encouraging the best use of the country's linguistic resources in order to enable South Africans to free themselves from all forms of linguistic discrimination, domination and division. To this end, the Pan African Language Board is required to promote and create conditions for the development and use of the official languages mentioned above, as well as of Khoi, Nama, the San languages and sign language. In addition, it is required to promote and ensure respect for all languages commonly used by communities in South Africa, including German, Greek, Gujarati, Hindi, Portuguese, Tamil, Telegu and Urdy, and languages used in South Africa for religious purposes such as Arabic, Hebrew and Sanskrit.

In the field of adult basic education, this multilingual policy generally translates into the initial teaching of mother tongue literacy, and learners are encouraged to continue with the acquisition of mother tongue literacy while a second language, usually English as the language of the local economy, is being introduced as an additional language.

It is clear, with the complexities of South African language policy, that teachers are required to be extremely well trained to teach learners in their first language and, in multilingual, non-homogeneous settings (usually in the larger urban/metropolitan centres), to teach in multilingual classrooms.

The gap between policy and implementation

Sadly, in the midst of all this legislation, the delivery of ABET in South Africa is dismal and does not appear to be making an impact. There is clearly a gap between policy and practice and it is necessary that this gap be bridged. The Human Sciences Research Council (HSRC) (1999:2) states that this gap is evident in the fact that in 1995/6, only about 334 000 people (of a potential 4 million adults in need of basic literacy) participated in ABET programmes throughout the country. Seven of South Africa's nine provinces spent less than 1% of their education budget on ABET in 1998 (HSRC 1999:4).[5] This is in spite of the policy developments and legislation (mentioned above) directed at the delivery and implementation of ABET. South Africa is now faced with the post-policy imperative of reducing the gap between policy and practice through the application of programmes and initiatives that will bring about the desired changes in the lives of many more South Africans. The HSRC audit indicates that participation in the state sector is 'disturbingly low when compared with the goal of universal access to ABET programmes' referred to in the multi-year plan (DoE 1998:7).

Clearly if universal access to adult literacy programmes is the goal, the ABET practitioner has a critical role to play in the education and training of adult learners in many different settings – including state, community, industry and other contexts.

Amidst the reluctant delivery in the sector, significant achievements have been made regarding the professionalisation of the adult educator, and this should provide a firm foundation for large-scale ABET delivery. (This is discussed further later in this chapter.)

The need for ABET in South Africa

How great is the need for ABET? Table 4 highlights the number of learners who have had little or no schooling and who might be considered as falling within the ABET target bracket.

Table 4 Number of ABET target learners

Education level	Aged 15 years and older	Between 15 - 65 years of age
Adults who have not attended school	1 621 214	1 024 870
Adults who have only completed Grade 1 - Std 4	4 472 390	4 117 525
TOTAL of adults who have less than Std 5	6 093 604	5 142 395
Adults who have completed Stds 5 – 6	4 758 723	4 490 464
TOTAL number of adults who have less than Std 7	**10 852 327**	**9 632 859**

Source: Adapted from Harley et al (1996) in Department of Education (1997: 64).

As is indicated in Table 4, more than 9 million[6] South Africans fall within the ABET target grouping.

A qualification framework for educators

The legislation discussed earlier has crucial implications for the educators of adults. It implies the need for well-trained adult practitioners who can play a role in addressing critical economic, political and social problems specific to learners across a variety of sectoral contexts (such as health and HIV/AIDS, the environment and labour) as well as across a variety of communal contexts. The legislation presupposes an educator who might understand her or his role as fitting in with the general principles of democracy, human rights, citizenship and development.

Well-trained practitioners will do much to enhance the quality of the learning experience for adults, and the 1990s saw a move away from 'makeshift' adult educators with little or no training towards a more professional cadre whose training is guided by the development of relevant qualifications and learning programmes. Several developments in the establishment of practitioner qualifications have taken place in the past four years. The establishment of the Standards Generating Body (SGB) and its recent development of unit standards for ABET practitioners signal a breakthrough in establishing a qualification framework and evolving a career path for ABET practitioners. The development of a qualification framework for Adult Practitioners by the SGB (adult learning NSB 05) can be regarded as one of the most significant areas of development in the training of practitioners for the ABET field.

Education, training and development roles of practitioners and educators

In addition to the complexities of language, the adult educator is required to assume a variety of complex roles and functions pertaining to education, training and development. The tasks and responsibilities below give some indication of the range these educators are expected to cover: (1) plan a learning event; (2) facilitate an adult learning event; (3) assess learners within a learning situation; (4) fulfil administrative requirements of a learning group; (5) evaluate own facilitation performance; (6) help learners with language and literacy across the curriculum; (7) identify and respond to learners who have special needs; (8) facilitate mother tongue literacy; (9) facilitate an additional language; (10) facilitate numeracy; (11) organise a programme of learning; (12) facilitate a programme of learning; (13) evaluate, select and adapt published learning materials; (14) develop, use and evaluate own supplementary learning aids; (15) design, implement and follow-up on internal assessment; (16) conduct research and liaison relevant to the learning situation; (17) mediate language, literacy and maths across the curriculum; (19) identify and respond to learners with special needs and barriers to learning; (20) promote lifelong learning; (21) facilitate communications and maths; (22) design learning programmes including curriculum design and materials development; (23) undertake a leadership role in an ABET division of an organisation; (24) supervise the work of other ABET practitioners; (25) apply extended skills around research, evaluation, quality assurance and community development; (26) facilitate learning areas; (27) offer specialist input on particular aspects of ABET provision.

In addition to these unit standards, practitioners may specialise in a range of electives from facilitating craftwork and subsistence agriculture, to workplace and occupational programmes and small and micro enterprises. Clearly, for a practitioner to assume the functions above, training has to be well conceptualised and presented.

Different training providers

While the NGO sector in South Africa has been pivotal in training adult educators and in the provision of adult learning, this sector is declining as a result of the decline in regular funding. After 1994 not many NGOs have become self-sustaining, making it difficult to estimate the number of literacy/ABET NGOs that have survived and the number of learners they serve. Many tertiary institutions have been involved in training adult educators in developing, *inter alia,* the above-mentioned competencies.

Since the focus of this investigation is on distance education and the training of basic education functionaries, the next section will present a case study of the programme presented by the Institute for Adult Basic Education and Training at the University of South Africa. Reference will, however, also be made to other university-based courses which make use of some distance components and which are directed at training adult educators.

At the tertiary level, various universities and Technikons are currently engaged in the training of ABET/adult education practitioners. (Leumer's chapter in this book refers to tertiary institutions with which the DVV has been associated in the training of adult educators.) However, the University of South Africa is currently the largest adult education provider, having trained over 45 000 adult education practitioners over the past nine years.

Distance education in South Africa – UNISA's historical position

The University of South Africa (also known as Unisa) is one of 11 mega distance teaching universities (universities with more than 100 000 students) in the world. Originally established as the University of the Cape of Good Hope in 1873, it is South Africa's oldest university. In 1946 Unisa became a pioneer of tertiary distance education in the western world, a move which heralded the beginning of Unisa as we know it today. Enrolments have climbed from the 1 250 who registered in 1946 to over 130 000 in 2002.

Unisa's ABET institute

The ABET Institute at Unisa was established in 1995 in response to the democratic government's expressed desire for reconstruction and development in South Africa. This required the Institute to be responsive to those areas where *education* could play a role in the development of communities. In order to fulfil this aim, the ABET Institute trains a cadre of practitioners who work in adult education programmes across various sectors and in different social contexts (such as health, environment, the workplace and water management) and in different types of settlements (urban, rural, formal and informal). This approach promotes key socio-economic benefits, especially for the most marginalised and disadvantaged communities, which are the Institute's primary target group. Training ABET practitioners in basic and generic skills allows them to work in a variety of specialised areas, including literacy, numeracy, primary health care and HIV/AIDS, English as another language, small business development and environmental education.

With development and the enhancement of livelihoods as the prime rationale for the courses presented by the ABET Institute, addressing the needs for, *inter alia*, literacy or numeracy could not occur without locating these needs within a broader development paradigm. This point of departure made the ABET Institute immediately different from programmes which focused primarily on literacy as a *method* or as a *technique* and rarely on literacy as a component of a development strategy.

The ABET Institute sees the practitioner as central to the enhancement of communities and directs its training at practitioners – in many instances nurses, community workers, literacy volunteers, trade unionists and so on – who will be able to teach skills like basic literacy, numeracy or health education but with a *developmental bias*.

For this reason, the ABET practitioner's programme is useful to a variety of practitioners, including literacy practitioners; trainers for water and sanitation; trainers in health, nutrition, HIV/AIDS, family planning; environmental educators; job skills trainers; trade unionists; worker educators; adult educators who teach in state programmes; agricultural extension workers; youth workers; community organisers; and materials developers.

How do we apply the programme in a way that can offer maximum benefit for the community while achieving maximum outreach? The programme trains up to 12 000 ABET practitioners per annum (and has to date trained more than 37 000 practitioners), who will work in a variety of fields in community development and community education. Attention is given later in the chapter to the way in which the methods of distance education make it possible to go to scale. It is, however, necessary to contextualise this discussion by referring to the view of the trainer which underlies the thinking and practices of the work of the ABET Institute.

The tenuous relationship between literacy and development

The Unisa ABET programme is informed by the premise that literacy does *not* equal development and that people who become literate do not necessarily enjoy a better quality of life: there is no direct link between literacy and development and no direct link between literacy and livelihood. It is for this reason that the ABET Institute couples its training of adult educators with developing the capacities of its trainees to initiate programmes for social development.

Traditional approaches to teaching literacy have not made deliberate attempts to forge links with development and livelihoods and where development has occurred, the linkages are usually coincidental. At the same time, the lack of literacy is often cited as being problematic in *development* programmes. Through conceptualising literacy and adult basic education and training more broadly and from a developmental point of view, the ABET programme has shown that it is possible to take on the challenge of bridging the gap between literacy and development.

In attempting to address such issues, it is crucial to focus on the import of *human agency* or *the will to act*. It is only through *human empowerment* and through enhancing peoples' *belief in their own ability* to participate that development can occur. Thus it is necessary to focus on the relationship between agency and participation, and accordingly this paper attempts to show how – within the framework of the programme presented by the ABET Institute at Unisa – the question of agency is addressed. In this sense, the ABET programme is contrasted with traditional approaches to teaching literacy.

Some of the failures of traditional literacy programmes can be attributed to the teaching of literacy as a *technical process*. This means that people are taught, for example, only to know the syllables and the mechanics of reading and writing – often using rote methods and a great deal of chanting. There is usually no connection with *local issues, local development* or *social change*. This is because, in the Freirian sense, learners or their teachers are not able to become engaged in *'reading the word and reading the world'*.

When we teach people to read words we do not automatically equip them to understand the world better, and therefore to change or develop it. The Unisa ABET programme regards the literacy practitioner as crucial to facilitating this understanding in order that people are able to make their mark on the world. The programme takes as its point of departure the principle that the facilitator is trained to become 'theoretically literate' – a precondition for engendering development.

While I am aware of the debate surrounding the concept of development and while I use the word loosely in this chapter to refer to an improvement in people's socio-economic situations and quality of life, I recognise the importance of the development of human agency in order that members of communities themselves participate in their own development. In this way, people are inextricably part of the development equation.

The development of human agency

This pertains to the need for ABET practitioners to encourage a sense of '*agency*' or what the well-known sociologist Peter Berger calls a *developmental consciousness* in order to address the problems of underdevelopment and also the 'human question'.[7] What Berger draws our attention to is that development has to be firmly based in human wellbeing, the quality of human life and a great deal of self-esteem. It has to touch on the aspirations and needs of people as defined by people themselves. Thus while social structures are transformable, the transformation has to be predicated on the basis of a meaningful existence.

The ABET programme recognises the importance of infrastructural features like the provision of water, sanitation and health facilities for development but emphasises that its ABET practitioners give equal recognition to the importance of developing *human agency* in the classes and in the development projects in which we are engaged. This is a way of 'awakening' at the local level. Agency refers to the importance of empowering people to determine their needs, to reflect on possible outcomes and to act on them. The Unisa ABET Institute has taken on the challenge of both the development of human agency and the necessity of social action. In practice, practitioners are made theoretically literate. They are trained to look at their learners' contexts through developmentally tinted spectacles. They are required to profile and analyse community contexts before embarking on any programme. It is for this reason that the curriculum developed by the ABET Institute (now aligned with the newly developed unit standards for ABET practitioners) begins with a module on contextual studies.

The ABET practitioner's training curriculum

The curriculum for the ABET course attempts to make practitioners aware of the variety of contexts in which they might work. They are also made aware of the choices and the necessity for debating knowledge and for acting. The curriculum presented to adult educators includes:

Box 1

Contextual studies	The uniqueness of the practitioner's course begins with a module on integrated social studies, or what we call Contextual Studies. The teaching of *contextual studies* is intended to make practitioners aware of the profiles and situations of different social contexts in which they might work. There is no one way of delivering ABET and there is no one correct curriculum. These have to be contextualised. We expose our trainees to various kinds of social and theoretical contexts which will make them aware of different types of areas (rural, urban, formal and informal/squatter settlements, etc) and to the types of problems faced by communities in these areas. They are also made aware of the discursiveness of knowledge and the importance of debating knowledge at every stage of their delivery. If teaching and learning are to be relevant, they have to be grounded in the communities the practitioners aim to serve, but the answers to relevance emerge from the knowledge arrived at through participation. This module pays attention to a variety of social issues – some of which may be relevant to practitioners' own contexts as well as to others that emerge, including health and AIDS, environment, women, employment/unemployment/ entrepreneurship. Practitioners of all varieties and

	persuasions need to have a degree of theoretical literacy if they are to play a role in social development.
Managing projects	The *Contextual Studies* module is coupled with the module on ***Managing Projects*** which, as its name suggests, deals with the basics of establishing and implementing a project as well as with issues like needs analyses and project impact evaluation.The programme aims to enable practitioners to look at their communities through *sociological tinted spectacles* so that they can take on their roles of agency in an informed way, with some understanding of the different contexts and issues.
Adult learning	We make a conscious effort to draw practitioners' attention to the importance of continuous self-reflection through teaching participatory methods; action research; ways of becoming a reflective practitioner. Through emphasising reflection and action research, the programme aims to encourage trainee practitioners to participate actively and to reflect on whatever project (or teaching practice) they are involved in. In this way the ABET programme is able to deploy students who can put into practice literacy/ABET programmes as being integrated into community development, income generation, food subsistence and health programmes.
Teaching literacy and mathe-matical numeracy	In these modules, practitioners are introduced to the various debates surrounding the teaching of literacy and numeracy. In the process, they enhance their own literacy and mathematical literacy skills. Students are required to develop materials for the teaching of these learning areas, to obtain teaching practice at adult learning sites and to determine the need for adults to acquire competencies in these areas in their life, family and work contexts.
Adult teaching and learning	In this module, the adult educator is trained in more advanced facilitation methods. He or she is trained in designing materials and assessment tools, identifying certain learning problems, teaching in difficult contexts (e.g. prison) and is schooled in advanced learner-centred approaches.

Teaching English as a second language Teaching health education	Here students are introduced to the various methods of teaching English as a second language. Students are given an understanding of health issues including hygiene, nutrition and HIV/AIDS.
Teaching practice	Students are expected to conduct about 10 to 15 classes. They are required to find a centre where they can obtain this experience and where they make certain observations. At these sites, students are assessed by their peers and by a teacher employed at the centre. The ABET Institute provides the centre with criteria for assessment.[8]
Specialised content courses[9]	Water and sanitation Applied science English Mathematics Environmental education Trade theory Educare Computer studies Business economics
Development studies	This module extends students' understanding of poverty and under-development. Students are exposed to models for development and to a range of developmental problems related to poverty, illiteracy, unemployment, environmental matters and the effects of globalisation.Students are also presented with cases on the relationship between education, technology and development. They focus closely on the role of women in development and on strategies for people-centred development and sustainable development.
Teaching adults about the environment and about small business development	These two modules relate to the module on development studies. Students are given practical guidelines for teaching adults how to establish a small business and on how their eco-environments contribute to a better quality of life.
Research methods	The student is trained in a variety of quantitative, qualitative, participatory and action methods of research. This extends their needs analysis skills and enhances their ability to profile communities. They are also given training in various research methods which support community development (eg participatory rural appraisal, Venn diagrams, mapping) and in designing a research project and writing up a research report.

Field project	Students submit a research project which demonstrates their ability to apply the research skills they acquire in the research module.They are required to submit a final research dissertation, which should demonstrate the application of the required knowledge, skills and understandings.

What specific outcomes should students on this course hope to achieve?

After successfully completing this course, students should demonstrate that they are equipped to do or possess several capabilities: undertake policy analysis; engage in policy debates; utilise a range of teaching/facilitation methods; utilise a range of assessment methods; counsel learners; identify and remedy learning difficulties; refer learners with complex learning difficulties to other professionals; develop teaching material; evaluate teaching material; profile learners; profile communities; identify target groupings. They must also be capable of adapting teaching and learning situations to target group's needs; improved knowledge in selected area of learning; facilitating adult learning in selected area of learning; planning a learning experience for group/individual learners; demonstrating teaching skills; demonstrating communicative skills; demonstrating assessment skills; relating teaching to social context; identifying areas of research; designing research approaches; compiling research reports; utilising a variety of qualitative, quantitative and participatory research methods; contributing to the development of a common, shared vision for ABET across sectors and understanding the situation within each district and its importance in terms of ABET. Moreover, they must be able to understand the usefulness of community profiles; know how to network and build partnerships with other stakeholders and institutions; form linkages between ABET and other developmental objectives and needs; have an understanding of terms like participation, development and people-centred development; know how to assess and prioritise needs and do a community profile; know how to collect information on relevant structures, organisations, institutions and other possible partners in an area; identify key roles that managerial staff may need to play; skills such as collaborative management, teamwork facilitation, counselling, monitoring and strategising. In addition to the specific outcomes listed above, learners are expected to achieve a number of *critical outcomes*: enable students to engage in problem solving; participate in group/syndicate task groups; encourage critical thinking; organise group tasks. These are the outcomes that are taught mainly indirectly but which should be achieved by all learners regardless of whether they are studying for a doctoral degree or a first-year certificate.

What are the methods of distance education?

In the teaching of this course, a variety of distance educational methods and techniques are employed.

Textual materials: All students are issued with study guides on registration. The study guides are complete (as opposed to wrapping around a particular textbook.) They are written in a way that invites the student to participate in a discussion on the various themes.

- The study material makes extensive use of case studies which engage the student in the 'story' before teaching certain concepts. Our research has shown that this method is extremely useful for students.
- Activities are included to encourage the learner to think about the matters at hand and to allow her or him the space to internalise the content and think of answers and solutions to the questions.
- Throughout the text, the often lonely student, usually from a disadvantaged educational background, is given hints on how to study. These may be practical hints, like working in a quiet place, but often they involve significant skills for learning.
- When we write our text, we assume we are addressing a student who is lonely and perhaps desperately trying to work through the material late into the night. We therefore try to speak to the student in order to encourage him or her to persevere.

Video tape: An effort is also made to incorporate video material into our teaching text. While we make use of a variety of videos which could help us get our message across, we also develop video material which we classify as being 'edutainment' and which entertain the students while making significant points.
Insert video tape activity

The Internet: In a small way, students are introduced to the world of the Internet. All our materials are included on our web site and students are encouraged to make use of the student online system to talk to lecturers at the university. Because of the lack of electricity and telephone infrastructure in many areas in South Africa, this method has had a slow start, although more recently students are making more frequent use of it.

Video conferencing: The university also provides video conferencing facilities which enable groups of students to talk to their lecturers from various sites. The limitations of this method for large-scale delivery are obvious (insufficient sites) but the facility works well with smaller groups of postgraduate students.

Satellite technology is currently being pursued for supporting our tutors and the SANLI campaign. These are discussed in greater detail below.

Radio: In the past the university made extensive use of radio broadcasts. Each broadcast was presented on two occasions in the same week so that students had ample opportunity to listen. Academics are not, however, always the best radio broadcasters and it is now believed that talking to students in this way was not as effective as it might have been. Academics would require a great deal of training before they could address students in a way that remotely compared with the broadcasters of the national radio stations.

In addition to various technological aids, the ABET institute makes use of a national base of tutors which enables the Institute to reach its annual intake of students around the country. In 2003 the ABET institute had 12 000 enrolled students supported by its tutorial system.

The Unisa ABET tutorial system

How does the ABET Institute manage to go to scale and to train practitioners nationally? Figure 1 illustrates how the ABET Institute is able to offer face-to-face tuition to students wherever they might be in South Africa.

As indicated in Figure 1, groups of students are formed in appropriate areas and each group is assigned a local person who acts as its tutor/motivator.[10] Because the teaching is delivered *in situ*, practitioners conduct needs analyses and carry out mapping and other research in their areas. They are also able to conduct practice teaching in their areas and to observe their peers and engage in group teaching initiatives. Since the final assessment requires that students engage with a local literacy/development project, the capacity on the ground is considerably enhanced. This has resulted in the emergence of a multitude of small income-generating, literacy/environmental projects in the local communities. The approach has proved to be so effective that the ABET Institute has now extended the cascade to participate in the government's national literacy campaign.

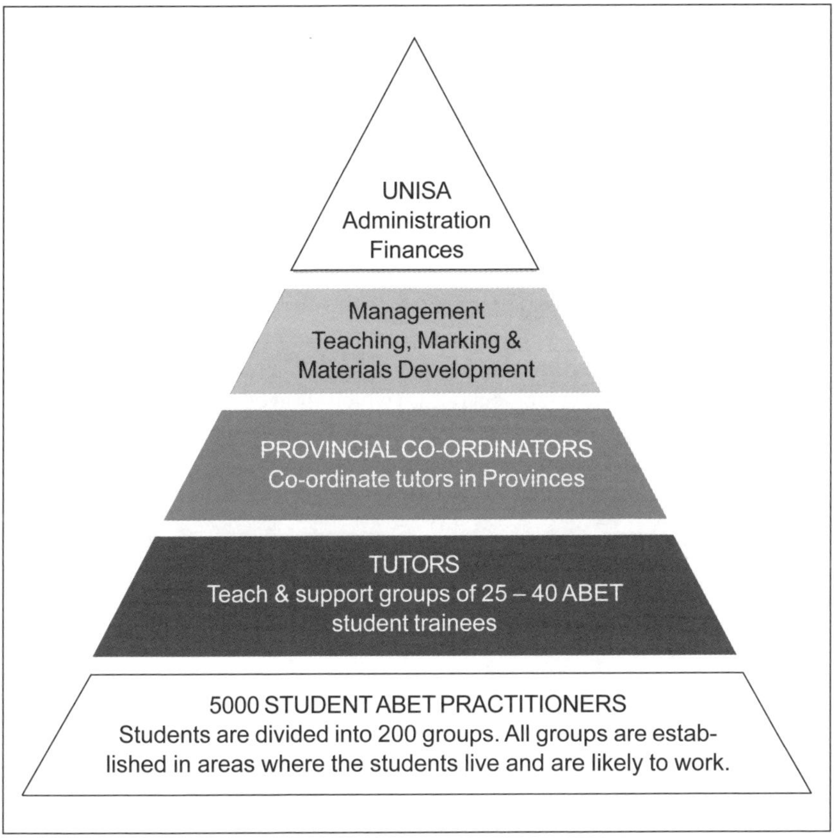

Figure 1 Unisa ABET cascade strategy

NAMCOL case study

In addition to providing training for South African students, the ABET Institute at Unisa formed a partnership with the Namibian College for Open Learning (NAMCOL) in order to jointly train adult educators for the Namibian government. Mensah's chapter elaborates on this partnership. As part of the initial arrangement, Unisa ABET provided training material to NAMCOL, which undertook to present the tutoring component. During the contact sessions, NAMCOL adapted and supplemented the programme to suit its own unique circumstances. The adaptation resulted in the following differences: NAMCOL developed supplementary material, which required that the course be extended for an additional year. The tutorial system was modified by NAMCOL to suit the Namibian context.

The course

In the first year, students worked through the Unisa modules. Their assignments were submitted to Unisa for assessment and they wrote the usual ABET examinations at the Unisa examination centres in Namibia. Students were required to submit a field project based on their own experiences of adult education and the projects submitted were uniquely Namibian.

Because of the unique circumstances, NAMCOL undertook to extend the South African course so that it would be more specific to its own context. This meant that NAMCOL developed and presented modules on research methods and development studies to students in their second year as part of their certificate qualification. At the end of the second year, students received a NAMCOL-Unisa Certificate in Education for Development (CED) which allowed them to be employed in development/literacy posts in various government departments, particularly in the Department of Basic Education (DBE).

The tutorial system

Namibia spans 825 118 km^2 and has a population of less than 1 million. The student population on the CED course was sparsely spread and due to the long distances to be travelled, it was not possible for NAMCOL to use the system of tutoring used in South Africa. NAMCOL presented training to its year intakes of students (usually around 30 students) at 2 two-week long residential workshops presented in Windhoek, the capital of Namibia. Students were accommodated by NAMCOL and they received tuition and worked with their peers during this period. After the block release programmes, students were expected to submit their assignments to Unisa and finally, to take the final Unisa examinations.

Unisa ABET's strategic response to the South African literacy campaign

The link between poverty and illiteracy is well known and SANLI (South African National Literacy Initiative) was established in 2000 to address the need for literacy. The illiteracy rate in South Africa is between 10 and 15 million people and SANLI aimed to reduce illiteracy by at least 35% by 2004.

The National Literacy Initiative of the South African Ministry of Education is presently in its second year of implementation. The objective is to enable approximately one million South Africans to become literate – an effort which will expand the participation of all South Africans in the new democracy. While the programme is aimed at all adults who have not had the opportunity to attend school, it endeavours to target, in particular, women and out-of-school youth.

SANLI's strategy for delivery is to harness the capacity of other agencies involved in the delivery of adult literacy. In this way the Ministry proposes to go to scale so that the project can reach its targeted number of enrolments.

Background to the Unisa-SANLI partnership

Recognising the value of the Institute's resource of trained personnel, in 2001 the South African National Literacy Initiative entered into a partnership with the Institute. This partnership focuses on stimulating and delivering literacy training to the most needy learners across the country in some of our most isolated and impoverished communities. On 7 February 2002, Unisa ABET entered into a partnership with the Ministerial SANLI project, in terms of which Unisa ABET undertook to make 75 000 adults literate – a target which was exceeded within the first few months of the partnership.

Since then, Unisa ABET has consistently achieved its targets and the widespread introduction of SANLI classes in all provinces has provided a critical mass of adults attending literacy classes, so that the process has taken on a momentum which was difficult to dampen. (In the first two years of this partnership, Unisa ABET has reached 307 000 learners.)

The Unisa-SANLI partnership has also been instrumental in developing the necessary management support systems to effectively control, review and evaluate activities across the country. This includes creating a database to facilitate payment of expenses to the volunteer educators, and to monitor the learners' growing competencies.

The figure below illustrates how Unisa ABET has used its human infrastructure to respond to the main components of the literacy campaign.

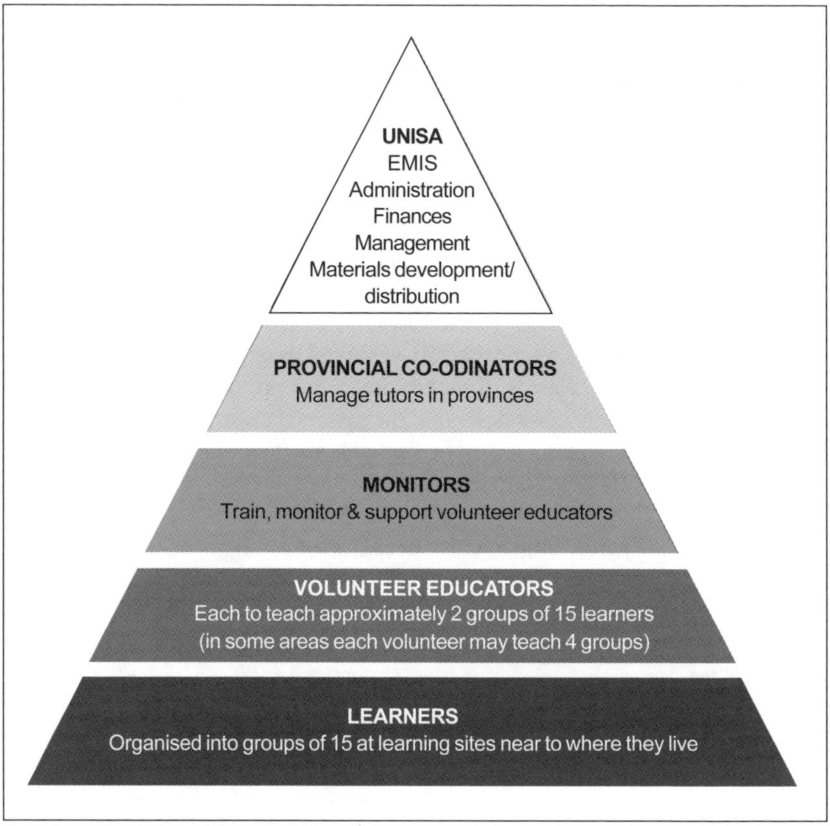

Figure 2 Unisa-SANLI strategy

Training, monitoring and supporting volunteer teachers

Box 2

Provincial co-ordinators	The cascade identifies co-ordinators in each province to oversee provincial monitors. The co-ordinators know the areas in which they work and are familiar with the main learning and development needs of the various target groups.
Provincial monitors	The number of monitors in each province is proportionate to the number of trained students. Monitors are required to: ◆ orient the already trained volunteer educators to the goals of the campaign and their own roles ◆ ensure that the volunteers in specific areas are co-ordinated and can map their targets and the need for literacy in their areas ◆ provide ongoing support and monitoring for established classes ◆ compile/gather reporting documentation.
Volunteer educators	The already trained volunteer graduates are oriented to undertake the a number of functions: ◆ compile maps, working with their peers and members of the community ◆ identify sites for presenting classes ◆ identify and recruit learners ◆ place learners at correct levels ◆ teach each class three times a week for two hours· present lessons using pre-designed and home-grown lessons and materials for up to six months ◆ motivate and ensure learner attendance[11] ◆ maintain records as required.

The partnership with the ABET Institute has constructed the necessary frameworks to underpin successful delivery of literacy and development opportunities throughout the country. By establishing learning centres located in the communities where the learners live, the partnership has created considerable momentum from the learners themselves. A specific indicator of this is that dropout rates have been minimal. A characteristic of the literacy activities implemented by the Institute, especially those developed through the relationship with SANLI, is the enthusiasm of the learners and their commitment to opening up new futures. Classes are held where the learners live and where it is convenient for them to attend. Unlike other initiatives, which rely on volunteers who have received only short periods of training, the Unisa-SANLI campaign volunteers have been trained for at least one year. In fact, many have been trained for up to three years and a significant number hold postgraduate qualifications.

Because the educators live in the communities from which the learners are drawn, they are intimately acquainted with the needs of their learners and the social challenges they face. This bottom-up approach ensures that the learners are able to feed in their concerns and that they have some control over the programme and its development. This makes it easier for learners to link with 'post'-literacy learning opportunities and income generating activities.

The statistical data gathered on the Unisa database and the detailed information collected from site visits and monitoring records suggest that: (1) Unisa ABET has achieved the benefits of scale and is delivering SANLI classes at a cost of R350 (US$59) per learner. (This includes all stationery, learner support materials, stipends for volunteers and monies needed for monitoring and supporting the programme. (2) The programme has been extremely well received by learners and communities. (3) Many learners are grateful for this, their first opportunity to learn to read and write. (4) Since the first classes started, learners have been subscribing in great numbers in what tutors have described as a 'SANLI-fever'. (5) The materials provided to the learners are extremely popular – especially the calculators, which for many learners represent their first exposure to any form of technology. (6) More than 400 tons of materials have been dispatched to the various sites across the country. (7) Learners are concerned about what will happen to them after they have completed the SANLI classes and the national ABET directorate has been earnestly requested to be ready to receive these learners into government adult learning centres. (8) Many educators are able to take learners beyond literacy into income generation programmes. While many classes have given rise to income generation projects, it is not unusual for classes to be formed around existing women's projects or community-based income generation projects. Since the educators are familiar with local contexts, they are able to integrate with other development programmes. (9) Volunteer educators value the stipend paid to them – this often constitutes their first (very welcome) form of income.

The process of delivering materials, capturing data for learner records, rolling out volunteer training, delivering classes and paying volunteers (who mostly do not know their bank details) has not been 'hiccup-free', but as a large-scale pilot it has nevertheless established parameters for future large-scale delivery.

Who are the volunteers?

Volunteer educators drawn from the ranks of Unisa ABET's graduate practitioners have been deployed to assist in the teaching of groups of learners at sites that are near to the learners' homes. The graduates have all had the minimum of a one-year course at certificate level. Many have, however, had training in ABET for three years at diploma level. A small but significant number of volunteers are post-graduate students or hold postgraduate qualifications.

The volunteers come from the areas in which they teach. They are encouraged to engage with community structures, to map the areas in which they live and to recruit learners from households in which they identify adults who could benefit from the SANLI classes.

Unisa's proposal is to recruit already trained ABET graduates who are currently unemployed. Since the Unisa ABET Institute does not align itself with the government's 'voluntary for no payment' philosophy, it was decided that only unemployed graduates be recruited and that they be permitted to teach more than one class in order that their monthly stipends would represent a meaningful financial contribution. Although the stipend is small, the suggestion has been well received, especially in the most poverty stricken areas. As one of the volunteers points out: 'At least when we wake up in the morning we will know what we are going to do on that day and this will help to buy food for the family.' Another volunteer states simply: 'We are all living off my grandmother's pension and this money [the volunteers' stipend] is more than double what she gets.'

Who are the learners?

Because of the wide Unisa ABET network and the broad spread of its student base, it has been possible for the programme to reach learners at a variety of sites across South Africa. Learners have therefore been recruited throughout the length and breadth of South Africa. They include rural dwellers; farm workers; prisoners; the disabled; people from urban townships; out-of-school youth; inner city dwellers; the homeless; hostel residents; women's groups; pensioners; church groups; children in AIDS-affected families; street children; traditional healers and so on.

What do they learn?

The programme aims to enable learners to become literate in their mother tongue and the ABET Institute has learner support materials in all 11 official languages. Learners are exposed to basic mathematic literacy, which includes a variety of life skills applications. They are also taught to speak and read in English – the main language of the local economy. All learners are taught about possible income generating opportunities and do a course in small business development – a course that is fondly referred to as the 'SANLI MBA'.

Because of the AIDS pandemic in South Africa all learners attend a series of lessons on HIV/AIDS, a programme intended to bring about behaviour change. The remote locations of a majority of the learners make it impossible for them to be reached by any of the mainstream HIV/AIDS interventions. Many learners report that it was through these classes that they first heard about HIV/AIDS and that they now know how to avoid contracting and spreading the virus. The fact that HIV/AIDS deaths are common fare in the areas has now been demystified. It is argued that the wide-scale outreach of the programme could have extended possibilities (if the Department of Health were to come on board) for use as a vehicle for condom distribution, voluntary counselling and testing and for extended care for those affected with the HI virus.

All volunteers are adequately trained to determine the learning needs of their learning groups, to contextualise their needs and to develop material to address these needs. Nevertheless, the topics dealt with in the learner support material supplied to the learners are extremely popular. This material covers a number of adult life skills, such as how to manage one's personal finances, how to read medicine instructions, how to treat a child suffering from diarrhoea, how to utilise existing resources to generate an income. In addition, learners are taught about their civic rights and responsibilities.

The training the volunteer educators undergo in development/contextual studies enables them to assist learners to understand their social contexts and to determine their own developmental needs. Thus in addition to the learning that takes place in classes, groups have formed around the learning to provide care for those affected with HIV/AIDS, craft projects where the goods might be sold, women's groups doing subsistence farming, childcare for preschoolers to free mothers to take on work opportunities.

What do learners say of their learning?

In our talks with the learners, a number of common themes have emerged. Many learners refer to the frustration of not being able to conduct financial transactions such as completing a bank form, working an automated teller machine or simply reading a price when shopping.

Almost all learners mention the frustration of not being able to interpret signs. One learner described how she was mauled by a dog because she could not read the 'beware of the dog' sign on a gate. The list of learners' frustrations goes on and on: 'I was not able to read destination signs when travelling by bus or train.' 'I never ever obtained an identity document because I could not fill in the forms. Now I have one.' 'I own a spaza shop but I could not work out the right change to give my customers. I never knew if I was making a profit. I now know and last month I bought a fridge from the money I made.'

Almost all learners interviewed said they were excited that they could check on children's homework. If they were not at the same level of learning as their children, this made no difference to their appreciation. As one mother remarked, 'At least I can now ask them if they have done their homework and even to show me what they have done.'

Another learner reports that she can now take advantage of the prices of 'no-name' brands (the labels of these products do not include pictures). Because the labels display only text and have no picture of the contents, learners were never sure about what the packages contained. 'It could have been washing powder or powder milk – I didn't know. Now I am able to buy these products, which are much cheaper than the other [better illustrated] products.' A priest says, with delight, that he can now actually read the bible rather than pretend to be reading from it. Another learner refers to the work he does in a factory. 'My work involves cutting metal. I can now use a tape measure to measure the lengths – I used to ask my colleague to do this for me.' A proud mother boasts: 'I can now write the names of all my children.' And a pensioner tells us that she can now sign for her own pension – and in this way avoid being cheated by her 17-year-old grandson who used to collect her money for her.

The joy of reading and writing goes beyond filling in forms for officialdom. A young woman whose lover works on a mine in Johannesburg says that she can now write private love letters to him and now has the joy of reading his letters to her without having to ask a literate member of the community to do this intimate task for her. For many learners, the ability to write their own name – to assert their identity on paper – was their first great achievement. While these sound like small achievements on people's wish lists, they are in fact great milestones and giant steps towards self-reliance and personal development.

Our partners

Since 1995, a main supporter of the practitioner training at the Institute has been Britain's Department for International Development. In 2001 DFID provided additional support for the partnership with SANLI, which has been extended for another year to assist a further 100 000 learners in 2003.

The Independent Electoral Commission has joined as a sponsor and partner in 2003, to incorporate awareness of democracy, human rights and voter issues into the literacy training. This adds considerable value to the critical life skills aspects of the courses being provided by the Unisa-SANLI programme, which are already having a significant impact on the understanding of other vital issues, such as HIV/AIDS.

The way forward

Important in the way forward is the consolidation of literacy support within a national framework for ABET. This has to be adequately funded to agreed standards and be available across all nine provinces. Meeting constitutional rights regarding the provision of literacy and ABET is a national priority, and the opportunity and means to do so have been convincingly demonstrated and enthusiastically received by the learners. The work that has been done through the Unisa-SANLI partnership has laid a solid base on which to accommodate the integration of the many diverse elements operating in literacy and thereby create a nationally co-ordinated programme. The main challenge now is to build on the impetus that has been generated to ensure that literacy training is provided where it is most needed and that it opens a pathway to ABET and life-long learning.

In conclusion

Distance education offers extensive possibilities for countries where large numbers of grassroots functionaries/educators are needed. The methods of distance education enable a country to go to scale with minimal per capita resources. They also open the way for countries to use and supplement materials developed by other institutions. While the Unisa experience demonstrates effective use of the cascade approach with minimal dilution at the lower end of the cascade, this is possible through the provision of materials prepared centrally and contextualised locally.

It is therefore possible for governments to present high quality training to grassroots functionaries by using distance education. The benefits of cost-cutting lie in the economies of scale.

Distance learning is not just about using media to reach a large number of learners. It is about ensuring that the teaching and learning materials are learner-centred, that the learning and teaching materials developed are of a high quality and that a network of professional tutors who can assist learners is created.

While an upfront investment is needed in materials and infrastructure, the Unisa ABET experience shows that the investment yields dividends in the long run. The choices of media and technology for learning need to be made on the basis of appropriateness to learning task and context rather than on fad and fashion.

References

Adult Basic Education and Training Act of 2000.

Employment of Educators Act No 76 of 1998.

Baartjes, I. 1998. *Accreditation of ABET practitioners.* Unpublished paper.

Constitution of the Republic of South Africa Act No 108 of 1996.

Department of Education 1998. *Policy for adult basic education and training.* Pretoria: DoE.

Department of Education 1998. *A national multi year implementation plan for adult education and training provision and accreditation.* Pretoria: DoE.

Department of Education 2000. *Criteria for the recognition of qualifications for employment in education.* Pretoria: DoE.

Department of National Education, October 1997.

Government Gazette 1994. No. 16085.

Harley, A., Aitchison, J., Lyster, E., & S. Land. *A survey of adult basic education in South Africa in the 90s.* Johannesburg: Sached Books.

HSRC. 1999. Annual survey of public adult learning centres. HSRC: Pretoria.

National Education Policy Act No 27 of 1996.

South African Qualifications Act No 58 of 1995.

McKay, V. & Romm, N. 1992. *People's education in theoretical perspective.* Cape Town: Maskew Miller Longman.

McKay, V. 1997. Reflection and development. *Educare Journal. Nov.*

McKay, V. 2001 The application of PAR to the assessment of impact. *Development and Education Journal. Vol 7.3. June.*

Whiteford, A., Posel, D. & Kelatwang, T. 1995. *A profile of poverty, inequality and human development.* Pretoria: HSRC.

Notes

1 The 2001 National Census was being conducted at the time that this article was being prepared.

2 Notwithstanding the impact of HIV/AIDS.

3 This is the official figure, which is always considerably lower than the de facto figure. This figure does not reflect the number of people who are under-employed or who are 'employed' in the informal sector – a colony for those unable to find employment.

4 The absence of these is recorded by the annual survey of public adult learning centres (HSRC: 1999), which refers to a significant lack of infrastructure and to paucity in ABET provision.

5 It is noteworthy that the HSRC audit refers only to ABET delivery in the public sector and does not focus on delivery within industry, other government sectors, the CBOs or other informal training programmes.

6 The approximately 4 million adults in need of basic education referred to in the HSRC report discussed above are indicated in this table as those adults who have completed between Grade 1 and Standard 4.

7 It is necessary that development programmes and community education programmes not only address structural solutions to social problems but that they also engender an awareness of multiple solutions and the ability to make choices.

8 The dissemination of these criteria contributes to the enhancement of teachers' capacities at the centres.

9 It is possible to teach these practical courses through the ABET Institute's partnerships with technical training organisations. Other non-institutional based courses, such as crafts and beadwork, are also accommodated through linkages with (mainly) NGOs.

10 Unisa ABET ameliorates the possible dilution of those at the lower levels of the cascade by training all tutors and closely monitoring all the levels of the cascade. In addition, the development of interactive material for students ensures a common curriculum which learners can apply to their own contexts. Learners' experiences are valued and there is much interplay between the various levels of the cascade. For example, learners' contributions towards materials are incorporated into texts.

11 In this regard, learners themselves are required to commit themselves to attending three classes per week. This form of learner commitment is usually not required in programmes.

5

How are training policies responding to training needs in Nigeria

Gidado Tahir

This paper is based on primary research into basic education in general, with particular reference to the use of open and distance learning (ODL) for grassroots facilitators. The paper presents the analyses of extant policies and practices on the training of fieldworkers for adult basic education (ABE) in Nigeria. It explores the potential use of ODL in the training of adult basic education staff.

The paper begins with a critical examination of the only known systematic attempt to use ODL strategies to train ABE personnel in the country, namely, the Interactive Radio Scheme (IRI) – put into practice on a pilot basis by the National Commission for Nomadic Education (NCNE). Drawing on the research findings, it then examines the training needs of ABE fieldworkers; analyses existing policies and objectives of the training of ABE fieldworkers; identifies and discusses the strategies used to train ABE fieldworkers; assesses the impact of existing programmes for the training of ABE grassroots workers; discusses the training of fieldworkers for the NCNE's IRI scheme; explores the potential of ODL in the training of ABE fieldworkers. The findings referred to in this chapter were obtained from a sample of ten training centres, their heads, five tutors and fifteen trainees from each centre.

Background

One of the significant outcomes of the 1990 World Conference on Education, held in Jomtien, Thailand, was the renewed commitment to meet the basic learning needs of children, youths and adults through 'Education for All'. Participants at the conference drew up a framework for action to meet the basic learning needs of all, based on this renewed commitment to the provision of access to basic education for all citizens who need it, irrespective of their sex, social status and/or creed. A key element in the promotion of access and equity is the recruitment, training and retraining of grassroots workers and educators who will apply basic education programmes.

ABE fieldworkers play a pivotal role in a variety of ways and for different goals. Their tasks are also varied and include imparting useful practical skills, knowledge, information and attitudes, the sensitisation of community members and social mobilisation of citizens for self-improvement and community development.

Through the wide range of activities in which they engage, these grassroots workers serve as a link between the people and the government and non-governmental agencies concerned broadly with national development. These activities include basic and functional literacy instruction, social work, basic health work, agricultural extension, running co-operatives, women's vocational education and community development.

However, these adult education grassroots workers can enhance their work and attain their objectives only if they themselves have the requisite knowledge and skills and the capacity to cope with the often changing needs and circumstances of the people they seek to assist. This can only be attained through training and re-training, using a variety of techniques and strategies, that will equip them for their tasks and that are also an integral part of lifelong learning.

Lifelong learning, which is a central facet of adult education, requires adults to upgrade their knowledge and competence in order to fit into the rapidly evolving economic and social situations around them. This has increased the demand for part-time training and distance education since a significant proportion of adults cannot afford to enrol in full-time, conventional, regular programmes. Distance education programmes are suitable for a variety of adults in need of a basic education because it is relatively cost-effective, promotes access and equity and is flexible enough to accommodate their diverse needs and circumstances.

While the pursuit of the goals and challenges of 'Education for All' (EFA) is the responsibility of us all, in the end it is the teachers, instructors, trainers and grassroots facilitators and fieldworkers who will be directly engaged in the task of achieving the EFA objectives. It is therefore essential that all those directly involved, particularly the grassroots fieldworkers, build the capacity to discharge their tasks by acquiring the necessary training and education.

Purpose of the research

From the above it is clear that training grassroots ABE facilitators and fieldworkers is an integral part of EFA. However, the nature and mode of their training vary from country to country and from time to time.

This chapter, which is based on primary research conducted in Nigeria, attempts to identify and analyse existing policies and practices relating to the training of

ABE facilitators and fieldworkers in Nigeria. In addition it explores the potential of ODL in training these grassroots ABE functionaries. The research study on which the chapter draws examines a number of sub-problems: to identify the training needs of ABE fieldworkers and facilitators in Nigeria today; to determine existing policies on and objectives of the training of ABE fieldworkers in Nigeria; to identify the strategies being used for the training of ABE fieldworkers in the country; to examine the impact of existing programmes for the training of grassroots ABE workers and to explore the potential of ODL for training ABE fieldworkers.

The significance of the study lies in its attempt to uncover the existing conditions and state of Nigeria's preparedness to train and reposition its grassroots ABE fieldworkers for the attainment of the goals of 'Education for All'.
The study provides baseline data for government and non-governmental agencies and educational planners on the efficacy and effectiveness of the existing programmes for these fieldworker. It highlights the gaps and areas of need with a view to informing present and future formulation of training policies, objectives and strategies.

The study also provides useful insights on the immense potential of the ODL mode in training ABE personnel.

Scope of the research

The study recognises that ABE is very broad and the fieldworkers range from those working for the traditional adult education agencies in the Ministries of Education to those in agriculture, health, social development, sub-sectors of the nation's economy and so on. The investigation was therefore limited to selected government and non-governmental training facilities and institutions, including selected tertiary educational institutions that train grassroots fieldworkers for ABE.

Concept, scope and significance of training grassroots workers

This section presents a summary of literature review, which examines the concept, scope and significance of training fieldworkers generally and in ABE in particular, and looks critically at the use of ODL in this area. This helps to clarify the level of activities and attainments or failures in training grassroots ABE fieldworkers through both the conventional training mode and ODL.

Training, like education, is an expression of people's desire to transmit their culture of knowledge, skills and attitudes or values from one generation to the next. This was the beginning of the traditional apprenticeship system. Modern day vocations also require workers, both high and low, to train and retrain in order to attain effective and efficient ways of doing their job and consequently improve themselves and their communities.

For all occupations above the absolutely unskilled level, entry into the labour force implies training (Awagu 1994). Training and retraining is a continuous process irrespective of the participants' attainments in knowledge or skills. It is therefore geared towards maximising workers' productivity and motivating long-serving staff by giving them the opportunity to renew their skills.

For the ABE worker, training is necessary, especially among recruits who are not necessarily well equipped to deal with the problems they face in their jobs or assigned tasks. Training helps these workers to rationally influence the members of the community in which they work to accept innovation, or useful new information, or the skills relevant to the needs of the community. It also prepares them to respond constructively to the expressions of needs by members of the community and to take useful initiatives. Training also equips the fieldworker to help people develop self-reliance and to work out co-operative endeavours.

The ABE fieldworker provides the link between policymakers and people at the grassroots level. Castle (1972) maintains that developing people's capacity through training to better cope with the imperatives of development is more important than material resources input both for community development and for national development.

In Nigeria, the National Centre for Adult Education (NCAE), an agency established by the Federal Government to train adult education personnel in the country, reported in 2001 that there was a preponderance of non-professionals and other untrained persons employed in planning and implementing adult education programmes – something many adult educators had known for quite some time. Moreover, no serious attempt to determine the training needs and competence of ABE personnel had been made.

According to the report: 'The desperate problem of untrained and incompetent human resources in the sector has been very discouraging. To date no comprehensive study has been done on the competence levels and training needs of adult education workers in Nigeria' (NCAE 2001:3).

The majority of adult education supervisors and organisers who participated in the NCAE study indicated their need for professional training, which they proposed should be *short* in duration and *relevant* to their work. Their preference for short courses is not unexpected since most of them have vocational, family and other responsibilities in the community which often make it difficult for them to enrol in lengthy programmes. Adults in any event usually prefer training which is of short duration and meets practical, short-term needs. The organisers and supervisors studied by the NCAE showed a preference for training packages on the following themes or issues: trainees' job descriptions and their roles and responsibilities; methods of introducing programmes to grassroots communities; monitoring and evaluation techniques.

Similarly, in an earlier study conducted by Oduaran (1987) in Bendel, Nigeria, it was found that, although the training objectives were being achieved, the training centres were hampered by a multitude of problems, among them inadequate physical infrastructure and poorly-trained trainers. Oduaran therefore recommended that training for adult education workers should be planned so as to minimise all institutional, social, physical and emotional impediments.

Distance education

At the beginning of the 21st century, the increasing demand for access to education and training, coupled with dwindling resources and changing circumstances, has made it imperative to adopt the distance education approach. Coombs (1978) and Saint (1999) believe that it is becoming difficult for governments to make huge capital investments in building educational infrastructure yearly to meet the rapidly expanding demand for education. This is more pertinent in the case of developing countries, like Nigeria, where the population grows at a very fast rate. Consequently, distance education is becoming a major component of the educational system of many countries.

Studies of open and distance education such as those of Coombs (1978), Keegan (1994; 1996), Butcher (1997), Bunza and Akintayo (1995), Tahir (1992) and Saint (1999) have highlighted some of the reasons for its use. Distance education is relatively inexpensive when compared to the conventional school system approach. The absence of expensive infrastructure such as lecture halls, classrooms and laboratories means less capital investment Its curricula and modes of delivery are flexible and sensitive to learners' needs and circumstances. This allows learners to choose what they want to learn, at their own pace and convenience. It reaches a wide range of learners simultaneously across larger territories. Distance education is therefore a very sound option that does not involve any sacrifice in quality. The rapid development of information and communication technologies has made it even more feasible.

Distance learning is part of lifelong learning. Lifelong learning, which is a central facet of adult education, requires workers to upgrade their knowledge and competencies in order to fit in with the rapidly evolving economic and social situations around them. This has increased the demand for part-time training and education since many workers cannot afford to enrol in full-time training programmes. Distance education has become a viable option for such trainees in many countries around the world. No wonder many governments today are providing or considering distance education to complement conventional or traditional provision. In 2000, for example, Nigeria developed and adopted a five-year Plan of Action to put into practice and institutionalise distance education. The major points of focus of the Plan are the resuscitation of the National Open University and the establishment of a National Open School and a National Open Polytechnic that will address the increases social demand for formal and non-formal education and the educational needs of diverse groups of learners (FME 2000).

In a study of ODL in the European Union, Keegan (1994) found that 2.25 million Europeans were engaged in ODL, about 50% of whom were in government organised training institutions. This excluded in-house or corporate distance training provision, which involved a further 366,212 learners in the Open Universities and an estimated 130,000 in distance education programmes of conventional universities in Europe. These developments can be attributed to the major advances in the use of communication technologies in ODL including universal mobile telephony, satellite virtual classrooms, universal personal telephony, fibre-to-the-local loop, two-way video Codec systems, video conferencing to the desktop, broadband ISDN, the Internet and multimedia in the home (Keegan 1996).

In Africa south of the Sahara, only a few countries have strong and vibrant distance learning programmes (Saint 1999; Bunza & Akintayo 1995). For instance, Saint (1999) indicates that only South Africa, Ghana, Zimbabwe and Tanzania have significantly developed distance education systems. Nigeria, the biggest African country of all, is lagging behind despite the fact that its population is larger than those of all four the above countries put together.

Nevertheless, Bunza and Akintayo (1995), Tahir (1992) and Saint (1999) all confirm that some forms of distance education have existed in Nigeria for quite some time and that it is certainly not new to the country. Correspondence schools, in particular, have existed for decades. The Universities of Ibadan and Lagos have been offering distance learning programmes in Nigeria for over two decades through, respectively, their External Degree Programmes (ESP) and the Correspondence Open Studies Institute (COSIT). During the early 1980s distance learning received a boost when the Federal Government attempted to establish the National Open University. Later, in 1989, a Centre for Distance Learning was established within the newly opened University of Abuja. Similarly, the National Teachers' Institute (NTI) was established in 1976 to train teachers at all levels using the distance learning mode. Tahir (1992) reports that the National Policy on Education and the Federal Constitution in Nigeria both advocate egalitarianism and the use of alternative modes of education, including distance education.

Unfortunately the available literature shows that distance education, especially in Nigeria, appears to be an exclusive preserve of tertiary educational institutions and is often directed towards the formal education sector. Adult and non-formal education are seldom included despite the huge potential benefits the approach could engender. This is especially pertinent for developing countries that are grappling with the universalisation of basic education at minimum cost to their citizens.

Methodology

The study used the descriptive survey method and focused on the major elements of the training of grassroots adult education fieldworkers in Nigeria as identified under the sub-problems. Salient details are provided here.

The sample for the study was drawn from the population of institutions that have training programmes for grassroots ABE workers; federal and state government owned training centres; and NGO training centres. A total of ten training centres were selected from five of the six geopolitical zones of the country. The heads of the training centres, 5 tutors and 15 trainees from each training centre were selected for the research sample. This translated into 10 heads of centres and 50 tutors. Government and NGO representatives and proprietors of training centres also participated. The trainee sample consisted of 150 people enrolled in training programmes with the training centres. The study was conducted using questionnaires, interviews and documentary materials. All the training centres (listed below) were visited during August to October, 2001: Department of Adult Education, University of Ibadan; University Village Association (UNIVA) – an NGO at Ibadan; Department of Social Development and Co-operatives, Kaduna Polytechnic, Kaduna; Federal Co-operatives College, Kaduna; National Adult Education Centre, Kano; Rabiu Kwankwaso Vocational Training Centre, Gorou Dutse, Kano; City Women Centre, Kano; Adult Education Training Institute, Bauchi; Adult Education and Social Development Institute, Kumo, Gombe State; Federal School of Social Development, Enugu; a number of government officials, policy chiefs and representatives of proprietors of training centres/institutes were interviewed: Executive Secretary, National Mass Education Commission, Abuja; Director, State Agency for Mass Education, Bauchi; Director, State Agency for Mass Education, Gombe; Director, State Agency for Mass Education, Kano; Chairman, University Village Association (UNIVA), Ibadan

Discussion of the research data

Training policies and objectives

Policies. There appears to be no single body of policies on the training of ABE fieldworkers. This might not be unconnected with the often narrow conception of the meaning and scope of adult education practice in Nigeria. The National Policy on Education (1998 revised edition) seems to contribute to this by unwittingly upholding the traditional meaning of adult education as the provision of literacy, vocational and continuing education programmes only, which are often provided by government ministries responsible for education. Thus other adult education activities in the health, agriculture, social development and co-operatives sectors are hardly mentioned or regarded by the policy and other government documents as part of adult education. Consequently, many adult educators involved in health, agriculture or social welfare departments do not see themselves as serving ABE even when they are involved in public enlightenment, social mobilisation, diffusion of innovation and so on.

Meanwhile education is on the concurrent legislative list and both the Federal Constitution and the National Policy on Education have placed it in the hands of all three tiers of government and of the private sector. However, the formulation of broad policy on education rests with the Federal Government. This is to ensure quality control, uniformity of standards and unity of purpose.

As regards training policies, the National Policy document has committed government-owned institutions and training centres and NGOs to the training of all categories of adult education personnel. The Policy places the training of adult education, particularly senior and intermediate adult education staff, in the hands of the Federal Government, while 'grassroots adult education personnel' are to be trained by the state governments (FME 1998:37-38).

The general objective of the training of grassroots level workers in adult education in Nigeria is to improve learners' knowledge, skills and attitudes for personal and community development. The specific objectives include: to enable grassroots fieldworkers in adult basic education to improve the quality of programme delivery; to update workers' knowledge on the current and most innovative ways of discharging their duties; to equip fieldworkers with skills and knowledge that will enable them to function effectively in (modern) society; to train fieldworkers in the techniques of organisation and management of ABE; to acquaint trainees with monitoring and reporting skills in ABE. Accordingly each training centre or institute is expected to work towards attaining all or some of these training objectives. While this is often dictated by the type and mode of training any given centre has employed, both NGOs and tertiary educational institutions are nevertheless expected to follow policy guidelines which include the objectives listed above.

Training practices

Types of training programmes. The ten training centres sampled for this study offer the ABE programmes below:

Table 1 ABE programmes offered at training centres surveyed

Programme offered	No of centres (N=10)
Literacy instruction/supervision	5
Social work	3
Basic Health Work	2
Agricultural Extension	3
Co-operatives	4
Women's Vocational Education	5
Others:	
◆ Community Development Officers	2
◆ Various Artisanship Training	1

From the table above it may be seen that half of the training centres have programmes for literacy instruction. Half also offer programmes for women's vocational training. It is not surprising that the frequency of literacy-related and women educational programmes are higher than the others since the two constitute the core activities of traditional adult education activity in Nigeria. The nation's high illiteracy levels have been a source of concern for quite some time both in government circles and in the international community. The ongoing national mass literacy campaign is enjoying the support of the government, NGOs and international development agencies such as the UNDP and UNICEF.

Similarly, women's vocational education has gained support and acceptance throughout the country over the last two decades. Activities of feminist groups, NGOs and women's development agencies at national and state levels have, no doubt, contributed to the popularisation of women's vocational training. This promotes the attainment of the goals of the national literacy campaign, particularly the reduction of gender disparities in adult education programmes.

Even though there is a preponderance of literacy and women's vocational education programmes in Nigerian adult education, the others forms of adult education are also quite significant. It is however, noteworthy that the diverse nature of training programmes for grassroots ABE fieldworkers reflects the amorphous nature of what constitutes the subject matter of adult education and the lack of consensus on its definition.

Training centres and institutes in Nigeria. The training of various grassroots ABE fieldworkers in Nigeria appears to have been taking place mainly by conventional means. The training patterns range from the formal curricula used at the traditional educational institutions to less formalised capacity-building workshops and seminars. The most prominent centres for training ABE fieldworkers are briefly discussed below.

Quite a number of tertiary educational institutions, especially universities, polytechnics and monotechnics, engage in training grassroots fieldworkers for adult education. The universities at Ibadan, Lagos, Zaria, Benin City, Calabar, Nsukka, Port-Harcourt, Maiduguri, Kano, Jos, Ile-Ife, and Sokoto in Nigeria are known to offer certificate and diploma programmes in adult education besides their degree and postgraduate programmes. The Kaduna Polytechnic also offers certificates and diploma courses in adult education with an emphasis on community development and co-operatives. The University of Ibadan and Kaduna Polytechnic were both selected for this study.

The University of Ibadan offers both full-time and part-time diploma courses in adult education. Its part-time students are mainly adult education fieldworkers such as literacy organisers, rural librarians, social workers and community development officers. Kaduna Polytechnic offers only full-time programmes.

There are also several monotechnics which train adult education fieldworkers. The Federal Co-operatives College, Kaduna and the Federal School of Social Development, Enugu were included in the study. A few NGOs also engage in training grassroots fieldworkers: UNIVA at Ibadan, PIERT-N at Abuja, NICE at Lagos and NIPRANET at Ilorin.

The National Adult Education Centre, Kano, established by the Federal Government, and other adult education training institutes and centres owned by state governments, are mainly concerned with literacy, vocational and continuing education programmes under the supervision of the Ministries of Education. These are the traditional adult education training outfits and may be found in Adamawa, Akwa Ibom, Bauchi, Borno, Edo, Gombe, Kano, Katsina, Kaduna, Plateau and Rivers states.

However, many of these centres are dormant and in a derelict condition. The National Centre at Kano, for instance, has yet to commence regular training since its inception in 1985. Only a few ad hoc training programmes have been organised by the Centre and the last of these was held five years ago. As regards the state government-owned training centres, the premier institution, namely Bauchi State Adult and Non-Formal Education Institute, has neither the resources nor the required support to regularly organise training programmes. The relocation of the Institute from the town of Bauchi to Kangere village a few years ago deprived it of basic infrastructure, such as electricity, audio-visual laboratories and studios and so on, vital to its operation. The difficulties posed by the inhospitable conditions at the school have resulted in a high dropout rate and a significant decline in enrolments.

Generally, both national and state training institutes lack adequate infrastructure and facilities that would provide the minimum conditions for training. They are therefore under-utilised and receive only minimal support from their proprietors. A few of the government owned training centres visited appear to be vibrant, although they also lack adequate infrastructure.

In the last decade training for adult education grassroots fieldworkers has increasingly taken the form of capacity building seminars and workshops. These are often sponsored by governments, NGOs, universities and external funding agencies such as the UNDP and UNICEF. The UNDP, for instance, granted Nigeria some US$5 million between 1995 and 2000 to assist with the country's national mass literacy campaign. Part of the money was used to sensitise and train literacy instructors, literacy organisers, co-ordinators, community leaders, rural librarians, social development workers, NGO personnel, and management staff of state agencies for mass education, all of whom were involved in conducting the campaign.

Instructional media and methods. The trainers of ABE fieldworkers sampled for the study were asked to specify the instructional methods and strategies they used. Their responses are summarised in Table 2 below.

Table 2 Instructional methods and strategies

S/No	Type of instructional method used	Frequency of responses (N=50)
1.	Lecture	42 (84%)
2.	Discussion	36 (72%)
3.	Project	21 (52%)
4.	Field trip	21 (52%)
5.	Simulation	13 (26%)
6.	Demonstration	33 (66%)

The table shows that the most common methods of delivery are lectures (84%), discussions (72%) and demonstrations (66%). Simulation, despite its huge potential for teaching concepts, principles and processes, is used very rarely and only 26% of the instructors claimed that they used it in their lessons.

The ABE instructors were also asked to indicate the type of audio-visual media they used most frequently in their lessons. Their responses are summarised in Table 3.

Table 3 Utilisation of educational media

S/No	Type of educational media used	Frequency of Responses (N=50)
1.	Audio recordings	28 (56%)
2.	Video	10 (20%)
3.	Slides	29 (58%)
4.	Slide	0 (0%)
5.	Radio	0 (0%)
6.	Television	0 (0%)
7.	Overhead projector	1 (2%)
8.	Charts and diagrams	42 (84%)
9.	Computers	5 (10%)

Table 3 above shows that charts and diagrams, slides and audio recordings were the most frequently used media. From this data it is clear that the use of educational radio and TV, video and computers is not widespread in the training of ABE fieldworkers in Nigeria. This is because there has been no systematic attempt on the part of the state, NGOs or any other organisations involved to use these media or the new information and telecommunications technology to broaden access to formal and non-formal education, or to train ABE fieldworkers. It is hoped that when the Abuja Declaration on ODL and the Plan of Action on ODL are put into practice, educational broadcasting and other technologies will be more generally harnessed.

Training needs of fieldworkers

The trainees surveyed were asked to specify their training needs in the context of their responsibilities as ABE fieldworkers and the challenges they face in their day-to-day activities. A training need is here defined as the discrepancy between a trainee's existing knowledge and skills and the required knowledge and skills. Table 4 below summarises their responses.

Table 4 Training needs of ABE fieldworkers

S/No	Training needs	Frequency of responses (N=120)
1.	Literacy instruction	70 (58.33%)
2.	Literacy supervision	40 (33.33%)
3.	Communication skills	46 (38.33%)
4.	Basic health work	25 (20.83%)
5.	Modern techniques of extension education	50 (41.66%)
6.	Innovative methods of teaching women's vocational education	62 (51.66%)
7.	Use of audio-visual media in adult education	60 (50%)
8.	Others	
	◆ Community development	15 (12.50%)
	◆ Home economics	12 (10%)
	◆ Vocational skills	16 (13.33%)

The diversity of the training needs indicated in Table 4 reflects the different interests and professional backgrounds of the respondents – literacy workers, social workers, community and co-operative development workers, public health workers and others. The most common needs were instructional methods for the teaching of literacy, innovative methods of teaching women's vocational education, and the use of audio-visual media in adult education.

It should be noted that training of ABE fieldworkers is neither regular nor based on a systematic analysis of their needs.

Trainees' expectations

The trainees sampled for the study were asked to specify why they had enrolled in the training programmes. Their responses are summarised below.

Table 5 Trainees' expectations in terms of knowledge gains and skills acquisition

S/No	Knowledge and skills expectations	Frequency of responses (N=120)
1.	Enhancing knowledge of the subject matter	78 (65%)
2.	Upgrading occupational skills	60 (50%)
3.	Improving interpersonal skills	72 (60%)
4.	Broadening communication skills	55 (45.83%)
5.	Increasing eligibility for employment	68 (56.66%)
6.	Facilitating promotion at workplace	59 (49.16%)

Table 5 above indicates that the motivation for training encompasses both personal expectations regarding professional growth as individuals and the expectation that training will lead to greater effectiveness in the discharge of their duties.

From the responses of all those consulted in the study, but especially those of the grassroots adult education fieldworkers themselves, it is clear that they needed training and retraining to increase their capacity to do their job and enable them to grow professionally. This would reposition them as agents for national development in a rapidly changing world.

Impact and utility of training

The grassroots fieldworkers or trainees sampled for the study gave their impressions on the practical usefulness of the training in improving their skills. Eighty-five respondents (i.e. 70.8%) believed that the training would improve their skills. Thus, the majority of the trainees believed that the training was a useful exercise and expected it to adequately equip them for the realities of their jobs. Most of them, for instance, expected to increase their knowledge of the subject matter, upgrade their job skills and improve their communication abilities. But perhaps more significantly, many believed that the training would enable them to earn a promotion upon graduating and the unemployed among them hoped it would enable them to secure a job.

While 77% of the trainees believed that the training facilities in their centre were inadequate, 89% (76 respondents) expressed satisfaction with the teaching methods used by their tutors. So while they expressed confidence in the abilities of their tutors to deliver, they were unequivocal in pointing out the inadequacy of facilities and educational media. While government officials believe that government is doing well in meeting the training needs of adult education grassroots officers, the latter appear to disagree, citing the derelict conditions at many training centres. Even the more active training centres (usually those based in tertiary educational institutions and offering a variety of regular training programmes of study for a wide range of clientele) are inadequately equipped to fully meet the basic learning needs of grassroots workers in adult education.

On the duration and content of the existing programmes, the trainees appeared to favour short, practical programmes that would meet immediate needs and have a direct bearing on their primary duties. Except for the UNDP sponsored training and sensitisation workshops and seminars held in the mid-1990sthis type of training was rarely available. The one-year or longer training programmes were too formal and were usually geared towards the acquisition of formal qualifications. Lack of resources or sponsorship prevents many grassroots workers from participating in such courses, particularly in view of the relatively long periods involved. In a recent study, the National Centre for Adult Education (2001) reported the preference of grassroots adult education fieldworkers for short training programmes that are relevant to their professional pursuits. These adult education organisers and supervisors stressed the need for training that dovetails with their job descriptions and responsibilities, uses the most effective methods of teaching adults, and provides programme monitoring and evaluation skills.

In the study under discussion here (Tahir 1992), all the tutors who responded reported that they participate and indeed influence the process of determining trainees' needs. However, although trainees are also supposed to be consulted in the preparation of the training packages, in reality they were hardly involved in curriculum development.

Distance learning strategies

Very little information can be directly found on the training of ABE fieldworkers by means of distance education strategies. In fact the only known instance is the interactive radio scheme being conducted by the National Commission for Nomadic Education (NCNE), which is discussed in the next section of this chapter.

None the less, distance learning is not entirely new in the Nigerian education system. Correspondence courses at the GCE ordinary and advanced levels of the University of London have long been in place. In addition, the External Degree Programmes (ESP) of the University of Ibadan and the Correspondence Open Studies Institute (COSIT) of the University of Lagos commenced providing tuition in the mid-1960s. The Federal Government opened the National Open University in the 1980s, although this was later downgraded to a Centre for Distance Learning of the University of Abuja.

The university distance learning programmes were, however, rarely targeted grassroots ABE workers. They were simply formal programmes aimed at workers who needed to acquire additional qualifications but who, for some reason, could not afford full-time, regular, conventional tuition.

The establishment of the National Teachers Institute (NTI) by the Nigerian Government in the 1970s with a mandate to train, upgrade and improve teachers' qualifications at all levels through the distance learning approach was a major step towards the training of grassroots facilitators. Through its Distance Learning School (DLS) the NTI has succeeded in improving, upgrading and training thousands of primary school teachers in Nigeria. Since the DLS programme is part time, the NTI's effort has broadened access to education for thousands of teachers who would find it difficult to study on a full-time basis. However, the NTI appears to focus mainly on school teachers and makes little or no effort to train ABE facilitators, who also need to be trained, retrained and upgraded for better performance and personal growth.

Thus most of Nigeria's distance learning programmes tend to focus on formal, conventional training for the purpose of certification. Training adult education grassroots personnel is minimal. There is, however, a growing recognition of and appreciation for the merits of distance learning for both formal schooling and non-formal adult education.

As mentioned, the training of fieldworkers usually takes place in conventional formal educational institutions using conventional androgogical techniques. However, there is at least one promising instance of the use ODL, namely, the Interactive Radio Distance Learning Scheme (IRI) for nomadic pastoralists in Nigeria, which was put into practice on a pilot basis by the National Commission for Nomadic Education (NCNE) Kaduna. The next section briefly describes the scheme and the training of ABE fieldworkers for it.

Interactive radio for adult education among pastoral nomads

The objectives of the IRI scheme were to sensitise the nomads on the nature, causes and possible solutions to their problems; mobilise them to take collective action in order to solve their socio-economic, political and educational problems; provide them with relevant coping skills and knowledge to deal with the complexities of modern society, including functional literacy and vocational skills and 'new' income generating activities which integrate traditional and modern techniques of dairy production and pasture management, among other things and give them a critical understanding of their rights, duties and obligations as citizens of Nigeria.

The components of the IRI delivery system included radio broadcasts; print (posters, broadcast guides, discussion guides, workbooks, worksheets and a specially designed functional literacy primer); audio and video cassettes; radio cassette recorders; extension agents and radio listening and discussion groups.

The nomads were organised into radio listening and discussion groups. Each group had fifteen members and a chairperson and secretary. There were 88 groups as at December 2000. Only fifteen groups took part in the pilot phase of the scheme.

Fieldworkers

Two types of fieldworkers were used in the IRI scheme, viz. the 49 extension agents, who were specialists in animal husbandry and rural development, and the chairpersons and secretaries of the fifteen radio listening groups selected for the pilot phase of the IRI scheme, who were members of the nomadic communities and specially selected and trained by the NCNE for the IRI scheme.

The extension agents' tasks included providing technical advice on animal husbandry to the groups; conducting demonstrations of procedures and processes as required by the radio broadcasts; explaining any difficult issues and concepts contained in the radio broadcasts; and assisting the radio listening and discussion groups to take concrete action to solve the problems or issues raised in the broadcasts.

The chairperson's responsibilities were to lead the radio listening and discussion sessions; ensure that the group carried out all the learning activities specified in the broadcasts; collect learning materials from the NCNE on behalf of the groups; and submit a weekly report on the group's progress and activities.

The secretary took minutes of meetings, wrote reports on the activities of the group and assisted the chairman in the management of the group.

Training needs of IRI fieldworkers

As mentioned above, there were two types of ABE fieldworkers: the extension agents and the chairmen and secretaries of the radio listening and discussion groups. The two groups differed in their educational and professional backgrounds. All the extension agents in the IRI project were employees of the NCNE. They had completed secondary school and had at least a certificate, diploma and/or Higher National Diploma in animal husbandry. The secretaries and chairpersons had only Secondary School Leaving Certificates or Grade II Teachers' Certificates and were employees of the Local Government, serving as, for instance, teachers and clerical assistants. These differences inevitably engendered differences in training needs.

Training needs of extension agents. The annual surveys of the training needs of the extension agents conducted in 1998, 1999 and 2000 indicated that their needs covered diverse areas such as animal husbandry, communication skills, group dynamics, social action and the use of audio-visual media in extension work, particularly the use of audio and video recordings. Table 6 below summarises their training needs.

Table 6 Training needs of extension agents

S/No	Training needs	No (%) of respondents expressing the need(N=49)
1.	Use of audio-visual media in extension work	49 (100 %)
2.	Formation and management of co-operatives	43 (87.75%)
3.	Participatory approaches to extension work	36 (73.46%)
4.	How to execute adult literacy programmes for nomads	30 (61.22%)
5.	Modern techniques of fodderbank development	43 (87.75%)
6.	Current tsetse and trypanosomiasis control techniques	49 (100%)
7.	Communication skills	41 (83.67%)
8.	Techniques of interviewing	32 (65.31%)
9.	Improvisation of instructional materials for extension work in nomadic communities	49 (100%)

Source: NCNE Kaduna 2000.

The most interesting thing about this is that certain needs featured prominently in the annual surveys of extension agents' training needs. These were the use of audio-visual media in extension work; current tsetse and trypanasomiasis control techniques; and communication skills.

Discussions with the extension agents indicated that this was connected with the challenges they faced in their daily interaction with the nomadic pastoralists. They believed that updating their knowledge and skills in these areas would enhance their practical effectiveness as helpers of the nomadic pastoralists.

Training needs of chairpersons and secretaries. As mentioned earlier, the educational qualifications of the leaders of the radio listening groups were somewhat lower than those of the extension agents and their identified needs in the context of the execution of the IRI scheme were less diverse. This is not surprising if it is remembered that these were volunteers who were not paid by the NCNE and were employed by Local Government authorities. Their expressed needs were mainly to do with the concept of IRI and the implementation of the IRI scheme in nomadic pastoralist communities, viz. the concept of IRI; the rationale for and objectives of IRI in nomadic pastoralist communities in Nigeria; implementation of the IRI scheme: delivery mode and roles of the NCNE headquarters, extension agents and chairmen and secretaries of radio groups; how to use the audio-cassettes, the broadcasts, the broadcast and discussion guides and the adult literacy primer; social action programming; interviewing/discussion techniques; and report writing.

These were the needs identified by the NCNE before embarking on the training of the chairmen and secretaries of the radio listening and discussion groups.

Existing training policies and objectives

Decree 41 of 1989 which set up the NCNE empowered it to use face-to-face conventional modes of instruction and ODL techniques, not only to provide tuition to nomadic children and adults but in all its other operations.

In 2000 the NCNE, in its determination to use radio to broaden access to basic education to nomadic adults, developed an IRI scheme which also included the training of fieldworkers for the scheme. The objectives of the training of IRI fieldworkers were to: give trainers a basic understanding of the use of radio in adult education, particularly the concept and operational modalities of Interactive radio; promote sufficient understanding of NCNE's IRI scheme, particularly the components of the delivery system; engender an adequate understanding of their roles in the execution of the IRI scheme; disseminate appropriate interviewing skills and enable fieldworkers to manage the radio listening and discussion groups; give them sufficient understanding of the concept of social action programming and its specific form in the NCNE's IRI scheme; provide practical training on the use of the broadcast guides, discussion guides, posters, audio-cassette recordings, worksheets and literacy primer; enable them to acquire basic report-writing skills.

Strategies used in training IRI fieldworkers

The main components of the training were two five-day workshops at the NCNE's headquarters, a learning package made up of video and audio recordings, workbooks, the literacy primer, worksheets, discussion guides and broadcast guides, and two intensive contact sessions of two days' duration each at the NCNE headquarters. Each of the components is outlined in turn.

The five-day workshops. These workshops were organised twice, in May and July 2000, and attended by both groups of fieldworkers. The objectives of the workshops were as specified in the previous section. The training materials included recordings of the radio broadcasts, broadcast guides and discussion guides, radio curriculum, workbooks and the literacy primer and video recordings showing how to use the broadcasts, broadcast guides, discussion guides and literacy primer.

The teaching methods used include lectures, discussions, demonstrations and micro teaching sessions. The resource persons used included experts on animal husbandry, adult literacy and educational radio.

Learning packages and intensive contact sessions. At the end of the five-day workshops, the fieldworkers were provided with the learning packages described above. The packages were to be used as resource materials in the field and each fieldworker had the opportunity to study the materials at home at his or her own pace, preparatory to a subsequent intensive contact session. The fieldworkers were also expected to carry out specific tasks contained in the packages. They then recorded their performance of the tasks and presented them at the intensive contact session held at the NCNE headquarters in Kaduna.

The learning package did not contain new information nor was it intended to be used to teach new skills. It covered all aspects of the operation of the IRI scheme and sought to reinforce what was learned at the five-day workshops held earlier.

Impact of the training

A post-training survey of the fieldworkers indicated that the training was very useful and had facilitated the acquisition of knowledge and skills that enhanced their field performance. The 79 IRI fieldworkers were asked in separate interviews to indicate the specific way in which the training programme was most useful. Their responses are listed below (see also Figure 1): 'I fully understand the objectives of the IRI scheme' (78%): 'I have a clear understanding of the mode of delivery of the IRI scheme' (72%); 'The training has enabled me to play my roles satisfactorily in the implementation of the scheme'(84%); 'The training has enabled me to use the teaching-learning materials effectively' (68%);

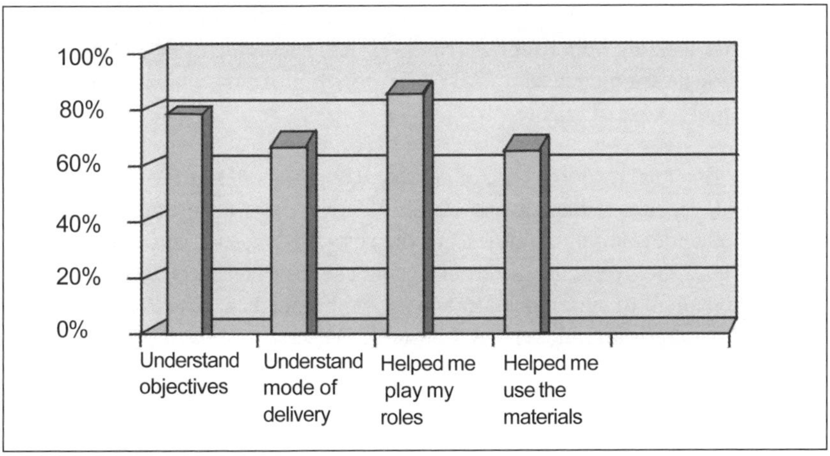

Figure 1 Most useful aspects of IRI training

The fieldworkers were also asked to rate the three components of the training programme in terms of usefulness and effectiveness. The five-day workshops received the highest rating (72.68%), followed by the learning package (70.18%) and the intensive contact session (52.82%).

The effectiveness of the training can also be partly determined from the NCNE's (2000) report, 'Post broadcast survey of the pilot phase of the IRI scheme'. One of the issues addressed in the survey was the impact of the scheme on the learners. The report clearly indicates high levels of success in terms of skills acquisition, knowledge gains and social action, partly attributable to the good training received by the IRI fieldworkers.

Harnessing the potential of open and distance learning

The IRI scheme executed by the NCNE, albeit on a pilot basis, clearly demonstrated that ODL training programmes for ABE, if properly planned and supported, can address the diverse training needs of ABE workers. ODL schemes such as the one discussed above offer viable options in the context of the current attempt to seek cost-effective methods of meeting the training needs of ABE personnel. This is particularly so in view of:

The training of ABE personnel in Nigeria has become not only an irregular and largely chance event, but is also very often of poor quality due to the dearth of equipment and facilities.

There are tens of thousands of ABE personnel whose training needs are not being met by the existing programmes offered by formal educational institutions and who, in addition, cannot enrol for these courses on a full-time basis. Thus as the demand for training opportunities increases, it is becoming more and more clear that meeting the training needs of ABE workers requires new, unconventional strategies, namely those of ODL.

The poor financial resource base of nearly all Nigeria's ABE training institutions suggests the need to harness the potentials of ODL which, according to the experiences of other developing countries, is more cost-effective than conventional methods, more responsive to the different learning styles of learners, can provide tuition independent of time, location and space, broadens access to ABE training programmes, and can train tens of thousands in a short period of time.

Given the poor condition of infrastructure such as roads and postal services, ODL strategies to train ABE workers offer perhaps the only way of actualising the nation's commitment to equal educational opportunities and of broadening access to training to ABE personnel who operate in remote, inaccessible regions.

What these observations point to is the need to draw useful lessons from the NCNE's IRI scheme and to design and apply nationwide, ODL schemes that can cost-effectively meet the nation's needs for well-trained ABE staff in all parts of the country.

Conclusion

Adult education appears to be somewhat narrowly conceptualised in Nigeria, particularly regarding meaning and mode of delivery. Examination of educational policy provisions reveals the absence of explicit guidelines on the roles and expectations of the various units and levels of government with regard to adult education practice. A variety of educational institutions and centres such as universities, polytechnics and monotechnics provide a wide range of training programmes geared towards enhancing or building the capacity of grassroots fieldworkers in adult education.

The number of ABE training centres in the country is not really known as the Federal and State governments, private institutions and NGOs all render different forms of training which could be regarded as adult educational. There appears, moreover, to be little or no co-ordination in terms of the roles and duties of the various agencies involved in the training of adult education grassroots fieldworkers. This might led to duplication of efforts and some wastage of meagre resources.
Adult education grassroots fieldworkers and their trainers have strongly expressed the need for training and retraining. However, much of the existing training takes the form of traditional, school-type programmes leading to formal qualifications such as diplomas and certificates. Since formal qualifications are the main yardstick for employment and promotion of workers, the extrinsic motivation to ac-

quire them is inevitably high and grassroots adult education workers, like other categories of workers, strive to enrol in the formal programmes.

Short-term capacity building seminars and workshops are virtually absent except for the UNDP assisted sensitisation and training programmes on mass literacy held between 1995 and 1999. There has been no systematic effort to train ABE fieldworkers on a massive scale using ODL strategies. The exception is the IRI scheme which was implemented on a pilot basis by the NCNE. However, lack of funds and inadequate qualified personnel have stifled the nationwide execution of the scheme. There is thus an urgent need to develop and put into practice other ODL programmes for the training of ABE workers nationwide, if the nation's need for well-trained ABE personnel is to be met.

References

Akinyele, J. O. (1988). A Comparative Study of Cost-Effectiveness of Instruction: Television and Conventional Classroom Instruction in Non-Formal Education, Unpublished Ph.D. Thesis, University of Ibadan, Nigeria.

Awagu, C. G. (1994). An Assessment of Staff Training Programmes and their Effect on Workers Productivity at Union Bank, Ibadan unpublished M.Ed. Thesis, University of Ibadan, Nigeria.

Butcher, N. (1997). The Use of Technologies in Education and Training: South African Policy Perspectives, Pretoria: South African Institute for Distance Education.

Bunza, M. M. and Akintayo (1995). *Perspectives in Distance Education,* Ibadan: Abisega Pubs.

Castle, A. B. (1972). Education for Self-help: New Strategies for Developing Countries, London: Oxford University Press.

Coombs, P. (1978). *The World Crisis in Education*, Oxford: Oxford University Press.

Eradajaye, S. E. (1987). Life Long Education and Motivational Factors: A case study of young Farmers Training Centre. Iseyin, Unpublished M.Ed. Thesis, University of Ibadan.

Federal Ministry of Education (revised 1998*). National Policy on Education* (2nd & 3rd editions), Lagos: NERDC Press.

Federal Ministry of Education (2000) 'Plan of Action for A Decade of Distance Education in Nigeria 2001-2010.' Abuja: FME

Federal Government of Nigeria (1999). *Constitution of the Federal Republic of Nigeria*, Lagos. Federal Government Press.

Haggis, S. M. (ed.) (1995). *The Education for All Teacher Training Package*, Vols. 1 & 2, UNESCO and UNDP.

Keegan, D. (1994). Distance Training in the European Union, Hasen: ZIFF.

Keegan, D (1996). *Foundation of Distance Education*, London: Routeledge.

National Centre for Adult Education, Kano (2001) Report of the Assessment of the Training Needs of the Staff of the Agencies for Mass Education in Nigeria (Unpublished).

National Commission for Nomadic Education (2000) 'A Report on the Post Broadcast survey of the Pilot Phase of the Interactive Radio Distance Learning Scheme.' Kaduna: NCNE.

National Commission for Nomadic Education (19989, 1999, 2000)

Reports on the Training Workshops for Extension Agents. Kaduna: NCNE

National Mass Literacy, Adult and Non-Formal Education (undated) *Trainers Manual.*

Oduara, A. B. (1987). A Comparative Study of Cost-Effectiveness of Instruction:

Television and Conventional Classroom Instruction in Non-Formal Education, Unpublished Ph.D. Thesis, University of Ibadan, Nigeria.

Okuwa, E. O. (1986). Training as a Factor of Manpower Development: A Case Study of ITF Ibadan Area Office, Unpublished M.Ed. Thesis, University of Ibadan, Nigeria.

Olaniyi, A. A. (1991). Training and Staff Development in the Private Sector: A Case Study of Co-operative Bank Limited, Ibadan. Unpublished M.Ed. Thesis, University of Ibadan, Nigeria.

Otegwu, C. A. (1986). *Workers Education Programmes of the N.A.S.U. of University of Ibadan*, Unpublished M.Ed. Thesis, University of Ibadan, Nigeria.

Saint, W. (1999). Tertiary Distance Education and Technology in Sub-Saharan Africa, Washington D.C: The World Bank.

Tahir, G. (1992). 'Education and Politics In Nigeria: The Open University of Nigeria in Retrospect' *International Journal of University Adult Education*, Vol. XXXI, No. 2, Pp. 39-51.

UNDP (1989). Education and Training in the 1990's: Developing Countries' Needs and Strategies, New York: UN Publications.

6

An NGO perspective on training grassroots facilitators in literacy and adult basic education in Bangladesh

Harun ur Rashid and ANS Habibur Rahman[1]

This chapter gives an overview of the kinds of literacy and basic educational programmes available in Bangladesh. The chapter starts with a historical overview of adult basic education programmes in Bangladesh, and then gives a comprehensive description of programmes that are currently conducted.

It is argued that the minimal outreach that characterises these programmes could be expanded if open and distance learning methods were employed. The chapter concludes with an elaboration of a proposed structure for large-scale delivery, a training curriculum for educators and a number of recommendations for shifting from face-to-face training to distance education methods.

Introduction

Bangladesh, like the other countries mentioned in this book, has a high level of illiteracy. Even though many programmes have been undertaken to provide literacy and basic education programmes[2] over the past five decades, Bangladesh still has a literacy rate of only 50%.

Today, the provision of literacy and basic education is more necessary than ever before. There are presently about 500 organisations involved in the delivery of adult literacy and basic education programmes in the country, with about one million grassroots level facilitators engaged in these activities. In terms of the need, the present outreach is still not adequate and we argue here that if distance education were used as a vehicle for training, the required numbers of adult educators would be reached and the quality of training would be higher. This would also enable Bangladesh to achieve a 90% literacy rate within five years.

Before discussing the need for literacy and basic education in the Bangladesh context, it is necessary first to consider this matter in a historical context.

History of literacy and basic education in Bangladesh

British period

Literacy and basic education in Bangladesh has a long history going back almost one hundred years. Adult literacy interventions were first introduced in this region in 1918. By 1926 there were more than 1 000 night schools run by 140 co-operative societies. In 1935 some eminent Indian civil servants and scholars initiated the expansion of adult literacy centres throughout the region. Three years later the then Indian government established a department called Bengal Reconstruction Department, which proclaimed that it would eradicate illiteracy from the society. In the 1940s, when Frank Lubach's slogan 'Each One Teach One' became popular, the wave of educating adults touched this country too. The East Bengal government established a wing of 'Adult Education' under the Department of Rural Development.

Pakistan period

India and Pakistan became independent states in 1947 and what is now Bangladesh became a province of Pakistan. At that time a tiny Mass Education department existed. In 1954 the government integrated this department with the package of development employed by V-AID, an assistance agency of the United States of America, and in 1956 the East Pakistan Adult Education Co-operative Union was formed and adult literacy and post-literacy policy and activities started to take shape. As a result, it became possible, for the first time, to provide statistics on adult neo-literates. By 1960, a total of 10 000 adults had been rendered literate though the Union's programme. This number was very insignificant considering that 27 million adults were illiterate adults at that time.

Comilla, a district town 100 miles from Dhaka, became well known in 1960 when the Bangladesh Academy for Rural Development (BARD) was established in the town. The Academy embarked on pioneering research into various aspects of rural development and initiated the foundation of the Education and Community Organisation to co-ordinate adult education efforts. In 1962 BARD conducted a seminar on the role of adult education in rural development in which many of the country's leading academics and development personalities participated. One outcome was the decision to establish a Department of Adult Education in Comilla. In the following year a powerful division of the Ministry of Education was established in Comilla to enhance adult education. This division developed primers, charts and post-literacy materials to run adult literacy centres. Within a period of five years it had enabled 40 000 of the 30 million illiterate adults to become literate. This adult education initiative, which became popularly known as the Comilla Approach, continued for fifteen years, during which time it achieved significant results in the Comilla region. The literacy work of the V-AID was inherited in the early sixties by the Pakistan Academy for Rural Development (now BARD). BARD's project area was in Comilla. A pilot project for adult education was started under the office in 1964, working in four *thanas* (sub-districts). It was reported in mid-1969 that almost 40 000 literacy certificates had been awarded through the programme. This programme was piloted in the Comilla district and so it is popularly known as the Comilla Approach. It should also be mentioned here that the Comilla Approach was not replicated in other places under that project.

Also during that period, the East Pakistan Adult Education Guild was established in Chittagong. The Guild promoted adult literacy through publishing materials and journals.

The people of Bangladesh were involved in a war of liberation for nine months in 1971. During this liberation war an adult literacy programme was run in the border district of Kurigram by an Adult Education Committee that received financial support from Oxfam and the Gandhi Foundation.

Post-liberation initiatives

In 1972, after the liberation, the National Co-operative Union of Bangladesh started an extensive adult literacy campaign in 52 *thanas* (presently *Upazila*). A *thana* or *Upazila* is a unit of administration. Bangladesh is divided into 64 districts, each of which is divided into five to nine *Upazilas* or sub-districts. The Union appointed 520 facilitators and 52 organisers, and within six months 13 000 men and women became literate through this programme. Unfortunately the government chose not to continue with the programme and several NGOs subsequently became involved in revitalising and running it. Some used their own approach while others followed the Comilla Approach. Literacy materials in the Comilla Approach comprised three primers of three months' duration each. The curriculum was considered roughly equivalent to Grade Three of formal primary school. The primers were taught along with two accountancy learning books and followed by 57 post-literacy books.

BRAC (Bangladesh Rural Advancement Committee), a leading national NGO in Bangladesh, which was established immediately after independence to work in remote areas of the country to rehabilitate the people who had lost their houses during the liberation war, ran an extensive programme using the literacy and adult education materials available at that time. Although primers were designed for the programme, little or no consideration was given to the needs of adults and the key words used in the primers were in no way related to the learners' socio-economic situation. This was one of the reasons for the high drop-out rate among learners before they broke through to literacy. In 1975, BRAC developed a functional literacy package following the principles of Freirian pedagogy. This approach required illiterate people to critically analyse their own life situations, and literacy lessons were based on the discussions arising from these analyses. As a result of the subsequent success of BRAC, many of the other NGOs who were working towards integrated development of the poor initiated adult literacy classes following the BRAC approach.

Expansion of functional adult literacy. In 1980, a reputable NGO, Friends in Village Development, Bangladesh (FIVDB), conducted an experimental study of the approaches to adult literacy provision that were being employed in the country at that time, particularly the Comilla and the BRAC approaches. The researchers concluded that with the Comilla approach the attainment of literacy was better than with other approaches, while the BRAC approach was effective in raising learners' level of consciousness. It was also found that after relatively short exposure to literacy classes, learners developed a strong desire to read books, and were able to write their own words and keep track of their accounts – which emphasised the importance of relating literacy to learners' developmental needs. Based on these findings, FIVDB developed a method and approach, in 1981, that was followed in literacy and adult education classes for about a decade.

PROSHIKA, one of the leading NGOs in Bangladesh, started its adult literacy programme in 1990 using materials developed by FIVDB. PROSHIKA's practical experience in conducting the programme soon identified many gaps in the approach. Gender, environment, health and sanitation, empowerment of the poor, poverty alleviation and disability issues were, for example, not adequately incorporated in the FIVDB materials. PROSHIKA therefore developed a new package of adult literacy materials based on their experience in the field, into which issues such as these were integrated. The PROSHIKA approach has, since 2000, been adopted by approximately 400 small organisations in Bangladesh.

Government initiatives since the 1980s. Adult literacy was given some emphasis in government policy in 1980 when a five-year plan to enable 40 million people to become literate was announced. Key features of the plan were that local government representatives were given the responsibility to educate the people, and all secondary and higher secondary students were tasked with enabling two persons to become literate. However, this approach was abandoned in 1982.

A bid to highjack power was successful and there was a change of government. In 1987 government piloted a new adult literacy programme. The Mass Education Programme (MEP), a wing of the Ministry of Education, was set up to operate the pilot phase.

The Jomtien Conference on Education for All (EFA) in 1990 stimulated greater official concern about countrywide adult literacy efforts and as a result the MEP involved NGOs in developing primers and training materials for conducting a large-scale adult literacy programme. In addition, from 1991 400 NGOs received financial support to run adult literacy centres. In 1992 MEP increased in size and was renamed the Integrated Non-formal Education Programme (INFEP), and in 1995 it became a Directorate of Non-formal Education (DNFE) within the Ministry of Education and was charged with the delivery of all non-formal education, including literacy, post-literacy and continuing education for adults and adolescents. In order to expand its outreach, DNFE also sponsors NGOs to execute programmes. DNFE's curricula and materials are developed by senior NGO personnel with the necessary expertise. The NGOs also provide training for the master trainers of the NGOs involved in executing DNFE programmes. So far, however, DNFE has not considered using distance and open learning (ODL) methods in literacy and adult education provision. Use of this mode would enable it to expand its outreach considerably.

Until June 2001, the DNFE funded NGOs to run adult literacy centres in the rural areas. In running adult literacy programmes with government funding, the centre-based approach has now been abandoned to free the country from illiteracy in the shortest possible time, and a new programme, the Total Literacy Movement (TLM), is being run directly through the administration on a district basis, instead of through NGOs. TLM requires the mobilisation of volunteers from all spheres of society, and the plan is to use NGOs to incorporate and implement the post-literacy and continuing education components of the programme. At the time of writing, the pilot phase of this programme had just been completed.

Table 1 Summary of the history of literacy and adult education in Bangladesh

Period	Major programme	Programme objectives	Teaching methods	Training of trainers
Immediately after First World War	Night schools established by Bengal Reconstruction Department	Strengthen co-operative societies	Alphabetic method	None
1940s	'Each One Teach One'	Enable more people to read simple messages	Educated people involved in teaching in traditional method	One or two hours' orientation
1954-1960	V-AID	Promote literacy as part of an integrated development approach	Charts	Orientation

Period	Major programme	Programme objectives	Teaching methods	Training of trainers
1960-1970	Comilla adult education approach	Arrange literacy and post-literacy programmes for organised group members	Primers developed based on specific contents	Two to three days' face-to-face training to enable trainers to train teachers
1975-1980	BRAC functional education approach	Conscientise non-literate men and women through literacy programme	Literacy derived through discussion of learners' own life issues	Two weeks' training for supervisors based on participatory methods
1981-1999	FIVDB functional education approach	Integrate development programme and literacy with emphasis on building awareness	Integration of discussion and literacy using primer and facilitators' books	Two weeks' training of supervisors
1990 to present	Government sponsored, centre-based approach	Disseminate literacy and development messages	Primers, charts and instructional guide	As above
1994 to present	Government initiated Total Literacy Movement (TLM)	Increase the rate of adult literacy in shortest possible time	Completion of primers by appointing volunteers from the community	Six days' training for Master Trainers
1999 to present	PROSHIKA approach to functional education	Empower participants in different aspects of development	Charts, flashcards, primers, workbooks and guide for facilitators	As above

Training grassroots level workers

The authors are of the opinion that a comparison of the curricula, methodologies and training presented by NGOs and government agencies reveals no fundamental difference between the various providers with regard to the training presented to grassroots level facilitators. Facilitators are generally from the same socio-economic background as the learners, with an average of eight years' schooling. In many cases female facilitators have a lower level of education than male facilitators. The age range of the facilitators is 25 to 35 years. With few exceptions, male classes are run by male facilitators and female classes by female facilitators.

In the last thirty years, NGOs have operated about 100 000 adult literacy centres, 70% of which were for women learners. The average centre caters for 23 learners. The success rate for a six-month course is 75% for women learners and 66% for men.

Many female facilitators are chosen from among the neo-literates. They are given intensive training to assist them to read the instructional materials. More often than not, the facilitators who go through the ranks of adult literacy classes are very familiar with the processes of delivery because they have been trained in same way. They are often able to enrich the training sessions because they can recount and express the real needs of learners in the classroom situation from their own experiences as learners. Once trained, facilitators need ongoing training – a need which could be best responded to by the introduction of in-service training using ODL methods.

Training of facilitators in general

Generally, the training provided to grassroots facilitators follows the same general format. They attend an initial pre-service training course which is defined as foundation training. Presently these courses are designed to be presented over two weeks. The first two or three days are usually devoted to discussions of social, cultural, economical, political and educational issues. Methods include lectures, visual presentations, small group discussions and classroom discussions. Participants are encouraged to think critically about local social structures and to analyse what, if anything, can be done to change them to favour the poor and the marginalised, particularly the non-literates who will be attending their centres.

Facilitators are introduced to the concept of different types of education for different purposes and are asked to question traditional roles and methods of education. Through their involvement in group discussions, trainees are encouraged to adopt new models of two-way learning and to recognise that the participants at their centres will also have much to contribute. This stage is crucial for sensitising facilitators and establishing programme goals. Unless trainers are convinced of their role as facilitators rather than as traditional, authoritarian teachers, they will be incapable of effectively leading discussions in an open learning course.

A major task of the initial training is to create appropriate attitudes so that a dependency relationship does not develop. The literacy and adult education materials are introduced on the fourth day of training. Through lectures, self study, demonstrations and practice the facilitators are helped to understand the underlying principles and methods inherent in the course. Much of the training involves demonstrations and practice of the lessons. Each discussion topic is thoroughly analysed and the lesson steps are demonstrated. In adult education courses discussion sessions are conducted in a non-directive manner whereas literacy lessons call for a more direct, instructive approach. Non-literate learners cannot identify new letters unless the facilitator instructs them; accordingly, facilitators are required to direct the learning process and select methodologies that are appropriate to the specific outcomes.

Training of supervisors and trainers

Another essential element of the programme is the supervision of centres to ensure the proper execution of the training and effective use of the materials. All the facilitators are required to record their learners' progress and problems on a regular basis. Generally the supervisors use the three-point scales (good, fair and poor) to measure the progress made by learners in acquiring literacy, numeracy and functional knowledge through their learning experience. Supervisors see to it that all the learners of a centre take a test at least once a month, and they record the progress in a format which helps them to take appropriate measures to improve the quality of facilitators. Facilitators' meetings are held each month. They discuss their reports and the supervisor assesses and records the overall progress being made with the programme. Frequent supervisory visits are essential for the effective running of the centres. Facilitators find the visits encouraging and useful for discussing any problems they may have encountered.

Another task of the supervisor, as already indicated, is to monitor the progress of the centres and ensure that facilitators are using appropriate methods. Classroom visits enable the supervisor to identify problems and to work with the facilitator to resolve them.

Recruiting and maintaining staff who understand both literacy methods and the dynamics of group discussions and co-operative action is a significant responsibility of the supervisory system. Supervisory staff need to be oriented to the philosophy of the organisation first and then they should participate in the facilitators' training. A three to four-day training course is necessary to develop supervisory skills. It is possible for a supervisor to become a trainer after participating in the facilitators' training programme and then demonstrating competence in supervisory activities.

Methods and techniques

Facilitator training undertaken by organisations that have professional trainers are based broadly on a participatory approach. A variety of methods are used by the different organisations in presenting the different lessons. Some of these are brain storming, small group discussions, lectures and discussions, role-plays, question-answer, buzz group discussions, card collection and clustering, games and simulation exercises, field visits and environmental walks, study circles, case analysis, picture analysis and expert interviews, demonstrations, value mapping, visualised presentation, problem solving, micro-teaching, alphabet song, chain drill, flashcard games, three-station discussions and story telling. The methods are invariably adapted to learners' daily life situations, which makes the sessions more lively and relevant.

Policy implications in facilitators' training

In order to organise, put into practice and supervise adult literacy and basic education programme activities effectively to attain the set objectives, a two-week long training course is organised for the staff members of service providers and NGOs. These trainers ultimately train the course facilitators at grassroots training centres (GTCs).

The main actors in running and operating adult literacy and basic education centres are the course facilitators. They are chosen from the community and in most cases from the same socio-economic status as the learners. They receive a small honorarium for conducting a course of six months' duration. They are usually the casual workers of the organisation. Men and women who can read, write and understand the reading, writing and learning exercise materials properly are selected as facilitators. They are generally between 20 to 35 years of age. Training plays a vital role in enabling facilitators to conduct adult literacy and basic education courses in the desired manner.

NGOs that have their own curriculum and materials design the training courses for the facilitators. The foundation training for the course facilitators is generally for two weeks, and they have to undergo this training before a centre starts. Besides foundation training, in-service and refresher training courses are also organised for them. Twenty-five to thirty facilitators participate in one course. The course is conducted by at least two full-time trainers and four to five guest speakers as resource persons on different issues. The full-time trainers are the regular staff members of the NGO. They receive the Training of Trainers (TOT) input and training on the literacy and basic education approach. The NGOs who are using the method and approach of other organisations, first arrange training for their supervisors and trainers by the trainers of the organisation that originally developed the curriculum and materials. These trained personnel ultimately conduct training for their facilitators.

DNFE has organised a group of Master Trainers from different NGOs to conduct training of the supervisors and trainers of the NGOs who execute their projects. DNFE commissions them when any training is required for the executing agencies. The trainers subsequently train the facilitators.

The policies of the DNFE and the NGOs have some limitations. To maintain the quality of training it is essential to develop the trainers through classroom training and observation of ongoing centres, and by creating opportunities for intensive supervision of the centres to find out the problems that learners and facilitators face.

The TOT course on adult literacy and basic education helps equip the participants with the methods and techniques of using primers, conducting classes and running learning centres effectively and efficiently. Participants also learn the methodology of training so that they can train the course facilitators at grassroots level. This course also covers the issues relevant to rural development, the causes of poverty, the aims and objectives of adult literacy and basic education and, at the same time, monitors and follows up on the techniques of the programmes. It also assists the courses facilitators with operating literacy centres.

The grassroots level course facilitators do not attend this TOT course. The participants of TOT course are supervisors as well as trainers who ultimately provide training to the course facilitators at GTCs. These trained course facilitators are entrusted with the responsibility of organising and conducting the literacy centres.

Some system loss is sometimes experienced because of this cascade system of conducting top-down training from TOT to grassroots level.
It is really very difficult to directly provide a huge number of course facilitators with training courses at central level.

The success of adult literacy and basic education largely depends on the facilitators, and their efficiency depends on the training they are given. A well-equipped facilitator can make the learning environment lively and effective by using appropriate techniques and methods. So training of the course facilitators is an essential aspect of this programme and is, in fact, essential in this type of non-formal education in general.

Box 1

Nasreen – From Learner to Facilitator: A Case Study

Nasreen is a young girl from Salirmahal village under Ghoramara in the working area of FIVDB. She did not have the opportunity to go to school. At the age of 15 her parents tried to arrange a marriage for her. They could not find a husband, however, because of her dark complexion and their inability to pay dowry.

In 1982 FIVDB opened an adult literacy class at Salirmahal. Nasreen and 19 other girls joined the class. For six months Nasreen attended every session of the course. Each session was divided into three parts – 45 minutes for discussion, 60 minutes for literacy and 30 minutes for numeracy. Nasreen was an active participant in all the components.

She became self-reliant and more aware of the problems and injustices that exist in society. Her enthusiasm helped her to complete the course successfully and at the end of it the adult literacy worker chose her to become a facilitator. In the next cycle, Nasreen was selected to participate in the two-week facilitator training course which she received with self-confidence. In addition to the time she spent going to lessons, she also took the time to read the content of the facilitators' manual.

As a facilitator, Nasreen conducted 25 cycles of the adult literacy course, each of six months' duration, and more than 400 learners were taught by her. She became a very important person in the village. She got married and as an earning partner she was able to be a decision-maker in the family, which further empowered her.

Every year FIVDB arranges several TOT (training of trainers) courses for the NGO's mid-level personnel. Nasreen is one of the grassroots facilitators who join them to share their experiences in different sessions. Their input is so interesting that a two-hour session becomes very interactive and the participants want to know more from them. By the end of the session they feel more confident about working with non-literate adults.
In the remote rural areas, it is very difficult to find female facilitators to run adult literacy centres for female learners. Proceeding from learner to facilitator is a solution to this problem. The facilitators have learnt in the same way as the present learners are being taught, so they feel good about doing their jobs.

PROSHIKA's approach

Training curriculum

The training of almost all the NGOs' grassroots level workers has taken on a more or less uniform structure. The DNFE developed its module with the assistance of leading NGOs working in the non-formal education sector. PROSHIKA was involved in that process and in fact developed its training curriculum in 2000. As a result it incorporates the essence of all the other curricula developed by the different NGOs, such as RDRS, FIVDB, Jagarani Chakra, VERC, DAM and CCDB (see the List of Abbreviations for full names).

PROSHIKA'S training of grassroots-level adult literacy workers includes the content summarised in Table 2.

Table 2 PROSHIKA curriculum for grassroots adult literacy workers

Module	Content
Awareness of the socio-economic and cultural situation	• Education and its usefulness • Different types of education, formal, non-formal and informal • Liberating education which develops critical awareness • Gender equity • Development and education
Concept of adult education and literacy	• Definition of literacy • Definition and scope of adult education literacy • Literacy methods and adult literacy approaches literacy • Content of the adult literacy materials • Delivery technique
Managing adult education and literacy	• Responsibilities and duties of the facilitators • Management of a literacy centre • Role of community
Materials and approaches	• Using real literacy materials • Identification of the adult's learning needs • Learner-centred education • The role of popular culture in adult education • Processes for conducting refresher training • The differences between the learning of children and adults • Adult literacy programme curriculum • Developing materials for adult literacy programmes
Adult education and empowerment	• Ensuring the success of a post-literacy programme • Access to public resources and institutions • Uses of literacy

The PROSHIKA programmes are presented and supervised by a large number of Universal Education Workers (UEWs) who play a significant role in the programmes. Currently about 900 UEWs are involved in supervising 11 450 adult literacy centres and training the course facilitators.

In order to ensure that the UEWs are properly trained, PROSHIKA has developed a distance education course for them. This is presented using written text and through a three-day orientation contact block at which the training manual is introduced. Thereafter, UEWs are required to work through the manual independently (or with their peers) whilst working at the various sites. The use of the distance education approach enables them to make site visits whilst simultaneously studying the relevant manual.

In addition to the distance component of the UEW course, PROSHIKA also expects them to participate in a 14-day facilitator course, which includes practice sessions in which participants try out their teaching skills. They also have to complete a number of written assignments. The course evaluation indicates that 80% of the participants felt that they were able to apply what they had learnt to their classroom situation.

In the first week of the course, the trainer demonstrates the lessons to the facilitators, who participate as learners. In the second week participants are divided in two or three groups and are required to practise teaching by presenting their lessons to their small groups. After the lesson the group analyses the lesson and engages the facilitator in the necessary self-reflection process.

Organisation of the adult literacy centres

PROSHIKA starts working with the poor men and women by organising them in groups, known as people's organisations. The non-literate members of the people's organisation are eligible to join the adult literacy and basic education courses. PROSHIKA's adult literacy centres are organised with non-literate members selected by their respective groups. There are 20-25 learners aged between 15 and 40 years in each literacy centre. PROSHIKA targets non-literate learners from poor households. Centres are normally held at Resource Centres established by PROSHIKA. Group members donate a piece of land and the cost of labour for building the Resource Centre premises, or the organisation uses rented houses in the community. The female literacy centres are held during the day while male literacy centres are held in the evening. The cost of the adult literacy centres is covered by PROSHIKA and part of the expenses are borne by the group. (PROSHIKA does not receiving government funding). Group members who have had formal education up to grades eight to ten are selected to facilitate the adult literacy classes. Classes are organised separately for male and female learners, with same-sex course facilitators. The curriculum and the teaching-learning materials are developed by PROSHIKA. The course is for six months, six days a week and two hours per day. Activity-based learning exercises, charts and flash-cards, among other things, are employed to make learning sessions more inviting. Learners also enjoy a great deal of leeway to set new learning areas for themselves. Literacy serves one of the felt needs of the learners. The content of the learning materials is life-related and needs-based. The centres are organised in such a way that every participant can share ideas and views, with enough scope for interaction among the participants. Currently 11 450 adult literacy centres with an enrolment of 254 695 learners – 60% of whom are female – are being run in 190 PROSHIKA programme locations.

Box 2

Jaynab – Now an Efficient Course Facilitator: Case Study

Jaynab, a woman from Dhankura village in the Manikganj district, is a facilitator of PROSHIKA's adult literacy centre run by the Saturia Area Development Centre (ADC). Her experience and wisdom, ignored for so long, blossomed when she joined a PROSHIKA group.

Jaynab started as a member of a PROSHIKA-organised group, 'Agrani Landless Group', in 1993. She then attended various training courses which broadened her vision, understanding and values. This empowered her to become an effective and efficient course facilitator.

Along with 20 other group members, Jaynab then took part in the field testing of adult literacy material developed by PROSHIKA. That was when she drew everybody's attention with her intelligence and understanding. She was very keen to see that the new literacy materials properly reflected the values and beliefs which PROSHIKA advocates, particularly community desires and issues like environment, gender, democracy and poverty alleviation. She kept asking questions and was eventually happy when she was answered in simple language. Since she had been a facilitator of an adult literacy centre, she could easily compare the difference between the existing materials and the new materials developed by PROSHIKA.

'The non-literates who participate in the course will not only become literate, they will be very conscious members of the grassroots organisations,' said Jaynab while commenting on the materials. 'They are not merely passive learners, rather very active in changing their present situation,' she added. Besides being a successful manager of the adult literacy centre, Jaynab leads a study circle for the women of her own village. Hers is a very well-known face in the village. 'What I do has brought so much change in my life – socially and culturally and economically', says Jaynab.

Materials used in training facilitators

Facilitator training is generally held at the *Upazila* (sub-district) level where there are residential facilities for the participants. Unfortunately training materials like VIPP cards, flannel boards, overhead projectors, videos and so on are not available in many of these venues. Training providers[3] are, however, very keen to use locally available materials.

Some materials are developed centrally, such as the manual for trainers, flip charts and learners' materials. When learners' materials are developed, a number of significant steps are followed, namely writing, illustrating, field testing and editing.

In Bangladesh more than 500 NGOs have adult literacy and adult basic education programmes, but only fifteen organisations, or thereabouts, have their own training materials. Most organisations rely on the training materials developed by PROSHIKA and FIVDB. The education programmes for adult literacy and basic education are designed together and may therefore be referred to as 'adult literacy and basic education'.

Type of training

Training of adult literacy and basic education personnel is available for course *facilitators, supervisors at the implementation level and management personnel*. As regards Facilitator's Training, an agreed principle of all the NGOs is to arrange foundation training of at least two weeks for facilitators, followed by two or three refresher courses of three to five days each. Supervisors Training are the workers who train, supervise and monitor the facilitators. They undergo training of at least two weeks, which includes topics like content of facilitator's course, monitoring, supervision and evaluation techniques and training methods. The monitoring and supervision system covers recording primary enrolment, regular attendance, maintaining the learning environment, preventing drop-out and assessing learners' abilities after completion of the course. It also includes grading the level of attainment. In supervision, techniques relating to smooth running of centres and evaluation are done to ensure follow-up programmes for the participants.

Management Personnel Training entails the overall orientation for planners, organisers and other management personnel who have experience but need more detailed information about the adult literacy programme.

In addition to the above, training and workshops are arranged for the materials developers, illustrators and trainers. These are conducted by people with the necessary experience and knowledge in the respective fields. A six-day training course and two to three workshops are held in a year. Materials are analysed in the workshop and some draft materials of different formats are also developed.

Providers of adult literacy and basic education

The Asia Pacific Programme of Education for All (APPEAL) has designed training courses for different levels of adult literacy personnel in the region. In Bangladesh the training planners use many aspects of the APPEAL approach. The organisations that provide adult literacy training in Bangladesh are mostly NGOs and they utilise this training as part of their integrated development approach. In such a model adult literacy and basic education are not the entry point at which facilitators start working with the people. There are a lot of factors such as group formation, income generation, skills training and so on that first have to be attended to. The APPEAL model, on the other hand, is designed for organisations whose primary and first focus is adult literacy, with other subsequent programmes based on that.

CAMPE (Campaign for Popular Education) is a coalition of NGOs in Bangladesh working in the non-formal education sector. CAMPE was founded in 1990 by a group of education activists who were advocating the liberation of education. The coalition has identified 55 organisations as capable of imparting adult literacy and basic education training. These are categorised in three grades. There are seventeen organisations in this *Grade 1*. They arrange regular training for their own and other organisations' personnel. Their training centres are often used by other organisations as training venues. Organisations of *Grade 2* arrange regular training programmes for their own workers and facilitators. They are capable of conducting training for the personnel of other organisations, but they cannot render this service because of time constraints. Eleven organisations are identified in this category. *Grade 3* includes fifteen organisations which have the capacity to train their own personnel and facilitators, but cannot train outsiders.

Content of an ODL training course

Based on the research undertaken for this study, and given the acute shortage of adult educators and the concomitant lack of funds, it is proposed that a two-week training session of grassroots level workers for ODL (open and distance learning) be designed with the curriculum content set out in Table 3. This content is currently used in different ways by the NGOs in Bangladesh.

Table 3 Proposed ODL curriculum for training grassroots adult literacy workers

Definition of literacy
Functional education and open and distance learning
Functional education and development
Different types of education system – informal, formal and non-formal
The status of literacy in Bangladesh
Literacy movements – problems and prospects
Skills obtained through ODL
Concept of literacy programme management
Socio-economic analysis of target group for adult education
Literacy personnel of different tiers
Curriculum and materials

Classification of materials
Steps followed in developing materials
Organisation and forming of literacy centres
Supervision
Monitoring and evaluation
Post-literacy – concepts and basic principles
Continuing education and learning society
Culture of continuing education and implementation strategy
Concept of People's Resource Centre
Role of literacy personnel in implementing CE
The concept of training
Principles of participatory training
Role of trainers
How to plan and organise a training course
Training methods
Theory and practice on different methods: lectures, brain storming, small group discussions, simulation exercises, case studies, role-play, question-and-answer, etc
Managing field visits
Process of developing session plans
Development of literacy materials
Group exercise on developing Learner Generated Materials (LGM)
Concept of training evaluation
Formative evaluation
Course evaluation

Training different tiers of literacy personnel

To conduct a successful ODL programme an appropriate personnel structure must be selected or designed. Literacy personnel (such as fieldworkers, facilitators, co-ordinators, managers and planners) need to co-ordinate closely with one another in executing the programme. The structure below is suggested for the four different levels of literacy personnel that are proposed:

Table 4 Learning outcomes and responsibilities for suggested four tiers of adult literacy staff

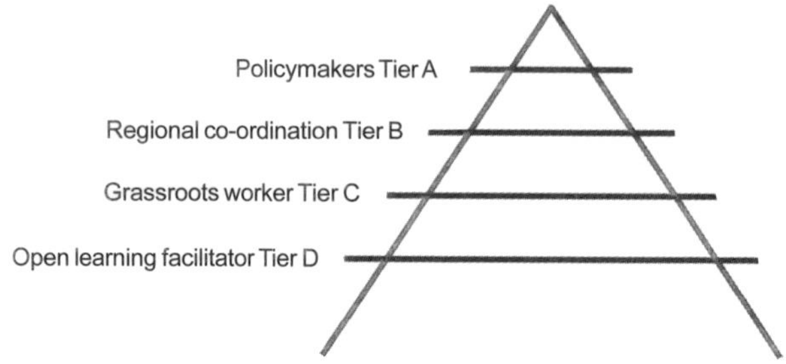

Tier	Responsibilities, roles and duties
Tier A personnel Mainly policymakers and planners	National policy-making for adult literacy and basic education Advocating government policy Planning overall national training; preparing a national training programme Identifying training needs and developing a curriculum Developing infrastructure and resources for a training programme and a training network Arranging staff development Approving training budgets and manuals Developing monitoring and evaluation systems; creating scope for research Ensuring co-ordination at all levels; initiating and maintaining contact and liaison with agencies providing adult literacy and basic education and development agenciesIntegrating the literacy programme with other development programme Making national and international contacts
Tier	**Responsibilities, roles and duties**
Tier B personnel Supervisors, trainers and material developers	Giving feedback on policy to policymakers Collecting information for planning national training courses Surveying training needs of the trainers and grassroots workers Identifying potential trainers Arranging training for the grassroots level workers Planning training programmes, developing curricula for different levels of literacy personnel Deciding on methodologies, selecting training equipment and determining the use of local resources Piloting training materials Motivating the training participants, community leaders and learners Supervising, monitoring and evaluating the activities of grassroots level workers Planning for action research Conducting study for improving the life situation of participating learnersUndertaking liaison with other NGOs

Tier	Responsibilities, roles and duties
Tier C personnel Grassroots workers who follow up the regular activities of learners and their facilitators	Gaining knowledge, understanding, skills and appropriate attitudes vis-à-vis the national training programme Involving local community in developing the programme and accessing local resourcesImplementing grassroots training Motivating learners and local leaders and ensuring maximum participation at all levels Selecting learners Organising the centres Assessing the progress of the learnersAssisting neo-literates to apply their skill in their daily lives Arranging skills training for graduates
Tier	**Responsibilities, roles and duties**
Tier D personnel People who directly facilitate the learners	Managing time effectively Compiling lesson plans Distributing materials Facilitating adult learning exercises, using appropriate teaching methods Maintaining sound interpersonal relations with the learners and ensuring good participation Keeping learner records Sharing the problems with other colleagues

Box 3

Profile of an Organiser – Nijera Shikhi: A Case Study

Nijera Shikhi (Let's Teach Ourselves) follows a self-learning mobilisation approach based on the principle of self-help. The organisation was established in 1993 with the objective of eradicating illiteracy by mobilising human and material resources. Self-education is carried out by means of a three-step method. The first step is spread over two to three months, during which time learners are assisted by a *Shebi* (volunteer) to acquire simple literacy and numeracy skills. During the second step the knowledge learnt in the first step is applied in operating a small business, health awareness, family planning and other improvements in life-style. In this step Nijera Shikhi distributes books free of cost. In the third step 80 to 100 learners acquire advanced knowledge by becoming members of a mini-library that has a good collection of books and journals. This helps learners to develop their literacy levels.

Mahera is a trained Nijera Shikhi volunteer who has been involved in eradicating illiteracy through developing volunteers in her area. She motivates people to participate in Nijera Shikhi's three-step literacy programme. She also recruits volunteers among educated people to assist non-literate men and women to become literate and to sustain their knowledge. She helps people to utilise local resources. She believes that in two years' time, she will be able to eradicate the curse of illiteracy from her own programme location. Mahera is very well known in the community as a result of her involvement in the self-learning movement. She tries her best to help community members sustain the literacy they attain. She dreams of a learning society which will solve the problems of poverty and remove the inequalities which exist in society.

Scope of distance education and open learning

A good many grassroots NGO personnel in Bangladesh are involved in training literacy and adult basic education facilitators. The mode of the training is a mixture of face-to-face and open and distance learning. The personnel have a background of formal education with very good foundation training to enable them to teach adult learners. Some of the characteristics of ODL in existing literacy and education programmes are mentioned below:

Adult literacy and basic education curricula are designed around life-related subjects including agriculture, health, nutrition, justice, dowry, poverty alleviation and so on. Most of the learning is delivered by means of instructional materials which are generally self-study materials, and where possible, the facilitator supplements the learning material.

Open learning for the adult is entirely free of the formal characteristics of schooling. The commonly seen hierarchical teacher-student relationship is avoided in this way of teaching and learning, in which the facilitator also learns from the participants.

Open learning for adults in Bangladesh starts with a functional literacy course that generally lasts for six months. The facilitators play a vital role in enabling learners to study independently, either in groups or individually.

Manuals developed by non-formal education personnel are used for educating the adults. Course facilitators use these open learning manuals during face-to-face sessions with learners.

The small organisations that run five to ten centres in a year with 100 to 200 learners, procure guidebooks for the trainers to use in conducting training courses of their facilitators. Facilitators mostly depend on the guidebook when they attend the training sessions.

In Bangladesh the NGOs and the government agencies use the term 'functional literacy' to refer to both literacy and adult basic education. The curricula of functional literacy courses therefore include all the essential life related topics.

Suggested design for a pilot adult literacy and basic education programme

In Bangladesh adult literacy and basic education for non-literate adults is mostly delivered through literacy centres. A batch of 20 to 30 adult learners participate at one centre, with one course facilitator for each literacy centre.

Course facilitators are selected on the basis of certain predetermined qualities and qualifications and they attend a two-week foundation training course. Each literacy centre operates for a minimum period of six to eight months, five or six days a week for two to three hours a day. There is one supervisor for each cluster of 25 to 30 adult literacy centres. Supervisors are trained in the teaching of basic literacy and more specifically in centre supervision, monitoring and evaluation. They are also required to conduct the training of the course facilitators in their organisations.

The following are usually necessary for running an adult literacy centre in the community: organising at grassroots level; selecting a house or other venue as a learning site; appointing supervisors; recruiting learners; appointing facilitators; organising training courses for supervisors and facilitators; procuring or developing primers and notebooks and supplementary reading materials; developing a comprehensive facilitators' manual; developing teaching and learning aids; acquiring teaching aids like blackboards, chalk, dusters, pencils, sharpeners and erasers; acquiring mats for seating and lanterns and kerosene oil for centres that function in the evening; developing monitoring and reporting forms and paying facilitators' honoraria and supervisors' salaries. Over the past three decades, this mode of delivery has allowed three million men and women to participate in adult literacy and basic education centres.

However, Bangladesh now needs a system which can deliver a faster, more effective method for educating adults. Such a system should also pay attention to the rapid reduction of gender disparity; awareness of the environment; using arsenic-free water; involving learners in tree-planting campaigns; active participation in poverty alleviation programme; rights of children; HIV/AIDS awareness; access to information and access to public services and resources. The list above reflects the learning requirements of more than half the country's adult population.

Bangladesh cannot wait years to disseminate such essential knowledge among the poor and an effective mode of delivery is therefore essential. ODL can play this role. So far Nijera Shikhi is the only organisation that has promoted literacy and adult basic education by means of an ODL system.

Nijera Shikhi introduced ODL for literacy and adult basic education to help build a learning society. The primers, teachers' books and other instructional materials are developed in such way that they can be disseminated by training grassroots level workers. All the materials make liberal use of the term 'self' to convey the idea of learning as a self-motivated activity. From its inception Nijera Shikhi has used a platform of volunteers from national to local level to work for the cause of educating the people at the lowest levels.[4]

The ODL approach initiated by Nijera Shikhi is quite different from other approaches that are employed, but it needs to be popularised among the development organisations as well as among individuals. Nijera Shikhi could create a strong literacy and adult basic education movement through ODL if it could procure the necessary support from national and international agencies.

Pilot open and distance learning programme

Suggestions

The following suggestions and guidelines are put forward with the aim of giving some impetus to the idea of piloting an ODL programme of adult literacy and basic education. An organisation such as UNESCO could possibly initiate a pilot project such as this in Bangladesh.

Five zones could be chosen, taking the country's geography into consideration. Within each zone a union (a population unit of around 30 000 adults) could be identified, and from this 5 000 non-literate people could be selected to participate in the programme.

Fifty workers would have to be appointed to carry out the programme at grassroots level. They would receive two weeks' conventional training and the remainder of their skills would be acquired through distance education. Adult literacy and basic education practitioners would be consulted and involved in the design of the training manual they would use.

Guidelines

The steps for starting such a programme include informing participants of the programme objectives, recording baseline information on participants, distributing the manual and seeing to it that it is collectively studied and that there is co-ordination among the workers. Two supervisors are recruited to supervise every 25 workers, and they are also trained in the same manner. Materials for the participants are developed in such a way that they get two-hour group lessons twice a week with scope for self study on the remaining days of the week. The Bangladesh Open University campus may be used for planning the programme, developing the curriculum and materials, co-ordinating the training courses and maintaining a central monitoring evaluation system. A representative group of experts from government, NGOs and the Open University are members of the project's steering committee. After analysing the findings of the pilot project, the programme could be disseminated countrywide. Well-written, comprehensive manuals are vital for the success of adult literacy and basic education using an ODL approach. The manual should include written objectives for each session, a comprehensive summary of the contents of the session, self-assessment exercises with each section of the course, clear direction for participants on self study and a variety of activities.

Recommendations

Based on the conclusions drawn in this review of adult literacy and basic education in Bangladesh, a number of recommendations are made.

Bangladesh is a country with millions of illiterate people. Of every three adult men and women, two are non-literate. In spite of all the efforts that have been made to promote literacy, many non-literate people remain out of reach. The rate of literacy can be significantly decreased by involving educated people from all walks of life, so an open learning system should be introduced and strengthened for the delivery of an extensive literacy programme in Bangladesh. The Open University of Bangladesh can play a vital role in this regard.

The existing adult literacy and basic education programme is being run as one of the components of non-formal education. Bangladesh has earned a good reputation for its delivery mechanism but the pace of coverage in this process is very slow. The open learning and existing approaches should therefore be more closely integrated.

Grassroots level workers need to be well trained so that they can create adequate learning opportunities for the non-literates and semi-literates who participate in their courses. Training courses offered by different government agencies and NGOs should be reviewed so that new avenues can be opened up and learning can be made more attractive and effective.

In ODL electronic media frequently play a significant role in disseminating life skills on a national basis. These media are becoming more effective and better established, and radio, television and other audio-visual technologies should be used in a planned manner to train grassroots workers. Availability of such technology also encourages non-literate members of the community to attend literacy and adult basic education centres.

The Open University of Bangladesh has so far been engaged in offering certificate courses for the formal education sector. The university's infrastructure could be a valuable resource in developing literacy and adult basic education personnel using ODL methods. The capacity of the Open University should therefore be assessed.

A decision has been taken to establish an Institute of Non-formal Education under the DNFE. The proposed institute could assist with the development of adult literacy and basic education personnel by establishing satellite training centres in all 64 districts of Bangladesh. This would also ensure the expansion of open and distance learning.

A uniform curriculum should be developed for disseminating training to grassroots workers throughout the country. The materials need to be eclectically developed and the mode of presentation should be participatory.

Grassroots level workers must be able to develop different types of local materials that can be used in their lessons. They need to have a strong commitment to ensure community participation in implementing adult literacy and basic education in the field.

Government sectors such as health, co-operatives, agriculture, livestock and forestation all employ extension workers. Concerted efforts on their part can play a significant role in an ODL education system.

UNESCO could initiate a five-zone pilot ODL literacy and adult education project with the involvement of reputable organisations. The capable NGOs, the Open University and DNFE could work jointly during the pilot phase.
There should be a continuous process of reviewing and developing adult literacy materials to meet the current need and for the ongoing process of human resource development.

References

Action Aid (1999–2001) REFLECT documents. Dhaka, Bangladesh.

ASPBAE (1999) Innovative and good practicing in adult literacy, Mumbai, India.

CAMPE (1996–1999). Training of Trainers Manual and other documents. Dhaka, Bangladesh.

Dhaka Ahansia Mission (2001). Adult Literacy and Basic Education Manual. Dhaka, Bangladesh.

Department of Non-Formal Education (1999), Manual for Supervisors, Dhaka, Bangladesh.

FIVDB (1990) Functional Education Materials and Approach Khadimnagar, Sylhet, Bangladesh.

International Conference Report on Open Basic Education (2001), Hydrabad, India.

Jenings, J. (1990) *Adult literacy – Master or servant?* Dhaka, Bangladesh: University Press Limited (UPL).

Maddox, B. (1999), *Learning and Using Literacy in Rural Bangladesh.* PROSHIKA, Dhaka, Bangladesh.

PROSHIKA Training Manual (1999). Section 2, Mirpur, Dhaka 1216, Bangladesh.

Volunteers Guide Annual Report and other Documents – Nijera Shikhi, Dhaka, Bangladesh 1996 to 2000.

Notes

1 The authors have been involved in organising and implementing a non-formal education programme and developing curricula and materials for children and adults. The following people were consulted: Professor Shuraiya Siddiquy – Nijera Shikhi; Mr Ashok Kar – Nijera Shikhi; Mr Shahnewaz Khan – Dhaka Ahsania Mission; Mr Tapan K Das – CAMPE; Mohammed Mohsin – FIVDB.

2 Many of these have in some way contributed to the reduction of poverty and other social injustices by engaging the active participation of the poor.

3 In most cases Universal Education workers and in some cases central Universal Education Programme personnel are the trainers for facilitators.

4 John P Hastings, a devoted missionary, pioneered this programme and was able to mobilise funds to expand it. Five years after founding the organisation he died in 1998; this was a great loss for the organisation.

Section II

The relevance of training in the framework of international development goals

7

Can open, distance and flexible learning assist with adult basic education? Pursuing the concept of quality in the context of education for all

Christopher Yates

Introduction

This paper focuses on quality and adult basic education (ABE) and literacy in sub-Saharan Africa. It argues that the most successful approaches to distance education have achieved quality outcomes by using a mass-based industrialised model – and that the mass-based industrialised model has been most successful with adults working at the tertiary level of provision. It is less well tested with adults learning at the basic level (defined as the first nine years of education). In fact, the distance teaching models that were used by many African states shortly after their independence, though showing early promise (e.g. radio-based campaigns and the correspondence and study group model), have often failed to go to scale. As a consequence they often have not had access to the resources they needed to offer sustainable high quality education. ABE, long the Cinderella of the education world, continues to be severely under-funded. The end of the 1990s saw a number of developments emerging from research and practice that may yet support more positive changes in ABE programming – in terms of quality and availability.

However, what role distance learning may play in the process remains problematic – partly because of changing views of how adults best learn at this level, but also because of the need to integrate that learning in a way that serves to improve livelihoods. The growth and popularity of more participatory and democratic methods of ABE, the stress on the applied nature of the learning and the increasing use of constructivist epistemologies raise questions about the relevance and utility of a standardised 'one size fits all model' of distance education. It may be that the centralised and industrialised model of distance learning is not the most appropriate to take ABE forward. Mass media might best be used in a secondary role, deployed in an integrated manner to support a range of smaller-scale group-based methods involving loosely co-ordinated local and international providers, working to nationally agreed and monitored quality standards and outcomes.

Quality and the industrialised model of distance education

Conventional large-scale forms of distance education (like the dedicated distance teaching universities and more recently the open schools) have traditionally achieved educational quality by combining carefully structured multimedia-based forms of education – printed study booklets and broadcast programmes – with a variety of different kinds of human interaction, provided either at a distance or face to face. The product-based elements have traditionally been developed using industrialised principles of production. To achieve a quality product, the task of designing and preparing the learning material was broken down into different stages and specialist skills deployed at each point. For example, researchers established the need and demand for the learning programme and provided details of the potential audiences and their study contexts; curriculum planners planned the curriculum and provided course outlines; specialist subject authors drafted the study units; and editors, graphic artists and instructional designers all then helped to transform them into self-study materials.

The interactions between these different specialists pursued the quality goal using a process of iterative and progressive improvement, achieved through continuous critique and peer support. In countries with effective mass postal and broadcasting systems the model worked well. It ensured each learner could receive the same quality of printed package, broadcast or tape recording no matter where they lived.

To these one-way learning products (standardised printed texts or broadcasts) is added a judicious mix of the more interactive, two-way, personalised, elements of a learning experience. The interactive elements are provided either directly through face-to-face meetings, or remotely through telephone conversations or correspondence (letter or email). But once again, industrialised principles are used to assure quality. Tutors are recruited to set qualification requirements and then employed on defined contracts in support of fixed group sizes (1 to 15-30). In the better systems tutors receive standardised training courses and given periodic in-service support derived from researched practice. Their tutorials and assessments are given according to principles contained in pre-defined tutoring guides and they apply the fixed criteria provided in the assessment mark schemes when grading students' work. More experienced colleagues may periodically monitor tutors. Examiners complete the process through the assessment of the terminal elements (examinations and projects), again according to predetermined mark schemes and assessment guidelines. Hence, the quality of the process elements also relies on a mix of rational planning, professional review and specialist division of labour (Peters 1983). Many distance education organisations have become successful national institutions using this industrialised model. It has succeeded in providing quality education in many contexts.

However, it should be noted that this success was often, though not always, achieved serving relatively well-educated, well-motivated adults who were learning at the upper secondary or tertiary levels. These included professional groups like teachers, nurses, accountants and business managers, or well-motivated adults seeking other forms of qualification such as school matriculation in order to access further study. The model has much less experience of working with adults at the basic level.

During the late 1980s and throughout the 1990s, to this mass-based, largely standardised model of education was added a highly interactive personalised approach based on the new information technology (computers and telecommunications). The new computer-based information technologies offered relatively cheap two-way synchronous and asynchronous communication to growing numbers. To the mass standardised products of the first media (print, broadcasting and tapes) was added the potential to incorporate high-quality personalised elements, made available through computer conferencing, email and modular knowledge banks.

Such developments in communications technology and learning design may enable us to offer both mass standardised learning and mass personalised learning in the future. The two-way computer-based communication technologies currently available certainly offer more promise in meeting this challenge than did the earlier one-way technologies like radio or TV, and they may yet achieve a paradigm shift in learning achievement for all. However, even if the technical possibilities exist to use knowledge information systems for more personalised learning, people still have to have cheap, easy access to the relevant technologies if they are to benefit from them. 'Scalability' will ultimately depend on cheap universal access, which is particularly problematic in the context of mass-based adult education in poor countries. That said, a number of ABE programmes may be able to benefit directly from open and distance education (ODE) based on information technology. These include the planning, training and supervisory staff who are likely to have increasing access to new technologies through their employers. And learner groups themselves could also gain limited access on a small scale, through the growing networks of community learning centres (Perraton & Creed 2002). However, we all recognise that any IT-led model of mass ABE faces considerable challenges, not least financial ones, if it is to provide quality ABE at affordable cost.

One programme currently investigating this area is the Bridges to the Future (BFI) initiative based at the University of Pennsylvania in the USA. This programme is working on the appropriate application of new information technologies to ABE in collaboration with agencies like UNISA in South Africa and the Community Services Foundation in Ghana – and a number of other agencies in India and Mexico (Wagner 2002; see also www.literacy.org). The extract in the next paragraph is taken from the BFI website (December 2002).

Three overlapping target phases of the BFI activities are envisioned: (1) development of tools to improve basic education and literacy through teacher training in selected countries; (2) development of community learning and technology centres (CLTCs) for lifelong learning and income-generation; and (3) development of specialised ICT-supported tools for improving the quality of human development in health, agriculture, HIV/AIDS prevention, etc. Throughout these phases, the BFI will utilise ICTs as 'enablers' both to deliver resources and to monitor progress and effectiveness of the results.

The BFI is a public-private collaboration of national and international agencies, non-profit institutions, corporations and foundations whose main focus is to remove the joint barriers of literacy and technological literacy, thereby assisting the world's poorest peoples to gain a stronger foothold in determining their own social and economic future.

A provisional budget is under preparation, and is expected to total approximately US$3.7 million over its first three years. Outcomes over a full five-year period are expected to include: increased basic and ICT skills an estimated 6.5 million youth and adult learners, creation of 240 CLTCs – some new and most built upon existing ICT resources in schools, community centres (MPCCs) and other centres which have been established and supported previously. Software solutions for teacher education in multiple languages; and end-user solutions in multiple languages for cross-sectoral and broadbased self-help learning. SchoolNet South Africa will serve as the South African secretariat and lead agency for this project. Support for the preparation of this global effort has included, among others: J. P. Morgan, Inc., IBM, Multichoice, Ford Foundation, Kellogg Foundation, UNESCO, OECD and UNICEF. Public and private funding is currently being sought for the implementation phase of the project in South Africa.

The BFI in South Africa will be the first major project in literacy and adult basic education to utilise ICTs to help illiterate, unschooled and out-of-school youth and adults in South Africa. (http://literacy.org/bfi_ili/countries_southafrica.html) Given the tremendous potential for developing highly up to date and interactive education at a distance through the new information technologies (e.g. see Stephenson 2001) it would seem essential to fund such initiatives, particularly in the context of growing EFA needs of the African states (Daniel 2002).

Quality and ABE: A review of some early distance-based approaches in sub-Saharan Africa

ABE using distance learning has a long history in sub-Saharan Africa (Kabwasa & Kaunda 1973; Dodds 1999; Siacewena 2000). Two main approaches can be identified: (1) the mass radio campaign; and (2) the correspondence course plus study group model. In many of the programmes, radio has played a significant role. These approaches have been used for both ABE and literacy development and for various forms of vocational training and development, particularly in agricultural extension and health promotion (Hornik 1988; Dodds 1996; Yates 1998; Perraton 2000). Both the campaign and the study group models try to achieve quality by using a mix of media and structured programming – combining printed materials (self-study units or group flipcharts and learner assignments) with radio broadcasting or cassettes and/or co-ordinated face-to-face group meetings. Specially selected and trained study group leaders or facilitators usually support the groups. The Listen/Read, Discuss, Decide, Apply and Review process has frequently underpinned the quality of the education on offer.

Campaigns

Shortly after independence a number of African states used the radio campaign approach to promote development. In the 1970s Tanzania held five campaigns – two for political purposes, one on health, one on nutrition and one on forestry. At the same time Botswana used similar techniques to raise awareness of its national development plan and ran one campaign on cattle management on tribally owned lands and another on good health practices. In 1982 the Zambian co-operative movement ran a campaign to stimulate interest in co-operatives. However, none of these three states used radio campaigns in the 1990s (Perraton 2000:20). Possibly this is because of the increasing privatisation of the mass media and cost of the airtime under the requirements of structural adjustment, rather than any technical or pedagogic failings. Funds have been hard to find. Many of the Western funding agencies have been unsympathetic to the overtly socialist ideals of some of the campaigns. More recently, Ghana has used radio to lead a literacy campaign in the north, but despite a commitment to multilingualism it has proved virtually impossible to transmit material in all fifteen of the languages identified. And administrative and co-ordination problems have hindered the potential impact of the chosen media mix (Siabi-Mensah 2000; Siacewena 2000). Recently, Mattee, writing on the early Tanzanian campaigns, has argued: 'These [three] campaigns demonstrated beyond doubt the potential of radio as a powerful medium for reaching a wide mass of the people within a short time and without much investment in infrastructure' (Mattee 2000:69).

Apparently, as Hornik (1988) suggests, we have long known how to develop and provide effective quality adult basic and vocational education using mass media:

> In sum an information service with the most promise depends on a mass medium as its central delivery mechanism, incorporates field agents as passive channels, is linked with a substantive ministry, and spends much of its energy and budget gathering and analysing information in order to respond systematically to the heterogeneous needs of its audience … It addresses

> important targets that justify the expense of a slow and intense materials production process and require patience toward the pace of consequential change. (Hornik 1988:163, cited in Perraton 2000:21)

And Mattee, lamenting the decline of farmer training in Tanzania, has also commented:

> Such radio programmes have had limited impact because they are not linked to the agricultural extension or farmer training programmes of the Ministry. Also, since farmers are not organised into radio listening or discussion groups, the information so broadcast is not adequately internalised by farmers. Farmers, therefore, have had limited opportunities for accessing agricultural knowledge and information, particularly considering the agricultural extension services are quite inadequate and the farmer training programme within the Ministry of Agriculture and Co-operatives has virtually ceased to operate. (Mattee 2000:70)

The fact remains that radio based campaign programming has rarely been expanded or built upon during the 1990s. Its potential remains unrealised.

Correspondence education and study groups

There are many kinds of correspondence course plus study group operating in sub-Saharan Africa. They use distance learning materials for a wide range of learning purposes. These include the farm forums (e.g. in Zambia), the adult correspondence colleges and institutes (e.g. the National Correspondence Institution and the Correspondence Department of the Institute of Adult Education, both in Tanzania) and the alternative and open schools (e.g. Namibian and Botswana Open Schools). The INADES and AMREF organisations have maintained their adult agricultural and health promotion programmes using distance education throughout sub-Saharan Africa for over 30 years and Zambia has maintained its Radio Farm Forum programme for a similar period.

INADES-formation

Over the years INADES-formation (the training wing of the African Institute for Economic and Social Development based in Côte-d'Ivoire) has developed outreach programmes (particularly in agriculture and civics) in a number of francophone African countries, and in Kenya, Ethiopia and Tanzania. Since its establishment in 1962, it has worked on a continuing programme of educational provision based on research. Its distance activities rely chiefly on correspondence courses with tutor marked assignments, supported by face-to-face seminars. Seminar programmes are decided in consultation with those who have requested them and with local authorities. They typically last up to three days. Seminars use problem focused enquiry and discussion-based methods suited to adult learning and are often facilitated by local field staff. Over the years INADES-formation (IF) has succeeded in localising its staff, who in theory are more sensitive to the cultural complexities of learning in their own contexts than the foreign priests who used to form the professional backbone of the programme. It has modularised its distance courses and tried to integrate them more closely into the sector-wide rural development programmes with which it is associated. It has responded to changing audience demands by developing marketing courses as the demand for cash cropping outstrips the more traditional agricultural practices. And it has shifted its education emphasis away from the capacity building of individuals, to strengthening groups within society (Perraton 2000:22-25).

Nonetheless, these responses to changing perceptions of need, relevance and quality in training provision have not been sufficient to stop the decline of correspondence education, and it seems that a more radical 'epistemological' break has occurred.

The correspondence courses were seen as merely facilitating the transfer of knowledge from experts to farmers without really creating the necessary capacity for managing change in the rural context (Mattee 2000:71).

Consequently a new training approach has been developed which is more context sensitive – Training Integrated in Peasant's Actions, Challenges and Organisations (TIPACO).

> In this approach training is rooted in the actions being undertaken by the farmers – that is identifying what farmers' development activities are, or what they are interested in doing, identifying necessary skills and working with farmers to develop a training programme that will provide these skills. With the TIPACO approach, IF-Tanzania has redefined its mission, from being a provider of technical knowledge and information to a passive audience of farmers, to one of supporting farmers through building their capacity to identify challenges and opportunities and to take steps that will analyse the development process. Using this approach IF-Tanzania has reorganised its training activities into Training Projects, whereby for each project, trainers work with farmers to learn together through research and training and to act together to implement specific actions. This is known within IF as Action Research Training (ART) … The trend in recent years has been to document the learning process with farmers, which has led to the production of booklets with less technical content, and with more emphasis on methodologies and processes. As a result, correspondence courses are seen as merely playing a supplementary role to the main approach … *Thus currently, correspondence courses no longer form the core of the IF activities, but are rather seen as*

supporting the training projects and benefiting those who cannot be reached directly (Mattee 2000: 72 – emphasis added).

There is no doubt that in the IF context, correspondence course enrolments declined markedly during the 1990s in favour of other more participatory methods. In 1996/7 there were 11 853 trainees enrolled on correspondence courses compared with more than 25 000 in 1989/90. The correspondence self-study model is now seen as a supplement to the more direct, action orientated, participatory methods of basic farmer education.

The Zambian radio farm forums

The Zambian Radio Farm Forums (RFF) offer another experience. A recent research study by Sibalwa (2000) provides the information from which this example is developed. The radio farm forums are run by the National Agricultural Information Service of the Ministry of Agriculture Food and Fisheries. They were first introduced in 1967. The audience for the programme was defined as the rural non-white farming community involved in subsistence agriculture with the potential for increased productivity. The programmes are broadcast by the Zambia National Broadcasting Corporation. Farmers establish listening groups under the guidance of agricultural extension officers. Each radio discussion group has up to fifteen farmers who identify a chairperson and a secretary from among their number. The 30 minute radio discussion programmes are broadcast in English and seven additional Zambian languages (Tonga, Nyanja, Lozi, Bemba, Luvale, Kaonde and Lunda). By 1992, about 1 000 RFF were taking part.

The objectives of the programme have remained the same since the programme was started. Listeners should be able to correctly apply the technical information received; correctly identify and describe some of the common crop and animal diseases and pests; and effectively advise other farmers on good farming practices.

Sibalwa (2000:115, 125) reports there is little evidence that the farmers were involved in the design of the RFF programme or in the production of the radio programmes. However, he says, the RFF do play a vital role in transferring agricultural information to inexperienced rural farmers and in helping them apply new ideas successfully without the direct help of the Agricultural Extension Officers.

Initially (1964-1990) the government encouraged the formation of listening groups using a variety of incentives. It supplied the groups with free radios and batteries. It provided subsidies on seed and fertilisers to encourage farmers to apply what they learned through the radio programmes. The groups, in their turn, sent feedback reports to the extension officers using a government prepaid mail service.

However, since 1991 the government no longer provides these incentives and the policy is one of self-help/reliance. The free market economic policy has also meant that the ZNBC now charges for the airtime for the broadcasts. All these factors have led to a decline in the RFF. Despite the many problems with the model there can be no doubt the RFF are valued by those who do make use of them.

And Sibalwa's (2000:123, 127) study shows there is evidence that they have reached poor farmers with low levels of education and improved their attitudes and farming practices:

> The survey shows that members of the radio farm forum attend meetings regularly mostly after harvesting but in most cases they meet and listen to the programmes as long as they have batteries and good reception. They described the meetings as very important because they learn a lot of new farming methods like crop rotation and soil conservation … the men had recognised the fact that their wives benefited from the Radio Farm Forum programme and had given their permission to listen to the programme.

Despite the potential of the RFF there is no evidence that the programme is sustainable on a self-help basis. Or that the farmers gain an improved standard of living as a result of the new learning – mainly because the government offers no support to small-scale farmers for accessing inputs or for marketing their produce. Further the restructuring of the civil service means that many experienced agricultural extension officers are being laid off because they lack the required qualifications. Eventually there will be nobody to produce the radio lessons.

Despite introducing a national system of basic education that was well suited to the needs and circumstances of the Zambian rural poor farmers, it seems the future of the RFF in the neo-liberal, market driven age is uncertain. It is unlikely it can be sustained on a self-help basis alone.

Contexts: Some recent developments and challenges that affect quality in ABE

In this section I discuss six recent developments that have a 'macro level' bearing on how quality is defined and achieved in ABE: (1) recent World Bank research on ABE; (2) globalisation and the provision of state education; (3) the challenge to the human capital theory of development; (4) the new social literacies; (5) declining linguistic diversity; (6) how we define illiteracy.

What does recent research suggest about how to provide effective/quality ABE/literacy?

Over the last three decades the approach to providing literacy has shifted from the mass campaign approach (which in some cases was highly politicised), designed by an external international body, implemented by a government ministry and focused on the eradication goal, to more demand driven, community orientated pluralistic approaches which have stressed longer-term social gains to individuals and groups. Such models have also tended to use more context sensitive, localised and participatory models of action and learning. These approaches have further served the good governance goal through a deepening of popular democratic processes. In the 1970s the campaigns were designed by international bodies like UNESCO and implemented through government adult education departments. Today, the design and implementation of many ABE and literacy programmes are much more complex affairs – involving a more diversified range of stakeholders and organisations including local community organisations, central government ministries, international funding agencies and international or indigenous NGOs and capacity building organisations (CBOs) with detailed specialist knowledge and experience of basic education provision (e.g. ActionAid and BUNYAD). They use local participatory forms of analysis for programme design and learning such as Participatory Rural/Rapid Appraisal, Participatory Needs Analysis, Participatory Learning Appraisal (see Rifkin & Pridmore 2001 for a recent discussion). Recent debates appear to be swinging away from literacy and education for its own sake to a more vocationally driven and applied rationale. The need to help people develop better livelihoods for improved income generation and poverty alleviation, as determined by the local people themselves, precedes other more decontextualised educational purposes. It is argued that literacy is best derived out of the experience of developing livelihoods rather than being developed first as prerequisite programming (Oxenham, Diallo, Katahoire, Petkova-Mwangi & Sall 2002).

Recent research by Oxenham et al (2002:2-3) suggests some basic prerequisites for developing successful ABE initiatives: (1) … the diversity of possibilities for improving established livelihoods and developing new ones appears so wide as to demand extreme flexibility, imagination and resourcefulness …(3) The program should be well run with competent, reliable and adequately supported instructors, and second the program is well adapted to the interests and conditions of its participants … (4) Education and training programs for very poor adults need to offer very clear, concrete and immediate reasons to justify enrolment and ensure perseverance. (5) Programs that start from livelihood skills seem to stand a stronger chance of success… (6) Organisations that are more concerned with livelihoods and other aspects of development seem to be better at designing and delivering effective combinations of livelihoods and literacy than organisations more focused on education. (7) NGOs seem to be more flexible than government agencies in responding to local and changing needs … (8) Deriving literacy/numeracy content from livelihood skills and integrating it with livelihood training from the very start seems more promising than running the two components in parallel… (9) Livelihood-plus literacy/numeracy programs can greatly improve their chances of success, if they incorporate training in savings, credit, and business management, along with actual access to credit. (10) Chances of success are even greater if a program works with established groups of people who share a common purpose, rather than with individual applicants… (11) Early evaluations of … the use of vouchers to buy training are very favourable (12)… programs that are well negotiated with their prospective learners in association with local authorities and leaders are likely to be more effective than programs that are simply put on offer …(13)… the minimum period needed by a really illiterate person with normal learning abilities to attain a degree of literacy and numeracy sufficient to support advancement of a livelihood seemed to be some 360 hours of instruction and practice… (14) arranging for both livelihood specialists and literacy instructors is more prudent than relying on literacy instructors to undertake livelihood instruction or income generating activities in addition to teaching literacy and numeracy.

Some of these findings echo the conclusions of UNESCO's own Experimental World Literacy Programme, implemented three decades before (Coombs 1985). It is vital to assess new findings against what is already known from earlier work.

Globalisation and declining state sovereignty

Oxenham et al's (2002) recommendation to develop more flexible relationships between NGOs and state institutions to facilitate the provision of ABE is an interesting one in the increasingly diversified nexus of state/private educational provision. Such unions would certainly seem to have the potential to improve the quality of ABE in many settings (Unterhalter & Dutt 2001). But such a move could also generate unproductive state and NGO tensions if not dealt with sensitively, as a recent sub-Saharan African study has shown (Miller-Grandvaux, Welmond & Wolff 2002). The forces of globalisation are relentlessly assailing state autonomy. In conjunction with, and parallel to, the grassroots pressures from below (from community organisations and NGOs), we can also see an increasingly prominent and closer coupling of international macro level planning, monitoring and information sharing through the EFA (education for all) process, with state level planning and action through Poverty Reduction Strategy Plans (PRSPs) and Education Sector Strategic Plans (ESSPs). Both these processes (the top-down pull from the supra-state EFA bodies like UNESCO and the World Bank and the bottom-up push from increasingly global NGOs like ActionAid and Oxfam) can be thought of as examples of globalisation processes which are simultaneously squeezing the sovereignty of the nation state. We should be careful to consider some of the implications of these processes and recognise that we have no viable alternative to the nation state as the primary adult education provider. There is no other entity which can build and deliver the EFA promise in the same way as the nation state. Certainly supra-state bodies and NGOs can complement, encourage and enhance state provision, but neither yet has any legal mandate to enforce their will, or necessarily the means to raise the resources needed or to substitute for those provided through state taxation. International bodies will undoubtedly encourage, professionally support and where necessary publicly shame and cajole states which fail to make progress with EFA. But they have no mandate to enforce the targets. Whatever is achieved will primarily have to be done through, and in partnership with, national state education systems. And as Lauglo (2001) points out, it is imperative to develop ABE systems that build capacity within the state at all levels of the administrative, support and delivery services, both centrally and locally, if the more favoured participative approaches are to be sustainable and offer quality.

Investment in ABE has remained low during the 1990S: The continued dominance of human capital theory

It has been accepted orthodoxy for many years that helping a person become literate is cheaper through primary schooling than through adult provision, such as literacy campaigns. We know that when ABE programmes and literacy campaigns have been judged in terms of their cost efficiency or effectiveness compared with primary schooling, they have been found wanting (Perraton 1983). However, this position has tended to prioritise the economic value of state action over other, more ethical, aspects of the development purpose. The finding has long suited those wedded to the historically dominant neo-liberal human capital theory of development. The position conflates the means with the ends of development, privileging the former to the advantage of elite social groups. Such a view does little to stem rising tensions on the periphery of factionalised or collapsed states. And it is now more clearly accepted that the provision of primary schooling alone is unlikely to solve the problem of adult illiteracy and marginality. Adult illiteracy will not just fade away as universal schooling gains ground (UNESCO 2002).

Recently a number of commentators, including Perraton and Creed (2002:27) and Lauglo (2001) have pointed out that adult education has been a neglected aspect of EFA since the Jomtien commitments were made. Lauglo's study, in particular, is significant because it shows how earlier World Bank analyses of the performance of ABE programming and its subsequent lending policies and practice may have been misguided. It is now thought that the cost effectiveness of much ABE programming is much better than first assumed (Lauglo 2001:12-22). However, the persistent low rate of investment in adult education is hardly surprising, given the continued dominance of the modernisation paradigm and human capital model of development. Policymakers in many Ministries of Education understandably have not questioned the World Bank argument that investment in ABE is less effective than investment in primary schooling for children. Consequently during the 1990s many governments and donors have prioritised primary education over adult basic provision.

The new social literacies

Over the last decade the way one defines and understands the meaning of literacy has also come under scrutiny. The latest UNESCO EFA Global Monitoring Report (2002:17) indicates that there has been a change in what counts as being literate: 'The meaning of literacy has developed radically since the World Conference on Education for All in Jomtien in 1990. Conceived now in the plural as 'literacies', and embedded in a range of life and livelihood situations, literacy differs according to purpose, context, use, script and institutional framework acquired' (UNESCO 2002:17). 'Literacy is no longer seen as a singular concept, but rather as plural 'literacies'... As individuals we all use multiple literacies – for example, for work, for personal matters, in different languages, and so on. Within any community there will be a range of literacies – understanding what these are and how they are structured is necessary for negotiating whether and how literacy might be acquired' (UNESCO 2002:60).

The challenge of achieving quality ABE has been made more complex by recent debates about the nature of adult literacy. In the past, such discussions have often been regarded as a largely technical matter, as in the development of an individual skill. It was thought that basically people needed to be taught to decode letters and numbers. Once they could do that and build up, represent and communicate meaning using these newly acquired signs and symbols they could then be said to be 'literate'. But this technicist, somewhat reified, position on literacy implies a deficit view of learners and their life context. It has tended to assume that nothing was actually going on in the learner's life setting, and so any literacy programme would have to *introduce something* in order to stimulate and 'create' literacy among potential users. It has been argued that such a model disguises its assumptions about how people learn and what they ought to value. And there is some evidence to suggest that the approach has essentially been used to impose a particularly Western conception of literacy on other cultures, promoting a kind of universal view of what is required for effective citizenship in the modern world (read western/capitalist free market economy – see Street 2001). The promotion of such a model contributes to the continuing process of social and political homogenisation and cultural convergence, evidenced most dramatically by the death of so many of the world's languages (May 2001).

More recently, it has been suggested that literacy is much more of a social process, which is constructed from epistemological principles that are embedded in a wide variety of contexts, all of which are suffused with power. 'The ways in which people address reading and writing are themselves rooted in conceptions of knowledge, identity and being. It is not valid to suggest "literacy" can be "given" neutrally and then its "social" effects only experienced afterwards' (Street 2001:7-8).

To this school of thought (labelled by Street the 'ideological model'), literacy is not simply a neutral technical process which develops certain kinds of skill. The assumption here is that there is something already going on in the context, and what those charged with fostering literacies need to do, is to discover what this is and build on it. Curricula and programming are thus developed out of an analysis of what already exists – rather than developed from assumptions of deficit and that something needs to be added to the context in order to 'create' literacy. Hence the task 'can be seen less as eradicating illiteracy and more as creating increasingly literate environments and learning societies' (UNESCO 2002:60).

It is necessary to consider the power dimensions of these reading and writing processes by considering how people take hold of literacies – what do they do with them and how do they put them to use? Where are people going if they take on one form of literacy rather than another? If one regards literacy as a singular, apolitical, largely neutral, technicist concept, 'the contestation over what counts as literacy and whose literacy is dominant gets lost' (Street 2001:9).

Literacy, according to the new social literacy theorists, is embedded in other social practices and is hence acquired alongside and through other life skills, while at the same time enhancing such life skills. Literacy, in a technical sense, refers to the ability of an individual or group to interact successfully through various kinds of communication practices with wider society. Low levels of literacy indicate low levels of wider social interaction. But this does not mean that people are not engaged in highly successful and diverse forms of communicative practice within their own, narrower, more localised community groupings.

These two positions on literacy (literacy as a technical skill and literacies as essentially social constructs) have been labelled the autonomous and the ideological models. However, views about what constitutes literacy and consequently how people become 'literate' remain much contested, and the view of the new literacy advocates is not yet widely accepted.

Marginality and identity: Some implications of the decline in language diversity for ABE

It is evident in the present period of globalisation that we are also in a period of accelerated language decline. Currently 96% of the world's 6 000 languages are spoken by only 4% of its people (Crystal 1999a, 1999b, cited in May 2001:4). A recent survey by the US Summer Institute of Linguistics estimates that as many as 5 000 of the world's 6 000 languages are spoken by fewer than 100 000 speakers. Krauss (1992, 1995) suggests that at the end of this century, less than 600 and maybe only 300 languages may actually survive. In a period of language death/ language shift and subsequent cultural homogenisation, it would not be surprising that a proportion of the 850 million adults who are presently categorised as 'illiterate' are actually defined as being so due to their inability to communicate with literacy surveyors or census takers using research instruments written in an official state language. There is a particularly small number of officially recognised state languages: 'around 120 nation states have adopted either English, French, Spanish or Arabic while another 50 have a local language as the language of the state ...and there are another 45 languages that are accorded regional status. In short, currently less than 1.5 per cent of the world's languages are recognised officially by nation states' (May 2001:5).

The increasing congruence here between the total number of nation states (presently around 200 and growing) and the number of languages in the world should not go unnoticed. It has been argued that this is a natural process of selection, and that language death, like species death, is merely a process of 'survival of the fittest'. But languages are not biological entities, they are political forms, forms which are socially, politically and historically constructed, privileged and maintained by those with the power and resources to do so. As May (2001:5) reminds us, 'Languages are "created" out of the politics of state making, not – as we often assume – the other way around'. One can argue that a reduction in language diversity undermines the cultural and symbolic capital of millions of people. The process inevitably serves to further marginalise the cultures and identities of those who do not speak the increasingly narrow range of official languages. This homogenisation of language and culture presents ABE with significant ethical, pedagogic and political challenges, which lie at the heart of any debate about educational quality, relevance and effectiveness.

How literacy is defined has implications for making judgments about quality

Literacy is not something that is easily defined or universally understood. For Rogers (forthcoming:3) literacy means 'working with texts. Be they on paper, on a computer screen, blackboards or some other surface or medium'. This seems a reasonable definition to work from. But how literacy comes to be defined and subsequently measured can be significant when making judgements about provision and ultimately quality. For example, the recent UNESCO Global EFA Monitoring Report (November 2002) gives details of the results of the first Lao National Literacy Survey. This survey defined a literate person as 'one who can read and write simple sentences in Lao and perform simple arithmetic calculations'

(UNESCO 2002:67 Box 2.13). At first glance this would again seem a not unreasonable definition to use. However, the definition serves to illustrate two points: How far is the Lao state, in defining literacy in terms of reading, writing and calculation, using a narrow interpretation of literacy in its singular form rather than regarding literacies as plural forms? And is literacy being defined in terms of the ability to communicate largely through a single official state language – Lao?

In the report the adult literacy rate (age 15 and over) in Lao PDR in 1999 is given as 64.8% (76.2% male – 53.4% female) (see UNESCO 2002 – Annex table 2: 208).

One might ask how many of the 35% of the population currently defined as 'illiterate' by the national survey are actually literate in languages other than Lao? Similarly, how many of those people might also demonstrate other forms of literacy that have not been recognised because they were not measured by the instruments used in the national survey? To what extent is the illiteracy/literacy instrument actually constructing the level of literacy by the way it is choosing to define and measure it? The point is a general one and stems from the recent debates over whether literacy is a single universal technical skill – or a series of communicative practices which derive their purchase and meaning from diverse socially and politically determined situations (cf. Street 2001 above).

Progress on the Dakar Adult Literacy Goal – Who are our 'Illiterates' and Where do They Live? The World Education Forum held in Dakar in April 2000 pledged to halve adult illiteracy levels by 2015. The goal was stated thus: 'Achieving a 50% improvement in levels of adult literacy by 2015, especially for women, and equitable access to basic and continuing education for all adults' (UNESCO 2000 para 7).

Are we on track to do this? Relatively speaking some progress is being made – albeit slowly. In 1980 we had a 70% global adult literacy rate which has increased to 80% in 2000. But the absolute figures still remain very high, because of continued population growth: 870 million people were defined as 'illiterate' in 1980 and 852 million are categorised this way in 2000. Further, over one third of this number live in India and a further 27% live in China, Pakistan or Bangladesh. Hence 61% of the people who lack literacy live in just four countries. If we look at the youth literacy situation (15-24 years) it is estimated there will be 107 million youth without literacy in 2015, of whom 67 million will be female. There are estimated to have been 140 million youth (86 million female) regarded as illiterate in 2000.

In 2002 it was reported that there were 97 countries with adult literacy rates of below 95%. It is estimated that 18 have a high chance of achieving the Dakar target by 2015 and of the remaining 79 some 40 countries have literacy rates below 70% and based on their 1990-2000 rate of progress are not expected to reach the Dakar target. Twenty-two of these 40 countries are in sub-Saharan Africa, eight in the Arab states and North Africa and four in South and West Asia. We can see that adult illiteracy is more concentrated in South and East Asia, compared with Africa. (UNESCO 2002:17-18). But these aggregate percentage figures at the international level do little to convey the scale of the challenge at the individual state level. What is the situation at the national level in sub-Saharan Africa? Lauglo (2001) presented figures for levels of illiteracy in sub-Saharan Africa. Which countries have the highest absolute levels of illiteracy in terms of total population figures? Table 1 shows absolute levels of illiteracy by country by size of illiterate population.

Table 1 Illiteracy levels in sub-Saharan Africa

Country	Illiterate population (000s)	Illiteracy rate %
Nigeria	22 803	36
Ethiopia	20 664	61
Sudan	7 675	43
Mozambique	6 101	56
Burkina Faso	4 845	77
Niger	4 688	84
Tanzania	4 551	25
Côte-d'Ivoire	4 457	53
South Africa	3 916	15
Mali	3 604	60
Uganda	3 565	33
Ghana	3 426	30
Senegal	3 290	63
Kenya	3 015	18
Malawi	2 296	40
Guinea	2 186	59
Cameroon	2 099	25
Benin	2 066	63
Chad	1 937	46
Burundi	1 867	52
Sierra Leone	1 732	64
Rwanda	1 394	33
Central African Republic	1 113	54
Togo	1 073	43
Zambia	1 065	22

From Table 1 it can be seen that 25 sub-Saharan African countries have more than a million people within their borders who are presently categorised as 'illiterate'. But precisely who are the 7.7 million people in Sudan who are regarded as illiterates? Or the three million or so in Kenya who are so categorised? What languages do they speak? What communicative practices are already going on in their communities and how do they maintain themselves in their present livelihoods? What is the nature of their literacy situation? How might open and distance education programmes work from and build on their life situations in ways that do not demean or devalue their community circumstances or personal achievements? Let me now introduce two case examples from recent work the International Extension College has been involved in to illustrate possible approaches. These are the Building Literacy with Solo Press Project (BLSP), a post-literacy project, and the Women in Fishing Industry Project (WIFIP), a livelihoods and social development project involving radio-based distance learning and study groups.

Case 1: The Building Literacy with SOLO Press Project (BLSP). Twenty-five years of civil war have had a huge impact on the Sudan, displacing thousands of people from the south into the north. Settlements for the displaced populations are scattered through the desert, around Khartoum, Omdurman and Gezira state. Eritrean refugees fleeing the struggle for independence first started arriving in Sudan in 1965. They live in established camps in the north-east. Generations of children have been born in these camps and whilst voluntary repatriation is an option, many Eritrean refugees are choosing to stay in Sudan, sometimes only 16 kilometres from their 'home' (Thomas 1996:18). Overall, there has been a lack of education provision and basic resources in these settlements. The refugee camps have had some UNHCR programmes offering activities. Settlements for the internally displaced are often unofficial, meaning that even less provision and basic services have been available. Community members are mostly excluded from formal education and employment due to language barriers, gender barriers and prejudice. In addition, there is a lack of basic skills, due to interruption of education as a result of war, drought and famine.

The Sudan Open Learning Organisation (SOLO), now a Sudanese NGO, was set up by the International Extension College (IEC) in 1984 to respond to some of the needs emerging in camps and settlements, and has been working with these communities promoting and delivering a range of non-formal and open learning programmes. SOLO delivers programmes in partnership with NGOs and governmental agencies, including teacher assistance courses, primary health care, and literacy classes. Through face-to-face adult literacy classes SOLO has reached over 6 000 learners.

Even with the initial success of SOLO's literacy classes, barriers to learning have remained. Whilst SOLO was providing basic education for adults, there was no follow up to the literacy classes, no 'next step'. Once the course was over, people were considered 'literate', and provision ceased. In addition to this, the profound lack of reading and writing material available to the newly literate populations and their exclusion from 'mainstream' society, meant that applying the literacy in a functional capacity was near to impossible.

In response to this, SOLO and IEC planned the Building Literacy in Sudan with SOLO Press project (BLSP). The BLSP model is based around the creation of community-based reading and writing circles facilitated by Community Liaison Workers (CLWs). CLWs are selected from the settlements and camps themselves and trained in a variety of community development skills. This training includes the development of the circles, generation of participant ideas and facilitation of discussion. Most central to the model is the facilitation of writing and reading in the circles. Particular assistance is given with the production of pieces of writing, which reflect the interests of the circle members.

Difficulties in retention of skills, inappropriate primers and 'staged' literacy classes, with post-literacy often being considered a cover for 'the deficiencies of initial literacy training', (Rogers 1998:2) are being overcome through a community-centred literacy and development process in an open learning, non-formal environment. In effect what is happening is that momentum is growing and BLSP is including participants beyond the initial target group, to include neighbours, daughters, cousins, friends and community leaders, who are creating their own groups and writing their own stories.

BLSP is about the *practice* and process of post-literacy.

It is about *practice* in the sense that the model was created in response to a lack of resources for newly literate refugees and internally displaced people. BLSP occurred as a layer over a literacy 'foundation' (Wrightson 2002:1). The project therefore was initially aimed at graduates from SOLO's literacy classes who were not retaining their literacy skills due to a lack of reading and writing materials. There has also been little opportunity for neo-literate people to apply functional literacy to the wider environment.

BLSP is creating a model whereby participants can gather together, at times convenient to them, to practise literacy skills. The writing and reading of their own stories of peace, war, marriage customs, legends and histories enables people to practise the technical skills of literacy and apply them to texts reflective of their lives and therefore meaningful to them. The pieces of writing created in the camps and settlements go through a comprehensive and recently tested selection process, which includes editing, designing and revising by the circles and community liaison workers, before being printed and published by SOLO Press.

The *process* of post-literacy is arguably the most central and exciting element of the model. BLSP goes beyond the act of retaining practical functional elements of literacy. Rather it set out to facilitate the means by which community members benefit from the actual process of learning, of gaining knowledge and understanding of their environments. Moving through the BLSP process is enabling people to have access to a forum where their voices are significant. They begin to shape the direction of their own learning and development by discussing issues, concerns and ideas in a supportive and autonomous arena. The model is not top-down, but an example of open learning. This openness allows for a flexibility and responsiveness, which in turn allow the participants to create the experience as they move through it.

BLSP has just begun its fourth year of a total of five. A review, which took place in the third year, revealed a high level of self-confidence amongst participants. The expansion of the model has been phenomenal, as in addition to the original circles, built and cultivated by the CLWs, more groups began to form naturally. These new groups are facilitated by Group Leaders, who are former circle participants. Now for every original circle there are between three and five groups.

The Arabic word *quiraeya* (pronounced: queer-ae-eeya) has been adopted to describe the BLSP model. It is derived from the Arabic verb to read (*iqra*) and was first used by adult educators in Tunisia to replace a word meaning the 'eradication of illiteracy'. The positive connotations of *quiraeya* go beyond its meaning as the 'name' of reading, to also describe the *process* of literacy. The model goes beyond the technical ability to read and write words, to include the process of exchanging ideas, gaining knowledge, the ability to think critically and the nurturing of active social and political commitment. *Quiraeya* is about the knowing, learning, thinking, discussing and creating that come with literacy. In BLSP we are able to observe people's growth in 'knowing' and applying what they 'know' to activities which enhance their lives and the lives of the wider community and they are doing this in their daily lives. BLSP as a post-literacy project goes beyond post-literacy as the 'next step' to formal literacy classes. *Quiraeya* is also a model with its own momentum, a momentum which is created and owned by the communities themselves. The ownership of the process by participants is due largely to the fact that their words are transformed into tangible, published works, distributed throughout camps and settlements. Their voices, their words, are 'out there' for people with no previous access to resources to read, and they are reflective of their experiences and their lives. *Quiraeya* recognises the different dimensions of 'literacy' and 'post-literacy' and facilitates the process of learning, knowing and engaging in the world and all of its texts (Lockwood, 2002).

Case 2: Women in Fishing Industry Project (WIFIP). WIFIP is a non-formal programme offering education via radio and audio to women who work within the fishing industry along the shores of Lake Victoria, Kenya. An HIV/AIDS survey in 2000 carried out by WIFIP's Project Manager established that women in these communities had expressed the need for information and education on health issues, in particular HIV/AIDS and sexually transmitted infections (STIs). The women said that although they were aware that HIV/AIDS information was available mainly in larger towns, they were unable to get adequate access to it. Through the survey, the women also voiced a desire for education and help to develop their business skills within the fishing industry.

Currently, men within the community undertake fishing on the lake. The women's role on the beaches is focused on purchasing fish from the fishermen, which they then clean and, on more rural beaches, preserve through sun or smoke drying. They then sell the fish at markets, which can be up to three hours walk from the beach. Many women who join the fishing industry have migrated from other communities as widows, divorcees or young mothers. Before they are able to work in this market system, they are allocated to one fisherman with whom they can trade. As many women have to trade on credit through lack of funds, they are left vulnerable to the sexual demands of their supplier when they are unable to pay and consequently risk contracting STIs and HIV.

Through a partnership between the Tropical Institute for Community Health and Development (TICH), Kisumu, Kenya, and the International Extension College, Cambridge, UK, a non-formal radio education programme is being co-ordinated and managed to deliver health and small business management education. Ultimately the project aims to enable these women to have a voice within this development by creating a supportive environment in which they can realise their educational, economic and social potential.

WIFIP is currently approaching the end of its first year of implementation. Radio programmes are being designed and produced locally in a dramatic format supported by tutorial presentation. The drama storyline that has been developed for the broadcasts is strongly influenced by scenarios that the women have described, and much of the recording of the programmes has been on location on the beaches, to provide a sense of reality and familiarity to the listeners. At the beginning of the project's second year, the pilot phase will commence, in which the radio programmes will be transmitted twice a week through the local radio station to the Kisumu region. The broadcasts will be transmitted at times which suit the routines of the women and their families.

The programmes will also be distributed on audiocassette to women's learning groups. The learning groups have developed from recognised welfare groups of 15 to 20 women who work in the fishing industry. The groups meet daily, under a chairperson and a secretary and a treasurer for an established revolving fund scheme, whereby one woman can benefit from contributions from the group to support her household for that particular week. It is the individuals who take a lead role in these groups who have been identified by the women to act as group leaders for the learning groups. The group leaders will receive training through WIFIP to facilitate discussions arising from the audiocassettes. Audiocassettes allow the programmes to be stopped and discussed or replayed when necessary, and accompanying flipchart materials provide visual backup to prompt debate or reinforce messages within the programmes.

The group leaders will also be integral in compiling feedback from the groups during the pilot phase, to ensure the programmes are meeting the needs of the women, are at an appropriate level and are of interest. Programmes will be revised in response to this feedback for the expansion phase in year three. The small business and health education incorporated in the dramas will demonstrate alternative ways in which situations can be dealt with and provide the skills to do so. The development of skills in small business management will increase the women's confidence and allow them to manage their financial situation without dependence or vulnerability to men in the community. Through information on health issues, women will become more aware of situations which may put their health at risk and be provided with the knowledge to avoid this.

Through the learning groups, over the pilot phase and the expansion phase, more than 700 women will have access to the programmes. It is envisaged that over 100,000 people within the community, women, men and youths, will also benefit from access to the programmes through the twice-weekly radio transmissions.

The project is also designed to give financial support for the women to top up whatever little money they are already trading with. It is envisaged that with improved business skills, and being better informed on health issues, the women will be able to manage and sustain a revolving fund and even increase their capital base. A baseline study has been carried out during the first year of WIFIP to ascertain the level of knowledge and current practices of women and others in the community. Impact studies will be undertaken in the pilot and expansion phases to measure changes in comparison to the baseline study and consequently the impact of the education delivered by radio and audio (McCulloch and Kere, 2002).

Analysis of the BUSP and WIFIP cases

We now briefly analyse these case designs in view of the research offered by Oxenham et al (2002) and consider them in relation to some recent writing on adult learning theory (Rogers, forthcoming). We do this in an attempt to identify some key principles for the design of *quality* ABE projects and learning experiences that might also draw on open and distance learning elements. Table 2 below offers an analysis of the two projects in relation to the design suggestions identified by Oxenham et al (2002).

Table 2 Analysis of BUSP and WIFIP projects

Findings/suggested features	BUSP	WIFIP	Comments/explanation
Building on established livelihoods.	No	Yes	SOLO builds on its established education materials development and printing capacity, and the reading materials generated through the project are sold in the market by the authors and the CLWs. Funds go back to the writing circles managed by SOLO's Post-Literacy Co-ordinator and CLWs. But it is not a learner livelihoods programme. WIFP is offering information and education in the context of a livelihood development project.
Run by competent, reliable, adequately supported instructors.	?	?	SOLO offers training and support to Community Literacy Workers. The work of the CLWs is monitored and their impact assessed by the Post-Literacy Co-ordinator. WIFIP have Group Leaders who are identified by the women's circles themselves and then trained in study circle facilitation techniques around the radio programmes.

Discussion: Towards Some Principles for Achieving Quality in ABE Through ODL. A number of principles seem to emerge from this brief review of using ODL for enhancing ABE quality: (1) the importance of putting participatory approaches at the centre; (2) treating adults as equals; (3) ensuring learning remains context sensitive; (4) emphasising curriculum as process over curriculum as product; (5) making learning active and applied to tangible livelihood goals; (6) keeping participation at the centre of the process

Putting participation at the centre. It would seem ABE learning programmes need to derive from needs assessments which involve the learners themselves directly in analysing their interests and identifying areas of need (Participatory Needs Assessments). Perhaps quality ABE programming approaches should also work to identify what literacy and livelihoods already exist in the communities they are intending to serve and build on them. But participatory approaches should not

Findings/suggested features	BUSP	WIFIP	Comments/explanation
Adapted to the needs and conditions of the participants.	Yes	Yes	Both projects were designed on the basis of participatory needs assessments involving local potential participants and stakeholders. This is a continuous, on-going process – the projects are shaped in response to expressions of changing needs.
Offering clear, con-crete reasons to justify enrolment and continued participa-tion.	Possibly	Possib-ly	BLSP was established in response to requests from neo-literates to practise their skills. In both projects there was field advocacy.
Beginning with liveli-hoods first. Derive and develop literacies from the development of livelihoods.	No	No	No – the BLSP project begins from an assumption that literacy comes first/runs parallel with livelihoods. WIFIP focuses on livelihoods – it is not a literacy project – but it took the lack of literacy into account in its design (e.g. use of radio as lead medium).
Developing partner-ships with livelihood organisations in preference to educa-tion organisations.	No	Yes	Both projects were developed in partnership with local service provider organisations. TICH is more a develop-ment through health awareness organisa-tion. SOLO is education focused.
Where feasible involving flexible NGOs	Yes	Yes	Both SOLO and TICH are NGOs. How flexible they are is debatable. TICH has not yet integrated WIFIP into its programming. SOLO has integrated BLSP.
Deriving literacy/ numeracy from livelihoods and integrating it into the livelihood training programmes.	No	Yes?	Projects were essentially planned on the assumption that literacy is needed for livelihood – literacy precedes livelihood. Some evidence of literacy integration into livelihood training evident in WIFIP.
Incorporating training in savings, credit and small business management.	To come	Yes	WIFIP has this as a major strand of its programming (merry-go-round savings). Not in the original BLSP design but this need has emerged and been recognised during implementation.

Findings/suggested features	BUSP	WIFIP	Comments/explanation
Giving access to credit.	No	Yes	WIFIP gives access to small credit advances. SOLO does not.
Working with established groups who share common goals.	Yes – they are graduates of SOLO's literacy courses	Yes in some cases	SOLO works with established refugee groups. WIFIP works with migrant workers seeking to integrate into new social systems and develop new local support groups, e.g. women's fish smoking groups. However, some groups had to be established through the project.
Using vouchers to enable participants to buy training.	No	No	Neither project has introduced voucher co-ordinated training purchase systems.
Providing a minimum of 360 hours of instruction and training for literacy to support a livelihood.	NoBLSP works with people who are already 'literate'	No	Study group programming variable lengths – often determined by the length of the radio programmes.
Employing separate specialist literacy and livelihood trainers –not combining the roles.	Yes – in some ways	Yes – to a limited extent	BLSP incorporates local expert trainers in livelihood skills in response to specific requests from different groups. WIFIP uses specialist livelihoods experts to ensure programmes are accurate.

stop there. They also need to infuse the whole curriculum development and implementation experience so that learners are themselves directly involved in the design, development, experience, and critical assessment and improvement of their basic education programmes. Information transfer from outside is still necessary – but it should be matched to the defined needs and experiences of the recipient users themselves.

Treating adults as equals. Adults construct identities while learning – at the same time they also have identities constructed for them by others (e.g. peers and learning facilitators). They try out new concepts of self and of being and becoming while learning. The hierarchical relationships that exist between the teacher and the child in schools often sit more comfortably with the child's concept of self in relation to a teacher than they do with adults in relation to their tutors As such, stronger, more horizontal relationships need to be promoted within which adults are recognised and treated as equals – whatever their background, expertise or previous experience (Rogers forthcoming).

Ensuring learning is context sensitive: deriving *content from experience and applying what is learned.* Where appropriate, programmes might try to build out of learner literacies and post-literacy. This might be done after close analysis of the context, which involves the learners themselves, and by facilitating the development of authentic materials designed and where feasible written by the learners, as in the BLSP project in Sudan. The Zambian Radio Farm Forums project showed that the programming was developed by agricultural extension officers without the direct involvement of the farmers themselves – and although it achieved some positive changes, this approach appears out of kilter with the latest thinking on multiple socially constructed literacies and the more participative approaches to adult education. Although Sibalwa's (2000) study reports the relevance of the programme and provides some evidence of the adoption of innovation, the fact remains the programme is not growing and it appears unsustainable on its present model. Further, the INADES-formation experience shows that the programme leaders in Tanzania have now rejected the old transmissionist correspondence model of distance adult education in favour of more action research orientated and participatory approaches.

Emphasising processes over products. ABE programmes might perhaps try to give more emphasise to curriculum processes over products. We know that many distance education institutions have produced excellent self-study texts. These have worked well to guide independent learning. Where there is a need to introduce new ideas, externally generated materials will still play an significant part in the development process. But effective quality ABE is more often group based, and therefore probably needs to develop approaches which produce texts that help stimulate and record the more participatory and applied forms of learning (ideally derived from participatory reflective analyses of practice).

Well-designed individual self-study materials might be used to supplement group-learning processes. These should build in active and applied learning using 'reflective action guide' and 'dialogic' type activity designs (see Lockwood 1992), as these can help to further the personal construction of meaning. Texts that rely too heavily on the 'tutorial in print' activity approach (Rowntree 1990) would seem to (1) place learners in a strongly hierarchical social situation in respect of their tutors – relationships which may not suit the learners preferred identity constructions; and (2) serve to develop and reinforce overly transmissionist and dependent pedagogies.

Too much directive pedagogy may undermine or devalue, rather than celebrate, the more tacit and implicit knowledge bases of ABE participants, to the extent that such tacit knowledge fails to surface or be recognised or valued.

It would seem the introduction of new content is in the ABE context often best used to support and supplement reflective action rather than to try to lead it. The use of expertly crafted and essentially 'transmitted educational product' to lead the ABE process has long been challenged. In an age of socially constructed multiple literacies, it looks even less appropriate.

Making learning active and applied to tangible livelihood goals. The linkage between learning and what one does with that learning is at the core of ABE. The new literacies for livelihoods movement would seem to place the development of the livelihood benefit at the forefront of the curriculum planning process. If the learning does not result in tangible, visible and quite immediate gains to learners, why should they persist with devoting the significant time investments needed to gain skills that may not help them? Clearly there is a strong tension in ABE between learning for vocational application and economic gain and learning to enhance wider life goals, as Singh (2000) points out. However, deriving rapid and beneficial feedback from learning is particularly significant at the ABE level. Programmes should focus on building in the rapid application of new knowledge and should ensure that learners review and reflect critically on what has or has not been achieved as a result of their learning investment.

Endnote – can radio do more to help?

Perraton and Creed (2000:27) recently reported that radio is experiencing a revival in ABE and non-formal education, through both national and community broadcasting. It is true that early experience with radio showed that the medium could provide effective educational inputs to ABE programmes – for example Radio Santa Maria in the Dominican Republic, Radio ECCA in the Canary Islands and the UK's 'On the Move' literacy project all reached large numbers with positive effects (Yates 1997). And we know that several Latin American radio schools served adult populations at the basic level very successfully for many years in Columbia, Honduras and elsewhere. However, where such models are only weakly linked to the state, their sustainability is often precarious, as the Zambian Radio Farm Forum account (see above) and the Colombian ACPO experience illustrates (see Fraser & Restrepo-Estrada 1998 for an interesting account).

Nonetheless, there is little doubt that, if used appropriately, radio could do much to improve the quality of ABE. Radio has the obvious advantage that it is much more widely available to isolated rural people than other media (e.g. audiocassettes, TV or computers). And the recent availability of wind-up radios which work without the need for batteries, though initially expensive to buy, could significantly extend access. Radio can be used to promote awareness of the availability of ABE programming and in theory it may also be able to assist with the language diversity challenge, in that radio programmes broadcast in the local languages in which ABE is taught could help improve the status and perceived value of these languages. The recent Ghanaian literacy experience demonstrates that this remains problematic in resource poor contexts. Radio may also be able to help with motivation and with enlivening the learning inputs through the use of local actors, and with the immediacy of the information it can provide.

Radio programming that is derived from outreach work articulating local priorities and agendas, and that responds to requests for information through phone-in, letters or email, is clearly in line with the more participatory approaches to ABE being advocated today (Mattee 2000; Rogers 2001; Oxenham et al 2002). And radio talk shows combined with newspaper supplements and/or local discussion groups, sourcing part of their content from local concerns, have long been used successfully for community development. Examples are 'O Povo' in Forteleza, Ceara in North East Brazil and 'Dr AMREF' in East Africa (Pridmore & Nduba 2000; Yates & Bradley 2000).

However, experience with projects based on predetermined curricula and combined integrated multimedia approaches has sometimes shown it can be difficult to keep a broadcast schedule effectively co-ordinated with the other elements (Siabi-Mensah 2000). Further, as Lauglo (2001:38) has recently remarked, *radio alone* cannot teach literacy and is unlikely to foster long-term, sustainable ABE. When used, radio needs to be deployed in ways which draw on its unique attributes and should be flexibly combined with other media, such as printed materials and face-to-face discussion groups (work groups, church groups or other forms of social or vocational group) if it is to be effective. The mass media, with their standardised approach to messaging, do not easily accommodate the more participatory and personalised approaches to education. The call for participatory educational provision sits more comfortably with small-scale localised educational designs, and as such it may be difficult to locate the role for radio and to justify its use – particularly in an era of increasingly privatised airtime. Local community radio stations may be able to offer a way forward here.

Conclusion

It would seem, at the ABE level, that the concept of 'open and flexible learning' could be more relevant than that of 'distance education'. How forms of openness and flexibility are achieved and sustained and how the many and varied barriers to learning achievement are reduced, may be much more essential to understand than overcoming spatial distance by learning how to transfer mass-produced texts. Effective ABE may well need to combine information transfer via externally developed products with local participatory analysis and application. In this case traditional distance education approaches have something to offer. However, at the adult basic level, the strongly product focused approach of distance learning may best be deployed in a more secondary and supportive role to the more participatory, group-focused and discussion led models of conventional adult education.

References

Coombs, PH. 1985. The Tarnished Literacy Myth in *The world crisis in education: the view from the eighties*, New York/Oxford: Oxford University Press.

Daniel, J. 2002. Progress towards the goals of education for all. Paper presented at the Institute of Education International Centenary Conference, Education for All: Enhancing Educational Quality and Ensuring Excellence. University of London, 22 November,.

Dodds, T. 1996. The use of distance learning in non-formal education. Vancouver and Cambridge: Commonwealth of Learning and International Extension College (Research Report).

Dodds, T. 1999. Non formal and adult basic education through open and distance learning in Africa: developments in the nineties towards Education for All. Unpublished study. Vancouver and Cambridge: International Extension College for the Commonwealth of Learning.

Fraser, C & Restrepo-Estrada, S. 1998. *Communicating for development: human change for survival*. London: IB Taurius.

Hornik, RC. 1988. *Development communication*. New York: Longman.

Kabwasa, A & Kaunda, M. 1973. *Correspondence education in Africa*. London: Routledge & Kegan Paul.

Krauss, M. 1992. The world's languages in crisis. *Language* (68):4-10.

Krauss, M. 1995. Language loss in Alaska, the United States and the world: frame of reference. *Alaska Humanities Forum* 6(1):2-5.

Lauglo, J. 2001. *Engaging with adults: the case for increased support to adult basic education in sub Saharan Africa.* African Region Human Development Working Paper Series. African Region: World Bank.

Lockwood, F. 1992. *Activities in self-instructional texts.* London: Kogan Page.

Lockwood, N. 2002, Quiraeya: literacy and post-literacy as process. *Open Praxis Vol., 2.*

Mattee, A. 2000. Tanzania: INADES-formation-Tanzania, in *Case studies of non-formal education by distance and open learning*, edited by R Siacewena. Vancouver: Commonwealth of Learning. Available at http://www.col.org/Consultancies/00nonformal.htm

May, S. 2001. Language and minority rights: ethnicity, nationalism and the politics of language. Harlow: Pearson Education Limited.

McCulloch, V. and Kere J 2002 Women in Fishing Project (WIFIP). *Open Praxis Vol. 2*

Miller-Grandvaux, Y, Welmond, M & Wolff, J. 2002. *Evolving partnership: the role of NGOs in basic education in Africa.* Washington: United States Agency for International Development.

Oxenham, J, Diallo, AH, Katahoire, A, Petkova-Mwangi, A & Sall, O. 2002. *Skills and literacy training for better livelihoods: a review of approaches and experiences.* Human Development Working Paper Series. Africa Region: The World Bank.

Perraton, H, Jamison, DT, Jenkins, J, Orivel, F & Wolff, L 1983. *Basic education and agricultural extension, costs, effects and alternatives.* Washington DC: World Bank, World Bank Staff Working Paper 564.

Perraton, H. 2000. Open and distance learning in the developing world. London: Routledge.

Perraton, H & Creed, C. 2000. Applying new technologies and cost-effective delivery systems in basic education. Paris: UNESCO.

Peters, O. 1983. Distance teaching and industrial production: a comparative interpretation in outline, in *Distance education: international perspectives*, edited by D Sewart, D Keegan & B Holmberg B. London: Croom Helm.

Pridmore, P & Nduba, S. 2000. The power of open and distance learning in basic education for health and the environment, in *Basic education at a distance*, edited by C Yates & J Bradley. London: Routledge.

Rifkin, SB & Pridmore, P. 2001. Partners in planning: information, participation and empowerment. London/Oxford: Macmillan.

Rowntree D (1990) Teaching Through Self Instruction London – How to Develop Open Learning Materials, London, Kogan Page/New York, Nichols Publishing Company

Rowntree, D. 1994. Preparing materials for open, distance, and flexible learning. London: Kogan Page.

Rogers, A. 1998. Changing post-literacy in a changing world; Report for DFID, Education for Development Reading

Rogers, A. 2001. Afterword: problematising literacy and development, in *Literacy and development: ethnographic perspectives*, edited by BV Street. London: Routledge.

Rogers, A. (forthcoming) *Constructing adult learning and teaching.* Leicester: National Institute for Adult and Continuing Education (NIACE).

Siabi-Mensah, K. 2000. Ghana: the use of radio in the National Literacy and Functional Skills Project in the Volta and Northern Regions, in *Case studies of non-formal education by distance and open learning in Africa*, edited by in R Siacewena *Vancouver, Commonwealth of Learning* Available at http://www.col.org/Consultancies/00nonformal.htm

Siacewena R. (ed). 2000. *Case studies of non-formal education by distance and open learning Vancouver, Commonwealth of Learning* Available at http://www.col.org/Consultancies/00nonformal.htm

Sibalwa, D. 2000. Zambia: the Radio Farm Forum, in *Case Studies of Non-Formal Education by Distance and Open Learning edited by* in R Siacewena, *Vancouver, Commonwealth of Learning* Available at http://www.col.org/Consultancies/00nonformal.htm

Singh, M. 2000. Background paper to the UNESCO conference, The Potential of distance and Open Learning in the Training of Adult Educators and Grass Roots Workers Involved in Literacy and Non-formal Education held in Pretoria, South Africa, 7-9 January 2003.

Stephenson, J. (ed). 2001. Teaching and learning online: pedagogies for new technologies. London: Kogan Page.

Street, BV. 2001. Literacy and development: ethnographic perspectives. London: Routledge.

Thomas, J. 1996 Distance Education for Refugees: The experience of using distance and open learning in Africa, 1980 – 1995 Cambridge: International Extension College

UNESCO. 2002. Education for All: is the world on track? Paris: UNESCO.

Unterhalter, E & Dutt, S. 2001. Gender, education and women's power: Indian state and civil society intersections in DPEP (District Primary Education Programme) and Mahila Samakhya. *Compare* 31(1).

Wagner, D. 2002. 'What works' in information technologies and education for the poor in Africa (ITEPA): developing evidence-based research and evaluation guidelines. Project Proposal. Philadelphia: International Literacy Institute.

Wrightson, T. 2002, *Building Literacy in Sudan with the SOLO Press: Outcomes and what now?* Unpublished paper, International Extension College, Cambridge

Yates, C. 1997. *Review of open and distance learning research in primary and adult basic education*. Cambridge: International Research Foundation for Open Learning. www.col.org/irfol

Yates, C & Bradley, J. (eds). 2000. *Basic education at a distance*. London: Routledge.

Yates, C. 2000. Adult education at a distance. Imfundo Knowledge Bank Paper, London DFID Imfundo.

8

Open learning in basic education for adults and the contribution of international co-operation

Wim Hoppers

Introduction

A discussion on the role of international co-operation in the promotion of open and distance learning (ODL) for the purpose of training adult educators needs to start with wider questions about adult education and the role of open learning. Major among these are: what developments and prospects in adult education affect the training of educators? What is ODL all about and what is its relevance for adult education? Are the issues only relevant for adult education or do they concern basic education as a whole? Attention to these questions, focusing both on the policy discourse and on the resource inputs, can promote interest in the contribution of international co-operation. Here the issues relate to the nature of the international discourse about adult education and ODL, to the actual contribution of international co-operation to shaping agendas and programmes, and to the agencies' possible roles in new initiatives in adult education and open learning.

This chapter, without being exhaustive, will raise a variety of issues and pointers regarding the above, starting with notions of the learning society, basic education and ODL, and then zooming in on the training of educators and the role of international policy discourse and collaboration. It concludes by posing a range of challenges for action.

The learning society and basic education

The concept of the 'learning society' assumes that all people – children, youth and adults – are actively involved in ongoing learning, using a wide variety of more or less structured opportunities for doing so. The concept also assumes that learning is not just an individual affair, but that it also has a social dimension in terms of both process and benefits. Learning as a social process, while it is often very informal, tends to take place through institutional arrangements – be it a school, a play group, an initiation programme or a workers' association – and is intended, at least in part, to serve the interests of the community or the wider society. The Hamburg Declaration states a variety of social and economic development goals for adult learning which, albeit in a more passive form, also tend to be reflected in school curricula (UNESCO 1997).

The broad and inclusive interpretation of the learning society and the related concept of the learning community presuppose a fundamental openness to the many forms, approaches and visions about learning – its substance, its pedagogies and its institutional formats – that have been part of people's heritage the world over or have been recent additions to people's learning (such as ICTs). Many of these forms, whether traditional or cutting edge, are regarded by the communities involved as essential components of a 'complete education' or as elements of lifelong learning. Thus an orientation towards the learning society implies openness, flexibility, recognition of diversity, and complementarity – concurrently as well as over time.

Through CONFINTEA V, adult education has placed itself unequivocally within the paradigm of the learning society. It thereby indicates an interest to serve the learning needs of adults as widely as possible and at all levels of lifelong learning, including basic education, continuing education and other forms of acquisition of competencies or skills later in life. Even though there are *de facto* differences of emphasis – whereby in the industrialised north lifelong learning has come to refer particularly to adaptive learning later in life, such as 're-skilling' and 're-training', and in the south there is greater attention to *basic* learning – adult educationists tend to take a broad perspective and would argue that all these needs have to be viewed and addressed within an integrative framework.

There is, however, a special case to be made for adult education as it relates to the needs for *basic education*, namely that part of organised learning that deals with foundation knowledge and awareness, skills and competencies, mores and values. These are the ingredients that prepare people for effective participation in their community and society: socially, economically, politically and culturally (WCEFA 1990). They are meant to constitute the building blocks for the capabilities that enable people to effectively work for their own development (Sen 1999). Basic education is special in that, more than further levels of education, it is acknowledged as a fundamental human right. Article 26 of the Universal Declaration of Human Rights states that, while everyone has a right to education, at least elementary education shall be free and compulsory (Daudet & Singh 2001:13). Later texts have come to define this right as completion of a good quality primary education or 'appropriate' alternatives (WCEFA 1990; Dakar Framework for Action). Arguably this right is applicable not only to children, but to youth and adults as well.

The challenge to adult education is to place its efforts within the wider discourse as to what this 'basic education for all' should be about, in terms of commonly acceptable outcomes, approaches and methodologies. It can be argued that the broad and diffuse interpretation of the learning society, while it is important conceptually, has allowed widely differing views and interpretations of basic adult learning, resulting in rather divergent deliveries on the ground. The 'adult route' of basic education tends to constitute different sets of learning tracks fanning out in different directions and producing very unequal benefits to participants. In pursuing this it has remained distinct from mainstream education provisions and has rarely managed to come close to being an equivalent and effective educational alternative for young people. The vagueness as to what is appropriate education is particularly problematic for those youngsters who are under 18 and under the Convention of the Rights of the Child still therefore have a full entitlement to education (CRC 1989).

It is argued here that a more integrative perspective on learning opportunities, as is implied by the learning society, within the context of rapidly changing social and economic conditions resulting from globalisation and from the threats of poverty, marginalisation and HIV/Aids, requires adult education to engage with the much broader spectrum of learning, education and development issues. It would, therefore, have to place itself, as *basic education for adults*, within the EFA movement and bring its insights and experiences related to lifelong learning to bear on efforts to make basic education equitable, meaningful and effective for everyone.

Challenges for adult education within this broader debate include its contribution to a clearer delimitation of purpose, content and scope of basic education in general, in such a way that it can live up to an equitable adherence to the universal right to such elementary education. A further challenge is to generate a stronger articulation of the complementarity between basic education for adults and that for children. The justification for this has been spelled out many times in the research literature and in policy intentions. Nevertheless, largely because of separate jurisdictions and resource constraints, the provision of basic education across different beneficiary groups tends not to be the focus of integrated development planning.

Adult education is confronted in particular with changing notions of adulthood, which are increasingly at variance with 'age'. In many countries in the developing world, poverty and inequality are increasing; and while in some areas and among some population groups more children are now able to attend schools, elsewhere they are staying away or dropping out in larger numbers. Many children continue to be forced to work, whether inside or outside the home, whether legally or illegally; and ever more of them are directly or indirectly affected by HIV/Aids. The phenomenon, particularly visible in the south, that large numbers of 'children' of school-going age – for social, economic, cultural or health reasons – effectively function as adults, with all the responsibilities that this entails, is unlikely to disappear for a long while to come. Since formal education systems, with all their idiosyncrasies, regulatory frameworks and constraints have structural and cultural problems in responding effectively to the needs of these children, the risk of these categories being offloaded on to adult provision is very great. Rather than insisting on maintaining a differentiated and effectively unequal system, adult education can be a major voice in opening up the mainstream and working towards an integrated and more diverse, yet in principle equitable, system for basic education.

The relevance of ODL in basic education

It is argued here that for adult education to make effective contributions to the inclusive promotion of lifelong learning, a deeper and systematic engagement with 'open learning' is of great necessity. The Hamburg Declaration does not refer to the concept of open learning, but it puts much emphasis on its basic principles of creativity, flexibility, diversification and responsiveness to diverse needs in the social, economic and cultural spheres. In its wording the Declaration follows the common practice of referring to ODL systems in one sentence along with the media and ICTs (UNESCO 1997:23). This restrictive use of the term 'open learning' is unfortunate as it emphasises openness in terms of sources of information while excluding other dimensions of openness. Open learning has tended to be lumped together with distance education, and ODL has come to be associated with resource-based learning where the teacher and learner are either removed from each other in space and/or time, or the teacher is absent altogether (Yates & Tilson 2000:7).

Open learning in a wider sense can be seen as an approach to education whereby openness is not only about removing constraints in terms of space and time, or of methods of study, but also refers to a general flexibility in creating structured learning situations. In these learning situations key ingredients for teaching and learning (such as teachers, sources of information, technology, space, time) are mixed in a manner that responds to people's learning needs and circumstances while adhering to essential criteria of quality, outcomes and entitlements. This specification includes the removal of barriers, but also allows for flexibility of substance, pedagogical practice and organisation (Hoppers 2000). The use of distance education is only one element within the context of open learning; the judicious mix of technologies (including ICT) in providing resource materials and/or pedagogical support is another.

Within a frame of open learning the role of the educator is not automatically defined. It will depend on the provision, nature and quality of other ingredients (such as information and resource materials) and the type and situation of learners. Thus the role may be more directly instructional or facilitative and the educator may be present on a continuous basis or only at certain times for specific purposes. The latter applies whether or not the learners by themselves or learners and educators together interact in a face-to-face situation. ICTs may be used to serve a variety of purposes for either or both educators and learners, but the actual choices will and must be context-specific.

Distance education and the use of ICTs have an important place in open learning. But their place and usage must be defined. The general promotion of openness, flexibility, quality and effectiveness often means that mixed-mode arrangements including elements of ICTs are being constructed. In the process, the distinction between distance learning and conventional learning can disappear. This is particularly the case in further and higher education, and in the training of educators (Nielsen 1991; Thorpe & Grugeon 1994; Rumble 1994).

While in the past there have been examples of (school) teacher education and training programmes through distance education (Yates & Tilson 2000:20), in more recent years distance modes have come to be complemented by a wider variety of face-to-face teacher support and development initiatives. This has followed criticisms of distance learning as being ineffective in shaping pedagogical practice in basic education situations and the allegation that its relevance lies only in upgrading teacher qualifications. Major characteristics of new and composite programmes have become the linking of distance learning with the development of school clusters, often with small teacher resource centres attached to them, giving teachers the possibility of supporting each other in their own professional development. Moreover, external education and training inputs have become mixed-mode arrangements whereby face-to-face modules taught by external providers are combined with on-the-job assignments and intermittent mentoring at the local level or through itinerant professional support personnel (Hoppers 1998).

Where distance programmes existed for teacher training or upgrading, these have gradually been incorporated into this wider support frame (as in Mozambique). Elsewhere, like in South Africa, different ICTs (including satellite technology) are used to provide complementary information and resource materials as well as teacher development modules to teachers learning jointly in the job situation. An important result of this open learning approach to teacher (and management) development has been the increased autonomy of schools (individually or jointly) with regard to utilising a diversity of available resources and improving their professional performance.

During the last few decades, distance education in basic education for children has come to reach beyond the conventional correspondence schools (which unfortunately are still referred to as open schools or open classes), and has gradually come to penetrate school education itself. Its use was problematic, however, due to the importance of the socialisation role of basic education for children, the need for greater supervision and support and the complexity of designing appropriate materials for children (Nettleton 1991:103). Nevertheless, in Africa during the 1980s, two types of programme emerged which were implemented with some success: in-school programmes of interactive radio instruction (IRI), and programmes of educational radio as an outreach for out-of-school youth. In the latter case it involved a combination of joint listening and group work, led by para-professionals (Nielsen 1991: 125/6). In-school usage of IRI was limited to serving as an optional supplement to conventional lessons by 'recreating the talking teacher format', as its basic purpose was to help compensate for poorly qualified teachers (Anzalone 1991:43).

Anzalone (1991:45) identified three ways of using instructional radio in basic education for children: (1) *Supplementary*: to improve quality by adding to regular school instruction in existing subjects or by enriching the curriculum in subjects otherwise difficult to teach. (2) *Stand-alone direct teaching*: to improve effectiveness and appeal by substituting for under-qualified teachers. (3) *Complementary*: to complement conventional instruction in particular subjects by using radio to support specific instructional objectives.

While in practice the major arguments in favour of introducing distance modes into school education were related to efficiency and cost-effectiveness by improving quality of learning, in Africa other concerns have been raised about the social, cultural and professional dimensions of such modes. These concerns include: (1) Mass production of learning and the feeding to learners of easily digestible chunks of pre-selected information are at variance with the human interaction dimension of learning and the social construction of knowledge. (2) There is less space for relating learning to the local context and orienting activities towards empowerment for social change. (3) Distance education tends to be individualistic and emphasises the written word in a foreign language; in this it is at variance with traditions of communalism and oral interaction, and knowledge generation in the local language. (4) Many young people are insufficiently prepared or motivated for autonomous learning, which is a condition for successful participation in distance learning. (5) Distance modes have a lesser status than conventional modes, as they deviate from prevailing conceptions about education. (6) Teachers often fear being replaced by externally produced media and seeing their profession downgraded. (7) Programmes tend to be produced outside the purview of mainstream education management, thus creating difficulties for institutionalisation and funding. (8) Distance programmes are seen as stopgap measures, the need for which disappears when there are enough school places and teachers. (Nielsen 1991:136/139; Gundani 1992:3-4)

The above illustrates that the use of distance education modes has not only been limited in the context of child education, but that there is as yet very little evidence of more systemic reflections on principles of open learning in terms of its potential contribution to access, participation and quality. As outlined above, the aforementioned concerns are not insurmountable. An open learning approach would consider at what point and for what purpose pre-selected materials would be utilised in the learning process. The application of ICT would have advantages in adapting generic materials to group needs and to the local context in its various dimensions. In situations of social learning, individual work would be complemented by learner interactions, whereby the educator would have a strongly enhanced role. Clearly there is a requirement for extensive work to be done at the policy and planning levels in order to establish the frames for the organisational (roles, responsibilities) and pedagogical (substance, methodologies) dimensions of open learning approaches, together with the management and financial implications for the system as whole.

Where is the relevance of all this for adult education? This lies partly in finding entry points for promoting open learning approaches (with or without ICTs) at the levels of adult learning as well as educator development. Partly it lies in defining the context within which dialogues with mainstream education about basic education and lifelong learning need to take place.

It can be argued that the space for further development of open learning approaches is much greater in adult education than in the mainstream formal education system, since the regulatory framework and bureaucratic constraints of the latter tend not to apply in adult education. At the same time it is also evident that adult education suffers from lack of recognition and attention from government, and that its development is severely constrained by the lack of resources and, in many instances, by demoralisation resulting from marginalisation. Thus the freedom from bureaucratic interference is at the same time a major problem in adult education. It is therefore questionable whether lack of attention and marginalisation can be addressed effectively without at the same time engaging the state and its institutions in a dialogue about the very nature, scope and functioning of education within current processes of (and policies for) social and economic change. In the final analysis it is the state that has to play the leading role in the move towards an integrated, inclusive education system.

In this context it would be essential for adult education organisations to embark upon systematic explorations of the purposes, scope and substance of adult education, its modalities and pedagogical practices, and concomitant technological, organisational and legal (rights) aspects, all within a frame of lifelong learning and open learning. Here the 'lifelong' part refers to the nature and purpose of different learnings (plural) *over time*, while the 'open' part refers to the diverse modalities and pedagogical practices of different learnings *concurrently*. In undertaking this exploration the operational parameters for adult education and its adult perspectives (following the Hamburg Declaration) could be defined in such way as to protect its pedagogical autonomy while at the same time enabling adult education approaches and provisions to be embedded within an (expanded) education mainframe.

A key issue in these investigations would be the status, professionalism, and training and support for the cadres of adult (field) educators. The improvement of the quality of adult educators would have to take cognisance of the underlying principles: either they remain volunteers, with great commitment but little education and training, or core groups are nurtured to the point that they can be recognised as professional educators with corresponding status and conditions. The choice would determine whether educator training would be limited and ameliorative or more extensive and radical. Furthermore it would define whether the bulk of the open learning development work will take place at central level, with central direction of the work to be done by grassroots educators, or at the regional and local level (as professional workers can work more autonomously, with central backing, on new programmes in collaboration with one another and with local professionals in related fields).

Given the argument in this chapter for closer engagement of adult education with the wider education system, the preference would be for the latter option, as it helps to improve quality and effectiveness at local level and enhance the standing and visibility of the adult education perspective. The development and continued nurturing of professionalism among adult educators is not only important from an equity perspective, but also has great relevance in relation to the diverse roles that adult educators play in communities. Such upgrading would imply following an open learning approach, which can take cues from related developments in the teacher development programmes in the formal system, as referred to above. This would give a major boost to arranging for direct and ongoing support for adult educators in the field, using ICTs not only as inputs in residential training but also in providing back-up services in the work situation. In turn, increased professionalism would open the way for greater co-ordination and collaboration between educators at regional and local level, and would enhance the dialogue regarding the promotion of quality basic education and community services across the board. Thus, the promotion of open learning approaches in the training and development of adult educators would become a major component of a wider engagement between adult education and mainstream child education.

International policy discourses and co-operation in ODL and adult education

The promotion of ODL in the context of enhanced training for adult educators is not helped much by the evolution of policy discourses in the last decade since the World Conference on Education for All at Jomtien. As a result, a good bit of reflective and sometimes rather painstaking policy and planning work will need to be undertaken to ensure a meaningful and effective application of ODL in the area of adult education. In this chapter attention has already been given to the problematics of the relationship between distance education and open learning, and it has been argued that the emphasis needs to be on the principles of open learning and their significance for the development of adult education within the broader context of basic education and lifelong learning. International discourse has given no more than cursory attention to such notions.

While this discourse has focused quite prominently on the importance of 'education for all' and the concept of and need for an expanded vision of learning in order to achieve this, it has been much less explicit on what such a vision means in terms of policies and strategies for implementation. In practice, emphasis has come to lie rather squarely on the expansion of primary school education as the major vehicle for ensuring basic education for all children. However, both the education and training for youth and adults, and the methodologies that could effectively be elaborated to ensure basic education for all, regardless of age and circumstances, have been seriously under-attended to (Unterhalter, Odora Hoppers & Hoppers 2000).

Jomtien's call for education opportunities designed to meet basic learning needs, and the recognition that an expanded vision is needed to reach beyond conventional delivery systems, should have given a major boost to the consideration of ODL as a philosophy and a strategy for realising rapid growth of participation in education. But while in this and later conferences there were explicit references to the growing international interest in ICTs for their potential to open up access to learning, this attention was not translated into an endorsement of a greater role for distance learning or non-formal education in enhancing delivery of basic education (Hoppers 2000).

Arguably there have been various practical reasons for this. It has been noted that in the late 1980s and early 1990s, the knowledge available on ODL in relation to basic education and teacher education was still rather limited, and that the experience to date has not been unequivocally positive, as has been illustrated above (Nielsen 1991). This lack of positive evidence applied not only to distance education but also to other forms of basic education using non-formal or open learning approaches (Hoppers 2000). The latter, coupled with the limited understanding of the workings, costing and benefits of alternative modalities in education among policymakers and agency personnel, has led to major hesitations about promoting these for the purpose of enhancing access and quality. The restricted focus of the international conferences on the idea of education for all and on advocacy for action also contributed to declarations remaining rather general, and not much was indicated about strategies for delivery (Unterhalter, Odora Hoppers & Hoppers 2000:31/3).

Nevertheless, it has also been argued that the over-emphasis on primary schooling and on formal education in general had arisen from deep-seated convictions in ministries of education and technical and funding agencies as to the contribution of education to development – in the context of structural adjustment. Formal education to serve the needs of economic change and the role of the state in providing this were seen as the priorities (Hoppers 2000). In this context non-formal and adult basic education came to be considered as inefficient or ineffective and programme support dwindled, in spite of evidence that demonstrated success in a number of cases (Lind 2002).

At the Mid-Decade Review in Amman (1995), none of the various commissions and sessions focused on the principles or potentialities of ODL. Instead, the final report noted that the use of media for educational purposes had delivered no more than a modest response to the challenges of the Jomtien Declaration. It further emphasised that while the use of such media and technology should be promoted, they could never replace the role of the teacher as the instructor, guide and example of and to the young (Hoppers 2000:20-21).

Yet the latter has remained an issue for debate and has become part of much more forceful efforts during the later part of the 1990s to make a case for the use of ICTs in basic education. This interest was associated with increased evidence of the apparent failure to reach the targets of EFA, and led to the proffering of new solutions that fitted into the market-oriented discourse and appeared to circumvent the institutional problem of delivering basic education (Unterhalter, Odora Hoppers & Hoppers 2000). In subsequent UNESCO and World Bank papers, ICT became the major attraction of ODL, offering many possibilities of access to quality education for all, including the poor, girls and adults (World Bank 1999). It was assumed that human agency and the appropriate supply of information technology could overcome complex structural problems in education provision. This view implied that ICTs are intrinsically inclusive and have the capacity to overcome the educational exclusions of the past (Unterhalter, Odora Hoppers & Hoppers 2000:38).

It was only the CONFINTEA V meeting that explored the wider social and cultural context of learning and looked at learning opportunities across the board in relation to development concerns. Through its promotion of lifelong learning, the Hamburg Declaration underscored the importance of open learning in its broader meaning as a basis for ensuring access, flexibility and learner-centredness. The Agenda for the Future was very clear on the need for better synergies between media, information technologies and adult learning. It urged that institutions of formal learning should open their doors to learners of all categories and adapt their programmes to meet learning needs, and that opportunities for adult learning should be created in flexible ways, taking into account the diverse nature of the clientele in new institutional formats (UNESCO 1997:13-4). Such statements clearly pointed to the need to explore possibilities for the application of open learning principles in a wider framework for inclusivity in learning, and to use these to prise open the doors of the formal institutions so as to engage with them on the direction and methodologies for adaptation.

The Dakar Framework for Action (2000) reaffirmed the commitment to education for all and referred to lifelong learning as the overall goal. It did not, however, attempt to build on the Hamburg Declaration or to arrive at firmer criteria for what would constitute relevant and equitable basic education. Instead, it left the different components of education to remain focused on their separate mandates, and what is considered 'basic' to be defined within the relevant contexts, including what is appropriate for children, youth and adults. It does plead for schools to be more responsive to the needs of children in difficult circumstances, and for greater synergies between different forms of learning in addressing the needs and circumstances of adults. While the Declaration recognises the peripheral position of adult education and pleads for its integration into the mainstream, it does not attempt to clarify what this would mean (World Education Forum 2000). Thus, the professed need for open learning and for harnessing ICTs for achieving education for all is not placed within an integrative framework that gives adequate cues for policy development. In its vagueness about quality the Declaration reflects the rather general and quantitative Millennium Development Goals set by the OECD.

The policy turn taken at Jomtien, with its stress on the need to prioritise basic education for children and adults, was rearticulated in a wide variety of agency documents. It subsequently produced a major intensification of initiatives by agencies to promote education for all within the formal system, as the universal access of children to primary school education was clearly the priority. In the course of the 1990s such initiatives became part of broader sector programmes in education. Within these frames only gradually some space began to be left for initiatives associated with youth and adult education.

The greater influence of ministries of education on such sector-wide programmes and their prioritising of programmes in which they themselves had a controlling interest contributed to keeping youth development and adult education initiatives firmly on the periphery. Bilateral agencies tended to follow this trend because of the accepted priority of formal primary education (as referred to above) and the massive financial inputs required for the achievement of EFA goals. Such explicit bias was also spurned by the apparent straightforwardness of the agenda for expanding quality formal schooling in the light of authoritative prescriptions about the appropriate mix of inputs to achieve expanded and workable school systems. By comparison, efforts to deal with the needs of out-of-school youth and adults not only had to be legitimised in terms of overall policy, but also required much more elaborate preparation in view of the complexities involved. Moreover they have been perceived to yield uncertain results while absorbing only low volumes of funds.

Where initiatives related to adult education and open learning were undertaken, these tended to remain in the margin of the agencies' agenda – having to establish their 'case'. In the prevailing policy climate they have also tended to find their justification in the link between an emphasis on life and vocational skills on the one hand and livelihood creation or maintenance and promotion of social cohesion on the other hand. In other words, the focus tended to move away from a systems approach in basic education to the use of a functionalist frame for the acquisition of appropriate skills, and from a rights-based approach to one based on the need for poverty alleviation, survival and social stability.

Thus, it should be concluded that the policy environment for applying ODL (with emphasis on OL) in the area of adult education, especially if the latter wishes to place itself within the context of the wider basic education agenda, lifelong learning and the move towards a learning society, is complex and often contradictory. There is much rhetorical reference to the expanded vision; to the need for openness, flexibility and diversity in relation to modalities for delivery; and to the importance of ensuring effective participation of the many groups who have been excluded. By contrast, the actual emphasis is on putting more children into school, on promoting simple access to whatever basic education is considered appropriate for various categories, and on bringing in the wonders of modern technologies in the hope that they will enhance access and quality across the board.

The challenges

The fundamental challenge is thus to place ODL efforts within the wider context of lifelong learning, i.e. as a 'process enabling people to unfold their human potential and to participate in the creation of learning societies' (UIE 2002:12). This requires further understanding of the nature of learning within the social, economic, cultural and political contexts, and exploring the essential learning rights and entitlements of all children, youth and adults. The rhetoric will need to be translated into tangible frameworks and indicators for defining the quality of process and outcomes of the many forms of learning and education that abound. Decision-making as regards such frameworks and how these are translated into actual deliverables within specific contexts cannot be left to agencies, nor can they, in fact, be an exclusive concern of ministries of education. Appropriate quality basic education needs to be defined through participatory processes, with reference to equitable and development-related criteria set by the state.

In the context of this effort there is a great need to engage in specific work around the contribution that ODL can make. Clearly it will help to differentiate between the wider principles of open learning and the practical specifics of distance education as one aspect of delivery. In the absence of international understanding about how new technologies can be used in different developmental contexts for lifelong learning, the principles and applicability of open learning to issues of access, participation and quality need to be understood first. Thus is irrespective of what technologies can suitably be invoked. Significantly, the use of ODL would need to be directly related to considerations of equitable outcomes and actual relevance of the intended impact.

The above is likely to require a fair amount of rather painstaking work on the many aspects of open learning; the merits and demerits of various modalities for delivery; their pedagogical, social and cultural dimensions; and above all, on their integration into (or relationship with) conventional mainstream provisions. The latter will throw up a wide variety of technical issues; but also issues of alternative costs, modes of institutionalisation, the handling of regulatory frameworks and legal provisions, as well as the provisions for professional and administrative, if not political, support.

Other challenges lie in relating the promotion of ODL in the context of educator training to the further articulation of the same in the process of teaching and learning on the ground. Educators (whether of adults or children) cannot be trained through ODL modalities if they do not understand their relevance and potential, or are not trained to apply open learning principles in their own work situations. Meeting these challenges would have major consequences for the organisation of the education and training of adult educators, and for the mobilisation of different professional networks. The latter, in turn, points to the need to redefine the relations and possible collaborations between the state, adult education organisations, training institutions, private providers of ICT programmes and services, community organisations, and the like. Given the prevailing discourse (as noted above), such collaborations will require very careful construction.

The positive factor is that in the world of adult education, distance education and open learning in more general terms, there is already a wealth of experiences – good or bad – that can be tapped into. This wealth would, however, need to be excavated, collated, thoroughly and systematically analysed, and repackaged for further discussion about policies and practices. The latter agendas would require major effort and, equally, the mobilisation and maintenance of a wide international network of partners.

Technical and funding agencies need to be challenged to support such international collaborative research and reflection, but on terms that are set by the participating partners themselves. Given that there is an increased realisation among a variety of agencies that ODL, lifelong learning and open learning somehow deserve further attention, if only to understand better the parameters for policy interventions to help achieve EFA and ensure greater inclusivity, there is a basis for serious dialogue to take place. Not only can such agencies contribute financially and technically, they can also play a modestly facilitative role in forging new coalitions among government and non-government and civil society partners. In addition, they can contribute to the legitimacy and visibility of the agenda agreed upon.

Moreover, as indicated before, there is at least some space – albeit rather constrained – in different countries to re-explore the position and potentialities of adult education as a necessary component of a broader framework for basic education. Such efforts do require parties other than ministries and agencies to be involved, in order to begin to raise fundamental issues about the nature of lifelong learning, the role of education for adults (in terms of programmes and adult perspectives) in basic education in general, the value of collaboration and synergies across formal and non-formal education, and consequently also the system-wide allocations of human resources and financial support.

If a shared concern for ODL in the training of adult educators can be an entry point for opening up ongoing policy discourses around basic education and lifelong learning, their current state and options for the future, it is as good a start as any.

References

Anzalone, S. 1991. Educational technology and the improvement of general education in developing countries. In *Educational technology: sustainable and effective use,* edited by ME Lockheed, J Middleton & GS Nettleton: 32-97. IBRD, PHREE Background Paper Series, no PHREE/91/32. Washington DC: The World Bank, 351 p.,tab.

CRC/Convention on the Rights of the Child. 1989. New York, UNICEF.

Daudet, Y & Singh, K. 2001. *The right to education: an analysis of UNESCO's standard-setting instruments*. Paris: UNESCO.

Gundani, CM. 1992. Increasing access and raising quality of secondary education using distance teaching methods. Paper presented at the International Extension College meeting on World Education Crisis: Roles for Distance Education, 20-24 September, Cambridge, UK.

Hoppers, W. 1998. Teachers' resource centres in Southern Africa; an investigation into local autonomy and educational change. *International Journal of Educational Development*, 18(3), May: 229-246.

——— 2000. Nonformal education, distance education and the restructuring of schooling: challenges for a new basic education policy. *International Review of Education*, 46(1/2): March/May, 5-30.

Lind, A. ABLE policies in an international perspective. Keynote Paper for International Conference on Adult Basic and Literacy Education (ABLE) in the SADC Region, 3-5 December 2002, University of Natal, Pietermaritzburg, South Africa.

Nettleton, GS. 1991. Uses and costs of educational technology for distance education in developing countries: a review of the recent literature. In *Educational technology: sustainable and effective use,* edited by ME

Lockheed, J Middleton & GS Nettleton: 99-147. IBRD, PHREE Back ground Paper Series, no PHREE/91/32. Washington DC: The World Bank. 351 p.:tab.

Nielsen, HD 1991. Using distance education to extend and improve teaching in developing countries. *Perspectives on Education for All*, IDRC: Social Science Division.

Rumble, G. 1994. Mixed modes of teaching and learning; structures, resources, and development. In *Open Learning in the Mainstream*, edited by M Thorpe & D Grugeon, Harlow, Longman.

Sen, A. 1999. *Development as freedom*. Oxford: Oxford University Press.

Thorpe, M & Grugeon, D. 1994. (Eds). *Open learning in the mainstream*. Harlow, Longman

UNESCO. 1997. Fifth International Conference on Adult Education (CONFINTEA V): *The Hamburg declaration on adult learning: the agenda for the future*. Hamburg: UIE.

UNESCO Institute of Education. 2002. Nurturing the treasure: the vision and strategy of the UNESCO Institute of Education, 2002 – 2007. Hamburg: UIE.

Unterhalter, E, Odora Hoppers, C, & Hoppers, W. The elusiveness of integration: policy discourses on open and distance learning in the 1990s. In *Basic education at a distance: world review of distance and open learning*, Vol. 2, edited by C Yates & J Bradley: 27-48. London, Routledge Farmer.

WCEFA. 1990. Final Report, World Conference on Education for All: Meeting Basic Learning Needs, 5-9 March, Jomtien, Thailand. Inter-Agency Commission.

WEF/ World Education Forum. 2000. The Dakar framework for action. Education for all: meeting our collective commitments. World Education Forum, 26-28 April, Dakar, Senegal.

World Bank. 1999. *Knowledge for development: world development report 1998/9.* Oxford: Oxford University Press.

Yates, C & Tilson, T. 2000. Basic education at a distance: an introduction. In *Basic education at a distance: world review of distance and open learning*, vol. 2, edited by C Yates & J Bradley: 3-26. London, Routledge Farmer.

Section III

Diversity in institutional arrangements and partnerships for effective delivery of training programs

9

The solidarity in literacy programme: A strategy for literacy training for the youths and adults of Brazil

Regina Célia Vasconcelos Esteves

The paper describes the principal characteristics and strategies of the Solidarity in Literacy Programme[1], which was created in 1997 as a tool for mobilisation for the reduction of illiteracy and for strengthening political policy for youth and adult education in Brazil and exported to other Portuguese-speaking countries. It analyses the successful partnership with higher education institutions, the private sector, civil society, government and non-governmental institutions, as well as deals with the pedagogical principles that guide the learning processes.

It is in the context of this immensely participatory literacy movement that the issue of training literacy teachers, the pedagogical content and the importance of continuous training for the literacy teachers is examined. The paper highlights significant qualitative and quantitative improvements in methods of literacy training and the important impacts on the students, teachers, businesses and universities involved in the project. The paper also highlights some projects in distance and open learning that enrich the literacy work in the classrooms and enhance the training of literacy teachers.

Background of the national programme

The Solidarity in Literacy Programme was created in 1997 by the Council of the Solidarity Community. This Council is a forum for the development of social actions. The Programme is part of a partnership between the federal government, private initiatives and civil society. It is currently administered by an NGO, the Association for the Support of the Solidarity in Literacy Programme. The Association is a third sector profit agency with a team of 220 consultants.

The Programme's goals are to reduce the indices of illiteracy in Brazil and provide wider access to education for youths and adults in the Brazilian municipalities with the highest indices of illiteracy. The Solidarity in Literacy Programme has achieved significant results since it began. In 2002 the number of beneficiary youths and adults that have been served by the Programme stood at over 3,6 million.

The Programme's strategy has become a model for the institutionalisation of the public offering of education for youths and adults in the poorest areas in Brazil. This chapter also explores the quantitative and qualitative impacts of the initiative in the context of Brazilian education. The model adopted to train the Programme's literacy teachers is also examined.

Since 1997, the Solidarity in Literacy Programme has undertaken development based on several criteria: An important *action criterion* is that the Programme acts in the municipalities with the highest illiteracy rates according to the ranking of the Brazilian Institute for Geography and Statistics. The municipalities involved are those that are most affected by lack of resources and/or unequal concentration of income. It is no accident that these municipalities have the highest illiteracy rates.

National mobilisation entails that the Programme's actions have sparked a permanent national movement. The multiplying effect of these actions in the fight against illiteracy has made a significant contribution to the process of institutionalising public education to youths and adults.

Creating and encouraging partnerships implies that the initiative has consolidated a model for solidarity, uniting partners from various sectors of society. This process has elicited the participation of public and private institutions that act according to their area of activity in society.

Youth mobilisation. When selecting literacy teachers, the Programme gives priority to youths from the communities involved. Preference is given to youths currently enrolled or who have completed secondary school or official teacher training. These youth literacy teachers are trained in the higher education institutions and receive a benefit for the teaching duties they carry out.

Pedagogical diversity has meant that each higher education institution partner (university, college or university centre) has autonomy in establishing methodologies that it deems adequate to the development of the literacy training modules. The Programme's parameters are found in the document *Guiding Principles for the Political-Pedagogical Proposal.* It is explored further on in this chapter.

Systematic evaluation of results is treated as an. ethical imperative and strategy of the Programme. This allows for social accountability of projects focused on improving the life of Brazilian citizens and means that eventual corrections in pedagogical directions may be made while the applied methods are entrenched. It also means the reach of the actions and the degree of involvement of the beneficiary communities are measured. This is all guided by the complete and consistent transparency that is needed in Brazilian society.

The programme's partnership model

The Programme model is based on six-month teaching modules. Each module begins with the process of choosing the literacy teachers, selected from the communities themselves. An average of one month is reserved to train these teachers. This process takes place on the campus of the higher education institution partner and is followed by five months of classes for the literacy students. The classes take place four times a week for three hours a day. At the end of the module the students receive counselling on entering the formal education system for youth and adult education in their municipalities. The Programme offers technical assistance to support the cities that do not have youth and adult education courses. It also helps develop and establish projects to present to the Ministry of Education. This support enables the Programme to give students the opportunity to continue their studies in their own cities, without interruption.

In addition, there is an administrative-technical co-ordinator that is responsible for the implementation of the Programme in each municipality. This local co-ordinator receives a monthly benefit of R$200.00 (US$57.14) for the five months of the module. The literacy teachers and the pedagogical co-ordinator receive a monthly benefit of R$120.00 (US$34.28)[2].

Each module includes recycling literacy teachers to allow other people in the communities to receive training. The Programme therefore naturally multiplies in the communities. Training new literacy teachers with every module means more opportunities for more people to receive training. It also encourages those who have already gone through the training process to become part of the official school system. In addition to the multiplying quality of the Programme, this model was designed to assure decentralisation and strengthen civil society.

Role of the partners

The structure of the Programme allows the institutionalisation of youth and adult education to be a natural result of the literacy training process. This is accomplished through strengthening civil society and reinforcing the relationship between civil society and the various governmental and non-governmental levels and entities.

A simple, innovative formula is established based on links of effective participation in numerous sectors of society. These include businesses, institutions, organisations, state governments, higher education institutions, individuals, mayor's offices and the Ministry of Education. These entities all take an active part in contributing to the Programme according to their specific areas of activity.

The first pilot project module was established in 1997 in 38 municipalities (with illiteracy rates of 63% to 82%). This pilot project included 38 partner institutions of higher education and eleven businesses. Today, the Programme is active in 2 010 municipalities distributed among seven metropolitan regions in over 20 Brazilian states. There are partnerships with 204 institutions (involving 1 700 academics) and 93 businesses. As of December 2002, 3 600 000 students had been served and 170 000 literacy teachers had been trained through the Programme. The majority of these (60%) came from rural areas.

The partnership model evolved both qualitatively and quantitatively. This occurred in terms of commitment, functions and partnerships that were formed. The role of each partner is defined according to the social function it performs. (This is discussed further below.)

Higher education institutions

The academic community (federal, state, community and private higher education institutions) has responsibility for the pedagogical execution of the Programme in the municipalities in which it operates. These institutions are free to choose the theories and pedagogical practices they wish to use. This independence in terms of choice is fundamental to the democratic nature of the Programme and is part of the Programme's political-pedagogical principles, which guide the pedagogical frameworks without dictating what they will be. These are developed by Council of higher education institutions and are approved by the entire academic community involved with the Programme together with the Programme's National Co-ordinator.

The higher education institutions are responsible for the project from the outset, through execution to the supervision of results. These institutions have the ability to select and train the literacy teachers. They also monitor and evaluate the progress of the classes as well as the quantitative and qualitative results of the literacy training. This includes language acquisition and reading and writing skills and their social uses. On-going evaluation is a permanent element of the Programme.

The partnership with the academic sector is institutional but the participation projects are often included in the activities of the dean's offices and the continuing study programmes of the universities. The teaching staff members who participate in the project work on a voluntary basis.

Private sector

Businesses, financial institutions, co-operative foundations and others participate in the Programme by providing the financial resources that allow it to carry out it activities in the poorest municipalities in the Brazilian North and Northeast. These resources go towards financing the training of the literacy teachers, including the monthly benefit payments, daily meal and travel expenses for the monthly and semester evaluations of results. These costs represent 50% of the cost per student enrolled in the literacy classes, around 17 *reais* (US$ 4.85) per month for six months.

The private sector has become more and more willing to fulfil its social responsibility by committing itself to building a better country in Brazil. The business partners place great emphasis on monitoring pedagogical results. This is an important tool in terms of student support and allows the business partners to monitor the entire literacy training process and to keep track of their investment. This monitoring takes place through visits to the adopted municipalities where they can verify results on location. It also takes place through annual reports that provide accounting information as well as semester evaluations.

Civil society

Civil society takes part in the Programme through individual membership that allows for the financing of students in the large urban centres. These 'Solidarity Citizens' are private individuals who adopt and sponsor students in the large urban centres. This is done through a credit card charge or a direct bank deposit of 17 *reais* (US$4.85) per month for six months.

The 'Solidarity Citizen' splits the cost of the Programme with the Ministry of Education in the cities of São Paulo, Rio de Janeiro, the Federal District and Goiânia. These are locations where illiteracy rates are not as high, but where there are large concentrations of illiterate people.

Non-governmental organisations

A number of NGOs are Programme partners in the 'Large Urban Centres' Project. Social projects that allow for a broad network of links with the Programme beneficiaries are developed in the underprivileged communities in these cities. These partners mobilise the communities for student registration and make spaces available for classes. They also provide the minimal infrastructure requirements and offer support to the higher learning institutions in the training of the literacy teachers.

Government

Partnerships with the different government levels occur in the following ways. The federal government, through the Ministry of Education, finances the acquisition of didactic and support material as well as the library kits for the municipalities. This represents 50% of the monthly cost per student, or 17 *reais* (US$4.85) per month for six months. The Ministry of Education also participates in promoting and financing youth and adult education in the municipalities. This is a fundamental part of ensuring continuity in the education of those who finish the programme. It also provides sustainability of results in the municipalities. Agencies, financial institutions, promotion agencies and public businesses finance the Programme implementation in the same way that the private sector does. This means contributing the 50% (17 *reais* or US$4.85) per month per student for six months, which covers the remaining expenses, such as meals, training and payment of the benefit for the literacy teachers as well as evaluation and monitoring. Brazilian state governments join the Programme in the same way that the private sector does by financing Programme implementation in the municipalities of their state. The Programme model is often adopted as a literacy training model in the municipalities. Municipal administrations are the primary governmental beneficiaries of the Programme. They serve as the Programme's liaison, providing the entire necessary local infrastructure. This includes classrooms and transport for the students and the literacy teachers. The relationship with the local government is constantly nourished and reinforced. Mutual trust allows the institutionalisation of education for youths and adults to be sufficiently straightforward to guarantee efficiency and effectiveness. All partner municipalities receive support from the Programme in order to carry out this process.

Programme business, institution or state government partners and the Ministry of Education thus cover costs in the municipalities. In the large urban centres, the costs are divided between the Ministry and private individuals who participate in the 'Adopt a Student' campaign.

Guiding principles for the political-pedagogical proposal

Transformations in today's working world have significantly changed the concept of literacy. It is important to sketch current world-wide academic discussion of *literacy* and *learning to read and write*. This discussion understands the process of reading and writing as more than just mastering the graphic elements of reading and writing. The process should be understood as something that allows for a broader worldview and one that is practised as the most consistent exercise of citizenship. This is why the learning process should take social, ethical and political issues into consideration. These issues are an integral part of the technical-pedagogical content that influences the literacy teachers in their actions. They are conscious of their roles as active agents of change.

The *Guiding Principles* document referred to earlier is a tool for the higher education institution partners. Its purpose is to provide political-pedagogical references for the practices developed in the classrooms and to give the literacy teachers methods that allow for improvisation as alternatives to empirical methods.

One Programme highlight, from a political point of view, is the concern for an education that favours the exercise of citizenship. The education practised in the Programme encourages continued training for the literacy teachers. An essential objective of the Programme is to educate individuals to exercise citizenship and this means students must be seen as citizens and not as simple receivers of information.

The pedagogical proposal that is practised in class should incorporate text and mathematics as live disciplines. Content needs to be meaningful to students in the context of their realities. Incorporating literacy and using it in daily life is what guarantees that literacy will become an important element in the process of exercising citizenship. The *Principles* are consistent with national and international debates on youth and adult education. They are consistent with the Law for Guidelines and Bases of Education in Brazil (1996) and with the Brazilian National Education Plan that was developed according to the goals established in Jomtien (Thailand, 1990) and Dakar (Senegal, 2000). The Programme wishes to respond to the educational necessities of the poorer levels of society, to facilitate their direct access to school and to encourage their permanence in school. The Programme also hopes to contribute to the process of building citizens and transforming society. *The process of reading and writing is practised as the most consistent exercise of citizenship*. The process is essential in developing a critical, contextual understanding that is responsible for conscious transformation in reality. Advances in information and communication combined with the alarming picture of illiteracy rates and the precarious reading and writing practices of the educated public demand activities that encourage literacy skills as a condition for exercising citizenship. The participation of a literate society depends on access to tools that express, identify or register accumulated knowledge. Keeping up with the modern world's changes and developments requires mastering the formats for communicating knowledge and the acquisition of information. The social use of these acquisitions is fundamental to their becoming concrete realities.

Intercultural dialogue is an ally in the pedagogical process. This principle points to the necessity for a dynamic of reflection on a community's culture. It involves linking information from different areas of knowledge. These different areas are all used by the literacy teachers and students to develop reading and writing skills and to build logical-mathematical knowledge. The pedagogical proposals require the literacy teachers to be prepared to plan their actions based on their daily contact with the literacy students. This contact involves intercultural dialogue and uses material that is relevant to the context of the students' lives in order to explore subjects such as history, geography, mathematics, politics, ethics, economy and social coexistence. The material is also used to study science and art. In this way, working with the Portuguese language and mathematics triggers analyses and reflections on language (oral and written). It also stimulates interest in the language of mathematics as an element that will contribute to understanding reality in a more complete way.

Literacy students and literacy teachers are subjects in the process of acquiring and forming knowledge. They adapt and build their knowledge by interacting with the communities they live in. The acquisition and development of reading and writing in the teaching-learning process increase the possibilities for access to new concepts. This contributes to the participating individuals' development and personal accomplishments and transforms the communities as well. Continuity in the reading and writing process as a social phenomenon allows for the forming of concepts and opinions that are necessary for critical thinking and action as citizens.

The solidarity commitment and social responsibility are included in encouraging partnerships and collective work. There is no doubt that overcoming problems in educating youths and adults goes beyond isolated, temporary or inappropriate actions. In order to confront the challenges that exist, a commitment must be made that involves all levels of society and all institutions in a collective, participatory movement.

Training the literacy teacher

Each literacy training module includes one month in which the literacy teachers are trained. The majority of them are lay teachers. They are selected from the municipalities by the higher education institution partners, which are also responsible for the training process and the systematic support of the project.

The selection of content and the basic skills related to them should be included according to the Programme model. Attending to basic learning requirements occurs according to the study undertaken (This information is currently in the UNESCO web site (internet) at www.unesco.org) by the World Conference on Education for All in Jomtien (Thailand, 1990), which requires taking into consideration a typology of content that goes beyond conceptual content like facts, concepts and principles to include content that is related to the development of abilities and attitudes.

In the dynamic of interaction that takes place between different types of knowledge it is important for the school to play an active role in developing knowledge in a way that encourages critical thinking and presents information in a conceptualised fashion. The school acts in a way that is responsible for conscious changes in the students' realities. The school must also take into consideration the pedagogical knowledge of the literacy teacher in relation to the literacy students. Know-how that is implicit in the organisation of the pedagogical project must also be considered. This organisation includes the selection of material, resources, and teaching and learning procedures. It also includes the evaluation process as a whole as well as identifying the skills that will be evaluated.

Language is therefore used as an essential link to explore different views of the world. This link incorporates analysis in a historical, geographic, political, ethical, socio-economic, scientific and artistic context. This means that learning a language and the fundamental principles of mathematics is a basic tool that allows students to gather a broader sense of knowledge. This is something they can take with them.

Intercultural dialogue depends on increasing the linguistic capital of the literacy teachers and the literacy students. This dialogue allows for information from different areas to be understood. The learning process should take into consideration the specificity of the adult as a subject who is already part of the working world and who has life experiences that must be respected in order to avoid 'infantilisation' in the selection of texts. This also demands the development of mathematical knowledge as more than just a formal concept. The first thing to be done is to understand and discuss the social context in which the literacy teachers and students live. Their historical cultural reality must be carefully considered.

Making this training operational is accomplished by courses in the higher education institutions involved and by systematic monitoring through visits by the academics to the municipalities. Contact with local cultural expressions, exposure to new experiences and new ways of learning encourage intercultural dialogue. This has repercussions for the literacy process itself in addition to having an impact on the academics' actions as teachers. Systematic monitoring allows the initial training to be broadened and for the pedagogical practice to take on new directions when necessary. This occurs through an active dialectic between theory and practice.

Profile of the literacy teacher

As mentioned previously, the literacy teachers are selected in the communities where they live by the co-ordinators of the higher education institutions. The selection is based on criteria such as education level, age, availability, previous education experience and residential area. Young candidates, people with higher education levels and individuals who live close to the classroom installations are given priority.

The data collected by the Programme in the course of semester evaluations demonstrate that the literacy teachers are primarily from the rural areas. They are usually between 20 and 24 years of age. Only a portion of the teachers (approximately one-third) have attended teacher training courses. This is a reflection of the national situation. Most of the municipalities present precarious education level indices as well as restricted reading and writing scenarios. On the one hand, these factors make the literacy training process more difficult; on the other hand, the literacy teachers undergo training in the partner universities and this trains them how to proceed within their reality. The training examines the specific difficulties of the local context. It then explores an appropriate way to address this reality without losing sight of the vast universe of accumulated human knowledge.

Training the literacy teacher

The profile of the Solidarity in Literacy Programme literacy teacher and the level of reading and writing in the communities make literacy teacher training essential. This training is developed in two specific stages. The first is an intensive course that includes an average of 120 work hours. The second occurs through local pedagogical support that is developed through the semester. Systematic visits are made by the higher learning institution co-ordinator in the municipalities and by the municipal co-ordinator together with the pedagogical support monitor. These visits allow for the establishment of continual training and qualification activities that are developed with the supervision of the higher learning institution partner.

The basic concern here is the development of a process of reading and writing for the literacy teachers and the study of existing theories that are used as a basis for pedagogical practice in the classroom. The municipal co-ordinator participates in both steps. Among the activities that form the foundation of the literacy teacher training process are courses developed in the higher learning institutions. Important components in this training process include: concepts of literacy and reading and writing: existing theories and practices; theoretical and practical bases of mathematics teaching; historical-cultural context and youth and adult education; theoretical foundations of knowledge acquisition; description of the specific demands of youth and adult education; organisation of pedagogical project (planning, procedures and didactic resources, evaluation); reading, producing texts and linguistic analysis; evaluation of the literacy students, pedagogical practices and involvement with the community.

Each higher education institution has the autonomy to plan and conduct its literacy teacher training, but these components should be incorporated into the pedagogical practices of the training. The *Principles* discussed above should also be included.

Intensive training for the literacy teachers

The history of reading and writing of most of the Programme's literacy students reveals extremely limited exposure to written language. This is due to the socio-economic conditions of the communities they live in. There are very few newspapers, magazines, printed advertising and libraries in these communities. Even among people who have some kind of schooling, such as the literacy teachers, the social use of the written language is restricted and usually involves letters and cards and some professional necessities. This is where the concern for developing the literacy teachers' reading and writing skills comes from.

The literacy teachers are not initially prepared for their work. This is seen in the selection phase and is a reflection of the distinct contexts of which they are a part. This indicates a necessity for adding to their education. It is a challenging task for the higher learning institution and involves developing reading skills and having the literacy teachers produce written texts. It also includes discussions of methods for teaching mathematics.

Reading and writing skills for the literacy teacher may be developed through reading activities and activities that involve the production of different types of text. These include journalistic, opinion and informative texts as well as essays, short stories, notes, cards, reports and poems, which may even be produced in groups. Literacy training must be understood as a process that is directly related to the social uses of language.

From this perspective there is an understanding that the use of reading and writing affects the way a person looks at and understands the world. That is why the literacy teachers are encouraged to plan and develop their pedagogical project giving priority to the social uses of the Portuguese language. This takes place based on studies of teaching approaches that incorporate the acquisition and construction of new concepts and knowledge.

During the intensive training period there are also proposals for how to develop plans that will promote the relationship between education and culture. An integral part of the training to be offered to the literacy trainers should involve museum and library activities and visits to theatres and movie theatres. It should include tourist visits in the cities where the training takes place as well as in nearby cities. These activities should be preceded by seminars on the locales to be visited. This preparation should also include videos with cultural and tourist information. Comments on any plays or films should be made and should be followed by debates. These activities can all be linked to other reading and writing activities.

Continuous training for the literacy teacher

Continuous training takes place through studies, workshops, analysis and reflection on the literacy teachers' practices. These sessions include reports on experiences, and are developed based on the actions of the higher education institution co-ordinator, the municipal co-ordinator and the pedagogical support monitor in the municipality. This is when the questions and issues raised in the classroom are explored and discussed in a theoretical context. The higher education institution co-ordinator visits the location with the local co-ordinator and the pedagogical support monitor. He holds meetings for studying and pedagogical support and; provides assistance and support at the diagnostic evaluations. He verifies if the classes have been established, detects problems and provides solutions. Another important role is to verify the development of the school calendar and anticipated programming. An important function is assisting in the pedagogical process. He also visits the classrooms in the urban and rural zones; collects quantitative data (current number of classes, attendance, dropout rates, reasons for dropouts, socio-cultural characteristics of the students and so forth); verifies the learning evaluation as well as the final evaluation of the modules (quantitative and qualitative results); and selects literacy trainers for the following module. The higher education institution co-ordinator also maintains contact with the local government agencies and with municipal leadership organisations and participates in local events.

The monthly visits to the municipalities become a forum for permanent discussion of the different teaching-learning issues. These visits encourage the establishment of training continuity. This is true not only for the literacy teachers but also for the literacy students.

Sub-projects in distance education

Radio school

To enrich the literacy work in the classrooms and to enhance the training of literacy teachers, the Radio School Project was established in 2001 in partnership with the Secretariat of Distance Education in the Ministry of Education. The Radio School produces a series of educational programmes for training and recycling literacy teachers. The programmes also serve as a pedagogical resource. The School thus employs the following tools: radio programmes, printed material and technical orientation. The printed material consists of a guide containing instruction and orientation on the use of the radio programmes. The orientation is performed by university co-ordinators from the Solidarity in Literacy Programme.

The main objectives of the project are to: reinforce the content applied in the training phase to the literacy teachers at the universities; provide inputs to the process of teaching; offer subsidies to the continuous training, in groups or individually; offer suggestions of strategies and activities applied to the literacy of youths and adults; expand the knowledge of the literacy teacher on specific themes which may be used in the classroom.

The themes are all linked to regional popular culture and literature. The theme of the series of the first semester of 2002 was *Reading and writing with much pleasure.*

The programmes are reproduced and distributed to the university co-ordinators of the Solidarity in Literacy Programme. Depending on the theme and the series format, the material is also relayed to a pool of selected radio stations which comprise the Communicators Net for Education.

Digital literacy

In implementing the literacy process in a municipality, the Solidarity in Literacy Programme stimulates more than the institutionalisation of education to youths and adults. It also sparks other needs in the communities, such as human resource training and access to new technologies. The Programme therefore devised a Digital Literacy Project, with the objective of reducing digital exclusion. The idea was to offer a room with five computer terminals to the communities covered by the Programme so that every member of the community, and not only the students who were being taught to read and write, could become familiar with the resources offered by such technology, which had until then remained beyond the reach of such small municipalities.

Twenty universities were selected to take responsibility for the co-ordination of the Digital Literacy initiative in 20 municipalities. The computers are donated by public and private corporations as they replace their own equipment and are invaluable aids in promoting digital democratisation.

Success of the partnership network

The strategy adopted by the Solidarity in Literacy Programme has made extensive, far-reaching impacts, with both vertical and horizontal effects, on the students, teachers, businesses and universities involved in the project. These impacts are currently being studied and some of the results show that the Programme is one of the most important initiatives yet undertaken in Brazilian youth and adult education.

Impact on illiteracy data in Brazil

The 2000 census done by the Brazilian Institute of Geography and Statistics confirms the positive impacts of the Programme on illiteracy indices. Published in December 2001, the data show that there was a reduction of 32,3% in the national illiteracy rate for adults over 15 years of age in the decade 1991 to 2001. In 1991, the national illiteracy rate was 20,7%, whereas for 2000 the figure was 13,6%.

According to the Institute, the Programme made a significant contribution to this decrease in illiteracy.

The final report of the Brazilian Institute of Geography and Statistics states that *(Censo Demográfico 2000.* Instituto Brasileiro de Geografia e Estatística. Dezembro, 2001) this improvement reflects, in part, the efforts of the Solidarity in Literacy Programme (non-governmental organisation) that has the objective of reducing the indices of illiteracy in Brazil and triggering the public offering of youth and adult education.

The most important reduction occurred in the North and the Northeast, where the largest number of the municipalities served by the Programme are located. In the Northeast the index dropped from 37,5% in 1991 to 24,6% in 2000, representing a decrease of 12,9%. In the North the drop was 8,3%, while in the South and the Southeast it was around 4%.

Another important figure is related to the reduction of illiteracy in the rural zone. This is where 70% of the Programme's classrooms are installed. The new census revealed a reduction in the illiteracy rate in the rural zone of 12,5%, compared with a national average reduction of 7%.

The Programme has also managed to guarantee continuity in results and in the institutionalisation of access to education for youths and adults. Over 74% of the participating municipalities had initiated youth and adult education by December 2000. Registration rates in youth and adult education courses had increased by 114% in the municipalities served by the Programme. The national average for registration increases was 42% for the same period. These data are from the school census 2000/2001, produced by the National Institute for Education Studies and Research/Ministry of Education *Censo Escolar (2000-2001).* Instituto Nacional de Estudos e Pesquisas Educacionais. Ministério da Educação, 2001.')

Impact on the partners

The success of the Programme's partnership engineering is demonstrated not only by the increase in numbers over the last five years but also by the impact the Programme has had on people's lives, on governmental actions and on civil society. The success of the model developed by the Programme is also evident in the concept of partnership that has been developed over the past few years by the third sector. The Programme's model demonstrates that partnership does not have to be limited to temporary actions or to local or regional actions. Partnership can be extended to important fundamental goals on national and international levels. The positive impact this partnership has on every partner must also be taken into consideration in any discussion of results.

Private sector partners: In the private initiative area, the strength of the Programme lay in its ability to salvage the meaning of social responsibility. This is a theme that currently appears on the national agendas of business professionals and members of Brazilian society. Although the Programme was conceived as a project to directly serve its students, it is clear that the benefits are mutual. The socially responsible businesses receive a positive response from society. This occurs principally because the Programme affects their market directly. The businesses invest in a Brazil that is far removed from their employees' reality and for the most part, from the reality of their consumers. Today over 50% of the Programme's participating businesses are in the large urban centres in the Southeast. The municipalities that they adopt are in a Brazil that is extremely distant from these urban centres regionally, socially and economically.

Education partner: Significant changes have occurred in the area of the higher education institutions. Participation in the Programme has resulted in prolific academic production concerning the illiteracy problem and youth and adult education in Brazil. Specific disciplines in this field have also been created in the higher education curriculum in addition to specialisation courses. These include new theoretical and practical guidelines in pedagogy courses and other related areas.

The higher education institutions have now moved into a place in society that had been neglected in recent Brazilian history. Before the creation of the Programme there were fewer than 10 institutions working with youth and adult education. Today there are over 204.

The Programme has also created a forum for discussion in Brazil and has opened channels of communication. The formulation of a political-pedagogical project and of a scientific magazine that is edited every semester by the Programme has contributed to the exchange of different theories and practices being used by the academic community. Programme seminars and meetings have also encouraged this exchange.

The numbers are clear: 42% of the partner institutions began to develop projects for youth and adult education after the Programme got under way; 46% developed scientific production in this area and 63,5% took advantage of the Programme experience to develop continuing education courses. In addition to these impressive figures, 44,2% established new partnerships, 40% began to participate in other social programmes and another 48% intensified their activities in these programmes.

With regard to the relationship between the higher education institutions and the municipalities, 38,5% took advantage of the on-going training of the literacy teachers to train teachers from the formal education network in their cities and 61% participated in other actions in these municipalities.

It can certainly be confirmed that the Solidarity in Literacy Programme brought the academic world closer to the reality of Brazilian communities that are very far away from the academic world. This was done by taking volunteer university professors to a Brazil they had never known before. The Programme's consolidation allowed 73% of these institutions to increase the number of states in which they were active. The number of municipalities increased by 84,6%, and the number of trained literacy teachers increased by 92%.

Government partners: The impact of Solidarity in Literacy has been evident in the governmental sphere as well. At the federal level, the Ministry of Education has created a specific programme to finance formal youth and adult education for students who have completed the programme.

At the state level, an awareness of the importance of the fight against illiteracy has become apparent. This fight has been defined as a priority item on the social agendas of state governments. Currently, seven states have developed plans of action in conjunction with the Programme in order to serve the illiterate population.

At municipal level, there has been a growing awareness of the importance of offering education to local populations. This has been demonstrated in the institutionalisation of formal education for youth and adults.

Furthermore, benefits to the participating communities have been clear. There have been increases in the educational levels of the population, improvements in infrastructure surrounding the schools and encouragement of community participation in municipal councils. There has also been better organisation in the schools and volunteer participation by the families.

Social partnership

In terms of pedagogical advances, the contribution to the formation of a literate society has been notable. This has occurred in that the process of written language acquisition has been approached as not just a linguistic objective in the educational process. It is seen as a social linguistic objective. The Programme's political-pedagogical project emphasises that literacy training should ensure written language acquisition is meaningful. This involves working with journalistic, scientific, poetic texts and texts from a number of other sources. It includes much more than just mastering the graphic skills involved in writing. Reading and writing are thus understood as a social function. The process of literacy training makes sense only if it takes place with the objective of introducing writing as a citizenship tool. Learning causes individuals to better understand themselves, others and the reality they live in.

It is clear that each action brings new demands and generates new alliances and new projects. This is what underwrites the Programme's effectiveness.[3] The fact that the Programme has created roots and promoted new initiatives has served to make it a cultural fixture and a differentiating factor in Brazilian youth and adult education.

Crossing frontiers

The international actions of the Solidarity in Literacy Programme have flowed naturally from the recognition the Programme has won in Brazil. The Programme has been recognised as a model of efficiency and effectiveness, and has received awards and international recognition. In November 2000, the Programme began to expand its borders with a technical Cupertino in East Timor. Since then, the Programme has also been established in Mozambique (July 2001) and in São Tome and Principé (August 2001).

The principal objective of the Programme is to provide support to local governments in the development of a national youth and adult education proposal.

The international project model is developed along the same lines as the national Programme. The international projects include modules and partnerships. Changes are incorporated into methodology and thematic issues in order to serve the needs of the specific situation of the co-operating countries and in such a way as to guarantee self-sustainability. The modules last twelve months: one month for training and qualification and eleven for classes. This includes selecting and training literacy teachers, giving them support and evaluating results. It also includes establishing a local structure that will allow for continuity in the process of restructuring youth and adult education.

The Solidarity in Literacy Programme passes on its experience in management, fund raising, data systematisation and evaluation. Sustaining the projects is based on a community and partnership model. The projects allow the literacy teacher responsible for data collection to assist in providing an understanding of the diversity of the languages and dialects of the countries involved.

The local governments do their part by ensuring the necessary infrastructure and by providing support to the project's progress. The initiative depends on a partnership with the Brazilian Co-operation Agency and with the national higher education institution partners in Brazil.

East Timor

This was the first country to receive, in November 2000, the Solidarity in Literacy experience. This initiative was locally christened the Community Literacy Training Project. It is regarded as an effective tool for reinstating Portuguese as the country's official language, and it will serve as a model for the local system to use in the initial literacy training of youths and adults.

Linguistic diversity is one of the challenges the Programme faces in East Timor. Only 15% of the population speaks Portuguese, which coexists with Indonesian Bahasa, Tetum and over 35 dialects.

The project began in Dili, the capital of Timor. There were 20 literacy teachers in this project and 300 students in 11 classrooms. In August 2001, 130 more classrooms were established in 13 districts and 3 500 people benefited from the project. In addition to this, 150 literacy teachers were trained. The universities of Santa Cecília, UNIRIO, UNIMONTES, Mackenzie and Faculdades Interlagos are the Programme's higher education institution partners in this country.

Mozambique

The partnership between the Solidarity in Literacy Programme and the Mozambique government aims at lowering the illiteracy rate in Mozambique of around 60,5%. In the pilot project that was established in 2001, the initiative benefited 1 000 students in 40 classrooms. In April 2002, the Programme expanded to 200 classrooms and 7 000 students have currently benefited.

Although Portuguese is the country's official language, over 25 national languages and 33 dialects are used in Mozambique. The partner universities in this international project are the Universidade do Vale in Paraíba (UNIVAP), Methodist University in Piracicaba (UNIMEP), State University of Bahia (UNEB) and Catholic University in Rio de Janeiro (PUC-RJ).

São Tomé and Príncipe

The Solidarity in Literacy Programme supports the São Tomé and Príncipe government in the fight against illiteracy. The illiteracy rate in São Tomé and Príncipe is currently 27%. The co-operation project began in September 2001 and took place in 10 classrooms on the two islands. This expanded to over 100 classrooms with 2 500 students and 120 trained co-ordinators and local literacy teachers in September 2002. This initiative counts on the partner universities of Braz Cubas, PUC-RS, PUC-MG and the Federal University of Paraná (UFPR).

Cabo Verde, Guatemala and Angola

In the second semester of 2002, in partnership with the Brazilian Co-operation Agency, the Solidarity in Literacy Programme initiated technical Cupertino in two other countries – Cabo Verde and Guatemala. Angola will receive Brazilian Cupertino from the first semester of 2003.

Conclusions

The Solidarity in Literacy Programme is an unprecedented presence in youth and adult education in Brazil. The Programme's methods have improved in quantitative and qualitative ways in every module.

In the year 2002 alone, the Programme's goal was to reach over 1,2 million students in approximately 2 010 municipalities. Among the targets that were reached and even surpassed, four deserve special attention because they convert results into numbers that have had a tremendous impact on the field of youth and adult education. This has contributed to lower illiteracy rates and a tangible improvement in people's lives.

One of these targets concerns the increase in the number of municipalities. In January 1997, the Programme was present in 38 municipalities. In 2001 the Programme reached 1 578 municipalities and the large urban centres of São Paulo, Rio de Janeiro, Brasília, Fortaleza and Goiânia. In 2002, 2 010 municipalities participated as well as the large urban centres of Belo Horizonte and São Luís do Maranhão.

Another target that was surpassed was the number of students served. By December 2000, the Programme had served more than 1,3 million students all over the country. By December 2001 there were 2,4 million students and in December 2002 this number had increased to 3,6 million Brazilians. This is a tremendous leap, especially when one considers how difficult it is to access these municipalities.

The number of participating universities is also growing. When the Programme started, it counted on 38 higher learning institution partners. Today there are more than 200 all over the country. In addition to co-ordinating the Programme's courses, the universities work to guarantee project quality and scientific production that will generate new knowledge. This brings about new pedagogical practices.

The fourth target that has been surpassed was action abroad. The pilot project established in Dili, the capitol of East Timor, has grown by leaps and bounds. In December 2002 activity in international projects had resulted in a total of 14 250 students served in 531 classrooms with 630 trained literacy teachers. This demonstrates the respect for the model and how effectively it can be adapted to other countries.

In Brazil and abroad, it is clear that the Solidarity in Literacy Programme has promoted and encouraged the use of the Portuguese language in a creative project that is innovative particularly in youth and adult education. This has occurred, from a structural point of view, by means of pedagogical practices performed by the higher learning institution partners. These practices have brought this creativity into the internal operations of the higher learning institutions. They have also had an impact on the social reach that is part of the institutions themselves. This has taken place in the intimate relationship between education, the incorporation of new values and new cultures and the strengthening of social institutions.

The Programme has shown that illiteracy should not be dealt with only as an educational issue. Illiteracy needs to be dealt with as a social issue as well. By creating an immensely participatory movement and creating links between demands and resources, the Programme has become an example both nationally and internationally. The steps that have been taken so far are precursors for a new Brazilian model. The driving force of this model is found in participation and shared responsibility on the part of all the partners in the process. Its effectiveness is a victory for all of the partners involved, who dream of a better Brazil and actively participate in making that dream come true.

References

Alfabetiz a Cão Solidaria. (n.d.)

Censo Demográfico (2000). Instituto Brasileiro de Geografia e Estatística. Dezembro, 2001)

Censo Escolar (2000-2001). Instituto Nacional de Estudos e Pesquisas Educacionais. Ministério da Educação, 2001.')

Guiding Principles for the Preparation of Political and Pedagogic Proposals, Brazilia.

Programa Alfabetiz a ção Solidaria (Mimeograph).

Solidarity in Literacy Program, Brazil.

Notes

1 The Association for the Support of Solidarity in Literacy. This is a non-profit civil society organisation created in 1998 to manage the Solidarity in Literacy Programme.

2 The Brazilian real and the North-American dollar exchange rate at the time of writing is 1 US$ = 3.50 reals.

3 Some of the projects flowing from the National Solidarity in Literacy Programme are: The Large Urban Centers Project, the To See Project, the Digital Literacy Training Project, the Radio School Project and International Literacy Training Projects.

10

Open and distance learning: Training and support for adult educators in the field

Tony Dodds

This article examines the under-utilisation of ODL in training adult literacy and non-formal educators. It is emphasised that ODL should be used as a strategy for adult basic education and training and non-formal education, rather than as just an approach. A number of projects are discussed, and from these as well as from the author's own experiences, recommendations and suggested guidelines are drawn. Particular attention is paid to the functional education of adult educators, the need for continuing training and support of these educators, and the importance of equipping them with recognised qualifications. The role of ODL in providing this education and training is highlighted, and both the pitfalls and advantages of exploiting ODL in this context are pointed out.

Background

For several years now I have been concerned – and have expressed that concern (Dodds 1999) – that open and distance learning (ODL) was not being exploited to reach out with education to the masses of adults in Africa who have had little or no formal education – about 182 million people. This is in spite of the fact that ODL is increasingly becoming accepted in academic circles throughout the world as a legitimate, effective and even fashionable approach to educational provision, especially at the tertiary level and, for example, for the education of teachers. It is not because of evidence that it doesn't work for adult basic or non-formal education; in fact what limited evidence does exist suggests it can be very effective (Siaciwena 2002). In 1980, in a book of which I was one of four co-authors, we concluded that 'while the record was patchy it was encouraging enough to suggest that [the methods of distance education, especially radio, could] create a whole new system of non-formal education which would complement the formal' (Young et al. 1980). In fact we went so far as to suggest that these new methods could help to take adult education from the tail to the head of the long column of educational provision.

Why, twenty years later, am I forced to ask the question which formed the title of my paper in 2002 to the Pan-Commonwealth Forum on Open and Distance Learning: 'Why is open learning at-a-distance failing the masses of Africa?' (Dodds 2002).

It is against this background, and in the hope and belief that this failure is being recognised and efforts being made to turn the tide, that I am writing this paper. The first title I was asked to write to was 'An overview of adult education programmes using the methods of ODL.' This article certainly isn't an overview: I am not in a position to form an overview; it is rather an 'underview' based on a very limited and selective set of recent personal experiences. It has three purposes: (1) to stress that ODL should not be seen exclusively as a training approach for adult basic and non-formal education; it needs to be seen in the much broader context of an ODL strategy for ABET and NFE, namely as a means of expanding provision through training and continuing support and the provision of self-study opportunities for adult learning. (2) to put forward possibilities for large-scale experimentation rather than to report on a proven track record (3) to suggest cautions and conditions for success in the same breath as expressing optimism about the possibilities in an attempt to avoid the 'panacea' syndrome.

Some recent personal experiences

Much of what I have to say here is based on my own experience in three recent or still in progress programmes of using the methods of ODL for adult educator training and support.

Network for advanced professional development in open learning for Southern Africa (NAPRODOLSA)

The first is a proposal, now at quite an advanced stage of implementation, to set up a network of universities in the SADC region to collaborate in the provision of postgraduate training and research in ODL, starting with a joint MA in ODL to be offered through ODL. Its intention is to combine resources in the region to provide locally affordable postgraduate programmes in this specialised area of adult educator training. Its purposes are fourfold: (1) to provide relevant advanced training for distance educators without sending them abroad or taking them from their work. (2) to maximise the use and sharing of local expertise in the region for this purpose (3) to ensure the continuing availability of such training and its sustainability at affordable costs (4) to make use of suitable existing materials from elsewhere and to adapt them to the regional environment

This is to illustrate that these methods can be used for continuing professional development.

University of Namibia diploma in adult education and community development

In 2001 the Department of Adult Education at the University of Namibia (UNAM) began to offer, through its Centre for External Studies, its pre-graduate Diploma in Adult Education and Community Development which it had been developing on a small-scale face-to-face basis for two years previously, through ODL methods. As well as having had some administrative involvement, I have recently completed writing one of the courses for this programme. The curriculum is the same as for the internal full-time programme, the qualification achieved is the same and most of the writers and tutors are the same as those who teach the internal students. I want to draw attention here only to three characteristics of offering the programme at a distance as compared to offering it full-time on campus face-to-face. These are: (1) It allows the Department and UNAM as a whole to meet the need for adult education training which it identified in its initial needs assessment study (Nyirenda et al. 1999), namely for a programme offered part-time and at a distance. (2) Thereby it is now reaching professionals in adult education who need such advanced training and who can now follow the courses without leaving their jobs (compared to younger pre-service students who may or may not eventually become adult educators). (3) It is possible to relate the courses directly to the working experience in the field of such students and to emphasise the links between theory and practice at the same time as supporting the workers in the field through training.

Use of radio and other media to support LITERACY and NFE programmes in Mozambique

The Ministry of Education's Department of Adult and Non-formal Education of the government of Mozambique is (at the time of writing) investigating the use of radio and other media to support their adult literacy, post-literacy and non-formal education programmes. A Working Group on Radio and Other Media, at the beginning of December 2002, put forward these recommendations: (1) That radio be used for three somewhat different roles, sometimes in combination with other media, to support the new adult literacy, post-literacy and non-formal education programmes. (2) That a general and continuing series of general information, mobilisation and motivational programmes on literacy and post-literacy activities be initiated; these would start well before the first new literacy classes were launched and would continue throughout the post literacy stages. (3) A series of regular facilitator training support programmes be introduced. These would aim first at training literacy facilitators (pre-service) and then at providing continuing support and guidance to facilitators. Such a series could well be combined with printed self-study materials to reinforce the training and support and serve as continuous reference materials. This would also make it possible to offer longer-term in-service training as a properly structured distance learning course, possibly leading to a recognised professional qualification.

A third series (or possibly two parallel series) would relate to the non-formal education themes incorporated (a) into the literacy curriculum and (b) into the post-literacy curriculum. This would give additional information, ideas and skills about these functional themes and would need to be designed in order to help the facilitators to lead discussions even about topics about which they themselves have limited expertise. Ideally the series should be accompanied by simple, carefully designed printed pamphlets which again would serve as continuous reference material both for the facilitators and for the students as they began to develop their literacy skills. At the post-literacy stages such a combination can be used to allow post-literacy groups to continue to study even where there are no facilitators to lead them.

Open and distance learning in adult basic education and training and non-formal education: a broad front approach

The struggle to define 'distance education' continues after nearly thirty years. Desmond Keegan, a few years ago, published the seventh edition of a book trying to do exactly that. The addition of the word 'open' to 'distance education' has complicated the issue even further; as several people have said, there is nothing essentially open in distance education. That is why the addition of 'open' is essential for me; any acceptable definition of ODL must stress the following four characteristics: (1) the opening up of educational opportunities to all, or at least to as many as possible, by breaking down barriers that prevent people studying what they want to study; (2) the use of media, of flexible delivery systems (i.e. the methods of distance education) to make this possible; (3) the inclusion of face-to-face communication and contact, at least on an occasional basis, either tutor-led or self-help, as an important component of the package; and (4) the presence of organised learning as its primary structure.

It is with these characteristics in mind that I want to urge that we approach the use of ODL for ABE and NFE on a broad front. My broad front, however, has four focus points, reflected in the recommendations I refer to above:

The media should be used in mobilising and motivating people to use whatever learning facilities are made available to them. All the media of ODL can be used for this somewhat informal educative role (mass media, printed media and electronic media). It is a process which needs to go on continuously throughout whatever programmes are on offer; and it can include their use for informational, administrative and counselling purposes.

ODL media and structures should be used to support ABET and NFE and in particular to support the work of the adult educators and facilitators: what I will describe later as the adult learning toolkit.

ODL structures, media and materials should be used to enable adults to study on their own, without tutors, at all levels, from pre-literacy to post-literacy continuing education.

ODL should be used in the pre-service, in-service and continuous professional development of adult educators and facilitators.

The next three sections deal with each of the last three of these focus points in turn.

ODL as continuing support for literacy and non-formal adult educators and facilitators in the field: the toolbox for adult learning

Most adult NFE, almost by the definition given to the phrase by its inventors, Ahmed, Coombs, Sheffield and Diejomaoh, in the late 1960s, and probably the majority of current adult literacy programmes, put emphasis on functional education. The subject matter or themes of such learning are about development, either personal development or community, social, cultural or economic development. In literacy programmes these themes are integrated with the educational skills of reading and writing.

Also, almost by default, the facilitators (or tutors or teachers) in such programmes, especially in rural areas of developing countries, who are expected to help adults to learn about these themes, cannot be expected themselves to be very highly educated, knowledgeable about or expert in such subject matter. In Mozambique, in the curriculum development process for adult literacy that was being completed at the time of writing, 40 development themes or activities have been identified for inclusion in the literacy courses to be developed. These cover practical day-to-day activities such as banking, writing and posting letters, telling historical stories, and reading the calendar; health education themes such as HIV/AIDS, nutrition, drugs, hygiene and mother and child care; and moral and civic themes such as ethics, vandalism and human relations. Lists of agricultural and other economic activities had not yet been added to the version of the list I saw! Presumably the same literacy facilitators will be expected to help their students to learn about all these themes.

It seems to me that we have only two options: either to leave the facilitators to do the best they can with limited training, to teach superficially and inexpertly about these themes or at least about most of them; or to provide them, through ODL methods and materials, with the tools, information and expertise needed and the skills to serve genuinely as facilitators, not teachers but discussion leaders, of their students as they study such themes together.

I support my claim that this can be done by reference to two examples. The first is the Tanzanian adult literacy campaigns of the early 1970s which coincided with that country's very large-scale radio study-group campaigns on health education. The two activities were brought together in ways that enabled millions of adults to combine literacy learning with learning about health concerns and preventive medicine which they could practise themselves in their communities (Hall & Dodds 1975).

The second is the Ghana literacy campaigns of the early 1980s in which there is evidence that radio programmes, where they were available, made significant contributions to the functional learning of the students who listened (K.Siabi Mensah, cited in Siaciwena, ed. 2000). There are other examples, though not as many as there should be. These lead even the self-confessed sceptic regarding ABET and NFE, Hilary Perraton, to conclude the most pessimistic chapter of his recent book *Open and distance learning in the developing world* (Perraton 2000) with the statement: 'Conclusions about methodology are also clear: the evidence from the field continues to support the view … that the use of distance education methods within non-formal education is well understood. The combination of study groups with prepared materials works in practice as well as in theory.'

What then can the toolkit I am suggesting consist of? I believe it has three essential compartments, though the tools in each may vary according to local access to media:

Electronic media such as radio or audiocassettes (or video or video-cassettes where these are available) and possibly in the not–too distant future (though, I believe, in most situations, not yet) the new computer-based ICT; these can be used to broadcast or narrowcast learning series about the development themes in question, including guidance and stimulation to put into practice what is being learned.

Simple printed materials which serve to elaborate the content of the media series and as long-term reference materials, both for the facilitators and the learners; these may be booklets, magazines, newspaper supplements, posters, flipchart series or handouts closely related to the radio or other media programmes.

Study groups, rural forums, radio (or video) clubs, reading circles or any other form of organised group meetings in which the learners, guided and led by their facilitators, study and discuss what the media are presenting and hopefully take decisions on how to put what they learn into practice.

There can be almost endless variations on the materials used and the structures in which discussion and learning take place. The main conclusion I wish to stress is that any such combination can make it possible for facilitators who have very limited expertise in the subjects which form the development or functional themes of literacy and non-formal education to enable meaningful learning to take place about these themes where otherwise it would be at best superficial.

ODL as the basis for self-study in ABET and NFE

In many ways this role for ODL is an extension of that described in the previous section. The only major difference is that here ODL is used to make adult non-formal learning possible outside the literacy context and often in situations where there is no teacher or facilitator present at all when the learning takes place. It is the ODL methods and media themselves that make learning possible.

The first is the well-known and widely practised Radio Farm or Rural Forum movement. This started in Canada more than half a century ago, spread first to India, then to Ghana and Zambia and to many other countries in both Africa and Asia. As is demonstrated in the case study on Zambia Farm Forums in a collection of studies on NFE by ODL in Africa (Sibalwa, in Siaciwena 2000) the pattern continues successfully to this day in some countries and forms an important element in farmer education.

The second example comes from Pakistan, where for more than a decade now the Allama Iqbal Open University has run functional education programmes using ODL methods (combinations of audiocassette series, flip-charts, printed hand-outs and study groups) for people in rural areas in situations where most of the learners are illiterate. The experience of the successful experimental programmes led the university to create a special faculty of mass education to run these as well as its functional literacy programmes (Warr 1992).

The third example is closer to where we are meeting and more recent. It comes from North Central Namibia where, at the end of 2001, UNAM's Northern Campus in association with its Centre for External Studies ran an experimental programme of farmer education entitled 'Cattle are our economy'. Here again, a combination of a specially produced radio series, flip-charts with handouts of the flipchart pictures for all learners and organised study groups, was used to provide information and guidance on modern cattle husbandry techniques and to raise questions and ideas about how to apply or adapt such techniques to the particular circumstances of the learners. The evaluation suggested that the programme was popular with the listeners, that they learned from the combination and that many learners were beginning to implement what they had learned. Moreover, interest from the Ministry of Agriculture in replicating the project in other parts of the country and on a larger scale has been encouraging (Nekongo-Nielsen 2002).

Other examples of such self-help study include reading circles to rural newspapers in Mali and Ghana.

In my opinion, at the centre of the philosophy and ideology of ODL is the commitment and the ability of these methods to open up opportunities for people to study at any time in their lives which they see as appropriate. This often requires opportunities outside the restrictions of traditional learning structures, whether these be schools, universities or face-to-face adult classes. These opportunities are just as necessary in ABET and NFE as they are at higher levels, where often a major constraint is the lack of qualified and expert teachers. This kind of use of ODL for ABET and NFE, to provide opportunities for self-study at pre and post-literacy levels, can offer a crucial way of extending such learning opportunities. I have suggested above that the evidence shows it can be done; it isn't being done very widely or on a very large-scale. Why not?

The continuing professional development of adult educators

My first point is that we can learn a lot from the now considerable experience of using ODL for the training and education of formal primary and secondary school teachers (see also Anita Dighe's contribution to this book). There is also a reasonable amount of documentation available on this experience. A recent wide-ranging book about this is the third volume of the World Review of Distance Education and Open Learning entitled *Teacher Education Through Open and Distance Learning* (Robinson & Latchem 2002).

In this section I highlight some suggested guidelines, from my own experience mainly in the three projects I referred to earlier, on the design and development of programmes for adult educator training by ODL, together with some cautions about possible pitfalls to avoid.

The major learning points which I believe we need to note as we set out to expand the use of ODL for adult educator training are discussed below. I group my observations under four sub-headings: (1) Why use ODL for adult educator training: what are its advantages and strengths? (2) What can we learn from formal teacher training? (3) What are the essential characteristics of good practice in educator training by ODL? (4) What are the potential dangers and pitfalls to be avoided?

Why? Advantages and strengths

As with ODL in other forms of educational provision, its greatest advantage is that it can reach large numbers of students at the same time and to do so requires a minimum of institutional infrastructure. In the process, it can reach out to trainees in remote and scattered areas over a wide terrain. This is a particular strength in

ABET and NFE, which is perhaps most needed in such scattered rural areas in developing countries.

Of similar importance to ABET and NFE is its ability to train facilitators without taking them away from their facilitation responsibilities. This characteristic has the added strength that it assumes that the training is given on the job: the training can and should be intimately related to the job of being a facilitator. As a result, it is possible to give long-term and in-depth training as compared to the traditional short, intensive training courses that are often all facilitators receive. From that it follows that such training can, if so planned, lead to professional qualifications which can in turn be a means of career development and thereby an important form of motivation.

Finally, though I believe this must be interpreted carefully, training by ODL can be a highly economical form of training. This is only the case if the number to be trained is large enough to allow for the economies of scale to come into play.

What can we learn from formal teacher training by ODL?

The first thing to say, I believe with confidence, is that teachers can be and have been quite successfully trained, in large numbers, using the methods of ODL. Robinson and Latchem (2002) conclude that: 'The use of distance education to upgrade the qualification levels of teachers has been widespread in both industrialised and developing countries ... Not all courses have worked well, or provided good quality, though enough have to demonstrate the capacity of distance education for training and educating teachers and for enabling new models of training to be explored.'

Secondly, ODL has been used in various forms both for the initial training of teachers immediately after their recruitment in ways that allowed them to become classroom teachers much earlier than is normally possible through college-based systems, and for the in-service training of existing untrained or under-trained practising teachers. There is more reported experience of the latter, though we must bear in mind that almost by its nature, ODL is an in-service form of training.

The third important lesson, and perhaps the most important, is that it can combine both content-based subject knowledge and expertise upgrading with providing understanding of the theories and principles of pedagogy (or in our case andragogy), and at the same time practical 'how-to-teach' training. However, as Robinson and Latchem (2002) point out: 'Developing skills in teaching requires a mixture of information, support for the development of understanding, guided observation, opportunities for experiment, practice, feedback, reflection and re-planning. Some of this learning can be assisted by the use of different media such as video or audio, but skill development needs practice over time, feedback, coaching and interaction on an individual basis.'

This leads directly to my fourth lesson: such programmes need significant infrastructural support networks, much of it part-time, to allow a lot of face-to-face practical support, tutoring and guidance. Such face-to-face support often seems most effective if it includes some form of local mentoring activity. These networks require significant financial and human resources and undermine the economies of scale I mentioned earlier.

Any system must be designed to use, as far as possible, delivery media which are already readily available to the students or can be easily made available to them by the providing institution.

A final and very important lesson is that such programmes take a large amount of time and resources to develop before they can be put into effective practice, and it is likely that students taking such programmes will take considerably longer to complete their training than if they were taking equivalent courses on a full-time, face-to-face basis.

Essential characteristics of good practice

The points I want to make under this sub-heading are inevitably somewhat repetitive of those made in the previous two subsections. The essential characteristics of good practice, in my view, are: (1) A combination of very carefully planned, well-designed learning materials using a variety of readily available media (print, radio/audio, TV/video, ICT as accessible) is the first prerequisite. (2) Well-organised, effective student support services, including regular face-to-face contact sessions, must be provided through a network of facilities easily accessible to the students. (3) Learning theory, subject content and classroom practice must be carefully and thoroughly integrated in the courses: what is taught as theory needs to be related to how it can affect practice in the classroom, for example, 'how does this particular bit of adult learning psychology help you to teach adults to write (or to practise agriculture) more effectively?' or 'how can you use this particular teaching method in making your teaching of numeracy more effective? Report in your assignment on your experience of doing so.' (4) Clearly, in order to make this work, there needs to be plenty of opportunity for feedback on student progress. (5) As mentioned above, an effective mentoring system, where students have as local as possible professional support from an experienced teacher or facilitator can make an enormous contribution to the success of such support though it can be very difficult to provide. (6) Finally, as has been said several times above, it is vital, I believe, that the result of successful completion of such training is some form of recognised accreditation or qualification which will contribute to career development.

Dangers and pitfalls to avoid

Most of these arise from underestimating the importance of the points made above. The most important to me are: (1) underestimating the development and preparation time required to set up the system and to prepare the materials; (2) underestimating the human and financial resources required to set it up, to make the preparations and to maintain the operation of the programme throughout its life; (3) concentrating almost exclusively on transferring knowledge and theory in an essentially didactic form (i.e. the easy bits of developing distance learning materials) to the exclusion of creating structures and materials that ensure the practical application and coaching of what is being learned to the business of being a teacher or facilitator; (4) under-utilising the greatest advantage of in-service ODL training, namely the opportunity to promote a learning-by-doing approach; (5) assuming, as the literature on ODL often claims, that students studying this way are automatically independent and self-motivated when they start their courses rather than providing them with study skills, counselling and guidance which will help them to become independent learners; (6) finally, failing to ensure, before the programme is launched, full, official and widely publicised recognition, presumably by the Ministry of Education and all other concerned authorities, of the programme, its qualification and what it qualifies completers to do.

Conclusion: where do we go from here?

In this final section I want to raise some questions and make some suggestions for research, networking and disseminating information. At the end of my paper to the Durban Pan-Commonwealth Forum on Open Learning in 2002 I raised the question of whether my pessimistic analysis of the status of ODL for ABET and NFE, namely that it was so far failing the masses of Africa, was correct and if so, what could we do about it. I want to end this article with similar questions addressed both to the community of ODL professionals and to the ABET and NFE professionals.

How can we contribute to turning the tide of failure into success? How can we ensure that decision takers get sufficient evidence of the possibilities, and of the requirements for success, to persuade them to make the resources we require available and to give us the chance to turn that tide?

I am sure that the four items listed below are vital: (1) research and evaluation; (2) networking of expertise and materials; (3) dissemination of information about experience; (4) promoting collaboration between institutions

I wish to raise here, as I did in Durban, the question as to whether there is a role, in promoting these three, for a professional advocacy and/or research body in this kind of educational provision such as an African (or intercontinental) Foundation for Open Learning at a Distance for Adult Basic and Literacy Education (AFOLDABLE). While pondering this article on a train in the depths of rural France, I thought of a non-exclusively African title for such a foundation: the Open Learning Foundation for Adult Basic Education and Training (OLFABET).

References

Dodds, T 1999. *Non-formal and adult education through open and distance learning in Africa: developments in the nineties towards education for all.* Windhoek: University of Namibia.

Dodds, T 2002. Why is open and distance learning failing the masses of Africa? Paper presented at Pan Commonwealth Forum on Open and Distance Education, Durban, South Africa.

Hall, B & Dodds, T 1974. *Voices for development: the Tanzanian National Radio Study Campaign.* Cambridge: IEC.

Nekongo-Nielsen, H Nd. Extending educational opportunities to people in North Central Namibia. In *Reader for Module 4: media for adult learning*, Windhoek: University of Namibia Centre for External Studies.

Nyirenda, J E et al 1999. *Developing professional adult education programmes in Namibia*. Windhoek: University of Namibia, Department of Adult and Non-formal Education.

Perraton, H 2000. *Open and distance learning in the developing world.* London: Routledge.

Robinson, B & Latchem, C (eds). 2002. *Teacher education through open and distance learning*. Vancouver: COL; London: Routledge Falmer.

Siaciwena, R (ed). 2000. *Case studies of non-formal education by distance and open learning*. Vancouver: COL/DFID.

Young, M et al. 1980. *Distance teaching for the Third World: the lion and the clockwork mouse*. London: Routledge and Kegan Paul.

Warr, D 1992. *Distance teaching in the village*. Cambridge: IEC.

11

The certificate in education for development: A direct response to the training needs of adult literacy promoters, agricultural extension and community development workers

Frances J Mensah

Introduction

The Namibian College of Open Learning (NAMCOL) is a state-supported educational institution which was established by an Act of Parliament to provide learning opportunities for adults and out-of-school youths. The College can trace its roots back to various continuing and distance education programmes available to Namibians before Independence. In late 1994, these programmes were consolidated under a single directorate within the Ministry, though this was but the first step in NAMCOL's transformation into an autonomous institution. In April 1998, the newly-established College took over responsibility for the programmes formerly provided by the Ministry of Basic Education, Sport and Culture.

Traditionally, the core activity of the College has been its programme of Alternative Secondary Education, which offers courses leading to examinations at two levels.

The Junior Secondary Certificate is the nationally set and marked examination taken by most Grade 10 learners. The International General Certificate of Secondary Education is an externally accredited, school-leaving examination taken by the majority of Grade 12 learners in Namibia. NAMCOL learners studying for these qualifications follow the same syllabuses and sit the same examinations as their counterparts in formal schools.

In 1997, NAMCOL initiated the Certificate in Education for Development (CED) programme jointly with the Adult Basic Education and Training Institute (ABET) of the University of South Africa (Unisa). The CED is a two-year programme that was designed to meet the professional development needs of adult educators, extension agents and community development workers. It is offered through a combination of distance education and residential workshops, and is recognised as the equivalent of two years of study at post-matriculation level.

Starting with the 2001 intake, NAMCOL has introduced a fully-fledged, Namibianised CED programme, offered through a similar combination of distance education and residential workshops. This is also a two-year programme.

The certificate in education for development

Background

Since Independence in March 1990, Namibia's development plans have been geared towards promoting the development of human resources and economic growth. Through its diverse policies, the government of the Republic of Namibia is committed to building institutional capacity throughout the country, while various government departments and NGOs employ personnel to do development work and promote democracy in Namibia. Enhancement of community participation and mobilisation requires a core of well-trained adult educators.
At the time of our Independence the country did not have enough adult educators with the required knowledge and skills to accomplish this task. The government of the Netherlands undertook to support the National Literacy Programme in Namibia (NPLN), by strengthening the capacity of the Division of Adult Basic Education in the Ministry of Basic Education, Sport and Culture (MBESC).

One of the main areas of this support was: enhancement of the capacity building of the NLPN by supporting its general staff training and in particular the development of a Certificate in Education (CED) Course for the mid-level staff of the NLPN and their equivalents in other ministries and NGOs.

The first objective of NAMCOL is to contribute towards the social and economic development of Namibia by upgrading the educational level of adults and out-of-school youths: (1) through programmes of open learning; (2) by designing, developing and offering programmes to address the diverse educational needs of such adults and out-of-school youths, and (3) by providing opportunities for adults and out-of school youths to upgrade their professional and vocational skills, as well as their general education, to attain economic self-improvement and managerial skills for the sound management of, inter alia, rural societies and NGOs.

The CED therefore falls under the third strategy of upgrading professional and vocational skills and it is NAMCOL's first venture beyond school-based qualifications.

The CED grew as a response to the needs of a particular target group within the MBESC. The original stimulus for the course was the necessity of upgrading the district literacy officers (DLOs) who are responsible for the management and training of the 3 000 literacy promoters throughout Namibia. This need was identified partly due to the job grading of DLOs as specialised teachers requiring relevant, accredited tertiary qualifications. Other potential users identified included government extension workers and non-government community workers.

Content

The CED has benefited from an agreement with the ABET Institute of the University of South Africa (Unisa) whereby student material, assignments, marking and moderation were initially all undertaken by Unisa. The course was a combination of ABET material and local workshops consisting of four modules: (1) Theory and Practice of Adult Education; (2) Development Studies; (3) Organisational Development Studies; (4) Basic Research Methods and Practices, supplemented by various workshops on Development Studies, Gender Analysis, Training of Trainers, Statistical Analysis, English Language Upgrading and Organisational Development.

The face-to-face aspect of the CED has added a different dimension to the course. An internal evaluation report of the CED found that over 80% of the respondents rated the workshops as useful, relevant, well presented and well organised. These supplementaries were designed to give a Namibian perspective to the course and to supplement the Unisa ABET materials in response to the specific training needs of the DLOs in particular. These workshops proved crucial for student support and the successful delivery of the programme.

Namibian CED

Towards the end of 1999, however, it became clear that the future of the programme was at risk, since most DLOs had been trained and funding was about to run out in March 2000. A feasibility study was then commissioned to establish, inter alia, the future demand for the CED programme.

Literacy promoters

***Tasks of literacy promoters*:** There are over 1 000 literacy promoters throughout the country who are responsible for offering literacy, English and adult primary education classes. They are required to mobilise communities to attend classes and to lead discussions on development issues within the class. Their numbers alone suggest that they could have a significant impact on community development through literacy and adult education in Namibia. According to the second overall National Literacy Evaluation report, the task of the promoter is immense. He requires a wide knowledge base to be able to guide discussions and come out with something new and related to the objectives.

The report explains that as adult educators, the promoters are responsible for adapting and even developing curriculum material to suit the particular needs of their community's literacy group. In many reports, it has been stated that the ultimate success of the literacy programme rests upon the skills and commitment of the literacy promoters. Unfortunately, it appeared that many of the literacy promoters were not well equipped to fulfil these multifaceted responsibilities and the training they received was still often minimal.

***Training needs of literacy promoters*:** Literacy promoters seemed an ideal target for the CED as the frontline adult educators in the country. The various reports and evaluations have all highlighted the need for more intensive training for them. If they were to be the main target for the CED, the course would have to be realigned with their particular needs in mind. The list below, culled from the five ERA reports and the two overall evaluations of the NLPN, provided a review of those needs in three specific areas: mobilising, organising, teaching.

***Mobilising*:** The ability to mobilise required a number of skills and abilities on the part of the literacy promoters: (1) communicating with community leaders; (2) motivating and inspiring potential learners; (3) relating literacy to development needs in community; (4) undertaking a needs assessment in the community; (5) continuing to interest learners in literacy classes; (6) continuing to motivate learners at all stages.

***Organising*:** This involved two skills: (1) keeping attendance records; (2) planning a lesson.

***Teaching*:** A skilled literacy promoter needed the following teaching skills and knowledge: (1) using a variety of methods suitable for adult learners; (2) relating relevant local issues into class; (3) speaking clearly, distinctly and understandably; (4) speaking clearly and confidently in English; (5) coping with multi-level skills in one class; (6) understanding and using a variety of assessment methods; (7) sufficient understanding of development issues to guide discussions and use codes

***Course requirements*:** The staff at the Directorate of Adult Basic Education (DABE) identified a few weaknesses in the CED that they wanted rectified before a large number of the literacy promoters went through the course. The main criticism was that the course was not practical enough, and though the DLOs might be able to talk about theories of adult education, they could not translate those theories into practical action in the field. This was a serious concern that had to be addressed for the CED to be effective in meeting the needs of the literacy promoters, and indeed of development in Namibia.

Agricultural extension workers

***Responsibilities of extension workers*:** NAMCOL was approached by the Directorate of Rural Water Supply with a request that it should provide training for agricultural extension workers. Most of the extension workers have a Grade 10 education, while a few have Grade 9.

There are six to eight extension officers per region. They are responsible for community-based water point management. This entails mobilising and sensitising communities concerning water supply, establishing and training water point committees and following-up on the committees.

The training programme for the committees included: leadership; record keeping; analysing problems and conflict resolution; roles, responsibilities and planning; managing funds.

***Training needs of extension workers*:** The extension officers required more training in the skills mentioned above to be able to transfer them to others in the community through workshops and classes. The Ministry undertook its own training of trainers' course.

A report from the MAWRD highlighted a number of additional training needs of extension technicians and workers: communication skills; training in how to transfer knowledge and skills to an adult, often illiterate, clientele; skills for working with groups; extension methodology skills; management skills; planning, monitoring, reporting

Some current training being given to these workers was criticised for containing massive content areas which encourage focusing on teacher-centred methods which reinforce the example set to students in the school system, which sees education and training as merely the one-way flow of knowledge from teacher to student.

The report suggested that any training given needed to produce high-quality generalists given an uncertain job market and possible satiation within the ministry for diploma holders; decrease content to allow for more student learning and practice and a focus on key competencies required to carry out the job and to allow for sufficient follow-up and monitoring of training.

There was an obvious overlap between the training needs of literacy promoters and those of extension workers. In addition many of the same problems with previous training – lack of a competency-based approach – were mentioned.

Community activators

Responsibilities of community activators**:** Community activators within the Ministry of Regional and Local Government and Housing (MRLGH) have three main areas of responsibility: to mobilise the communities to establish development committees, to mobilise the communities to establish early childhood development (ECD) programmes and to support these initiatives, and to mobilisc communities to establish income-generating activities and to support these initiatives.

Training needs of activators**:** Activators and liaison officers serve under the regional Chief Community Liaison Officer. There are approximately sixty community activators throughout the country. Community activators and liaison officers interviewed requested more training in the areas of: report writing, project management, budgeting and financial controls, early childhood development, leadership and conflict management and record keeping.

The Directorate of Habitat, Community and Early Childhood Development was interested in sending community activators and liaison officers to do the CED. Community activators are required to have Grade 12 and are usually given in-service training on community development. The CED would be relevant to their work in communities and would give them a greater appreciation of the mechanisms and theoretical basis of development.

As is evident in the discussion of literacy promoters and extension workers, many of the same training needs were mentioned.

NGO community workers**:** Rossing Foundation had already utilised the CED course for some of its community workers. Other NGOs also had community level workers and adult educators on their staff. For example, the Council of Churches in Namibia had a few trainers in early childhood development who could benefit from a course such as CED. Promoters working for Oxfam, previously students of !Nara, had expressed a need for more information on community development practice and theory to enlighten their practice in the community. The demand from NGOs would probably always be quite small, due partly to funding constraints and partly to the size of the sector.

The beauty of the CED course was, however, that it could bring together frontline workers from different ministries and different sectors. This would be a significant achievement. At village level there is a proliferation of groups set up by different agencies (including water point committees, Farmer Extension and Development Groups and Literacy Groups). This means duplicating efforts aimed at group mobilization and causes confusion among community members.

Other existing courses in Namibia

Although many NGOs and government ministries offered short courses and upgrading workshops to their employees, the CED had some unique advantages. The CED was offered through distance mode to community workers with Grade 12, or in some cases Grade 10 plus appropriate experience. The requirements of the course thus made it accessible to the vast number of community workers in Namibia. The CED was accredited by the NQA as 12 + 2 (community development) and could result in a higher job grading and subsequent salary increase for some government employees. This was a tremendous motivation for students. The accreditation of CED thus needed to be confirmed and the adjustments to job scale publicised.

Recommendations

Recommendations from the study at that time pointed out that there was indeed a need for a programme of this nature in Namibia and that the programme had a much wider application potential and great relevance in the sense that for instance literacy promoters, agricultural extension agents, and community development workers could all benefit from the programme.

Demand for the CED

Extension workers, promoters and community activators are the frontline development workers in Namibia. They required skills in a variety of areas in order to be effective. There was thus a substantial need for additional training and certification at this level. Although a multitude of short courses were available for most government community workers, these might not lead to the certification necessary for job grading; nor did they provide the depth and scope of a certificate level course. The CED distance programme was well positioned to fill that gap.

The CED was the only distance learning course available for community workers and adult educators in Namibia. The University of Namibia (UNAM), through its Department of Adult and Non-formal Education within the Faculty of Education, was developing distance materials for its Diploma in Adult Education. These materials were scheduled to be available for distance learners as from 2001. Although the diploma course would represent competition to the CED, others with insufficient points to gain admission to the diploma, for example the many literacy promoters, would still value and seek the accreditation and skills supplied by the CED.

Content of CED

The content of the current CED had to be revised to fulfil the requirements of the NQA in a coherent and consistent manner. The revised CED outline should incorporate all the supplementary material as a matter of urgency. The proposed programme outline should incorporate units to meet the training needs highlighted earlier: (1) project development and implementation; (2) a full English language course and (3) a stronger focus on development issues in Namibia.

In addition, the programme should be designed and presented in terms of a practical, competency-based approach.

Suitable materials for the CED

The ABET materials were user-friendly for distance delivery, but needed additional scope and depth to meet the requirements for the Namibian CED. In order to do this it was suggested that CED should rewrite the materials using local course writers. This was always part of the original vision for the CED.

Content of Namibian CED

Based on the findings of the feasibility study, the course outline for the programme was revised and materials were developed (addressing the training needs of a wider target population). A fully Namibianised CED programme was put into practice in 2001 and at the time of writing the first cohort of NAMCOL CED learners (82 in total from different sectors of the society) were due to complete the programme at the end of 2002. Forty-nine learners were currently enrolled for the first year.

Structure of the programme

This programme is offered through a combination of distance and face-to-face modes of study. There is a residential orientation workshop at the start of the programme, during which students receive study materials and learn how to study by distance learning. Two workshops are held in most parts of the country during the year.

Programme content

The programme consists of five courses: *Communication and Language Skills (CED 01):* This course aims at enabling students to use vocabulary correctly and confidently, communicate effectively and appropriately through the medium of written English, use correct grammatical structures in speaking and writing English, and understand and critically evaluate written information in English from the course material and from other relevant sources.

Development studies (CED 02): This course looks at what development means in our context. It investigates the relation of health, employment, the environment and education to development in Namibia. The course discusses development policies in Namibia and analyses the effectiveness of different approaches. It looks at specific development needs and suggests interventions.

Theory and practice of adult learning (CED 03): This course attempts to identify who your learners are. It looks at how adults learn, barriers to learning, recruitment, screening of learners and assessment of learners. It discusses different teaching methods and resources.

Theory and practice of community development (CE 04): This course looks at how we mobilise communities. It focuses on different target groups, namely women and youth. Special attention is given to people with disabilities.

Project development and management (CED 05): This course explains how you can manage community development projects. It looks at effective management skills and emphasises practical skills such as minute writing, proposal writing and organising meetings.

Conclusion: Future plan for CED

The idea to develop and introduce a third year for the CED basically emanated from first, a strong conviction on our part that it is crucial for CED graduates to be able to further their studies in the field of adult education and community development work after completing the programme. And second, from a request from the MBESC in this regard.

In order to address the first of these and thereby secure future pathways for our learners, a request was forwarded to UNAM in 2000 to formally recognise the programme. Although a visitation panel was sent to NAMCOL at the time and specific recommendations were made with regard to formal recognition, at the time of writing UNAM had not been able to conclude this matter. It is anticipated, though, that CED graduates will get some credits to enrol for UNAM's bachelor's degree in Adult Education.

With regard to the request from MBESC, we were informed that the Public Service Commission has great difficulty in placing people with a two-year qualification on salary/grading scales, since a three-year qualification (equivalent to BETD) is regarded as the minimum entry level qualification for teaching staff in the public service.

Prompted by the above considerations, a process was started to investigate the possibility of introducing a third year for the CED. After careful consideration, the ABET Institute of Unisa was approached and it was established that it would be possible for our CED graduates to enrol with Unisa for the third year of their Higher Diploma in Adult Basic Education and Training. The ABET Diploma is accredited by the South African Qualifications Authority (SAQA) as a matric plus 3 level qualification and our learners would, therefore, benefit from this accreditation as well. However, a formal request for recognition will have to be submitted to the NQA.

It is envisaged that learners will enrol with NAMCOL and that we will enrol them in bulk with Unisa for the year. Unisa will then distribute all course materials through us and will be responsible for assessment. NAMCOL will provide local support, primarily through vacation workshops. Upon successful completion, learners will receive the three-year Higher Diploma from Unisa (and if deemed desirable, a joint NAMCOL/UNISA diploma with the same status). At their last meeting in November 2002, the NAMCOL Board of Governors approved this direction and the course outline. This course will therefore be introduced in 2004.

*Please Note: The ABT104 course is given as an additional option to all students who have done the fully Namibianised CED programme with NAMCOL since 2001. All NAMCOL/ABET students have already done this course in their first year with Unisa (between 1997and 2000) and, therefore, don't have this as an option.

References

Beukes, J. (2002) Proposal for the Introduction of third year for the CED – October 2001.

Hess, C. (1998) CED Report.

Keeja, Tauanda Yates, Dee-dee (1999) CED Feasibility Study. NAMCOL Statistical Digest.

12

Adult educators' training in Egypt

Mohsen Kamal Abu Seif

Introduction

The NGO Service Centre is a developmental activity that aims to strengthen the capacity of Egyptian civil society organisations in order to increase citizen participation in public decision-making. Within this context the Office of Civil Society Strengthening and Promotion (OCSSP) is responsible for delivering training and technical assistance services to NGOs in Egypt. As part of its goal to strengthen civil society's structure and capacity, OCSSP has initiated different training programmes, including the Training of Trainers (TOT) for Adult Educators programme – the focus of this paper.

The TOT for Adult Educators programme is intended to develop sustainable and indigenous training and technical support resources for the NGO community in Egypt. TOT programmes are imperative for sustainable development in the developing world, as such programmes aim to develop a cadre of trainers and Adult Educators, as well as technical assistance providers in specific fields such as advocacy, management, gender and governance, in order to orient people who are working with the community and enhance their skills.

The NGO SC is the pioneer in designing a TOT certification programme in Egypt that includes adult educator selection, evaluation and graduation, starting from the selection stage and the preparation of trainers along different levels, namely: introductory, intermediate and advanced up to certification and graduation of candidates.

NGO service centre TOT programmes vision

The vision for the TOT Adult Educators programmes put into practice by the NGO Service Centre is to: (1)

develop a TOT curriculum using distance learning methodology; (2) develop a stand-alone TOT package to be used as a self-learning tool; (3) develop a website to provide registered participants with updated information; (4) develop videotapes to be used as a guide to help participants while studying their TOT package; (5)

hold regular general meetings to give the distance learning registered participants an opportunity to meet and discuss issues; (6) conduct a meeting towards the end of the course to provide face-to-face interaction and guidance; (7) using the TOT evaluation system, to assess the registered participants' progress and calculate their grades; (8) certificate participants who achieve a satisfactory level of learning and practice as stated in the TOT evaluation system and (9) follow up and upgrade graduated participants according to the rules of the TOT evaluation system.

Structure of the programme

The TOT programme comprises seven phases: (1) screening; (2) interview and collective meeting; (3) first training programme; (4) second training programme (specialised); (5) third training programme (advanced); (6) training exercise; (7) follow-up after TOT programme execution. These stages are described in more detail below.

Screening

The screening process consists of a review of CVs submitted by applicants to ensure that the best candidates are selected. The purpose is to increase the cost-effectiveness of the implementation of the TOT programme and to reduce the risk of participants' dropping out during the course of the programme.

Interviews and collective meeting

The best candidates are selected based on their participation and interaction with other colleagues in the collective meeting.

First training programme: introductory

During the first training programme, the participants are introduced to different training skills. These skills are appropriate to training functions such as needs assessment, curriculum development, implementation as well as monitoring and evaluation. Participants are also introduced to different presentation techniques and the actual subject matter, in order to familiarise them with the main concepts, viz advocacy, governance, networking, gender and management.

The objective of this phase is to ensure that participants understand and are able to effectively use training cycle and adult learning principles, session planning guidelines and elementary and basic issues of the subject matter.

Second training programme: specialised

During this phase participants are expected to understand and effectively use training curriculum development techniques as well as facilitation skills with a large group, together with specialised issues relevant to the subject matter.

Third training programme: advanced

Participants at this phase are expected to understand and effectively apply training management principles and marketing skills in order to commence their training careers.

Training exercise

During this phase the participants are required to design and put into practice a graduation project whereby they practice what they have learnt throughout the different phases. They basically design, put into practice and manage a one-day workshop for participants from NGOs, and at the end they carry out an evaluation of the workshop.

The objective of this phase is to evaluate the ability of participants to: apply training principles in real training; work independently as trainers; understand and clearly transfer the subject matter to participants from different backgrounds and levels of education; deal with unexpected situations.

Follow-up after TOT programme implementation

This last phase is the starting point for the participants as professional trainers. Through this phase we hope to enhance their capacity after the completion of the TOT programme as well as to assist TOT graduates to commence their training careers.

Programme evaluation

This process is complemented by evaluation procedures and tests that measure the readiness of the trainer in terms of knowledge, attitude and skills. Programme evaluation is used as a tool for assessing and modifying the programme's efficiency and effectiveness through: (1) assessing the participant's reaction; (2) assessing the participant's progress during the programme implementation; (3) identifying areas needed for development in the participant's performance

The evaluation dimensions can be divided into four levels: reaction, learning, skills and behaviour, and results. A maximum of 100 grades may be scored in terms of the evaluation system.

Based on a participant's total score, his or her grades will be one of the following: A (80-100 %); B (65-79 %); C (50-64 %); D (Less than 50 %).

On completion of this evaluation, the participants who successfully complete the programme become graduates of the TOT programme and are declared certified trainers at a graduation ceremony organised by the NGO Service Centre.

Training of trainers follow-up and upgrading

TOT alumni develop an action plan after receiving the graduation report. They work on their action plan using distance learning methodology (receive materials and indirect support from TOT co-ordinators, i.e. telephone or email). A general meeting is held for graduated trainers so that they can receive feedback on their action plan progress and can be given whatever support they need. In addition, a network is established among TOT alumni so that they can share experience and information with their peers. Based on progress and achievement, graduated trainers will be upgraded according to the TOT evaluation system.

Lessons learned

Lessons learned through application of the TOT programme are: more attention should be paid to the screening process at an early stage. In addition, a one-day orientation workshop should be conducted for the participants to make them aware of the commitment and efforts they will have to make during the TOT programme execution, and of their obligations during the course of the programme..

Another lesson learnt is that participant NGOs should have a more active role during the TOT programme implementation. Related to this is that participating NGOs should be assessed to develop training functions within the NGO structure to ensure the sustainability of the TOT programme effect.

Finally, participants should be assigned to develop training materials and manage training sessions at the early stages of the TOT programme to give them an opportunity to put the training into practice.

13

Training local government councillors in Tanzania mainland: A case study

Nderikyo Elizabeth Ligate

The Training of Local Government Councillors' Project was put into practice throughout Tanzania Mainland between 1996 and 1998 by the South African Extension Unit (SAEU) under the overall management of the Commonwealth Local Government Forum (CLGF). The Project was co-funded by the European Union (EU) under its budget line for projects relating to human rights and democratisation in developing countries and was allocated an amount of 207 700 Euros. Further funding included 15 390 Euros from the Irish government specifically for the pilot exercise, 26 373 Euros from the Dutch government for printing study modules, 7 588 Euros from the government of Tanzania for providing countrywide study venues and 5 341 Euros from the Carnegie Fund through the CLGF. The total costs of the programme therefore came to 262 392 Euros. The project is discussed below under three main headings: (1) Need for the project; (2) Process of organising the project; (3) Evaluation of the project

Need for a local government councillors' distance education project

The first multi-party civic elections were held in Tanzania in October 1994. The elections brought to power a total of 3198 new councillors. Unlike their predecessors, these councillors had to fulfil their duties under a new political order, that of 'multi-partyism'. The Tanzanian civil service reform programme, which was taking place then, recognised the reform of local government as an integral part of the process. In addition, training for councillors and local government staff was recognised as one of the eighteen essential elements of local government reform.

Commenting in more specific terms on the need for councillors' training, Ngware (1995) points out that the rules of the game in a mono-party council are different from those in a multi-party council. Ngware notes that in the latter, a council's deliberations and decisions take place through a process and culture guided by rules of the council characterised by participation, democracy, transparency, respect for minority views, collective responsibility and the need to put the electorate's interests above those of individual councillors. In order to do this, councillors need skills, knowledge and experience as leaders, politicians, negotiators, managers and coalition and consensus builders. Ngware also underscores these necessary skills are not acquired automatically but are learned and Councillors must be trained in order to acquire them.

A further problem was that councillors from different parties but serving on the same council did not always see eye-to-eye with each other and as a result some councils experienced serious conflicts.

From this account, it is obvious that there was an urgent need to strengthen the local government system in Tanzania through a systematic human resource capacity building project, among other interventions. While it was clear that such a programme was vital for both councillors and the staff, this case study considers only the councillors.

Taking into account the size of the target group (more than 3 000 councillors) and its geographical spread, the urgency of the need for training, and the importance of equity in educational provision and training, distance education (DE) was thought to be the strategy which could most effectively address councillors' training needs.

However, not every DE project can promise urgent delivery of the required goods. For instance, to be sure of timely delivery of effective materials, the DE provider has to be a quality provider. For this reason the next logical question to tackle was the extent to which the envisaged SAEU Distance Education Project for Local Government Councillors carried the hallmarks of a quality distance education project.

The challenges facing the formulation of a DE project

Whenever a quality training project is formulated there are various challenges which must be considered. There are, for instance, challenges associated with the target group, policy decisions, quality control mechanisms, training needs assessments; the training institution's capability, support mechanisms, the learning environment itself and how to evaluate it. The chart below elaborates on these challenges.

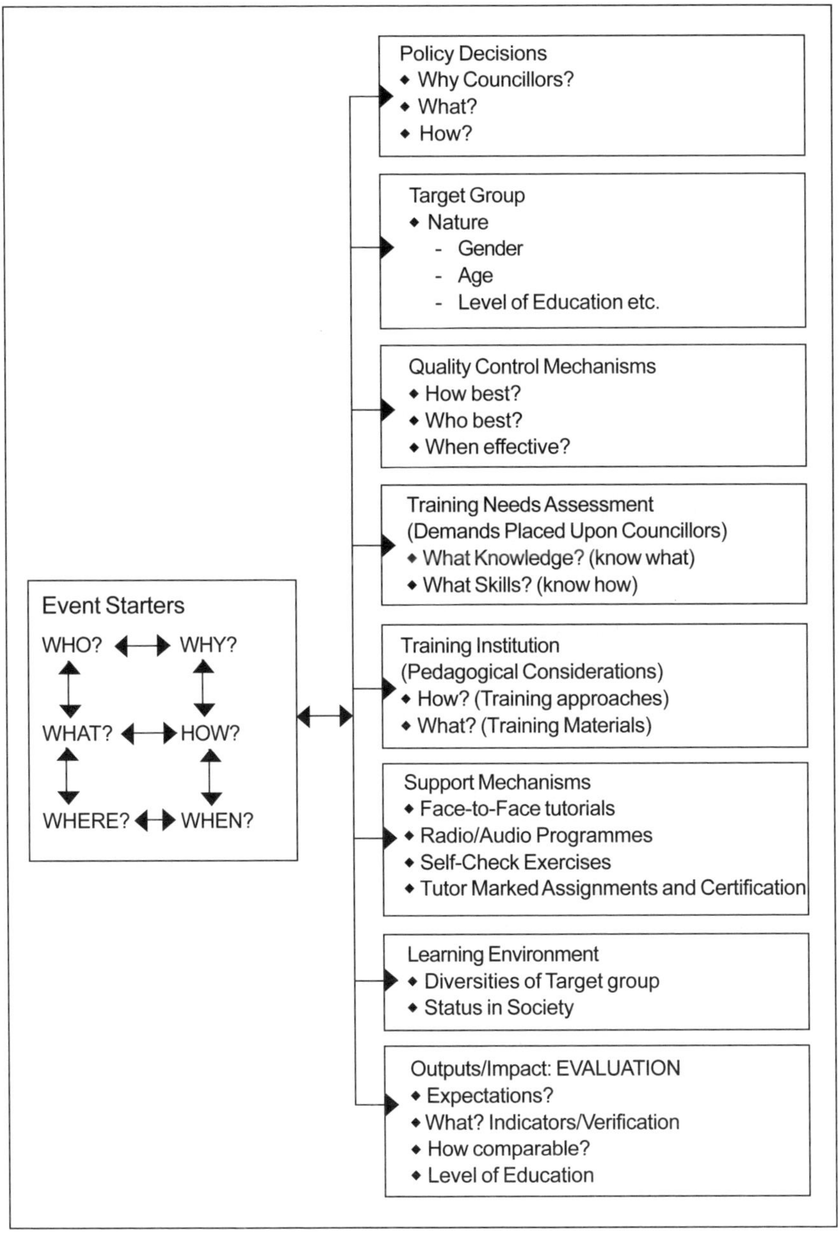

Figure 1 Challenges facing the formulation of the training project

Organising the project

Nature and needs of the target group

A sample consisting of one council from each tier of the local government system was studied to establish gender patterns, age groups, educational levels, training areas and current professions among councillors. The sample was made up of elected councillors from the City Council of Dar es Salaam (47), Moshi Municipal Council (14), Singida Town Council (26) and Kisarawe District Council (19).

Data collected from the sample showed that only a very small fraction of councillors in the country were women. This situation accounts for the provision in the electoral law that each political party must nominate women councillors for a council proportionately to the number of elected councillors in that council, to ensure gender aspects are mainstreamed in the activities of the councils.

The sample also indicated that the bulk of the councillors (92%) were literate adults between 35 and 54 years old. These were mature adults who therefore possessed the required level of discipline for distance learning. They would also have the necessary literacy skills to follow the course, which would be delivered primarily by print media. Whereas 3% appeared to have acquired literacy skills through functional literacy projects, 55% of the sample of councillors had primary education, 42% secondary education and 1% tertiary education. There was thus a significant range of educational experience among them. In spite of this, the course had been designed to be used by all the councillors, their different levels of education notwithstanding, by presenting the course in Kiswahili, which is the country's lingua-franca; focusing the discussions on areas of interest and relevance to all the councillors (their roles under multi-partyism) and presenting concepts in simple, common and clear terms.

Project design and development

The project was designed on the basis of a Training Needs Assessment (TNA), which yielded essential information on the needs and means of organising the DE project. The TNA meetings and workshops involving the relevant experts and field personnel were organised by the SAEU with a view to developing the training project. Experts and field personnel who took part in these workshops were drawn from the University of Dar es Salaam (Local Government Research Unit of the Institute of Development Studies and Department of Political Science), Association of Local Authorities in Tanzania (ALAT), Local Government Services Commission (LGSC), Prime Ministers' Office (PMO), Hombolo Local Government Institute and SAEU. The draft project worked out by these experts was further enriched by views and proposals collected from a cross-section of councillors in the country.

It was the consensus of some of the stakeholders (field personnel, councillors, ALAT, PMO), expressed at interviews, that the course should be entitled: The Conduct of the Councillors in a Multi-party Democracy System. Since there was an urgent need to provide it on an equitable basis to all the councillors throughout the country, the most rational course of action was to provide it at a distance through printed media, supplemented by face-to-face sessions as well as radio/audio programmes. The objectives of the project included: (1) Exposing the councillors to the history of the local government system in Tanzania, so that they could come away with a clearer understanding of the contemporary local government system and its dynamics (2) Assisting the councillors to enhance their knowledge and skills, thereby enabling them to fulfil their duties in a multi-party democracy more effectively; (3) Training local government councillors in their roles and duties in a multi-party, democratic system; (4) Providing councillors with the means to successfully access further training in local government management within and outside the country (SAEU 1995a).

In order to realise the foregoing objectives it was proposed that three self-instructional modules be written in Kiswahili (the national language): (1) A Brief History of Local Government in Tanzania; (2) The Roles of the Councillors in a Multi-party Democracy System; (3) Finance, Planning and Management.

Each module was written by an expert selected by the project design workshop. The writer was required to abide by an outline drawn up by the workshop. The first drafts were edited by editors selected by the design workshop. After the proposed editorial amendments had been effected, the drafts were submitted to a review workshop. In addition to the writers and editors, other participants of the workshop were drawn from the Institute of Development Management (IDM) Mzumbe, Hombolo Local Government Institute, Government Training Institute (GTI) Mombasa, Kenya, Civil Service Reform Programme, Frederich Ebert Stiftung (FES) Tanzania Office, City Director (Dar es Salaam), District Executive Director (Korogwe). There were also three councillors from the City Council of Dar es Salaam. The workshop came up with a list of proposals on how to further improve the modules in line with the stated course objectives (SAEU 1995b). These improvements were brought about before limited copies were printed for piloting.

The modules were piloted in five councils: one city council, one town council, one municipal council and two district councils. This sample was selected deliberately in order to assess the impact of the course at each tier of the local government system. The two district councils included in the sample varied markedly in terms of their performance and socio-economic environment. Whereas one was a high performer with a mixed economy (agriculture and pastoralism), the other was a low performer with a predominantly agricultural economy.

The pilot exercise revealed that: (1) The modules were clear and interesting. (2) They were interactive. (3) They met the course objectives. (4) The performance of the learners in modules 1 and 2 was good. Adjustments had to be made to module 3, 'Finance, Planning and Management', to make it more user friendly. (5) It was clear that learners would have liked more face-to-face sessions. This need could not, however, be fulfilled due to limited resources. (6) Student support services were sufficient and effective.

Feedback from the pilot was used in revising the modules for final printing. This thorough and vigorous approach to course design and development was a reliable recipe for the quality distance education project that was sought, as will be shown later under the discussion of the evaluation report of the project.

The chart in Figure 2 summarises the training modality.

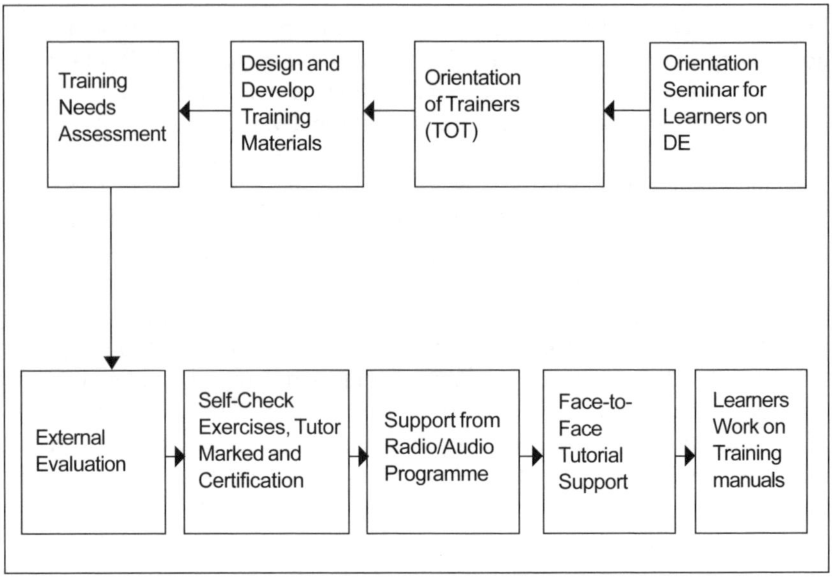

Figure 2 Graphical representation of the training modality

Student support services system

A good student support services system is not only essential for effective and successful distance learning but is also a means through which knowledge and skills are delivered to learners. An effective student support services system should break down all barriers which inhibit learners' access to knowledge and skills.

Such barriers include communication and transport problems, financial limitations, social constraints and so on. Irrespective of these and other barriers, the system should ensure efficient and safe delivery of study materials and other learning aids to the students. Besides this provision of quality, adequate tutorial support and prompt response to students' queries and demands are essential.

In the case of the Councillors' Distance Education Project, the student support services system consisted, at the top, of the Ministry responsible for Policy Formulation; the Consultative Committee for quality control; Regional Local Government Officers (RLGOs) and the Council's Directors. The RLGO body served as the Project's Regional Co-ordinator. Besides receiving and distributing the study materials and other learning aids to the field co-ordinators (council directors), the RLGO received students' progress records and submitted them to the SAEU for appropriate action. The field co-ordinator enrolled students into the project, provided them with study materials, organised tutorials for them, marked and commented on their assignments, responded to their demands and queries and kept students' records before submitting them to the RLGO. The organisation chart in Figure 3 gives a diagrammatic representation of the system.

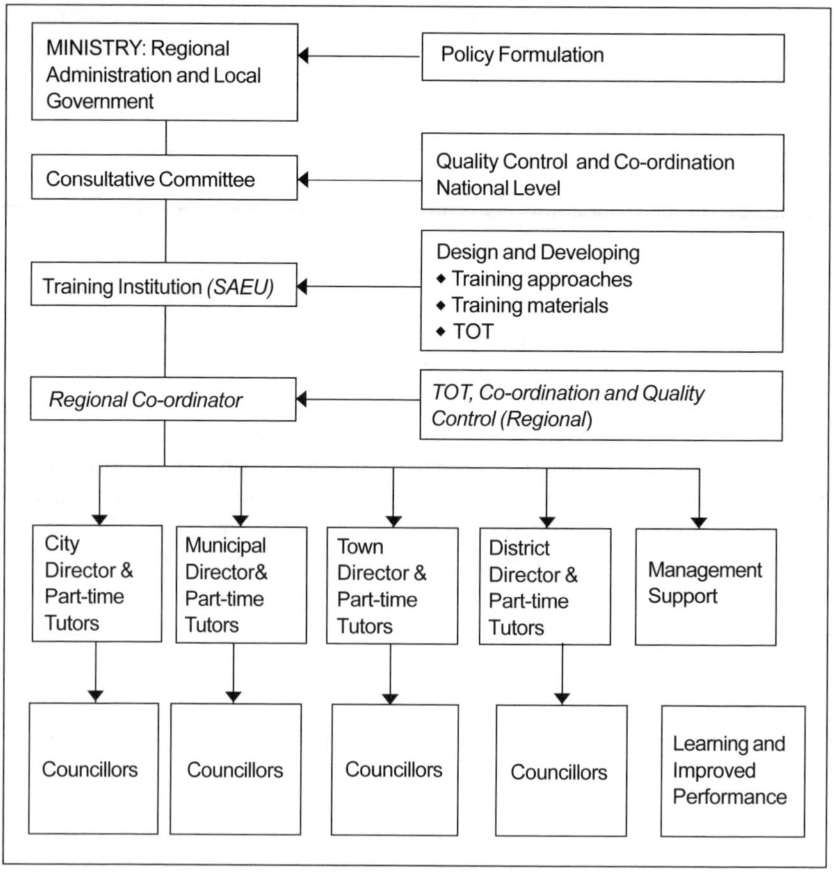

Figure 3 Organisation structure and inputs of key actors (support services system)

Essentially, the support system was designed to decentralise the implementation of the project by transferring its day-to-day management to councils. Besides solving logistical problems associated with centralisation, such as transport and communications constraints, the system was intended to make the project efficient and effective.

The project was allocated twelve months' duration, excluding the pilot stage. During this time over 2 324 (72%) of the councillors managed to complete the course.

Problems during the implementation process

The project confronted a number of problems during its implementation. First of all, Tanzania is a large country with an area of over 945 087 square kilometres. The technology (radio) that was utilised to support the printed modules could not be received countrywide. Some peripheral, border regions could therefore not benefit from the radio programme and for that reason the SAEU had to record it on audio cassettes. However, audio cassettes are less used than radio for lack of equipment. Hence it was left to the councils to ensure that councillors had access to the audio cassette programme.

Other problems were associated with poor literacy among some councillors. As noted earlier, some councillors had acquired their literacy skills from adult classes. This level of literacy permitted them to study only very slowly. To combat the problem, the SAEU advised and encouraged councillors to study in groups so that the more educated councillors could help the slower ones cope with the course. SAEU also encouraged councillors to improve their understanding by getting anyone in their neighbourhood, including family members, to read the modules and to discuss the content with them.

To give an indication of the success or failure of the project, the evaluation report is summarised below.

Evaluation of the councillors' training project

The evaluation of the project was carried out by a firm of consultants, 'Carl Bro Management', who were contracted by the EU under the Evaluation of EDF Support to Human Resources Development in Tanzania, 1990-1997 programme.

The team of evaluators looked at a number of aspects, among them: project relevance, efficiency, effectiveness, impacts and sustainability and replicability.

Each of these is briefly examined. *Project Relevance*: The project was judged to be relevant at the time of inception and implementation. However, the ongoing decentralisation process in Tanzania has made the understanding of roles even more relevant than at the time of inception. *Efficiency:* It was found out that, by and large, the project was implemented efficiently, and in the way it was designed and intended. It was observed that this was due to the relatively elaborate preparation process. *Effectiveness:* Effectiveness was discussed under parameters such as reaction, learning and behavioural changes, all of which were assessed positively. The most significant result mentioned by councillors and noted by the evaluation team was the improved co-operation and conflict resolution practices within the council itself. A typical remark by councillors was 'A councillor represents the community'. *Impacts:* It was reported that the most important impact was that the councillors had been able to educate other members of their constituency (ward) on the purpose and authority of the local council and the work to be carried out by it. They have therefore been able to motivate the community to engage in development projects. *Sustainability:* The team noted that an accelerated local government reform process will ensure that the necessary policy support measures will be in place to sustain the project results.

Lessons learned from the case study

From the evaluation of the project it will be noted that a number of lessons could be drawn from the training project and the paper concludes with a brief discussion of some of these.
The project was successful, firstly, because it was relevant. The introduction of a new political system created a need for councillors to acquire knowledge and skills for effective service delivery in a multi-party situation.

Looking at the training approach that was used (DE), it can be said that as long as courses are well prepared, with well-designed study materials, effective support services coupled with a good monitoring and evaluation scheme, there is bound to be success. The SAEU as a training institution has a good reputation with all the stakeholders of the project (namely councillors, ALAT, PMO) and was therefore well accepted. It would appear that for such success to be achieved the specialised institution must be accepted. It is also true that there is a certain amount of hesitation about DE which must be removed for a DE project to be effective. It would appear that the SAEU was able to remove this hesitation. Finally, a good funding base is essential for the project to be successful, as was the case with the project discussed here.

References

Ligate, NE. 1995. Problems and prospects of organising a distance education programme for Local Government Councillors in Tanzania. Paper presented at the Regional Workshop on Local Government Capacity Building through Education/Training Policy in Eastern and Southern Africa, Mombasa, 23 - 27 October.

Maslow, AH 1970. *Motivation and personality* (2nd ed) New York: Harper & Row.

Ngware, S. 1995. Councillor-political party relationship: the art and science of working together. Paper presented at a conference organised by ALAT, Dar es Salaam, 12 August.

Rogers, A. 1986. *Teaching adults.* Milton Keynes: Open University.

SAEU. 1995a. Report of the Local Government Councillors' Course Design Workshop, Dar es Salaam, 25 April.

SAEU. 1995b. Report of the Local Government Councillors' Course Review Workshop, Dar es Salaam, 15 September.
Tennant, M. 1998. *Psychology and adult learning.* London: Routledge.
World Bank. 1998. *Education in sub saharan Africa.* Washington DC: World Bank.

14

Partnerships in distance education for youth and adult educators

F Benito Fernández

This chapter describes an initiative launched in the late nineties by the Bolivian government to transform adult education in that country. The author emphasises the role of partnerships in the FEJAD Programme, which is the vehicle for this transformation initiative and gives attention, as well, to the use of distance education in training educators in the field of youth and adult education. A number of lessons are drawn from the experience gained through the programme, in particular the need for recognised qualifications and social and state acknowledgement of educators in this field.

Background

IIZ is the Institute for International Cooperation of the German Adult Education Association (DVV), founded in 1953. Today it represents 16 Popular University Associations in Germany that are regarded as public centres for lifelong education.

IIZ/DVV has worked in Bolivia since October 1986. Its overall goal is to give young people and adults in Bolivia who were unable, for various reasons, to pursue school education or were obliged to drop out early, the opportunity to receive general, vocational and social education through public (state) provision. The hope is that this will help them to feel valued by the community and society, and enable them to take part in social, economic and cultural life as autonomous individuals who are aware of their identity, rights and obligations.

Bolivia is situated in central South America and has an area of a little more than one million square kilometres and a population of 8 500 000 people, 60% of whom live in urban areas and 40% in rural areas. More than 50% are indigenous people comprising 32 different ethnic groups, with a very small 'Afro' group. Spanish is the official language. The educational level of the population as a whole is very low. More than 50% (about 4 500 000 people) are functionally illiterate, which means they have completed fewer than three degrees (or grades) at primary school. About 15% of people aged 15 years and over are illiterate, and among these women, rural and indigenous people predominate.

The consequences of this low level of education are poverty, illness, low social participation and unemployment.

Educational reform

In 1994 the Bolivian government embarked on a campaign of educational reform with a programme called 'Alternative Education'. The objectives were to reduce illiteracy, improve basic and non-formal education among youths and adults especially directed towards the vulnerable members of the population, such as the handicapped, street children and out-of-school children. However, the resources for the Alternative Education programme have represented about 4% of the state's budget for education. That is clearly insufficient.

In Bolivia there are approximately 350 adult education centres that depend on the Ministry of Education, and 50 private centres, with just over 4 000 teaching staff. In 1995, the Ministry of Education, supported financially and pedagogically by the IIZ/DVV, started a transformation process in adult education in which 100 centres are involved at present. The scope of the transformation included: (1) A new curriculum for primary (EPA), secondary (ESA) and technical education (ETA) has been developed. (2) Nine modules have been designed specifically for adult basic education, ranging from literacy to a sort of lower secondary school-leaving certificate. (3) Methodological guidelines have been drawn up for the development of modules, modular programmes, syllabuses and proposed final qualifications. (4) Further training has been provided for the teachers and directors of the experimental centres. (5) A manual dealing with procedural and operational issues has been written. (6) Many of these centres (*Centro de recursos educativos*) have been equipped with machinery, tools and teaching material, and improvements have been made to the infrastructure.

In this context the need for alternative training for adult educators becomes urgent for the following reasons: (1) The large majority of the adult teachers have received no pedagogical training in adult education. (2) The training offered at the experimental centres through courses, seminars and workshops reaches only a few of the teachers, at a high cost and with no clear sustainability. (3) Many of the teachers in service live in remote areas, where they have little or no access to advanced training.

Since 1996 a group of NGOs, the Ministry of Education, the Bolivian University and the IIZ/DVV have been sharing ideas about the training of adult educators through distance education so that people working in rural areas would also have the chance to take participate.

FEJAD programme

In 1997, two important international agreements were signed by the Bolivian Ministry of Education, the Spanish University (UNED), the Bolivian University (CEUB) and the German Adult Education Association (DVV), whereby the FEJAD Programme was set up. The programme began its academic activities in March 1998, with somewhat more than 400 registered students. Its aims are described below.

Overall aim

FEJAD's overall aim is to provide university level human resource training for youth and adult education at the level of a university degree, in order to raise the level of professional practice among teachers working in that field and to improve the range of provision offered by adult education centres.

Subsidiary aims

The subsidiary aims are as follows: (1) Creation of a programme of initial training in education for teachers at degree level, with the emphasis on youth and adult education. (2) Development of a model of professional training by means of distance education for youth and adult educators already working in the field. (3) Development and design of methods to improve teaching in youth and adult education. (4) Enrichment and improvement of pedagogical theory and practice among students taking part in the programme. (5) Production of a package of alternative, theory-based materials for youth and adult education appropriate to the distance education mode.

Syllabus

The syllabus is divided into 12 learning modules, each containing teaching units, amounting to approximately 1 200 hours spread over four semesters (two years). The syllabus covers techniques of study and self-learning, the situation in the country and in education, basics of youth and adult education, communication and education, grassroots education for youth people and adults, community development, sociological and professional aspects of youth and adult education, updating teaching methods, researching and writing the dissertation, pedagogical diagnosis, planning and curricula, administration and educational projects and monitoring, evaluation and systematisation in educational processes.

The 12 modules contain teaching guidelines, practical exercises, examination questions and bibliographical suggestions.

Qualification

The Spanish university, UNED, awards the title of 'University Specialist in Youth and Adult Education' to successful students and the Bolivian University, in conjunction with UNED, awards a 'Degree of Bachelor of Education, specialising in Youth and Adult Education'. Students thus gain two qualifications at once, one recognised in Europe and the other in Bolivia.

Management of the programme

The distance programme is supported by a national team in La Paz and a network of ten tutors based in offices in the nine Departments of Bolivia. This team provides individual student counselling and monitoring, supplemented by group meetings and dialogue between the students themselves, telephone advice, answers to postal queries and so on. Tutors have a university degree, and are also trained by means of seminars and workshop in the management of the programme. Examinations are written, with ten closed and two open questions per module. If a student fails a module, he or she may repeat it at the next examination.

During the second year of the course, students are given advice by the tutors on the preparation of their dissertation: choice of subject, arrangement of content, research needed, bibliography and so on. The subject must be agreed by the teaching staff of UNED before the dissertation can be submitted, and the students must have passed the 12 modules before doing so. It is a requirement for the award of a degree that a dissertation, which is subject to an oral examination, be submitted.

Costs and administration

The two-year course costs a total of Us.720, to be paid in monthly instalments of Us.30. This covers the 12 modules received by every student. This fee is very low in comparison with other degree courses. In order to assist students who have particular financial difficulties, 10% of the programme's entire income is distributed in the form of bursaries, in accordance with specified criteria.

Initial funding for the programme, covering the preparation, design and printing of the modules, was provided by the IIZ/DVV. The national team and the ten tutors are paid by the Ministry of Education. Since 2000 the programme has been running independently, without external funding.

The Ministry of Education has overall responsibility for the programme, while the universities (UNED and CEUB) are responsible for technical and pedagogical aspects. An inter-institutional supervisory board (or council) provides advice and support and has certain monitoring functions.

Student Statistics: 1998 to 2002

Table 1 Breakdown of students 1998-2002

Status of students	Women	Men	Total
Registered (Inscritos)	791	819	1610
Dissertation not submitted (Egresados)			500
Dissertation successfully submitted (Titulados)	99	107	206

Note: A third course, with 737 students registered, is still in progress.

Lessons and challenges arising from the Bolivian experience

The following important lessons are identified:

1. Distance education gives many youth and adult educators an opportunity to qualify themselves and get a professional degree.
2. The quality of distance education depends on good planning, monitoring, a well-qualified, well-trained corps of teachers, and useful, attractive and interactive (using multi-media and new technologies) learning materials.
3. The methods and pedagogical process must accord with the practice and cultural background of the educators. The main object of research and systematisation would therefore be the educators' unique contexts and practices.
4. Distance learning needs both individual and group activities to improve the quality of the training. Communication and exchange are important.
5. In Bolivia, training of facilitators and teachers by distance education was made possible by co-operation between the state, civil society, universities and international agencies, all having different roles: financial support being provided by state and international agencies, pedagogical support by civil society and the universities.

A major challenge, however, remains the moral, professional and economic recognition of youth and adult educators by government and by the society as a whole.

References

Ministerio de Desarrollo Humano- Asociación Alemana de Educación de Adultos (AAEA): 'Proyecto Formación de Educadores de Jóvenes y Adultos a Distancia' (FEJAD), La Paz abril 1997.

Molina, Renato : 'Programa de cualificación de recursos humanos', en 'Estado de Situación y proyecciones de la educación de adultos', Cebiae/Ayuda en Acción-Bolivia, La Paz , 2002, pp.32-36.

Pollinger, Hans: 'Educadores de adultos a través de estudios universitarios a distancia: una experiencia boliviana', en *Revista Educación de Adultos y Desarrollo*, IIZ/DVV, Bonn, 2000, n.55, pp.359-373.

Autores Varios.: 'Educación alternativa. Análisis y propuestas de política pública', Cebiae, La Paz., 2002.

Viceministerio de Educación Alternativa (VEA): 'Plan de transformación curricular y reorganización administrativa de los Centros de Educación de Adultos', La Paz 2001.

Módulos de aprendizaje a Distancia del Programa FEJAD:

FEJAD (1998): 'Módulo 1: Técnicas de estudio'.

FEJAD (1998): 'Módulo 2: Realidad Nacional y Educativa'.

FEJAD (1998): 'Módulo 3: Fundamentos de la educación del joven y adulto'

FEJAD (1998): 'Módulo 4: Comunicación educativa'

FEJAD (1998): 'Módulo 5: Educación popular de jóvenes y adultos'

FEJAD (1998): 'Módulo 6: Desarrollo comunitario urbano y rural'

FEJAD (1999): 'Módulo 7: Aspectos sociológicos y ocupacionales de la educación de Jóvenes y adultos'

FEJAD (1999): 'Módulo 8: Innovación educativa'

FEJAD (1999): 'Módulo 9: Investigación educativa y tesis de grado'

FEJAD (1999): 'Módulo 10: Diagnóstico educativo, planificación y diseño curricular'

FEJAD (2000): 'Módulo 11: Administración y proyectos educativos'

FEJAD (2001): 'Módulo 12: Seguimiento, evaluación y sistematización de procesos Educativos'

15

Networking among organisations involved in training adult education specialists

Wolfgang Leumer

This paper is more a collation and collection of innovative experiences than a paper on one single topic or aspect. It presents a review of the networking done by IIZ/DVV in southern Africa, it outlines IIZ/DVV's co-operation with REFLECT pilots, refers to a project aimed at the improvement of textbooks; and highlights endeavour to form a national network on adult education in South Africa and HIV/ AIDS as an adult learning concern.

In spite of efforts made by the German Adult Education Association IIZ/DVV to facilitate the networking efforts through its engagement with adult learning in South Africa and in the region, it is unfortunate that South Africans at an individual and institutional level seem to be unable to come together and identify the commonality of their interests and the need to work towards an adult learning movement.

The reason for this may be on the one hand the sad state of adult education in this country and in the region. However, it needs to be admitted that the state of neglect of adult education is no exception to the rule. Adult education in this part of the world, as in most other countries, is still a Cinderella, a fifth wheel on the wagon, a stepchild.

The SADC conference held recently in Pietermaritzburg on Adult Basic Literacy Education was a notable exception and one would hope that the recommendations made by this conference will lead to more networking in the region on urgent issues of quality of training, HIV-AIDS as a concern for adult education and other areas where it will make sense to join hands and put pressure on governments and institutions to fulfil what they committed themselves to in the Hamburg Declaration, in the Dakar Objectives and in many other noble commitments. The 2002 Pietermaritzburg Declaration was a result of the first *International Conference on Adult Basic and Literacy Education in the Southern African Development Community (SADC) region* held in Pietermaritzburg, South Africa in 2002, which included among its participants adult educators and development practitioners from governments, education and training institutions, NGOs, unions and donor agencies. The delegates expressed a commitment to the revitalisation of adult basic and literacy education for democracy and sustainable development in the SADC region and on the African continent. It urged the SADC member states to make adult education central to the education agenda and to allocate resources to deploy adult education for community development. Particular emphasis was placed on the devastation caused by the HIV/AIDs pandemic in the region, which has the potential to render all education and development efforts redundant.

Regional networking REFLECT

The REFLECT literacy approach could also be called Literacy Second, a term used by John Oxenham[1]. In spite of the critiques of recent evaluations of REFLECT literacy programmes (DFID, Rosa-Maria Torres, Agneta Lind), IIZ/DVV is still interested in knowing more about the benefits of adult learning approaches which do not necessarily start with literacy but with action points and development plans of our target groups; poor adults in poverty-stricken, rural areas of Africa (IIZ/DVV is particularly involved in programmes of this kind in Angola, Lesotho, Madagascar, Malawi, South Africa). In South Africa IIZ/DVV co-operates with Action Aid (AA) in carrying out five pilot projects (IDASA and Fair Share are two distinct operations), applying the REFLECT approach in South Africa. The project partners are as follows: IDASA and Fair Share (economic literacy and integrated development planning at local government level) are involved in a project whose final objective is community participation, with literacy and numeracy playing a role in local participation in understanding and shaping local budgets... Women for Peace Alexandra and Mid-Rand are co-operating with IIZ/DVV and Action Aid in a project focusing on the production of handicraft, urban agriculture, domestic violence and urban renewal (hostels). The Kruger to Canyons is a project for rural communities adjacent to the Kruger National Park, which is looking at how these communities can benefit from resource streams generated by tourism in the region, and at the production of handicrafts, the improvement of services in their own communities and income generation. Learning for Development in the Freestate/Koffiefontein used REFLECT as a training approach for agriculture and small business.

The South African pilot projects will be increased by two more projects dealing with family literacy in KwaZulu-Natal and the Casablanca informal settlements in the Western Cape in 2003. The main objective of our experiments is to show the role of Participatory Rural Appraisal methods in identifying action points. Literacy is introduced as and when learning circles identify the need for literacy for themselves and start to practise it in their attempts to improve their livelihoods. With the support of AA these experiences are linked with ongoing larger projects of REFLECT application in Angola, Zambia, Lesotho, Malawi and Swaziland. Annual meetings are held by supporters of this approach, in order to improve best practice and help develop a common understanding of strengths and weaknesses of existing practice. This is further networked into an international Circle of REFLECT practitioners under the name of CIRAC (Circle of International REFLECT ACTION circles).

Training adult educators in South Africa

IIZ/DVV supports at present the training of close to 100 practitioners in adult education via stipends and scholarships at four institutions (at a cost of not more than i32.000). University of Cape Town has 12 students enrolled for a Diploma in Adult Education; Peninsula Technicon has 15 students studying for a National Diploma in Adult Education; the Centre for Adult Education at the University of Natal has 34 students enrolled in a diploma course entitled *Participatory Development in Education,* while the Centre for Adult Continuing Education at the University of the Western Cape has 37 students studying for a Higher Certificate and Higher Diploma in Adult Education. Although all of these qualifications have been recognised by the South African Qualifications Authority they have not generated subsidies through the university grant system.

As the IIZ/DVV's funding ministry was reluctant to continue supporting the training of adult educators from 2003 onwards, the organisation had to invite its beneficiary institutions to put together motivations for the renewal of scholarship support in 2003 which constitutes for IIZ/DVV a cornerstone of ODA practices.

UCT diploma in education (University of Cape Town)

Since 1995, the diploma course (which was previously accredited as a certificate course) has provided a programme of initial professional education for practitioners who have work experience in adult education, community development or workplace education and training, but who have not previously had access to formal tertiary level study. In 2000, the Certificate in Adult Education, Training and Development was re-named the Diploma in Education in order to bring it in line with qualification level 5 on the NQF (National Qualifications Framework) and with the national Department of Education's 'Norms and Standards for Educators'. Students complete the following six courses over the length of the programme: (1) *Introduction to Adult Learning*: Introduces students to theories of adult learning through reflecting on their own experiences as learners and educators; (2) *Organisation Development*: Introduces students to theories of organisation development, and develops practical skills in areas such as goal-setting, planning and working in groups. (3) *Designing and Facilitating Learning Events:* Students carry out group projects aimed at developing their design, presentation and facilitation skills. (4) *Foundations of Adult Learning Theory:* Introduces students to some of the basic concepts of social theory, and explores different ways of viewing the relationship between education, social change and development. (5) *Fields and*

Sites of ETD (Education, Training and Development) *Practice:* Examines the different sites of adult education practice, and introduces students to recent policy developments in the field of adult education. This module also draws in a number of guest lecturers from different fields of practice. (6) *Field Study*: Students work in groups on a project designed to deepen their expertise in various ETD roles, e.g. designing and facilitating an education programme.

Given that the course is an initial professional qualification, the Diploma does not require formal educational qualifications for entry. Initial student selection is based on an oral and written Recognition of Prior Learning process and continuation into the second year of the diploma is based on successful completion of modules during year one. In addition, and importantly, participants need at least two to five years' experience in the education, training and development sector, and proficiency in English. These entry requirements are significant in that they imply that the Diploma recognises that the ETD field has been largely unregulated and many people have worked as Education, Training and Development Practitioners (ETDPs) in the field for years without formal educational qualifications. This is due to the history of apartheid education as well as the lack of formal qualifications in the ETD field itself. Gaining a qualification such as the Diploma therefore enables the participants to work as professionals more easily but also to bring capacity to the field, something that is sorely needed in South Africa.

A major factor hindering acceptance of student into a second year will be the lack of funding to support student bursaries, as students will not be accepted unless student fees have been paid.

Students on the programme: The profile of students has remained fairly constant over the past seven years: most participants are 'mature students' (with the average age ranging between 35 and 50 years), and are culturally diverse. In 2000 and 2001, three-quarters of the class were women, and over 70% of the class were first-language Xhosa speakers, with most of the remainder being drawn from communities historically classified as 'coloured'. Participants are drawn from a wide variety of ETD organisations and projects, as the table below indicates. Many of these organisations, while supportive of the programme, are unable to find the funding to pay student fees. In the next section, we discuss ways in which this might be resolved in the longer term. In the short term, however, the lack of funding for students in our Diploma remains a critical issue.

Table 2000-2001 students – by sector

Organisation sector	Number of Students
Health education/promotion	12
Trade union education	3
Workplace training: financial services sector	2
Small business skills development	2
Educare	2
Secondary schooling	1
Local government	1
Arts and culture	1
Media training	1
UCT Staff	1

***Building long-term capacity in the field of ETD at UCT*:** Training ETDPs on the Diploma course provides an opportunity for the development of 'critical reflective practitioners', ETDPs who can build the capacity of their organisations and ultimately, their constituencies through the training and education they receive. Because of its alternative admissions criteria, the Diploma also provides access to higher education to a group of adult learners who would otherwise not have such access.

The curriculum of the Diploma has been developed over a number of years and takes into account the requirements of the ETDP working in a poorly-resourced community organisation. As 'critical reflective practitioners' the participants leave the Diploma with renewed skills, confidence and knowledge. The Diploma enables them to see their own practice in terms of broader issues and in a more contextualised way. Participants are thus empowered to take more control over their jobs and to develop the capacity of their colleagues and other members of their broader community. They will therefore be able to support and drive national strategic priorities within their communities and actively participate in the wider transformation agenda in a meaningful way.

***Student evaluations*:** During the course of the year, students completed individual, written evaluations and participated in group discussions evaluating the course. Their final evaluation of the course was generally extremely positive: students felt that the course presented an enormous opportunity for personal development and that they learned as much from one another as from the course itself. Many also commented on the importance of the course in helping them gain communication, writing and computer skills and to learn to understand people from different backgrounds.

Besides providing further practitioner training and development, the Diploma also aims to open paths of further learning for students. The course enjoys formal recognition and accreditation from the University of Cape Town and students who successfully complete the course may apply for admission to the Advanced Certificate in Education (Adults), and thereafter the Master's programme, both offered by UCT's Department of Education. Over the years a number of the graduates of the Diploma course have proceeded to the Advanced Certificate course in adult education and some have continued their learning in the UCT Department of Education's BEd course and even on to the Master's course.

Bursary support: While a significant grouping of Diploma students in 2002-2003 will have their fees covered by a training grant drawn from new skills funds available to employers, the 'regular' grouping of students drawn mainly from smaller training organisations and community-based NGOs in the Cape Town area are more dependent than ever on bursary assistance if they are going to complete the programme and graduate with their Diploma. In the long term, some of the money to support students from under-resourced organisations on the Diploma could well come from the ETDP sector itself through its Sectoral Education and Training Authority (SETA). Through the SETA, organisations will in future be able to access Skills Levy funding for staff training and development. In the short term, however, it is precisely the organisations from which our students are drawn who lack the capacity to access this funding, given their limited capacity and stretched resources.

Bursary support for our students, who work as ETDPs in these very organisations, is an immediate attempt to support their development as ETDPs and thereby the contribution they might be able to make in their own organisations towards accessing Skills Levy funding.

The 2002-2003 course is already halfway completed, with a number of new developments. In late 2001, Diploma course staff were approached by the Clothing Chamber of the Clothing, Textile, Leather and Footwear SETA (Sector Education and Training Authority), which wanted to send 20 of its industry trainers on the Diploma course, drawing on SETA funds. In February 2002, in addition to approximately 25 new, 'regular' Diploma students (drawn from community, local government and industry settings), we registered a second cohort of students, who are trainers in the clothing industry. Also in 2002, we will be running the Diploma course for a *third* cohort of students – trade union educators sent through the national trade union institute. There will be approximately 65 students on the Diploma programme in 2002-2003.

We are convinced that the Diploma in Education (Adult Education) continues to make a significant contribution to reconstruction and development in South Africa, by providing an alternative access route into university level study for historically disadvantaged South Africans. Through the professional development of practising adult educators and trainers, it contributes to the development of deprived communities, to the building of a democratic civil society and to enhancing the capacity of this country to produce a skilled workforce.

IIZ/DVV's support for the Peninsula Technikon ABET (Adult Basic Education and Training) education partnership

IIZ/DVV has supported the ABET educator programme at Peninsula Technikon since 1996. The bursary programme provided the backbone for continued and sustained development work in the National Diploma programme and later the BTech degree in ABET. The positive influence of the programme and materials development, which cascaded throughout the national ABET sector, through the contribution of the Peninsula Technikon players in national and provincial policy formulation, curriculum development and materials development initiatives was largely thanks to the DVV partnership. We did, however, note the following problems: the provision of full-time working opportunities in the ABET sector did not absorb the throughput of students effectively. The education department ABET educator posts are mainly part-time and poorly paid positions, hence there were few opportunities for our graduates to enter into attractive teaching positions. Many of the Peninsula Technikon students were very young and not easily accommodated in the ABET sector. Most of the Peninsula Technikon students were from the Eastern Cape and it was difficult to track them once they had completed their studies. Although the demand for ABET provision dictates otherwise, the ABET sector has seen a decline in actual ABET provision over the past few years.

The motivation for a continued Peninsula Technikon/DVV partnership includes the changed approach to DVV bursary allocations (2002) and the targeting of more mature learners. The decision to target more mature learners for the bursary should contribute to greater value added to the ABET sector. Unemployed learners and learners working in community organisations and prisons are also targeted. This will contribute to sustainability and a wider reach of the partnership through on-the-ground participation of learners in ABET programmes. Trainee educators are increasingly expected to work in the ABET sector during their time of study. Another important consideration is the contribution the project is making to combat crime in South Africa. Training carefully selected prison inmates as ABET educators is very successful.

Given the fragile status of ABET educator development, the sector will be adversely affected by the termination of the DVV partnership. The DVV/Peninsula Technikon partnership is one of the important motivations for the continued provision of ABET educator programmes at Peninsula Technikon. As a strategic national player in the technikon sector (national ABET technikon convenor) Peninsula will continue to play a leading role in the provision of ABET educator training. It is anticipated that there will be an upturn in the ABET sector, and with increased activity in the Further Education and Training band, stimulated by new workplace training legislation, the demand for ABET provision will increase.

IIZ/DVV Scholarships for disadvantaged students to study at the Centre for Adult and Continuing Education (CACE-University of the Western Cape)

The three CACE qualifications, namely the Higher Certificate: Education Training and Development Adult Learning (HC), Higher Diploma: Education Training and Development: Adult Learning (HD) and the Advanced Diploma for Educators of Adults (Adv. Dip) have been receiving scholarships from the Institute for International Co-operation of the German Adult Education Association (IIZ/DVV) for the past seven years. All these qualifications are approved by the Council for Higher Education (CHE) and registered with the South African Qualifications Authority (SAQA). Two of these qualifications (HC and HD) are now recognised as university qualifications and will generate state subsidies by the end of 2003. These qualifications should be developed to create a career path for adult educators in compliance with NQF recommendations.

These qualifications are supported by IIZ/DVV because it believes that, given the continuing problem of high illiteracy, there is a great demand for adult educator qualifications in South Africa. More than six million South Africans cannot access information through reading. There are new policies, new laws in this country which are being developed and designed to redress the imbalances of the past, but the majority of citizens cannot access these documents because these citizens are illiterate. Through IIZ/DVV support CACE and other institutions of learning train facilitators, trainers and educators who work in communities as ETDPs.

These groups of learners are deeply involved in civil society work, actions and movements. Adult education knowledge and skills are needed in community-based development and organisations, and therefore continuous support creates the layers of cadres needed at grassroots, middle and upper middle levels.

The other reason for supporting this project is tuition fees. With high unemployment rates in South Africa, many students are unable to pay for their tuition fees. From our experience there are only a handful of students whose fees are paid by their employers and very few of them can pay their own fees. CACE would like to continue building the capacity of under-resourced and rurally-based practitioners, and for us to do this, students need scholarships. IIZ/DVV scholarships have ben-

efited students from as far afield as the Eastern Cape and Springbok who were registered in the Certificate course, and prepared to travel.
The materials used are developed to address learners' needs but also try to create an understanding of the past and present, theoretically, philosophically and practically. These materials have to be reproduced and/or further developed depending on circumstances. This is what makes the difference between Adult Learning Theories and Practices. This approach seeks to reconcile learner's needs with environmental demands and challenges.

The qualifications are offered through face-to-face and distance learning. For Higher Certificate and Higher Diploma, lectures take place on campus but students also meet locally as small groups. A tutor takes responsibility for facilitating the process of learning in a study group. This support is core to distance learning and it is mostly needed in the Certificate groups of learners.

The services of these adult ETDPs is crucial, particularly at the grassroots level. Many of these graduates continue working in non-governmental and community-based organisations, but the majority are in the ABET field, particularly in the Northern Cape. Adult educators are employed in several fields; some move to positions of power in local government authorities and a few enter the provincial government legislature, trade union organisations and political and religious organisations.

The CACE courses remain an important human resources development initiative, which serve a constituency many of whom have been deeply disadvantaged through the social and economic conditions of the past. We hope that IIZ/DVV will once again be able to offer the support needed to give students the opportunity to build their capacity through these qualifications. The level of commitment and desire to continue learning and teaching give one hope for a better South Africa.

IIZ/DVV scholarship programme Centre for Adult Education (CAE-University of Natal)

The IIZ/DVV scholarships are currently utilised within the Participatory Development Certificate in Education (PDCE) programme. The PDCE programme is an innovative programme emerging from three years of research, curriculum development and materials development. It has replaced the University Diploma in Adult Education (UDAE), which IIZ/DVV scholarships previously supported. The concept underpinning the PDCE learning programme outcomes is of a body of skills, knowledge and attitudes that are common across all sectors of people-orientated development. The compulsory courses of the programme aim to develop such competencies. On completing the compulsory courses, learners choose to specialise in either ABET, Land Care or Entrepreneurship. Three other specialisations, namely, HIV/AIDS Education, Peace Education and Leadership and Management of NGOs, are currently being developed as electives for the future. Learners gain a quarter of their credits from a service learning component (called Development in Practice) which places them within development-oriented organisations and projects.

The PDCE learning programme aims to build the capacity of rural and disadvantaged communities through producing qualified community development practitioners who understand and are equipped to plan and implement basic participatory, holistic and sustainable development projects at the community level. The programme was piloted during 2001-2002 with the first group of learners gaining the qualification at the end of 2002.

The lack of support for adult education under apartheid rule has been perpetuated under the present dispensation. Adult education continues to remain on the margins of the education system, receiving inadequate resources. There are still too few opportunities for adult educators to be trained. The virtual collapse of adult education provision within the university context makes the Centre for Adult Education (CAE) one of the few remaining resources for the training of adult educators within the country. *Education for All* targets become a dim hope without a strong, well-trained cadre of adult educators, particularly those trained within a participatory development paradigm.

The IIZ/DVV scholarships enable us to broaden access to tertiary education, specifically to community development workers from poor communities. The PDCE programme attracts learners from marginalised communities in KwaZulu-Natal, many students coming from rural areas where development needs are the greatest. It brings to the university some of the poorest learners that this university has. This is only possible through the scholarships that we are able to offer to these students.

KwaZulu-Natal has the largest proportion of South Africans who are infected and affected by HIV/AIDS. The pandemic poses the single largest challenge to development in the region and has highlighted the need for skilled educators who can work in non-formal and community settings. The PDCE programme is an ideal vehicle for developing such educators. CAE is currently collaborating with IIZ/DVV in South Africa in the development of HIV/Aids skills programmes and in the training of community educators who can deliver HIV/AIDS courses to learners with low levels of literacy. This will be formalised and developed into a specialised track that deals with HIV/AIDS education within the PDCE.

In a similar vein, the Land Care course within the PDCE addresses another critical need in aiming to produce development practitioners who are equipped to help communities work towards increasing the productivity and ecological sustainability of South Africa's natural resources. The Land Care course concentrates on developing institutional support for smallholder farmers by training development workers in the area of environmental management and small-scale, low-input food production. The Land Care course supports low-input as well as organic agriculture. Partnerships are fostered with other NGOs who are practising and teaching these forms of agriculture as well as promoting organic marketing. Future specialised tracks within the PDCE include an option that would allow learners to specialise in Peace Education. This course will be piloted during 2003 within the Human Rights, Democracy and Development (HRDD) project, a joint project of CAE, Tembaletu Community Education Centre and the Embassy of Finland.

Evaluation of the programme: The general conclusions and recommendations show that financial constraints are a significant factor in the lives of our students. In April 2001, when the University refused to budge over the issue of payment of registration fees, students were refused admission to our courses and we lost a third of our first cohort. Students' lack of confidence, their confusion and uncertainty, especially in the early days of the programme but also subsequently, at various times during the programme, came through very strongly. Facilitators need to be more sensitive to this but find it difficult to maintain a balance between being supportive and spoon feeding. They feel that the relationship between students and supervisors (especially supervisors from host organisations) during their learnerships could be improved. A more assertive initial contact with host organisations could address this.

Poor planning on the part of students created many of their difficulties during the learnership programme. They battled to overcome dependency and apathy during their learnership and interpreted the facilitators' insistence that they take responsibility for their own learning and logistics as a lack of support. Students themselves requested that facilitators should be strict with them from the beginning of the programme, and finally admitting to being too quick to complain before thinking and talking things through carefully. For example, after being initially very resistant to both the Lifelong Learning and Entrepreneurship courses, students came to understand the importance and value of the courses and wished they had realised that at the time. Arranging for some of the present cohort of students to present their own stories and evaluations of the PDCE to new students early on may help to address this. The value of the RPL/placement test workshop needs to be critically reviewed to ascertain whether it is fulfilling its purpose. A workshop will be presented in 2003. Facilitators need to ensure that the work students produce there is carried forward, and students' progress in relation to the workshop carefully should be monitored so that the workshop's usefulness as an indicator can be more accurately evaluated.

We need to examine our andragogy and perhaps look at making it more explicit from the outset (note that facilitators feel we tried very hard to do that throughout the programme but that somehow it was not fully understood or internalised by students). A focus group with all facilitators should be run in early January to discuss strategies to address this problem. Students strongly praised the facilitation practice of highlighting strengths and giving detailed feedback in response to assignments. We need to build on this strength and ensure the practice is continued.

Although the practice of reflection is actively taught and regularly encouraged, students admit that they fail to do this effectively. Stricter measures need to be applied to the submission for comment of reflective activities (like journals). Journal writing should be introduced as a *de rigeur* activity early in the Lifelong Learning course. Some students (and their employers) found weekly contact sessions inconvenient. We need to reconsider the block-week structure of contact sessions. It creates a sense of community, of sharing and provides opportunities that contact sessions of four to five hours once a week simply cannot do. We need to consider the possibility of running a block-type contact as a first contact with students at the beginning of the programme. We want to be creative about exploring opportunities for such cheap, relevant and practical sessions. A meeting will be held early in January to more formally explore the ideas already under discussion. There is a perception among students that there is often a discrepancy between what CAE says and what CAE does. We really need to guard against raising expectations that we are not sure we can deliver on, and making promises we cannot fulfil – it is extremely demotivating for students and tarnishes the Centre's image.

Textbook series: AFRICAN Perspectives in Adult Learning (APAL)

IIZ/DVV has been supporting the professional training of adult educators at numerous African universities. When in 1995 this training project was evaluated by Paul Fordham and Lalage Bowen, one of the evaluation recommendations was to improve the quality and relevance of study materials for Diploma and Bachelor degree students. Accordingly, in 2001 IIZ/DVV took the initiative to bring together African scholars, heads of departments and representatives of other interested institutions to start a project on improving teaching and learning materials for students in adult education in Africa.

This project is carried at present by the Department of Adult Education of the University of Botswana, the Institute for International Co-operation of the German Adult Education Association, and the UNESCO Institute for Education and Pearson Education. The project co-operation aims to develop a textbook series entitled *African perspectives on adult learning*. The purpose of the series is to provide accessible textbooks to students in Africa studying adult education, especially at the Diploma and Bachelor's degree level. The books will be co-published by Pearson Education and the UNESCO Institute for Education. Initially, there will be five titles in the series, namely *The psychology of adult learning in Africa, Research methods in African adult education; Foundations of adult education in Africa; Programme development in African adult education and The social context of adult education in Africa*. Each book is expected to provide an overview of the topic, introduce appropriate theory, provide discussion and examples rooted in professional practice, actual policies and empirical research and indicate further areas of inquiry and reading. A key principle is that the textbooks will reflect African social realities, theoretical and cultural perspectives, policies and modes of practice.

In conformity with the Editorial Board's decision in January 2002, the Secretariat of the text book initiative organised Writers' Workshops in April and August. These were attended by all the commissioned authors. The workshops helped to develop a clearer vision of the nature of the Series, which will not only provide up-to-date Afrocentric textbooks for students of adult education in Africa, but will also promote recognition around the world of a distinctive African perspective on adult learning. The workshops developed a strong sense of joint involvement and commitment by all involved and provided important intellectual direction as well as an induction into professional textbook publishing. A standard format and the pedagogical approach for all the books in the series and the outline for each title were agreed upon in the workshops. Each workshop received very positive evaluation by the participants.

The project is now at a stage where the writers are busy working on their manuscripts according to design criteria and deadlines agreed in the workshops. This is a critical phase of the project in which the capability and commitment of the writers are paramount. A number of writer support strategies are in place. The most important is the publisher's feedback on submitted drafts of chapters. Other strategies include the provision of books, journals and other reference materials to writers by IIZ/DVV, UIE and the Secretariat and the establishment of the African Perspectives in Adult Learning (APAL) listserve, which provides a vehicle for sharing information amongst both writers and the Series Editorial Board. A key issue raised by writers is the difficulty of finding quality time for writing and the possibility of writing fellowships and residencies is being explored.

Adult learning network (South Africa)

Another networking attempt supported by IIZ/DVV happens around the remainder of a once-vibrant adult educators and practitioners sector, which has gone through many crises in South Africa. Of several hundred NGOs and CBOs working in the field of adult education, according to a Database Collation of the Adult Literacy Basic Education and Development Foundation (ALBED), only 50 organisations remain today and are still working on the ground. The sector has suffered and is at a very low ebb. The Adult Learning Network, which currently has a membership of 200, is an attempt to remedy this deplorable state of affairs. It brings together at present eight provincial bodies, trying to constitute themselves as advocacy and lobbying bodies at provincial level (only Mpumalanga remains defunct for the time being).

The main activity in 2001 and 2002 was running an adult learners' week. This event and the preparatory phases leading to it, which showcase adult education and adult learning in South Africa, received financial support from the SETAs for the first time in 2002. We hope to be able to continue to make inroads into the SETAs and as a national Adult Learning Network offer services to the SETAs around advocacy and capacity building. An interesting feature of the Adult Learning Network is that they have seemingly been able to get the trade unions (before 1994 a staunch supporter of a non-Cinderella status for adult education) back on board. A further notable feature of this new network is that the notion of adult learning is beginning to be understood more holistically, embracing not only ABET but all fields in which adult learning happens.

Another notable innovation is the link between the Adult Learners Week as promoted by the Adult Learners Network and a provincial initiative on the Learning Cape Festival – a remarkable example of networking in adult learning and lifelong learning

The learning Cape Festival (LCF)

Learning for development: The Learning Cape Festival aims to promote a culture of lifelong learning that will enable people from all walks of life to develop their full potential. The concept of the Learning Cape was identified by the Provincial Department of Economic Affairs, Agriculture and Tourism as a key component of its economic development strategy in its White Paper, *Preparing the Western Cape for the Knowledge Economy of the 21st Century.* This follows a growing international trend, spearheaded by countries in Europe and North America, towards the development of *learning societies* that equip their citizens with the knowledge and skills needed to compete effectively on global markets.

A learning society: A learning society invests in people by creating learning opportunities that enhance the potential of all its citizens. Partnerships between state, business and civil society are used to maximise learning opportunities within and between different sectors of society, which in turn promote a culture of learning where personal and professional growth are valued. This commitment to developing a learning society goes beyond the marketplace demand for skilled labour. A learning society actively seeks to address the needs of all members of society. Programmes that promote tolerance and mutual respect, alleviate poverty, and address critical social issues such as crime, unemployment and HIV/AIDS all help to build the social cohesion necessary for sustained economic growth. United we stand, divided we fall.

***Towards a culture of lifelong learning*:** If we wish to develop a vibrant learning society, then we need to move beyond narrow definitions of education and training and develop *a holistic approach to learning*. Learning is not confined to the classroom: we continue to learn and grow throughout our lives – in our places of work, our homes and our community. Lifelong learning recognises the role of formal institutions such as schools, universities and technikons but also acknowledges the *informal learning* that takes place through the media, information technology and the work of NGOs and community-based organisations. Lifelong learning aims to create an enabling environment in which all members of society can acquire the knowledge, skills and confidence they need to become active participants in the social and economic development of our region.

The Learning Cape Festival is an advocacy campaign designed to popularise the concept of 'The Learning Cape' and promote a culture of lifelong learning amongst all sectors of Western Cape society. We see the Festival as the catalyst for a process of ongoing collaboration between government, business and civil society that will identify and meet the learning needs of our region. The Festival aims to promote a culture of learning throughout the Western Cape region; create viable partnerships between government, business and civil society that support integrated approaches to learning and development; expose people of all ages to a wide range of learning opportunities; showcase innovative projects and programmes; celebrate learners' achievements; and develop a tradition of an annual Learning Cape Festival.

The Festival aims to build on current initiatives such as National Women's Day, Small Business Development Week and Adult Learners Week, with the aim of strengthening these campaigns and promoting the links between them through a common focus on lifelong learning. As such, the Festival will celebrate learning in a variety of contexts: from formal institutions of learning through to skills training in the workplace and community development programmes.

***Proposed programme of events*:** We envisage a month-long festival of learning starting with Women's Day in August and culminating in Adult Learners Week and International Literacy Day in September 2002. The Festival will build on existing campaigns but also create the space and opportunity for individual organisations to promote their own learning programmes under a common banner or theme. It will draw on the following strategies to promote lifelong learning: (1) awards that acknowledge the achievements of outstanding learners, educators, projects and programmes; (2) Open Days where different centres of learning open their doors and offer short courses to the general public, free of charge; (3) cultural events that raise awareness of social issues such as gender equity, HIV/AIDS; (4) seminars and debates that address key learning and development issues; (5) development of a hotline or website that provides up-to-date information on the full range of education and training opportunities available in the Western Cape; (6) a high profile media campaign that includes coverage of the calendar of events, learners' success stories and innovative programmes; (7) encouragement of the media to produce educational supplements and programmes on a variety of issues central to social and economic development on an ongoing basis.

Effective partnerships are central to the success of a learning society. The Learning Cape Festival is envisaged as a broad-based and inclusive initiative that will promote ongoing collaboration among a broad range of stakeholders. We encourage participation from all sectors of society – including the state, business and civil society. The initiative originated through the collaboration of the Department of Business Promotion and Tourism and the University of the Western Cape and has now broadened to include participation from higher education institutions, the Adult Learning Forum, IIZ/DVV, Cape Online, Unicity, COSATU, Department of Education, Provincial Development Council, Chamber of Commerce, NGOs and the media. The aim is to draw in key government departments, libraries, museums, businesses, SETAs, civil society organisations and the media. In other words, all those who have an interest in learning and the social and economic development of our region.

The Learning Cape Festival provides an opportunity for organisations to promote a wide range of learning programmes and to strengthen the links between them. For example HIV/AIDS education, entrepreneurship, literacy, science and technology, management , computer literacy, human rights and gender equity, sustainable development and health and environmental education.

This follows a growing international trend, spearheaded by countries in Europe and North America, towards the development of *learning societies* that equip their citizens with the knowledge and skills needed to compete effectively in global markets.

When reviewing the Learning Cape Festival 2002 questionnaires were widely distributed to all the participating organisations. A follow-up review workshop was held with funders, education NGOs, business, labour and government. The following were viewed as challenges and concerns: need for the festival to have a wider reach and that rural areas need to be engaged; the involvement of the other two Cape provinces (Northern Cape and Eastern Cape); the lack of resources; the need for the Learning Cape Festival (LCF) to be more focused; more inclusive participation; the minimal involvement of the media; too much work and too few resources

HIV/AIDS networking

Funded from the Poverty Reduction Programme of the German government, IIZ/DVV has started to develop a holistic training programme for volunteers in HIV/AIDS which does not only look at the need for volunteers to provide palliative or home-based care. The programme is, instead, designed to look at the need for coping strategies and capacity of interaction with health bureaucracies and local government to deal with all aspects of HIV/AIDS: awareness, home-based care, caring for orphans and so on. It is interesting to note that one can possibly assume an increase of illiteracy in South Africa in the coming years because of the impact of HIV/AIDS leading to millions of children and adolescents being unable to obtain formal schooling.

The project aims to develop a qualification at NQF level 1 for volunteers (some of them will need support ABET training in order to be able to follow the package) of which St Johns Ambulance estimates there are about 100 000 to 120 000 active in South Africa. But without sufficient training they have no support structures, are unemployed, unpaid and without recognition. In the long run it is hoped to get accreditation for this qualification and to register it as a learnership such that local funding can carry the cost of training. It is hoped that local government and health hierarchies will be able to use these intermediary facilitators at local level once they have a qualification. They are adult educators par excellence. Learners' materials and facilitators' manuals have been developed and will be tested in the course of the next three months in three provinces in South Africa. Based on the first results of this project, we have also started to build a consortium of interested providers/partners in this important domain of adult education. This domain is important both because of the high impact of HIV/AIDS and also because the high level of stigmatisation against people living with HIV/AIDS impacts on their ability to be employed. Funding proposals are being developed to be submitted to the Global Fund and an expression of interest has been tabled by a regional consortium to the European Union.

Conclusion

Quoting from Harbans Bhola's paper presented at the Pietermaritzburg Conference, the challenge of Education For All objectives and poverty reduction as expressed by the declaration on Sustainable Development mean that: 'In the education of adults, one single more or less tightly packaged program such as ABE (Adult Basic Education), ABET (Adult Basic Education and Training), ABLE (Adult Basic and Literacy Education), or ALE (Adult and Life Long Education) would not do. Appropriate adult education packages will have to be designed and delivered in particular contexts to suit groups of individual, clusters of families and communities for overall community development' (Bhola 2002).

It is in view of diverse contexts and livelihoods that facilitation and training need to happen. The linkage between adult education literacy and development will not be an easy one as long as we only teach the nuts and bolts of ABET methods. The daunting challenge of making adult education instrumental in reducing poverty requires more in-depth and quality training and we need political support for this to happen. Distance education can in this scenario be only one element in a mixed mode delivery model of quality teaching for adult educators and development practitioners. More networking and exchange around existing innovative practice can enrich these delivery models.

Notes

1 The World Bank, Africa Region, Working Papers, *Skills and Literacy Training for Better Livelihoods: A review of Approaches and Experiences,* Washington 2002

Section IV

Implications of technology for literacy, open learning and information networking

16

Use of communication technology for literacy

Anita Dighe

Introduction

While there is considerable information available on the use of information and communication technology and distance education approaches in teacher education, little is known about their application in training adult education and literacy functionaries. This article describes a DFID funded project using ICT to promote literacy. Among the lessons learnt were that it is important to develop a vision at the outset and to choose suitable institutional partners. Further issues discussed include capacity building and hands-on experience and the need to do needs assessments so that technologies may be developed to respond to diverse needs. It was found that ICT helped improve drop-out and attendance rates in both expected and unexpected ways, and that the opportunity to become computer literate attracted young literacy students. The potential of ICT to create a learning environment and provide informal learning opportunities is examined, and the link between networking, communication and empowerment is explored. Finally the article raises questions about the sustainability of ICT projects in this environment, and the measurement of outcomes and key competencies acquired.

According to Perraton (2002), the one area where we have extensive, encouraging and reasonably solid data on the use of technologies and of distance education approaches is in the education of teachers. Perraton maintains that there is extensive international experience in the use of distance education, using a variety of technologies, for teacher education. The situation with regard to the use of technologies in training adult education and literacy functionaries, on the other hand, is not very encouraging. Shah's study (2002) has highlighted that while technology in one form or another has sometimes been used for training adult education functionaries in India, its use has been perfunctory and ad hoc, with little effort made to learn from such experiences and build on them. Given this, it was felt that it would be useful to base this paper on an on-going project that uses information and communication technology (ICT) for literacy-related work.

For the past three years, I have been part of a team that has been putting into practice a project funded by DFID on the use of ICT for promoting literacy education. This project is being implemented in India and Zambia under the overall leadership of Project Manager, Commonwealth of Learning, Vancouver. Considering how rare the project is in that ICT has been used for promoting literacy and the fact that the project cycle is now almost over, it seems opportune to reflect on the experiences of the past three years and to highlight some issues for consideration. This will help the team as well as wider audiences understand the implications of using ICT in training adult education functionaries and in implementing literacy and non-formal education programmes

Project description

Rationale and project set-up

Inadequacy of traditional adult literacy programmes. The project owes its origin to the high levels of illiteracy, particularly among women, in developing countries as well as the inadequacy of the traditional adult literacy programmes in responding to this challenge. It was recognised that the adult literacy programmes, by and large, lacked innovation in curriculum design and instructional materials and used inappropriate pedagogical strategies.

Project partners. In the implementation of the project in India, a national level organisation (earlier Indira Gandhi National Open University, and subsequently Commonwealth Educational Media Centre for Asia) was identified. This organisation, in turn, identified state level organisations in two states of India. These are the State Resource Centres (SRCs) of Rajasthan and Madhya Pradesh, based at Jaipur and Indore – the capitals of the two states. Subsequently, M.S. Swaminathan Research Foundation (MSSRF) was included as a third partner. The two SRCs were selected because they were part of large organisations that had long experience of working as NGOs in the field of adult literacy, had links with government as well as with other NGOs and were engaged in training adult education functionaries as well as in producing literacy and adult education materials for their respective states. Each SRC, in turn, set up two community-based centres – one in a rural area and the other in a semi-urban area. Decisions about the number of computers to be purchased, their peripherals and other technological appliances such as TV, VCR, digital camera and handy cam, were taken centrally. An important consideration was the type and kind of equipment that could be placed in a rural centre, to be accessed and put to use by the community and used for promoting literacy in the village. The equipment provided at each centre included two Pentium-3 computersone printer, one camera, one TV set, one VCR and one audio-cassette recorder. The equipment provided at the SRC level included one Pentium-3, one laser printer, one scanner, one photocopier, one digital camera and one handy cam.

MSSRF was selected as the third partner because, unlike the two SRCs with their literacy focus, it was concerned about sustainable livelihood issues. Also unlike the other two organisations, MSSRF's work was based on bottom-up and participatory approaches and it was envisaged that the self-help groups would take responsibility for setting up and maintaining the technology-based community learning centres.

The project is being implemented in four villages in two blocks of Tamilnadu.

Planned outcomes. The project outcomes included enhanced knowledge of what constitutes appropriate and sustainable use of ICTs in literacy education; the development of a cadre of fieldworkers who are knowledgeable in using ICTs in literacy education; significantly improved knowledge and skills in reading and numeracy due to the use of ICTs; the development of a set of materials for training literacy workers and the development of a set of literacy materials.

While these have been spelt out as the overall project goals, the special focus has been on the capacity building of the two SRCs in the use of ICTs for literacy related work. In the case of MSSRF, however, the focus has been on understanding how learners, as well as the community, have exercised control over technology and defined the 'what' and 'why' of technology use for the acquisition of literacy.

Implementation Activities. Implementation of the project involved several activities. A review of the experiences in setting up technology-based community learning centres highlighted the need to promote accessibility of technology, ensure its interactivity, ensure community ownership and plan for sustainability.

As a result, considerable time was spent on discussions and consultations with the community so that the community could select the site for setting up such a centre and take responsibility for its maintenance. Attempts were made to demystify the technology so that learners could eventually exercise control over its use. At the village level, meetings and consultations have continued to take place, various cultural programmes have been organised to create interest and sustain motivation among the community, and PRA (Participatory Research Approach) techniques have been used for community mobilisation.

Over a period of time, the technology-based community learning centres have given learners access to technological appliances. These centres have also provided a space for learners to meet, interact with others and participate in activities that entail use of technology. Gradually, the grassroots workers and learners have begun to acquire, adapt and develop learning materials of various kinds.

Lessons Learnt Thus Far. What has been our learning from this project so far? While the evaluation study undertaken by the national and international evaluators for the project is still awaited, the project experience thus far has thrown up some issues that may help us understand the implications of using ICT in literacy-related work. Rather than using ICT as a tool for training literacy workers, the focus here is on understanding the content, the processes and the skills that have to be developed among adult education functionaries and grassroots level functionaries if ICTs are to be meaningfully used.

Issues for consideration

Importance of evolving a vision

The importance of a vision that stresses the expanded concept of basic education as well the centrality of learning as a lifelong process that is multi-sectoral and diverse, has been repeatedly emphasised by practitioners, experts and policymakers. But if a vision is to guide us, it has to be based on consensus and an understanding shared by a broad constituency of stakeholders. Ahmed (2002) emphasises the need for a vision to evolve through a genuine, systematic and participatory consensus-building effort. According to him, rather than a one-shot affair, it has to be a continuous, iterative and evolving process. Our project experience has shown that although there was an initial workshop at which it was intended to define a common perspective and vision, it would have been helpful if we had subsequently reiterated and redefined the goals and objectives so that a common vision would have evolved over a period of time.

Clarity and consensus on an overarching vision are important for the literacy workers to avoid the danger that their work will be guided by a myopic vision.

Importance of suitable institutional partners

Our experience in working with the SRCs has shown that as government-funded institutions, their perspective and focus were confined to literacy skills work, with the emphasis on developing literacy primers and other print-based materials and the use of the 'cascading model' in training literacy functionaries. With such an orientation, it was an onerous task to change their perspective and mindset. Our experience has underscored the importance of seeking institutional partnerships with organisations that emphasise the centrality of the adult learner, believe in and practise bottom-up and participatory approaches, are open to new ideas and have a desire to learn.

A related issue is the attitude of the personnel of such organisations to computers and related technology. If ICTs are to be used for training literacy workers, it is desirable to have partners who understand and appreciate the use of technology for literacy-related work. In the absence of this, considerable time has to be spent on overcoming resistance and lack of interest.

Capacity building and hands-on experience

Computer training programmes. Rather than using ICTs to train literacy workers, our focus was on organising a number of training programmes that provided hands-on experience in the use of ICTs to SRC personnel and to the field functionaries. Accordingly, we organised regular computer training programmes. In the case of the SRC Indore, all four village level animators have now become computer literate and have learnt to make their own Power Point presentations. In the case of MSSRF, which is a computer-savvy NGO, their experience has demonstrated the use of technology in developing learner-generated literacy materials. MSSRF have, in fact, developed learner-specific materials for 150 learners. Learners have been using digital cameras and have learnt to make their own Power Point presentations.

Instructional design and development of multi-media materials. As an outflow of the workshop on multi-media courseware development, project partners have evolved a common understanding of the principles of instructional design and have begun to understand the processes for developing multi-media materials. This has considerably enhanced the capacities of SRC and field personnel to develop multi-media materials. The lack of relevant multi-media materials means these have had to be developed for training adult education functionaries. In the Bridges to the Future Initiative (BFI) of the International Literacy Institute that is about to initiate its work in the Andhra Pradesh and Karnataka states of India, an important component of the project will be the development of ICT-based tools to improve the quality of in-service training of literacy and basic education functionaries.

Training in audio and video technologies. Similarly, we have organised training programmes in the use of audio and video technologies at the village level. As a result, grassroots functionaries, village youth and women have been given hands-on training in the use of these technologies for developing locally relevant materials. Grassroots functionaries have shown great promise in using such technologies for developing their own materials.

Identifying diverse groups of learners and using technology to respond to diverse needs

Assessment of information needs. Our experience has shown that there are diverse groups of learners who have diverse learning needs. MSSRF had found, earlier, that extensive discussions with different sections of the village community to ascertain their information needs had highlighted that women wanted information about childcare, health, child rearing, education and reproductive health, whereas men were interested in information on the market prices of fertilisers and grain.

Assessment of information needs is useful in helping the project team to craft technology uses that are responsive to the needs of the villagers. The information needs become the starting point for procuring, adapting and/or developing a variety of materials. Clearly, this diversity is important in understanding why we need to move away from narrowly focused, 'one size fits all' education programmes and to use technology to respond to diverse needs.

Thus in the case of SRC Jaipur, a soil testing programme that was organised by the project led to a great deal of interest among the farmers, a workshop on reproductive health enthused women in the two SRC villages of Indore, and a booklet on potato cultivation raised some questions among the farm workers near Indore as this is a potato growing area. In each case, either information was put on the computer and a printout given to the learners, or an information booklet was provided. In the training programmes, it would be necessary to build the skills of the functionaries so that they can ascertain the information needs of different sections of the rural community. They would also need to acquire skills that would allow them high levels of adaptability in applying technology to support varying adult learning needs.

Role of ICT in facilitating adult learning

Experience of adult education programmes shows that even when adults join basic education programmes, they are very likely to attend sporadically and to drop out before completing the full cycle of the programme. This is particularly true of women learners, who drop out or attend the classes irregularly for various family and social reasons. Technology can help to remedy the problem of participation and retention in a number of ways.

The novelty and entertainment value of multi-media technologies in particular can attract adults into educational programmes and sustain their interest in learning. Thus a CD-ROM on basic literacy skills used by the project attracted a large number of learners due to its novelty effect and interactivity. A series of TV programmes, again on basic literacy, not only had entertainment value for adolescent girls, but also facilitated the learning process.

Does technology facilitate the acquisition of literacy skills? We are unsure whether technology necessarily does so. Hopefully, the evaluation study will throw some light on this issue.

On the other hand, what has drawn considerable attention among school and college-going adolescent rural youth is the possibility of becoming computer literate. Access to computers and to training in basic computer literacy is a motivating factor for the young adults, who recognise the market value of such skills. It is therefore possible that as an outcome of this project, a section of the village youth will not only become computer literate but that a cadre of such computer trained local youth may be created.

Technology can also give adult education programmes the necessary tools to more effectively track and monitor the progress of the learners who drop in and out of the programmes. SRC Jaipur has developed some formats for maintaining such records on the computers and the other two partners have evolved similar formats.

Potential of technology to create a learning environment

Beyond the utility of technology in literacy and non-formal adult education, existing and readily available information technologies can also provide unprecedented opportunities for informal learning by adults. Broadcast media, interactive video and the Internet can provide rich informal learning opportunities to adults in a wide variety of contexts. In order to create a learning environment, such learning must not only be attractive to adults but must also be designed to fit into their already crowded daily schedule.

At the rural centre of SRC Indore, a request from some learners who wanted to know how to ensure cleanliness in the cowsheds they maintained resulted in some of them using the digital camera to take pictures of the cowsheds in their neighbourhood. This led to a discussion of the prevailing conditions and the remedial measures they could take. At another centre, an audio recording was made of the old veterans who had participated in the freedom struggle, and used to honour the village's unsung heroes. There are neo-literate adults who have begun to use digital cameras and handy cams to take pictures and compose their own stories and materials. Such instances are beginning to show that technology has the potential to create an environment of learning in the community.

Potential of technology in empowering individuals and communities

Networking technologies have the capacity to open channels of communication and provide access to important resources for marginalised individuals and communities. Technology also has the potential to support a learning process that is transformative and empowers learners to become more critically aware of individual and collective interests and to pursue these interests more effectively.

There are interesting examples, both within India and abroad, of how the ICTs can be used by the poor for accessing information on issues that affect their lives.

MSSRF reports that women's self-help groups that are making bio-pesticides for a sustainable livelihood are using the Internet to find markets. The women are now saying that they would like to learn how to craft their own content for the website. Computerisation of the Self-Employed Women's Association (SEWA) Bank helped to expand self-help groups involved in financial services at village level. The use of computers in district level organisations to maintain up-to-date records helped expand business, which in turn increased productivity.

Computers opened up new markets for the craftswomen of Banaskantha and Kutch when the wares of these skilled artisans were displayed on the Internet, generating a lot of interest and bringing in more business. This has helped the women command a better price for their products and has benefited more than 40 000 women in these areas (Bindra 2000).

For the 800 Bangladeshi women to whom the Grameen Bank lent cell phones, the instrument became more than a means of communication: it became a weapon which they have successfully used to fight poverty. As a result, there are now a great many cases where the mobile phone has brought changes in their lives and in their social status as women (Thakuria 2000).

According to Johnson and Jain (1999), individuals and communities that use ICTs should hold a larger vision of learning. This vision should involve processes of critical self-reflection, thinking, questioning, exploring, interacting, creating, connecting and discovering. Such processes are directly linked to a notion of empowerment in terms of which individuals and communities engage in learning to create, appropriate and share knowledge, tools and techniques in order to change and improve the quality of their own lives and of their societies. Through empowerment, individuals not only manage and adapt to change but also contribute to and generate changes in their lives and in their environments. It is such a vision of learning that must guide the technology-based community learning centres if ICTs are to play a meaningful role.

Changing nature of literacy

Our understanding of literacy has changed from a technical concept focusing on the ability to read and write a simple text to the notion of a process that includes problem-solving and life skills. With the advent of technology, information and computer literacy are being associated with definitions of literacy. Information literacy has been defined as traditional literacy (reading, writing, numeracy) *plus* computer literacy (being able to use basic functions and software on a computer), *plus* using information to solve problems (Nishimuro, 1999).

Our experience has shown that there is yet another literacy, namely technological literacy. Very early on, SRC Indore started developing materials to train both grass-roots functionaries and learners in the use of the various technological appliances.

Literacy workers need to develop an understanding of the changing nature of literacy and the importance of contextual factors in determining this.

Holistic planning and planning for sustainability

An ICT project tends to focus exclusively on software aspects once the technological appliances have been put in place. Our experience has highlighted the need to plan for hardware and its maintenance and to seriously address the problem of non-availability of electricity in certain parts of rural India. MSSRF installed solar panels to augment the supply of electricity and thereby ensured uninterrupted power supply for about 22 hours a day. In the case of the rural centres of the SRCs in Jaipur and Indore, although it took some time to install telephone connections, this was ultimately achieved, whereas internet connections were not made available during the entire project cycle. Given the varying technological constraints from region to region, it is important to plan for technology choices that are feasible, cost effective and relevant to local needs.

According to Wagner (2000), there is much talk in development circles (broadly defined), especially in the Digital Divide domain, about 'sustainability'. This usually refers to how recurrent costs will be covered (e.g., by government, external agencies, user fees). Ahmed (2002), however, elaborates on the different facets of sustainability of a non-formal education programme: viability in terms of costs and finances; sustainability in respect of institutional arrangements, management of programmes and their ownership; and the question of the continuing relevance and effectiveness of programmes.

While concerted efforts were made in our project to plan for sustainability and to constantly raise questions about sustainability with our project partners, there are now serious doubts as to whether the technology-based community learning centres will survive beyond the project cycle. Some local communities have shown an interest in taking responsibility for running the centres, but financing has remained an unresolved issue. If user fees are charged, it is likely that the very poor will be unable to pay them and will be left out.

The problem of sustainability of such centres is very real and poses a serious challenge. Perraton (2002) quotes a 2001 study by Oestmann and Dymond that found that 'there is no multi-purpose telecentre in a developing country that has proved to be self-sustaining'. Clearly, this is an area where more research is necessary.

Measuring outcomes and impact of using ICTs in literacy programmes

A challenge posed by the use of ICTs in literacy programmes is that of measuring learning outcomes and the impact of the literacy programme on people's lives and well-being. This requires periodic monitoring and evaluation using credible and holistic indicators. According to Singh (2002), while statistical data on literacy skills are needed for effective assessment, a more critical question is related to the creation of learning communities and the development of critical indicators pointing in that direction.

Learning communities are first and foremost made by people who need and demand literacy and education, and only secondly by technologies that facilitate adult learning. The challenge lies in developing and refining indicators pertaining to a comprehensive and holistic notion of basic education for adults. Ouane (2002) addresses this issue when he indicates that the evaluation of learning will have to shift completely from an emphasis on narrow skills in teaching, transmission and memorisation to making generic or key competencies integral to learning. The key competencies he highlights include critical thinking, being able to communicate and live together, learning to learn, collective knowledge, scientific temper, creativity and emphasis on values. According to Ouane, while these key competencies can be seen from an individual's viewpoint, they can also be perceived from a social point of view. The challenge now would be to develop suitable tools and methodologies to measure such competencies.

Concluding remark

This paper has attempted to raise some issues on the basis of an on-going ICT project. While an external evaluation report for the project is still awaited, what the project has shown us are directions for future work and possibilities for using ICT meaningfully in literacy-related projects.

References

Ahmed, M. 2002. Lifelong learning and the learning society. In *Institutionalising Lifelong Learning*, vide Singh 2002.

Bindra, P. 2000. IT has great potential in alleviating poverty. *Humanscape* 7(6), June

Johnson, J & Jain, S. 1999. Community Technology Center for Learning and Empowerment. *Mimeograph.* November.

Nishimuro, T. 1999. Information literacy: how does it differ from traditional computer literacy? *TechKnowLogia Sept/Oct: 13.*

Ouane, A. 2002. Key competencies for lifelong learning. In I*nstitutionalising lifelong learning,* vide Singh 2002.

Perraton, H. 2002. Beyond the hype: a practical overview of the current applications and limitations of information and communication technologies in advancing education for all. Mimeograph.

Singh, M (ed). 2002. Institutionalising lifelong learning. Hamburg: UNESCO Institute for Education, Introduction.

Shah, SY. 2002. Using ICTs for training literacy workers: a case study from India. Mimeograph.

Thakuria, N. 2000. Here come the mobile ladies. Humanscape 7(6) June

Wagner D. 2001. IT and education for the poorest of the poor: constraints, possibilities and principles. TechKnowLogia, July/August.

17

ICTs and open and distance learning for training trainers in the context of the labour market and lifelong learning in Central America

Peter Gerasch

The poorest and most corrupt countries in Latin America are found in Central America and the Caribbean. A considerable part of the populations of Nicaragua, Honduras and Guatemala has to live on less than one or two dollars per day. These people face poor schooling and illiteracy, which are a constant barrier to further development in general. Official government policy is thus to emphasise the intent to ensure sufficient income and education/training for the poorest.

Many experts believe that the information and communication technologies (ICTs) have added a new dimension and provide opportunities in the field of open and distance learning (ODL) which have never been seen before. They maintain that this could contribute to significantly reducing illiteracy and poverty at a lower cost.

But reality tells a different story in most Central America countries. Generally speaking, Central American countries (or governments) are bankrupt. They are facing not only colossal external and internal debt but also the costs of widespread corruption. This affects every segment or sector and level in society and is felt on a day-to-day basis. It is therefore understandable that one simply does not find ICT playing a prominent role in a government budget where acutely marginalised segments of the population are a concern. ICT is found mostly in private endeavours (e.g. universities) that have some chance of becoming self-sustainable.

This applies also to ODL systems. In principle, we find such learning opportunities only in Costa Rica (one of the Central American countries) but they do not benefit the poor. In the other countries – Guatemala, El Salvador, Honduras and Nicaragua – there are just vague plans for a future distance learning system, mostly in higher education or at university level. Nevertheless, there are examples of the use of ICT in ODL available to the poor sectors of the population in Central America. The difference is that such projects are funded from abroad (by international development operations) and usually operate on a local, regional or ethnic basis for a limited period of time.

The 'Toolbox Network' is a joint Central American effort in the field of ODL, using ICT. Target groups are the marginalised micro, small and medium-sized enterprise (MSME) sector and consultants/teachers who train entrepreneurs or their staff, including unemployed people with Internet access. At present, the Toolbox provides mainly information data and material for education and training. Other components, like more interactive modules, are at the planning stage.

Introduction

The chapter opens with recent experiences in Central American and the Caribbean in non-formal adult education using some background on this beautiful but poor region of the world and then moves on to discuss various experiences with ICT and ODL for adults.

The circles in Figure 1 may illustrate the field of interest in this context.

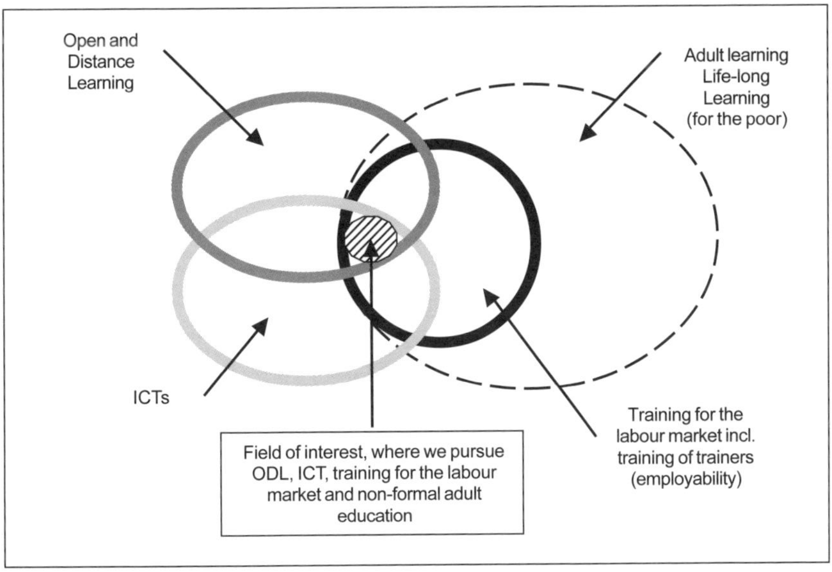

Figure 1 Field of interest

General information

Nicaragua and Honduras are the poorest Central American countries in Latin America (except for Haiti in the Caribbean). Per capita income in the region (Guatemala, El Salvador, Honduras and Nicaragua) is estimated at US$1370 per year (average for all countries) according to official World Bank statistics, which is about US$ 3.8 dollars a day.

These figures, however, do not reveal much, and they need some explanation. There are, for example, substantial differences between the different countries: thus the per capita income in El Salvador is four times higher than that in Nicaragua. Furthermore, an average per capita income expressed as a given number of US$ does not really mean that the people have that amount of money at their disposal. Most of the poor and poorest in Nicaragua would be grateful to the World Bank (WB) if they actually had the US$485 income in one year, as published in the WB statistics.

Table 1 Central America: some statistics

2000-01	Guatemala	El Salvador	Honduras	Nicaragua	Costa Rica
Population	11.9	6.4	7.0	5.2	3.7
Size (km²)	109000	21000	112000	130000	51000
GDP per capita	1.670	2050	900	485	3600
Illiteracy ♂	23 %	18 %	26 %	33 %	5 %
Illiteracy ♀	38 %	23 %	26 %	33 %	5 %
☎/1000	118	218	44	49	204
🖫/1000	11	19	10	9	102
Internet	75000	60000	40000	40000	250000

Sources: WB Statistics.

If you consider the poverty situation in the Central American region, it is clear why access to technology (telephone, fax, PCs, internet) is limited to a certain segment of the population.

In Nicaragua, where the author has lived for the last two years (since 2000), only five to six percent of the population use a telephone service (fixed line or cellular phone). Access to the Internet is confined mostly to the big enterprises, the international co-operation agencies and a growing number of private or state-owned telecentres.

In most Central American countries (except Costa Rica) teaching is conducted in ways that are very similar to the schooling of the 19th century. This is something to be seen, and ICT use has to be evaluated in terms of this situation.

Poverty reduction

At the beginning of this new millennium the wealthiest countries in the world felt it was essential to put themselves under pressure and to reduce poverty by half by 2015 (a goal which many experts already consider unrealistic).

In Central America the two poorest countries have, in a joint effort with the International Monetary Fund (IMF), prepared national strategies to fight poverty.[1] The central pillars of this strategy are economic growth and education (investment in the so-called human resources). Within this strategy special attention is paid to micro, small and medium-sized enterprises (MSMEs), including self-employment. Central to the strategy is the conviction that poverty and illiteracy cannot be reduced without improvements in these enterprises, which account for up to 85% of the urban workforce in the industry, trade and service sector.

The German government is also committed to the objective of poverty reduction, which is the main goal of its foreign aid policy. Thus, fighting poverty is the ultimate objective of the German Technical Corporation (GTZ), an organisation that implements a large number of projects of the German government. (GTZ is, however, also carrying out an increasing number of multilaterally-funded projects – e.g. of the EU.)

In Central America, GTZ is committed to supporting national antipoverty policies by focusing on certain priorities in the different countries. Priorities in Central America and the Caribbean include economic and employment promotion. In this field of activity, training and adult education play key roles.

ICTs and eradication of poverty

When we talk about ICTs we have to distinguish at least two kinds of technologies. One includes television, telephone, video (on demand or conferencing) and data transmission. The other is best represented by the word Internet.

The question at issue here is: Can ICT be useful in the struggle against poverty? In the literature we find an uncountable number of contributions (among them UNESCO, UNDP and ILO) on this topic. The main controversy is about the impact and effectiveness of ICT in the fight against poverty. This discussion cannot come to an end here and now as, particularly with the development of Internet, we can observe a host of activities and projects related to the poverty objective. The results remain to be seen.

Nevertheless, it can be said that there is a widespread belief that ICT at least provides an opportunity to bridge or, better, narrow the digital gap, accelerate growth, promote human development and finally eradicate poverty.[2]

ODL and ICT in Central America

Generally speaking, almost every country in Central America has some kind of experience with ODL. However, only Costa Rica has a working distance learning scheme, with a tradition of several years. This is the National University of Distance Education (UNED). As a state-owned institution, UNED is funded by the Ministry of Education and provided with almost state of the art technological equipment. UNED organises an international conference on distance learning every year. However, the main concern of UNED is higher education rather than basic teaching or training.

Universities in other Central American countries lag a long way behind the Costa Rican standard. But with emerging new technologies, all Central American universities are showing an increasing interest in developing their own distance learning systems. But again, such intent and effort are aimed at the university level, not at raising the schooling level in marginalised segments of the population.

But what about the experiences of the so-called national training institutions or agencies in several countries (Guatemala, El Salvador, Nicaragua), which are being at least partially funded by a tax paid by the private enterprise sector? So one finds a National Technical Institute (INATEC) in Guatemala, an INFOTEP in the Dominican Republic, an INSAFORP in El Salvador and an INATEC in Nicaragua. In these entities there are 'distance learning' departments that provide (or should furnish) training or courses in the distance learning method to poorer target groups (e.g. in distant rural areas).

The sad reality of these departments is that they all lack funds and well-trained staff and have to work with virtually no technological equipment or with technology that is hopelessly obsolete. For the time being, most of the courses offered by these institutions are still related to general administrative contents such as accounting, basic business administration, motivation, and English. Moreover, what is called a distance mode or method is in fact a sort of disguised contact teaching. In other words, the participants usually get the learning material (personally in the case of Nicaragua because the postal service is far from reliable) and then meet with a tutor at some time to check and prepare new material.

Using ICT in education and training, particularly in distance learning systems, requires a considerable investment in equipment. Except for Costa Rica, these funds probably do not exist in Central America.[3] So when it comes to ICT almost all projects seek external funds. The following undertakings are examples.

The *Spanish foreign aid programme* supports literacy and adult basic education efforts in Central America. In Nicaragua, where the Education Ministry is the official counterpart, some PAEBANIC (Programa de Alfabetización y Educación Básica de Adultos de Nicaragua) project funds go into infrastructure. Today, the Ministry has at its disposal a computer centre with more than 15 modern PCs with access to the Internet and a small distance learning project[4] has been started. The target group is ministry staff, that is, functionaries or teachers with access to the Internet. Thus most participants rely on the ministry's computer centre. The main purpose of this training programme is to improve performance in the ministry's labour force. The courses offered by this small project are tutored from Spain (Ministry of Education, Culture, and Sports). There is no teacher involved, just an administrator who manages information exchange and monitors the learning process. So far, these e-learning courses (of up to 4 months' duration) are exclusively related to Windows Software (Excel, Word, PowerPoint, Access) and general content in the field of informatics (for instance introduction, maintenance, internet). Additional courses are planned for the near future, covering not only the demands of the Ministry but also those of the public in general. For these efforts to be sustainable, these additional courses cannot be provided for free.

In Latin America, the World Bank operates 14 *Distance Learning Centres* (DLCs) as part of the Global Development Learning Network (GDLN). There are DLCs in all Central American countries (except for Honduras, which was due to be included in 2003). In Nicaragua the video conference centre is equipped to hold up to 30 participants. These centres use video conferencing and e-learning with state of the art technology to provide all kinds of events (relating to, for example, globalisation, decentralisation, health, and environmental issues) with some emphasis on the education and training sector. Several events concerning the use of the media (video conferences, e-learning) are aimed at organisations and institutions like ministries and foreign aid agencies. A recent example is an e-learning course entitled 'Teleformation or E-learning', organised by the World Bank and implemented by IFO,[5] Madrid, Spain. Its objectives are to create and experience different methodologies of e-learning and discuss the usefulness of e-learning, its advantages and disadvantages. The course duration is three weeks, and participants came from six Latin American countries and Spain. Central America was represented by Guatemala, Nicaragua and Costa Rica.

Language education: In Guatemala there are five different Mayan languages with an incredible variety of some 21 dialects spoken in this beautiful, relatively small country, which is going through unthinkable corruption and suffers under a completely unjust wealth distribution. Although few Mayans can still read in their language and even fewer of them can write in it, Mayans with little schooling prefer their native language over Spanish. Bilingual teachers are very scarce and have usually had little or no experience or training in bilingual teaching methodologies.

The 'Quiché Link' project got started in 2000 as a response to these problems and is part of the USAID programme, 'Better Educated Rural Society'. The project started by funding the establishment of five technology centres and then it created multimedia training materials, showing the use of the new ICTs in preparing and developing bilingual instructional materials. Technology is used to develop and prepare future teachers not only in learning to do, but also in learning to be. This idea behind the project prompted the slogan: 'Teaching with computers, not about computers.' More information about this interesting project can be found at www.aed.org/learnlink, www.usaid.gov, and www.TechKnowLogia.org.

In response to the enormous digital gap between Latin America and the developed world, bilateral and multilateral development organisations have recently put part of their budgets into the creation of so-called *telecentres*.[6] According to a recent study[7] these telecentres 'have the potential to help in ridding of some of the largest barriers to development that are currently faced by low-income populations, particularly in rural areas'.

Telecentres exist in every Central American country. In Nicaragua, for instance, there are about 60 telecentres offering services to the public, while over 200 new telecentres are planned. These telecentres are usually multipurpose. They provide an excellent opportunity not only to train trainers in ICTs, but also in using these technologies in their teaching in order to improve poor people's language, knowledge and capacity to make a living (employability).

The Toolbox Network

The complete name of this instrument is: Toolbox Network for MSME Development and Training.

Why a Toolbox Network?

National governments in Central America and bilateral and multilateral development co-operation are striving to close or at least bridge the digital gap between this region and the northern part of the world. Having access or not to new markets and being successful or not in creating and finding new sources of income or a new job to a large extent depend today on access to ICTs. So information and communication systems have a direct impact on the availability of knowledge and thus on current and future social conditions throughout the world.

Thus our knowledge-based economies require, as a first step, access to the technology. No less important than the technological question are the problems of creation and dissemination of information and know-how. Know-how and knowledge have to be made available to everybody.

As we have seen, access to the Internet in Central America and the Caribbean varies from country to country and as a rule it lags way behind developed countries. However, the number of Internet users is growing day by day and new possibilities are therefore being opened up to, for example, entrepreneurs, teachers and consultants.

In Guatemala, El Salvador, Honduras, Nicaragua and the Dominican Republic, up to 80% of the workforce, in MSMEs (in Spanish MIPYME), accounts for up to 70% of the workforce in the industry, trade and service sector. For this reason the MSME sector requires special attention in the context of antipoverty strategies and policies.

The number of MSMEs in Central America and the Caribbean is in sharp contrast to the quality of service, information and training available to them. An estimated 70% of all MSMEs discontinue their activities shortly after start-up, since they are unable to compete in the local market, let alone in the world market. One of the main reasons for this is the inadequate knowledge and use of instruments on the part of small entrepreneurs, which would enable: (1) entrepreneurs to manage their enterprises efficiently and in a market-oriented manner; (2) skilled and unskilled workers to acquire the necessary know-how to improve their employability; (3) teachers and trainers to convey adequate know-how, techniques and new competences, among other things, to their students.

These instruments include basic elements such as business plans, accounting systems, knowledge of demand structures and marketing strategy..

Thus, three major problems must be resolved to fight the information vacuum of MSMEs in Central America and the Caribbean, and these are: (1) absence of an MSME information system that adequately meets the demand; (2) inadequate use of modern information technologies for dissemination and use of knowledge; (3) lack of co-operation and communication between information providers in the region.

What is the Toolbox?

With the initiative of GTZ's projects network, 'Economic and Employment Promotion of GTZ projects in Central America and the Caribbean' in El Salvador, Guatemala, Honduras, Nicaragua and the Dominican Republic (see figure 2), a complex problem is approached with an innovative instrument: the Toolbox Network for MSME development and training. This is an enterprise management network for MSMEs in Latin America and the Caribbean, an Internet-based information and data system that provides selected and adequately prepared information to the target groups through an Internet website.

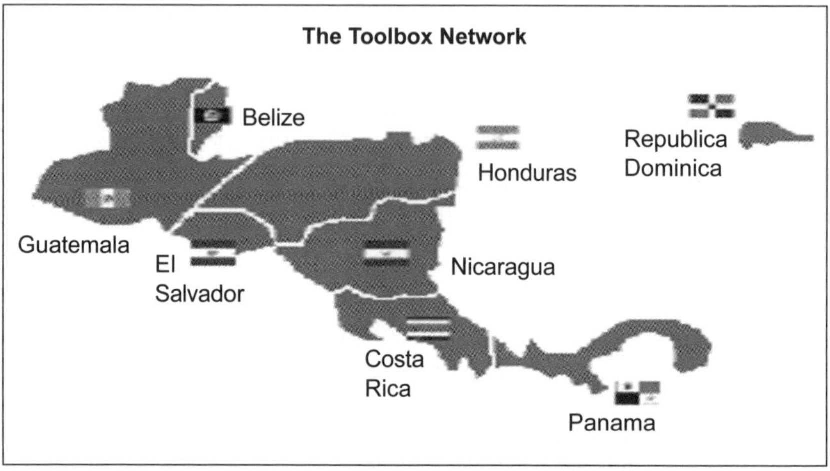

Figure 2 Five countries participating in the network

Two target groups are to be served through the Internet website: (1) MSMEs in El Salvador, Guatemala, Honduras, Nicaragua and the Dominican Republic. (2) institutions and organisations that support and promote MSME in these regions.

In practice, however, the structure of the target groups is much more heterogeneous, since the offer stretches over five countries. Moreover, different possibilities and known customs with which both target groups in the respective countries tackle the Internet medium have been taken into consideration at the project planning stage. Thus, regionally and nationally applicable instruments and content must be distinguished from one another, and a similar distinction must be drawn between information that is important to enterprises (the entrepreneur or his/her personnel), institutions/ organisations and consultants/trainers.

Website structure

Starting in FrontPage, the user can choose between access to the respective countries and access to a sub web page with regional information (see Figure 3).
FrontPage

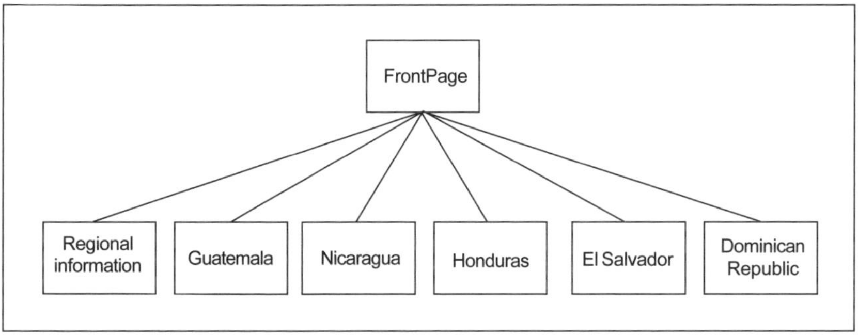

Figure 3 User access provided by Toolbox Network

The page with regional information contains a number of documents and many links on issues such as business consulting, good management, market indicators, certification, training documents, trade agreements, banking systems, financial participation in the project. This offer is of particular interest to experienced Internet users who provide consultancy services to MSMEs.

Country pages contain specific information about a country and provide two entries:

***For entrepreneurs*:** It is presumed that most entrepreneurs have little experience with Internet use and do not always have access to thc Internet. As a result, the segment for entrepreneurs for the most part contains simple, directly applicable documents that are saved as files within the page and can thus be used offline. The documents for entrepreneurs include, for example, information about business plans, book-keeping, procedures for completion of formalities, staff management, financing and training possibilities and much more. This section can be copied to the hard disk or burnt onto a CD, and it is up to 90% available offline.

For institutions/organisations/consultants/trainers: This target group has Internet experience and regular online access to the Internet. Here, mainly links to other pages are provided. These contain continuously updated information on topics such as import/export information, national guidelines, training modules, sector information, indicators, certification, market information, production, financing, and much more.

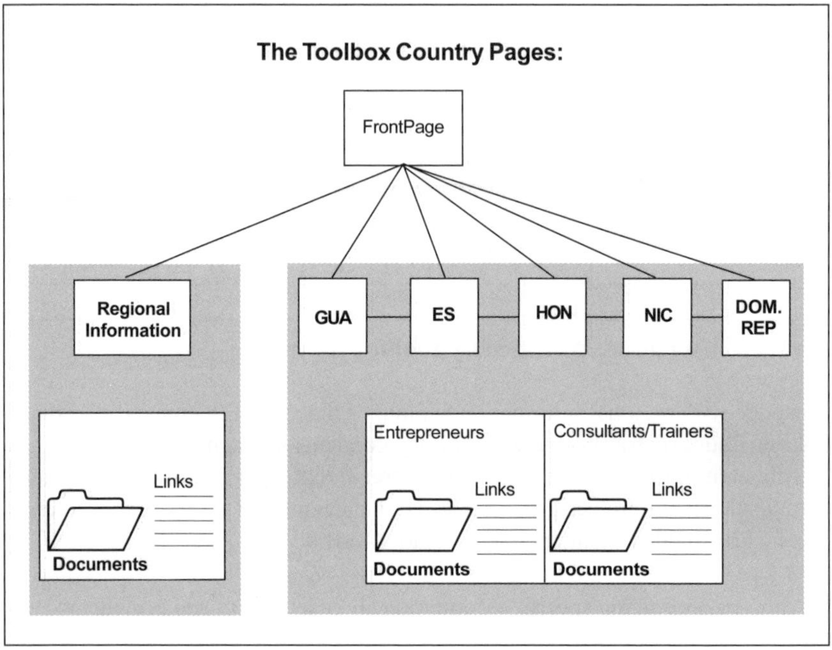

Figure 4 Specific information made available at country pages

What are the Tools?

***Download*:** Since not all interested persons or stakeholders have daily Internet access, the possibility of downloading the pages on a PC or CD-ROM has been catered for. *Translation*: A translation program makes it possible to use documents that are not available in Spanish. *Search*: The search mechanism gives users easy access to documents on a single page or in the whole homepage. S*ite map*: The structure of the national and regional pages will be clarified by a site map. *User Service*: Virtual support to the user should be furnished through direct email contact options with the Service Centre (*Centro de Servicios*), which will handle problems, questions and contacts and provide detailed information.

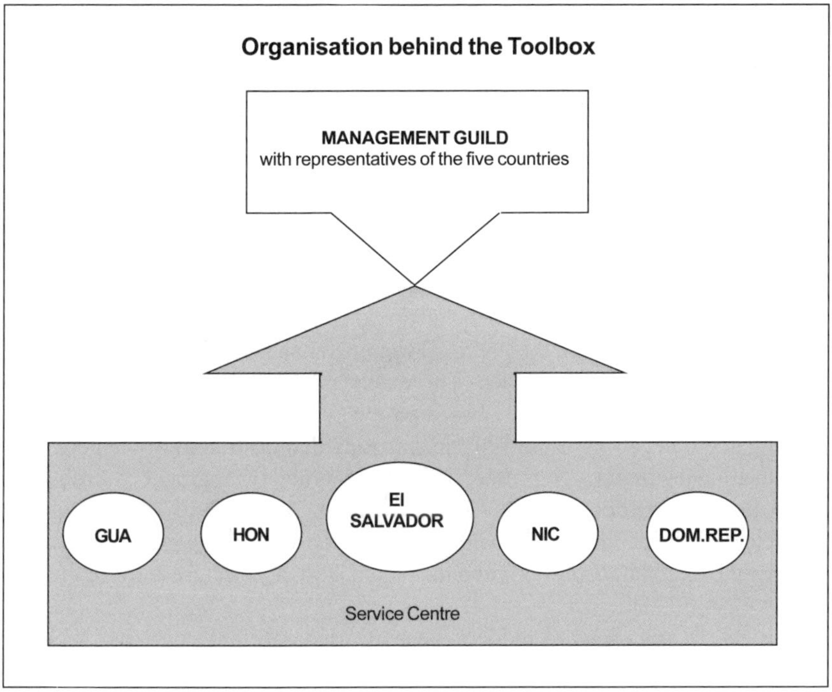

Figure 5 Toolbox Network Organisation

In each country, a different participating GTZ project started and supported the organisational structure of the information system, which is based on national and regional co-operation. All the participating countries have signed special agreements and have national working groups in place, with representatives from relevant MSME institutions (e.g. in Nicaragua, the INDE or Nicaraguan Small and Medium-sized Enterprise Institute; the INPYME, or Nicaraguan Institute for Entrepreneurial Development; the INATEC, or Nacional Technical Training Institute; the UAM, which is the Universidad Americana or American University; and the GTZ). The working groups meet regularly and are responsible for searching (and processing) instruments, maintaining the web page, co-operating with and co-ordinating other institutions and organisations, reaching target groups, carrying out impact evaluation, providing public services, and so on. Such groups are supported and strengthened by the respective GTZ projects.

A committee with national representatives of the working groups is in charge of the quality of this service, and it works on regional strategies for its improvement. A Service Centre has been established in El Salvador, which provides technical services for the whole regional network.

Sustainability

Institutional sustainability. Strategies for sustainability have already been implemented during the planning phase of these projects. Thus, the first steps in building up such a network usually include having stakeholders and interested sector institutions join in the process and signing agreements with them. The working groups thus established in each country have been involved in the planning and implementation phases from the very beginning and they are responsible for a successful project. Democratic decision-making processes, along with co-ordination by GTZ, have yielded outcomes that are in line with national requirements, leading to strong identification of the institutions with these projects. This method means GTZ projects have the potential to transfer successive responsibilities to national institutions or agencies. The extent of the outcome on institutional sustainability achieved so far is based on the systems for democratic decision-making and delegating responsibilities (already demonstrated) of the network's organisational structure. At present, GTZ projects and the regional co-ordination of the project network still play a role in planning, implementing and financing activities. However, this role will diminish as responsibilities are increasingly taken over by the national institutions and the organisational structure is strengthened.

Technical sustainability. A modern, decentralised online system gives working groups direct access to the respective national sites, which they can handle independently, i.e. change texts, set up links and documents, delete and change them. The Service Centre helps with technical problems in each country. This ensures that the quality and updating of the sites do not depend on a single site, but can be guaranteed directly and non-bureaucratically at national level, being controlled at regional level.

Financial sustainability. While the GTZ projects have taken a major part in financing for planning, implementation and technical assistance, national institutions have been involved at an early stage in funding small activities, such as covering travelling expenses for workshop participants, working on special, not yet existing, instruments as well as official launching of the sites. Furthermore, negotiations are under way with a regional MSME institution, which would like to take over ownership of the network at regional level, to accept responsibility for substantial possible costs until the sites have capacity to fund themselves. It is hoped that this financial independence can be achieved by selling advertising spots on the sites.

Quality assurance

The issue of sustainability is closely linked to the question of quality assurance methods: Only an updated and flexible offer will stay in the market in the long term and satisfy the needs of an increasing number of users.

In order to keep abreast of the composition of users, their needs and preferences, the following evaluation mechanisms have been included: *Counter:* Two counters, one internal and one external, automatically give the results as statistical data. They show the number of users, during which period they have visited, which themes and individual sites. In this way, preferences can be identified and the offer to users in particularly interesting areas can be expanded qualitatively and quantitatively. *Contact:* The contact option provides a user with the option of making suggestions, asking questions and making complaints. This gives network managers insight into users' additional needs and how to satisfy these. *Download*: When a user downloads the 'Box' onto the hard disk or CD for use offline, she or he will provide some data (name, place of residence, address, email, profession etc.), which are required for later evaluation and making contact with target groups. *Questionnaire*: As soon as the user leaves the 'Box Network', a pop-up window is opened asking for personal data, topics that are of particular interest to users, and for assessment of 'Box Network'.

Putting these options together provides insight into potential improvements and how extensively the target groups have been reached.

Future prospects

The Toolbox Network is far from being complete. At the current stage of development it still lacks some important features that will make it more efficient and effective in the future.

First of all, there is a need to evaluate the system. Particularly important are the recommendations made by users, especially teachers and trainers. These recommendations will be used as a basis for future development of a Toolbox. There are plans to include new, more interactive module training (using forums, chats, online training) to trainers in 2003. Here again, co-operation between several interested institutions will be needed within and between the participating Central American countries.

Visit us:

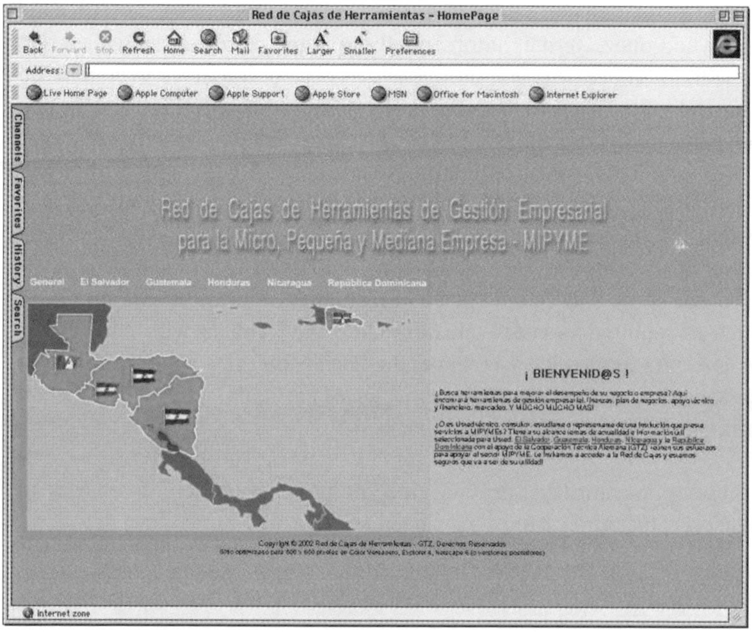

www.infomipyme.com / www.infomipyme.org

Data:

Planning	Phase:	05/2000	–	06/2001
Orientation	Phase:	07/2001	–	08/2002
Launching:				08-10/2002

Optimisation Phase: 10/2002 – 07/2003

Notes

1 These strategies (called PRSP, or poverty reduction strategy papers) are some of the requirements for the different countries if they want to benefit from the support of multilateral financial organisations in regard to foreign and domestic debt reduction and additional financial aid.

2 See: www.undp.org/rblac/ict

3 In most Central American countries, oligarchies with sufficient political power are not really interested in providing substantial budget allocations to education and training. Even worse, part of the small amount of money allocated to such purposes finally ends up in the pockets of corrupt politicians and functionaries or officials.

4 This project is called, in Spanish, aula mentor (classroom mentor)

5 Instituto de Formación Online (www.ifo.es/ceddet/)

6 Telecentres can be characterised by management type: commercial (e.g. cyber cafes), university, school, NGO-sponsored, franchise and others, and impact on sustainability.

7 Financed by FAO, IADB and others: Telecentres for Socioeconomic and Rural Development in Latin America and the Caribbean (www.iadb.org/regions/itdev/telecenters/index.htm).

18

Professional backup to adult educators through networking resources using technology and media

Vitalicy Chifwepa

Networking has made it possible to communicate and share resources across geographic boundaries. A number of cases that show the potential to apply this technology to the benefit of adult educators are cited, and it is argued that some of the difficulties with using technologies could be alleviated by networking. This would also mean that the resources of those who might have certain advantages over others could be spread for the benefit of adult educators.

Introduction

Adult educators include a range of people in formal employment and an equally wide range of people who are not formally employed. Those who are formally employed are, in general, associated with sectors such as agricultural extension services, health education services, continuing education units, environmental management and control, public awareness services and other units involved in some kind of public awareness. Those who are not formally employed include traditional trainers like those who teach young mothers and young adults traditional and cultural values and practices and volunteer literacy instructors.

The support such educators need varies, but methodological and basic information materials are required by all. The means to support adult educators depends on the environments in which they operate, and these environments pose a number of challenges. Some of these are technological while others are policy related. This paper deals with the technological issues and how some policies may influence or affect the technological factors. Professional backup refers to providing support in the form of information resources or materials as well as to forums for the exchange of information and experience (communication). The formal educators need basic teaching materials, such as literacy materials, for use in their work.

In most developing countries the availability of materials is affected by problems such as poor publishing infrastructure, a shortage of proficient writers, poor means of distributing materials and poorly stocked libraries. In Zambia, for example, a shortage of appropriate materials almost brought literacy work to a standstill

(Mwansa et al 2001). On the other hand, initiatives have been launched in some countries and have resulted in the production of basic literacy materials. The British Department for Education and Employment,[1] for example, has developed various materials that could be used by other countries.

The evolution of Information Communication Technologies (ICTs) has made it possible not only to produce materials in more flexible formats but also to make the materials more readily available and accessible so that the resources can be more widely shared. As Barrett and Wilkins (2000) observe:

> ICT can allow access not only to adult and continuing education programs but also to specific learning experiences that would otherwise be difficult to provide. For example, web-based, multimedia, virtual site tours can provide contextual information, promote insights, and bridge the gap between theory and practice just as actual site tours without the inconvenience of inclement weather, travel costs, scheduling and logistics, and safety or security arrangements.

However, despite the claimed benefits of ICT for Adult and Basic Education and distance education, it is perhaps best to approach these innovations with caution, as recommended by Kirkwood (1998):

> Media technologies can facilitate or support certain aspects of the teaching and/or learning, but … none is capable of supporting every aspect. For any teaching/learning situation, there should be an analysis of the educational activities needed to promote learning: only after that analysis should the media be considered in terms of contribution that each can (or cannot) make to the education process.

Networking of resources

There is no one institution or country that can claim to be able to satisfy all its educational requirements. Some countries, especially in the West, have been able to develop high-quality educational resources, but others have had to struggle with the various pressures of having limited means of meeting basic requirements.

One of the ways of maximising resource utilisation is networking, which aims at maximising access and minimising costs. A network is a forum on which educators may share and find information regarding the profession or relating to their duties as educators. Networking of resources refers to making resources available to educators and learners more widely than if they were localised. Networks make it possible to share large quantities of information, learning materials, ideas and experiences, and to do so more rapidly than by other means. A lot of institutions have therefore created local area networks and have also joined the wide area networks such as the Internet. Libraries are being urged to join with other libraries to share resources and increase the accessibility of their materials, and at the same time access the holdings of other libraries and enjoy their services.

Some examples that could be exploited or emulated in order to widen accessibility of resources for adult educators are discussed below.

The Internet

The Internet is the widest and most frequently used ICT network and covers almost the entire world. It has become a resource that provides a number of possible services. As Jensen (2002) puts it:

> Internet continues to grow rapidly in Africa, and local Internet access is available in all 54 countries and territories. The number of dialup Internet subscribers now stands at over 1.3 million, up from about 1 million at the end of 2000. The total international incoming Internet bandwidth is now well over 1 gigabyte per second, while outgoing traffic is estimated at about 800Mbps.

In addition to other universities in Africa, the universities of Mozambique and Zambia are now Internet Service Providers as well. With Internet access so widely available, Africa has joined the rest of the world in being able tap the information that is so plentifully available on the net. Internet access has also made it far more feasible for African researchers and scholars to publish widely.

Projects aimed at enabling university libraries to acquire ICTs and to train personnel in their management and utilisation have mushroomed. Once this is in place, it is hoped that Africa's university libraries will join the rest of the academic world in providing the dynamic information services that are so acutely needed. The services currently available are:

Electronic mail service (email). This service facilitates one-to-one communication, conferencing (a number of people may be connected and send email to each other in real time) and listserv groups (people with the same interests may discuss or share experiences and ideas on a given subject or on subjects of mutual interest).

Information resources (web sites). One of the major Internet services is the worldwide web (WWW), which is a network of information resources available worldwide. This makes it possible for adult educators to publish their materials and make them available for the rest of the world. It also makes it possible for educators to access materials on various subjects.

Some of the examples of programmes that have utilised the internet services are discussed next.

The Commonwealth of Learning Literacy Project (COLLIT), 1999-2003. COLLIT is a project currently running in India and Zambia under the Commonwealth of Learning and is funded by the British Department for International Development (DFID). Its objective is to explore ways in which literacy programmes can be enhanced through the use of appropriate technologies. The project officially began on 1 July 1999, and plans to achieve a number of outcomes: enhanced knowledge of what constitutes appropriate and sustainable use of ICT in literacy education; a cadre of tutors who are able to use ICT in literacy education and are aware of global media-based instructional resources; significantly improved knowledge and skills in reading, numeracy and the use of ICT appliances for learners who participated in the project; objective data regarding the role of ICT-based community learning centres (CLCs) in the education delivery model for the country; a set of materials for training literacy workers and a set of literacy materials

COLLIT aims to make the set of literacy materials for training literacy workers and the materials for learners available in the operating country centres and among the participating countries, and for participants to exchange materials. It also thrives on exchanging ideas between the project managers from the Commonwealth of Learning, India and Zambia. The medium through which this happens is the Internet and the means used is the COLLIT website (http://www.col.org/literacy/intro.htm) and email listserv services. Teleconferencing is conducted using telephones. Other media used are audio and visual recordings of lessons by means of video camera, audio-recorders and digital cameras.

The final evaluation of COLLIT has yet to show its impact.

Using ICT to Increase the Effectiveness of Community-Based Non-Formal Education for Rural People in Zambia (CERP Project), 1999-2002. This project was designed to take advantage of the COLLIT project. Its purpose was to develop and test new, cost-effective educational strategies in non-formal education in rural communities, by building on existing Zambian initiatives and local expertise in non-formal education. An example of these local initiatives was the University of Zambia community-based learning initiative to develop ICT capability and literacy programmes in regional centres in partnership with the Commonwealth of Learning. The intention was to explore the potential of poorer rural communities to benefit from a wide range of technological educational tools. Some of these may enable communities to leapfrog what might previously have been seen to be necessary stages in the development of educational provision and of a body of knowledge in a community. The main practical outcomes of the CERP initiative are the following:

Production of educational materials. Culturally acceptable paper, audio and web-based materials were developed in two modules focusing on basic education and health education, using examples that incorporate farming and health practices as appropriate to the community. The materials can be accessed via paper, audio and internet. The intention was to provide materials for use as well as to develop staff skills and web-based resources for more widespread use later as ICT (e.g. computers, CD-ROMs, email, internet) access grows.

Educational outcomes for the communities involved. Through sharing and creating knowledge, and new ways of doing things; study groups in the communities made up the sample that worked through the materials.
Educational outcomes for the young staff involved. These included skills development in the area of producing educational materials, research, evaluation, development, the use of ICT to support educational initiatives, technical skills in materials production for the web, skills in the management of electronic communication for professional development and knowledge sharing between professionals. Young people worked beside more experienced colleagues.

Educational outcomes for the educators involved. Models for providing education using ICT in rural areas were developed. The outcomes of the development and testing of models of community-based, non-formal education using higher-tech ICT than currently used were analysed. The final report will include an evaluation of initiative outcomes against the objectives above and will provide suggestions for further development in this area.

Sustainable networks. An electronic mailing list was set up for those who wanted to discuss non-formal education and information and communication technologies. It was intended that this would involve members of other initiatives with similar and complementary objectives (see http://www.unza.zm/CERP/index.html).

Like the COLLIT project, CERP developed training materials that were put on the website and communication took place using the listserv. Here too, audio-visual technology was used to develop and use recorded lessons. The project has come to an end and the final report is yet to be published.

Access to Internet resources

Accessing internet resources is not an easy thing and it has, in fact, become much more challenging as the number of resources has grown. One development that aims at alleviating the problem of accessing the resources is the development of subject gateways. A subject gateway has been defined by Stoklasová and Krbec (2001) as 'a Web-based mechanism for accessing a collection of high quality, evaluated resources identified to support research in a particular subject discipline'. It is a service that is accessed via a portal, through open standard protocols (such as Whois++, LDAP, Z39.50, Harvest Broker) which allow it to slot in seamlessly behind the scenes. What the end-user sees is Web-based, although behind the scenes it is more structured. Another definition of a subject gateway describes it as an 'Internet accessible collection of descriptions and location details for a range of information, generally available electronically, organised by subject or discipline, and selected for inclusion based on a published set of quality criteria' (http://www.nla.gov.au/initiatives/sg/servicetypes.html).

Continuing Education: libraries and the Internet (CELI). An example of such a service is the one being developed by the libraries of the universities of Botswana, Malawi, Mozambique, Tanzania, Lesotho, Swaziland, Namibia, Zambia and Zimbabwe, in conjunction with Lund University of Sweden and under the sponsorship of SIDA. The service is on the theme of 'Continuing education: libraries and the Internet' (CELI). An information gateway is being developed covering the use and application of ICT in education and information provision in Africa south of the Sahara. Although the target group comprises students, teachers, researchers and librarians at university level, any interested person could use the content.

The aims of the services are to provide structured access to quality online resources and enhance teaching and information provision. The scope encompasses materials with African content that are available on the Internet. Adult education is one of the subject areas although it is limited to those resources that deal with the use of ICT.

Other media

The other media that could be used to support adult educators include radio, television, audiovisual technologies like digital camera, video camera and recorders and fax.

Audiovisual recordings have the advantage of providing vision at a lower cost to the learner in that they could be used at learners' homes. A lot of countries have such media and use them locally. There are some broadcasting services, such as the British Broadcasting Corporation (BBC), that could reach almost the whole world. Most developing countries are struggling to reach the remote parts of their own territories. The degree to which such media could be networked depends on a high level of co-operation between governments. However, the recorded formats could be exchanged as audio and visual tapes, disks, among others.

A survey of the literature suggests that the most popular medium for education in Africa is the radio. In a study on distance education in Zambia, Siaciwena (1988) established that the radio was a satisfactory medium. Sibalwa (2000) found that radio has been extensively used in the transmission of agricultural extension information services. Siabi-Mensah (2000) also found that the radio was recognised as an important tool in literacy in Ghana. Apart from the cost of batteries for their radios, learners received free transmissions.

Radio could therefore be a useful backup for both the formally employed and the non-formal adult educators in providing them with information for their work. Radio, together with television, is in fact the medium that is most likely to be used by both groups of adult educators. As mentioned above, the COLLIT and CERP projects utilised audio and video materials and preliminary results show that the trainers found these very useful. It seems, therefore, that radio could be an effective means, provided the necessary funding was forthcoming. In Zambia there are some areas that do not receive the Zambia National Broadcasting Corporation services but they do receive transmissions from neighbouring countries. This could prove problematic and, in addition, Siaciwena (1988) found that time allocation for educational services was not adequate.

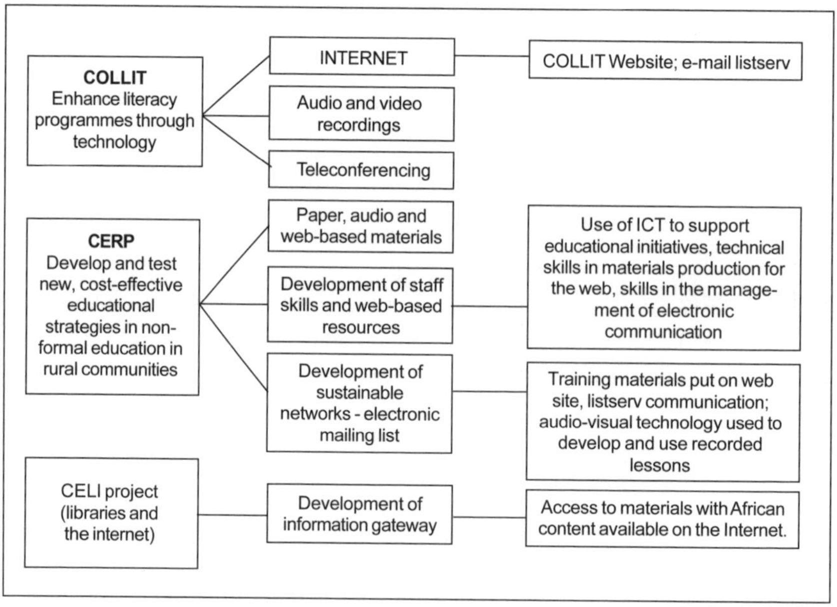

Figure 1 ICT Projects and Technologies Used

Library services

Print materials are the most-used medium in literacy and distance education. A big service provider that could provide print and non-print materials is the library. The different types of libraries, including academic, special and public libraries, can be used to provide backup services to both formal and informal adult educators. Libraries have the advantage of being able to use the economies of scale in that a large number of educators can use a limited number of materials. If the different types of libraries were integrated in a scheme of service, all adult educators would be able to access at least one library, be it a school or public library.

Given the developments in technology, libraries are able to network and share resources in order to maximise and widen their services. The new technologies have made it possible for libraries to access catalogues and digital resources in local and wide area networks. As has been illustrated by the CELI service described above, libraries are opening up to wide-ranging strategies of co-operation. However, a basic level of investment is required to allow the libraries to stock up with relevant and up-to-date resources.

While the Internet offers other methods of co-operation, postal services will continue to be an important means of networking and sharing print materials.

Care should be taken to ensure that the integration of these libraries is not derailed by debates on which institution or ministry 'owns' and 'controls' the libraries.

Challenges in the African context

Full networking and the use of technologies are not without their challenges, both technological and political. Uhomoibhi (2003) identifies the following challenges and problems: fear of technology; lack of financial proficiency in using e-learning; lack of awareness of opportunities offered by ICT-based teaching/learning to allow adequate exploitation; lack of a comprehensive, high-quality collection of online information resources to support teaching, learning and research; restricted access to the main information network and its services to learners; security: creation and maintenance of a secure teaching and learning environment and the Internet with authenticated access to required resources, enabling confidential transactions to be carried out conveniently and safely; a comprehensive set of advisory and consultancy services to help institutions explore and exploit the Internet safely, legally and effectively along with other IT applications for learning, teaching, research and e-business; collaboration: the need to encourage an appreciation of the global nature of ICT and associated applications to foster collaboration for effective international competition.

According to Deal (2002), online connection via dial-up modem can be a problem with very large graphic or video files; CD-ROM may be a better option. Brickman et al (2000) identify the cost of connectivity and hardware, time spent due to lack of staff proficiency in the use of technology and occasional hardware failures as the most significant barriers to effective use of the technology for learners, teachers and administrative staff.

A major problem that developing countries are likely to face is lack of policy on the availability of technology. In the absence of such policy, technology will not be available for education in general, let alone adult education. A positive development is, however, the formulation in Botswana of a policy on ICT in education that outlines the integration of ICT in formal and non-formal education (Magetse 1997).

Connectivity is a big problem in Africa. According to Jensen (2002):

> Due to high international tariffs and lack of circuit capacity, obtaining sufficient international bandwidth for delivering web pages over the internet is still a major problem in most countries. Until recently few of the countries outside of South Africa had international Internet links larger than 64Kbps, but today 23 countries have links carrying 2Mbps or more, and 10 countries have outgoing links of 5Mbps or more – Botswana, Egypt, Kenya, Mauritius, Morocco, Nigeria, Senegal, South Africa, Tunisia and Zimbabwe. Excluding South Africa, the total international outgoing Internet bandwidth installed in Africa is about 250Mbps.

Such problems make accessing the Internet painfully slow.

One way forward is to consider co-operation along the lines of the European project that aimed at the establishment of *Folkbildningsnätet* in folk high schools and study associations. The Swedish International Programme Office for Education and Training appealed to the National Council for Liberal Adult Education to explore the possibility of initiating and co-ordinating a Europe-wide project in which *Folkbildningsnätet* concepts for the use of ICT networks in adult education could be implemented in other European countries. The purpose of the programme was to promote the use of ICT in adult education by testing national, regional and local ICT networks for studies, meetings, discussions and access to information, and by examining the potential for a European adult education network (see http://www.adultstudy.net/summary.htm).

The issue of language will also need to be addressed. The English language currently dominates the Internet, and while this may not be a problem for educators, it could become a problem in the long run, especially for those educators who are not formally employed.

Conclusion

As technologies have evolved over the past few years, they have started to provide great potential for the support of adult educators, especially if used with reference to the distance education models in which the ICTs have been applied. Due to differences in endowments and environments, some countries will find different types of technologies more practical than others. The challenges related to the cost of the hardware, especially, will continue to affect developing countries more, but if the political will is there, some degree of investment could bring significant benefits.

Some of the challenges referred to here and above could be alleviated if adult educators undertook to share resources through networking.

As a way of summing up, it is important to reiterate that media application is very important in terms of desired results. As Saint (2000: 14) so aptly comments:

> How the media are used has proven to be more important than which medium is selected. Furthermore, multiple media appear to be more effective than a single, with interactivity between students and tutors contributing a major boost to learning. Because the choice of technology does not influence learning, technology cost and maintenance become determining considerations.

The use of print materials should not be arbitrarily discarded at the temptation of the apparent expediency offered by technologies, because print media will remain a reliable tool of learner support.

References

Barrett, JF. & Wilkins, B. 2000. Establishing a virtual building and construction site for education and training. Paper presented at the International Vocational Education and Training Association Conference, Hong Kong, China, August 6-9, 2000. (ED 446 247)

Brickman, A; Braun, L.W; Marge, S. 2000. An evaluation of the use of technology in support of adult basic education in Massachusetts. Available at http://www.alri.org/maltt/maltteval.pdf (seen on 3 January 2003)

Deal, WF. 2002. Distance learning: teaching technology online. *Technology Teacher* 61(8) May-June: 21-26.

Jensen, M. 2002 The African internet: a status report. Available at http://www3.sn.apc.org/africa/index.html (seen on 3 January 2003)

Kirkwood, A. 1998. Can information and communication technologies enhance learning? Paper presented at the 3rd International Security Forum and 1st Conference of the PfP Consortium of Defense Academies and Security Studies Institutes, 'Networking the Security Community in the Information Age', 19–21 October, Kongresshaus Zurich, Switzerland. Available at http://www.isn.ethz.ch/securityforum/Online_Publications/WS2/kirkwood.htm

Magetse, T. 1997. Information and communication technology policy in education context. Paper presented at the National Workshop on ICT in Swaziland Education, 2 October, Royal Swazi Spa, Swaziland.

Mwansa, D., Chifwepa, V. & Zulu, S. 2001. Needs assessment or participation in literacy projects: a case study of Kabwe and Katete. (Unpublished report)

Saint, W. 2000. Tertiary distance education and technology in sub-Saharan Africa. Education and Technology Technical Notes Series, 5(1).

Siabi-Mensah, K. 2000 Ghana: the use of radio in the National Literacy and Functional Skills Project in the Volta and Northern Regions. In Case studies of non-formal education by distance and open learning, edited by R. Siaciwena. Available at http://www.col.org/consultancies/00nonformal.htm (seen on 3 January 2003)

Siaciwena, RMC. 1988. A study of distance teaching at the University of Zambia with special reference to the effectiveness of degree courses. PhD thesis, University of Wales.

Sibalwa, D. 2000. Zambia: radio farm forums. In Case studies of non-formal education by distance and open learning, edited by R. Siaciwena. Available at http://www.col.org/consultancies/00nonformal.htm (seen on 3 January 2003)

Stoklasová, B. & Krbec, P. 2001 The CASLIN Uniform Information Gateway for Integrating Heterogeneous Resources. Available at http://jib-info.cuni.cz/eng/about/JIBENG.htm (seen on 12 December 2001)

Uhomoibhi, JO. ICT-Based Teaching and Learning and Adult Education at Queens University, Belfast. Available at http://www.qub.ac.uk/alpine/groups/group4/reports/ICTrep_UK.pdf (seen on 3 January 2003)

Notes

1 The Department for Education and Employment through the National Literacy Strategy has developed both print and electronic literacy materials both for learners and literacy educators.

Section V

Some reflections on adult basic learning from South Africa

19

Unisa and how it pioneered distance education

MS Makhanya

This chapter discusses distance education and highlights the University of South Africa (Unisa) as an open and distance learning institution. In the first part of this article, the author presents a case study describing an encounter with a sociology student. This case study is used as a starting point for highlighting in the second section the importance for lecturers to be able to guide, interact, communicate and enter into dialogue with their students as an important element of the distance education system. It describes how Unisa became geared to take up the challenge posed by the young students.

Case study: An encounter with a student

It was in 1994 that I first came across a 19-year-old student who was doing Sociology I at that time. She caught my attention when she approached me, after a number of tutorial sessions, to ask for assistance with a predicament.

She paid me a visit on the following Monday. She was there at eight in the morning. Her face struck me as very familiar, and I realised that this was so because she had not missed a single tutorial session. I invited her to tell me about her problem. I thought she had come to discuss the problem of, for example, finding sociology inaccessible, as was the case with so many of our students. Instead, she told me that she had come to ask for help from me because I was a black lecturer. I was taken aback by that remark, and I listened attentively to her story.

She said she was unhappy with the fact that Unisa, a distance education university, did not cater for the interests of its students. I was puzzled by this insinuation. She continued by saying that she wanted to know why we did not provide lectures for them, as did other universities. I realised that this was a genuine question from a concerned student and that I had to be sensitive in responding to her.

Her question told me two different things: that first year students, or at least the younger generation of students, see Unisa as a university that can offer lectures just like any other university; and that they see Unisa as deliberately sidelining them by not offering lectures.

I decided to ask her some questions about her background and history. She was from a rural village of Mpumalanga province. Her parents had decided to send her to live with her uncle in Tembisa township (Gauteng Province) so that she could be closer to Unisa. Her understanding was that being in Tembisa would at least facilitate her attendance at lectures. When I asked her why she had chosen Unisa rather than another university, her response was that it was relatively cheap and was the only tertiary institution her parents could afford.

This young student had moved directly from secondary school to the university, and she was finding it difficult to do without the classroom set-up and the guidance of a teacher. It was a shock for her to have to study on her own.

After listening to her story, I realised the urgency of attending to her need, that is, her lack of readiness to study at a distance education institution). *This is What I Did.*

The reality dawned on me that Unisa was at that time not ready to take up the challenge articulated by this student, so I had to consider an option that would mean losing her as our student. With this in mind, I wanted to know if she would be willing to leave Unisa and go to a residential university. She responded immediately that she would love to do so but the main hurdle was how to finance her studies. I suggested that she should apply for as many bursaries as possible and offered to act as her referee, and I helped her draft an application letter. Next, I supplied her with the addresses of all the bursars that I knew. Before she posted the applications, I telephoned Unisa's Department of Undergraduate Student Affairs and requested them to print an academic progress report for this student. I duplicated the report to equate the number of application letters, which were then posted.

She waited for about six weeks before receiving bursary application forms from the institutions concerned. As arranged, she then returned to me for further assistance, and I guided her in completing the applications. I wrote letters of recommendation, which we attached to all the application forms before returning them to the bursars. Then we had to wait for the outcome.

In the meantime, the student received an admission letter from the University of Pretoria. This university had arranged to enrol her for the second year of the BA degree pending the receipt of her examination results from Unisa. To expedite matters, I suggested to her, after another tutorial class at Thutong, that it would be advisable to make copies of the admission letter and send it to all the bursars to whom we had sent application forms. She was excited at this idea and the following Monday morning she visited me once again in my office. I requested her to start addressing all the envelopes to the bursars while I made copies of her admission letter. When this was done, I gave her the money to buy stamps and to mail all the letters.

After about two months, one of the bursars, Anglo American Corporation, wrote asking to meet the student at their offices in Johannesburg. She came to me to show me the letter. Her aunt was very supportive and offered to accompany her niece to Anglo's offices. I was happy with that arrangement. Two weeks after that meeting, one of Anglo's officials telephoned me to get my referee's report. In November 1994 my student received a letter from Anglo granting her a bursary. She was so elated that she could not believe that she had been granted a bursary. She was just on top of the world.

In the third week of December 1994, she received her first year BA degree results. She had been studying four first year subjects and had passed all of them very well, with marks ranging from 58% to 63%. Considering how new she was to tertiary level study, her family background and the environment she came from, I felt that she had excelled. I photocopied her statement of results, faxed it to Anglo's Johannesburg offices and used a fast-mail service to post the copy of the results to them. I then instructed the student to take Anglo's letter along with her when she went to register at the University of Pretoria in January 1995.

She followed my instructions and was registered as a University of Pretoria student. Anglo covered her tuition and residence fees while her family had the responsibility of buying her textbooks and stationery. This was a huge relief for her family, who felt that this was something they could afford to do for their daughter.

She passed all her second year courses in 1995. In 1996 she enrolled for three courses (including two of her majors) which she passed very well. Before the end of 1996, the heads of department of two of her major subjects persuaded her to do honours studies in their subjects. In 1997 she applied for a loan administered by the university to finance honours studies in either sociology or psychology. She informed me later that year that she had succeeded in getting a loan and had enrolled for honours studies in psychology. She completed her honours studies and the last time I had contact with her was when she was searching for employment.

I am happy that travelling an extra mile with this student gave her an opportunity that guaranteed her a career at a time when the majority of her peers could not afford the privilege of acquiring the knowledge that she received. When I look back now, I say to myself that had it not been for that first bold step of hers and my receptiveness, this student could have been thrown out of the education system.

I see what I did for this student as being part of my profession rather than as a task that was extra to my work of lecturing. I feel that a lecturer's failure to engage in his or her students' career development is a disservice to the nation, because lecturers meet the students more frequently than any student counsellor or vocational guidance consultant does or can.

Unisa was still comfortable with its traditional, simplistic view of itself as a distance education institution whose students worked on their own. However, a distance education institution is, by definition, not supposed to put learners into solitude. Instead, it is supposed to be dialogical: dialogue is integrated in the distance education system, which is premised on two-way communication. For Moore and Kearsley (1996: 201), dialogue is the interplay of words, actions, and ideas and any other interactions between teacher and learner. There was thus no reason for Unisa to be so distant from its learners during this period when my student felt completely isolated. Unfortunately, it had been overtaken by events and my experience clearly demonstrated to me that its traditional approach had become outdated.

The distance education scene in South Africa

What is happening at Unisa

Changing student population. South Africa is experiencing a trend whereby black people now constitute a larger share of the university population than white people. This is in stark contrast with the past when, as a result of apartheid legislation, the majority of black student struggled to get to a university because they were prevented from making it to matric. Those who succeeded were mainly from urban areas. Since the beginning of the 1990s, we have seen an increasing number of university entrants drawn from educationally and socially disadvantaged communities. However, the majority of these students cannot afford full-time studies at residential universities, and this is where we at Unisa are succeeding in attracting these students. Moreover, we are drawing in large numbers of young students, which means that Unisa is no longer attracting only the traditional distance learner.

However, the traditional students (the employed students who are furthering their education) have not stopped enrolling at Unisa. The rapid changes that are taking place within the world of work require a workforce that continuously sharpens its skills and can therefore never stop learning and furthering its knowledge. Hence the report of the National Commission for Higher Education that today we have a learning society and that institutions of higher learning have to make provision for ongoing learning so that learners can be competitive intheir world of work (NCHE 1996). However, these learners cannot leave the workplace in order to pursue their studies, nor could they consider giving up their jobs for this purpose, and distance education is the answer to their quest to learn.

Distance education and ODL defined. Unisa was established in 1873 as the University of the Cape of Good Hope, serving exclusively as an examining body. In 1916 the university relocated from Cape Town to Pretoria, and took a new name – the University of South Africa (or Unisa, as it is generally known). The institution became a federal structure incorporating almost all the university colleges that existed in South Africa at that time, and parented them until they were able to become autonomous. In 1946 Unisa transformed itself into an institution that provided postal tuition to non-residential students.

A distance education institution is one that is dedicated to providing education to those who might otherwise not be able to study at a university. Today, such institutions use a set of multimedia channels to deliver education that is didactically appropriate to their students. Moore (1973: 664) defines distance education as: the family of instructional methods in which the teaching behaviours are executed apart from the learning behaviours, including those that in a contiguous situation would be performed in the learner's presence, so that communication between the teacher and the learner must be facilitated by print, electronic, mechanical or other devices.

Keegan (1986: 49) adds to this, saying that distance education is a form of education characterised by: the quasi-permanent separation of teacher and learner throughout the length of the learning process; this distinguishes it from conventional face-to-face education; the influence of an educational organisation both in the planning and preparation of learning materials and in the provision of student support services; this distinguishes it from private study and teach yourself programmes; the use of technical media, print, audio, video and computer, to unite teacher and learner and carry the content of the course; the provision of two-way communication so that the student may benefit from or even initiate dialogue; this distinguishes it from other uses of technology in education; the quasi-permanent absence of the learning group throughout the length of the learning process so that people are usually taught as individuals and not in groups, with the possibility of occasional meetings for both didactic and socialisation purposes.

Unisa's most recent Tuition Policy document states that distance learning is a form of planned learning which provides learning opportunities aimed at limiting the constraints of time/place/pace. It involves the design and development of learning experiences using various technologies and student-support strategies to effect interaction among teachers and learners. It enables learners to become independent and critical thinkers, and to attain their educational goals (http://www.unisa.ac.za/internal/cs98/pol.html:1).

The role of distance education in South Africa is elucidated by the National Commission of Higher Education (NCHE 1996:118-119) in these words: A key challenge for higher education is to enhance the quality of higher education programmes ... This challenge must be met in the context of greatly increased access to a wide diversity of students at varying entry levels, and within a higher education budget that increases significantly slower than enrolments rise. The Commission believes that distance education and resource-based learning are a fundamental part of meeting this challenge ... A further challenge is to move the higher education system in the direction of becoming an open learning system organised for use by learners at various stages of their lives and careers, a system that promotes lifelong learning, not merely at the margins for small groups of 'mature' students, but in its basic shape and structure.

Distance education evolved from a mode that was known as correspondence education as it started to use a wider and wider array of media. This is captured clearly by Rumble (1991: 7-9), who says: 'Although the term "distance education" is now widely used in preference to "correspondence education", there is no inherent difference in the two methods. "Correspondence education" is the older term, reflecting the origins of distance education as a product of the development of a cheap, reliable postal service and the fact that the early means of communication was by letter. Nowadays correspondence education can be regarded as a particular form of distance education based on print and written assignments and letters, whereas distance education uses a wide range of media'.

Unisa is an open distance learning (ODL) institution. It provides quality open and distance learning opportunities in higher education, conducts research and serves the community through the expertise of its personnel. It enrols learners in a flexible manner without the barriers that a traditional university would put in their way. Having looked at the definitions of distance education, it is appropriate to define open learning in order to get a clearer picture of Unisa and how it functions. The Manpower Services Commission (1984: 7) offers a succinct definition: "Open Learning arrangements enable people to learn at the time, place and pace which satisfy their circumstances and requirements. The emphasis is on opening up opportunities by overcoming barriers that result from geographical isolation, personal or work commitments or conventional course structures which have often prevented people from gaining access to the training they need."

Wedemeyer's definition (1977:2117) of open learning reads: "All open schools have one principle in common: they are to a greater or lesser extent efforts to expand the freedoms of learners. Some are open only in a spatial sense ... while others provide freedoms in more significant dimensions - in admissions, selection of courses, individual adaptation of the curriculum and time, goal selection and evaluation."

Lewis (1988:257) defines open learning as "essentially a means to enable [learners], of whatever age, to take responsibility for their own learning". This is how open learning is described in Unisa's Tuition Policy document: "Open learning promotes open access to courses, flexibility in learning provision, and methods and criteria of assessing learning progress and achievement. Open learning denotes a shift of emphasis from the institutional lecturer or content-centred learning to a learner-centred and outcomes-based approach" (http://www.unisa.ac.za/internal/comserve/cs98/pol.html:1).

This presupposes a learner-centred approach in respect of curriculum development and the learning process itself.

Unisa as a mega-university. Unisa is the largest open and distance learning institution in South Africa and on the African continent. It is also one of the twelve mega-universities in the world, and in fact the mega-universities of the world: The Top Ten, an International Centre for Distance Learning publication, lists the following ten mega-universities as of 1995: Anadolu University, Turkey (AU); Centre National d' Enseignement à Distance, France (CNED); China Central TV and Broadcasting University, China (CCRTVU); Indira Ghandi National Open University, India (IGNOU; Korea National Open University, Korea (KNOU); Open University, United Kingdom (OUUK); Sukhothai Thammathirat Open University, Thailand (STOU; Universidad Nacional de Educacion a Distancia, Spain (UNED; University of South Africa (UNISA); University of Terbuka, Indonesia (UT); Unisa achieves economies of scale in an environment of ever-increasing budgetary constraints on higher education. The funding formula, and the subsidies paid to institutions of higher learning have, at the time of writing, been reduced to 50% of what they should be. ODL institutions such as Unisa are considerably cheaper than residential universities, and have the advantage of reaching multitudes of students. Unisa currently reaches around 134 000 degree students annually and about 50 000 diploma and certificate students.

Study material: Design and delivery. Unisa's success lies in its use of printed materials, consisting primarily of study guides and tutorial letters. Study guides are interactive materials with various activities aimed at keeping students actively involved in the learning process. Self-assessment exercises, for example, assist learners to practise what they have learnt in each unit or section of the guide, while additional reading lists complement the material, which addresses students in a direct, reader-friendly manner, and a range of activities provoke students to think critically about what they are learning and to apply concepts and principles to practical situations. Tutorial letters set out various assignments that students should complete. There are also a number of optional assignments aimed at giving learners a broader base of understanding of the course. They may choose whether or not to write these, although obviously writing them is to their own advantage. In addition to printed materials, we also use recorded audio programmes. Among these are audiocassettes, videos and CD ROMs. We also use radio, tele- and video conferencing, but we have not as yet experimented with television as a medium for delivery. We do, however, provide face-to-face support in the form of group discussion lectures and tutorials presented at various provincial and other centres throughout South Africa.

ODL institutions require a support system infrastructure that must operate smoothly if these institutions are to succeed. Unisa is no exception, and its infrastructure includes the following departments or sections: Call Centre; Examination Administration; Finance; Department of Student Administration; Postgraduate Student Affairs; Graduation Ceremonies; Bureau of Student Counselling and Career Development; Student Financial Aid Bureau; Assignments (the section that handles the administration of assignments, which includes implementing a policy of receipt and return of assignments to students in a workable timeframe); Despatch (which distributes materials); Computer Services; Library Services; Telecommunication Services; Corporate Communication and Marketing; Editorial; Bureau of Management Information; Bureau of Learning Development; Safety Services; and Student Support. *Unisa saw it fit to start a Department of Student Support in the mid 1990s, and I* would like, at this point, to explain what I mean by student support. There is no doubt that as an ODL institution we had to take the question of student support seriously if we wanted to be able to face the future with certainty.

To my mind, student support covers a wide range of support that the university renders to students, such as the provision of accessible study material, recorded audio materials such as audio and video, cassettes, tutorial letters, telephone discussions with lecturers and tutors and tutorials.

Accessible study material is also a means of providing support, which requires us as lecturers to move away from the kind of study material that students struggle to read and understand. Our materials need to be student-friendly. We need to make clear to learners, from the very beginning, what they need to know or what they should be able to do once they have completed their course of study. We need to give the learners a chance to see how well they are mastering the objectives of each unit or chapter by providing them with exercises that they can do after each unit or chapter. We need to provide them with support mechanisms such as a glossary that explains difficult concepts, and our style of writing should be consistently dialogical in order to stimulate students' interest in the material.

According to Moore (1973: 664-665), a student support system may be defined as "a programme within the dominant institution aiming towards bridging the distance between teaching and learning whereby the distance learner can control the pace at which he[she] receives information and at which he[she] must make his[her] response through face-to-face dialogical intervention.

Rowntree (1990) perceives distance learners as students who will not be in regular contact with the teachers responsible for course design, and with little or no face-to-face contact even with other learners. On the other hand, he points out that distance learners may include students who use the facilities of the institution sponsoring the course and who learn through self-instruction in a situation where they are able to meet one another, a tutor, and perhaps a more experienced colleague who can support their studies although he or she is not the actual course designer.

Moore's definition of student support corresponds with the approach adopted by Unisa when it decided to establish a network of learning centres from 1995 onwards, where tutors were hired to render subject-related and study skills support to students. Our understanding was that this would go a long way towards addressing the needs of our students but that it would also assist in improving the level of communication between lecturers and students. We were also following other ODL institutions that had demonstrated the value of limited face-to-face contact with students. Having co-operated very closely with the South African

Unisa took over DUSSPRO (Distance University Support Programme) from SACHED (the Council for Higher Education) in 1994. DUSSPRO was rendered in Pretoria and Johannesburg and this set the stage for the tutorial programme that Unisa has pursued since then. These programmes were also simultaneously extended to Cape Town, Durban and Pietersburg, where Unisa has regional offices. (These offices have since been renamed, respectively, the Western Cape, KwaZulu-Natal and Polokwane Provincial Offices of Unisa.) Since 1995 Unisa has committed itself to offering student support in terms of tutorials, counselling and administrative services (including library services) to reinforce the study package.

Tutorials. A number of tutors were brought on board to serve as facilitators of independent learning by students. They do not replace the study material but rather assist students to understand and relate to their materials. They provide explanations where required and diagnose problems students may be experiencing in grasping the material. Finally, they help students address such problems so that students can comprehend their work and ultimately pass their examinations at the end of each semester or year.

For the first time, therefore, Unisa started seeing tutors as an integral part of the university and as taking the distance out of its ODL endeavours in order to bring students and Unisa itself closer together.

In order to facilitate the effectiveness and efficiency of the tutorial programme, we decided to appoint tutor representatives or co-ordinators to represent the different faculties so that a relationship could be built between academic departments and tutors. Besides offering tutorials themselves, tutors are expected to oversee the tutorial support in terms of both content and process, and are also lecturers in their own departments.

Counselling. Student counsellors are required to guide and assist the students with study skills as well as to give them career guidance. Unisa has gone beyond counselling services provided by professionals only, the Bureau for Student Counselling and Career Development (BSCCD) having started a programme of assistance through peer helpers – a group of students who are specially trained to provide assistance to other students. The programme was developed for students who are nervous about sharing their problems with student counsellors and prefer to discuss them with the peer helpers, who are their contemporaries.

Administrative services. Unisa has extended library services to the regions by linking them up with the main library at the campus in Pretoria. An Assignments Section is equipped with facilities for receiving students' assignments. Students are being organised into local SRCs that will feed into the national SRC in Pretoria. The university has also started to formalise structures for financial assistance through bursaries and loans to students.

Learning centres. Learning centres have been established at the regional campuses and a number of other venues. These provide adequate study areas, seminar rooms (where tutorials and group discussion lectures take place); discussion rooms for students, offices for staff and local SRC, a post box for assignments, a recreation hall, micro computer facilities, as already mentioned, library services (the young students we are attracting need access to the library on a full-time basis), conference telephone, video and television facilities, and small cafeterias serving light refreshments.

Current successes at Unisa

Continental collaboration and networking. Unisa is particularly successful in its training of chartered accountants. In testimony of our expertise and capacity in training chartered accountants, the African Universities Association selected Unisa's Department of Applied Accountancy 2001 to assist universities in southern Africa in establishing departments to train chartered accountants. Currently, Unisa trains all the chartered accountants in Zimbabwe. We also have a collaboration arrangement with the Kenya College of Accountancy, which assists our students with tutorials in Kenya.

There are also numerous collaborative initiatives championed by our Department of Health Studies (previously known as Advanced Nursing Sciences) which have resulted in the postgraduate training of health professionals in southern, eastern and western Africa.

Our successes in Zimbabwe and Namibia are marked by graduation ceremonies that are held in these two countries every year, and we held our first graduation ceremony in Mauritius in 2002.

A co-operative agreement signed with Angola's University of Agostinho Neto allows for extensive collaboration between all departments of the two universities. Another agreement has been concluded with the Nigerian company, Management Education and Training, to make tutorial and administrative support available to existing and prospective Unisa students in West Africa. We also have collaborative arrangements with the Mascareignes Academy of Art, Law, Economics and Management and DCDM of Mauritius, who assist our learners with tutorials in Mauritius. We are currently exploring opportunities for collaborating with a number of public institutions in Mauritius to extend even further support to our students there.

Awards. Professional Management Review (PMR), which conducts research through personnel agencies and human resource executives (representing South African employers) across South Africa, has consistently placed Unisa among the top three universities in terms of academic excellence. Unisa's School of Business Leadership, which holds 30% of South Africa's MBL/MBA market, received the PMR Golden Arrow Award as the best business school offering these programmes on a part-time basis via ODL in 2001. In the same year, in the category for the best-rated degrees and degree courses offered at universities, the Faculty of Humanities and Social Sciences (then still known as the Faculty of Arts) received the following PMR awards: Golden Arrow for BA (General and Humanities) in Historical Studies/History; Silver Arrow for BA (General and Humanities) in Governance and Political Science; Silver Arrow for BA (Humanities) in Industrial, Organisational and Labour Studies.

The Faculty of Economic and Management Sciences received three Golden Arrow Awards: Golden Arrow (overall) for Distance Learning (Human Resources and Finance); Golden Arrow (specialised) for Distance Learning - Human Resources and Finance; Golden Arrow for Business School (offering MBL via distance learning).

Accreditation by the Distance Education and Training Council. Finally, Unisa was been accredited by the Accrediting Commission of the Distance Education and Training Council (DETC) of the United States. This means it has passed the stringent DETC tests on account of its quality multimedia instructional materials, tutorial support networks and highly qualified staff. The DETC's accreditation attests to the quality of our products, our processes, our delivery systems and our general organisational philosophy (these are the four aspects of quality referred to by Normann in his 1984 work on quality in educational institutions). Our accreditation gives us the right to use the DETC seal on all our learning materials, and gives us continued access to quality assurance and peer review, which will guarantee the maintenance of our high standards. Our accreditation is valid for five years, from 2002 to 2006.

Challenges

As a distance education provider, Unisa has faced three broad challenges in the past eight years or so. These challenges were the learning curve; innovation and refinement; and delivery.

Curriculum development. I do not plan to delve into these challenges, but I do want to identify questions that are critical in curriculum development. These are:

(1) What kind of curriculum can prepare students for participation in a global economy, while not losing sight of the specifics of the South African economy?

(2) To what extent should the curriculum accommodate previously marginalised knowledge, particularly indigenous knowledge, as opposed to knowledge that is characterised as global?

(3) How should the curriculum deal with traditional disciplines, interdisciplinarity, multidisciplinarity and transdisciplinarity?

(4) Unisa has committed itself to lifelong learning, as required by the new world economy. This means we need to know what comprises a lifelong learning curriculum.

(5) What forms of knowledge and skills do employers value and are we ready, as universities, to comply with those requirements?

(6) What kind of South Africans (who will not necessarily be excluded from global citizenship) do we intend developing and is the curriculum flexible enough to accommodate that?

(7) Are we ready for public accountability as universities and how does this correspond with our autonomy and the academic freedom of intellectuals?

(8) Are we ready to deal with the possible new demands and expectations of Unisa in the future?

Information and communication technology. With innovation and refinement, as well as with delivery, we have accepted the reality of a globalising world and have taken information and communications technology (ICT) seriously. We have already begun a project known by the acronym VMA (the Virtual Multimedia Academy) project. This is a UNESCO sponsored joint venture with Universidade de Eduardo Mondlane (UEM) of Mozambique and Sudan University of Science and Technology (SUST). At Unisa we have set up our own team of people who are to be involved in the project. The team includes three members from the ICT Directorate, three members from the Faculty of Humanities and Social Sciences' Art History department (these members are multimedia specialists), three members who are isiZulu, tshiVenda and isiXhosa language specialists, and an administrator from the ICT Directorate. In addition to this team, our Unit for Video, Sound and Photography has recorded the voice-overs and provided the digital sound clips. The three institutions involved in the VMA project have decided to use the learning materials of an existing print-based Unisa course - a first level Art History module – as the basis for the multimedia enhanced learning material.

The outcome of the VMA Project is to create contextualised multimedia versions of the Art and Technology (Study Unit 4) and Media and Advertising (Study Unit 3) components of a first level Art History module offered by Unisa. Contextualisation will be in terms of the language and culture of the three countries of the participating institutions. The plan is to present the content in English, Arabic, Portuguese and one South African indigenous language. It is also envisaged that the product will function in a web-browser, but will be produced on a CD-ROM.

Another of Unisa's dreams springs from a government initiative to build multipurpose community centres (MPCCs) in various disadvantaged communities in order to connect every South African to the Internet. We have decided to collaborate with government in this initiative so that our students will, in the near future, enjoy all the benefits of the Internet and its related services.

We have already made great strides in the area of ICT. Our Department of Computer Services has, for example, already completed a number of major projects in the following areas: *Networks.* All the buildings on Unisa's main campus have now been re-cabled with high speed networks to give all staff an access speed to workstations of 100MB per second; *Internet access.* We have doubled the bandwidth of our Internet access; *PC support.* We have done remote deployment of software as well as antivirus software; *Storage area network.* We have installed a huge storage area of approximately 1.2 terabytes to assist staff with storing their academic and research data; *Students-On-Line (SOL)*. SOL communication has taken off in the past three years and its value is apparent in the significant increase in the number of students who use this communication tool each year.

Last word

We anticipate that in the years to come in South Africa, the majority of Unisa's students will come already equipped with intense media experience acquired in their homes and from recreational activities. These students will obviously learn more readily in the technologically rich environment that Unisa is preparing for them today.

References

Http://www.unisa.ac.za/internal/cs 98/hd.html

International Centre for Distance Learning. 1995. *The mega-universities of the world: the top ten*. Milton Keynes: Open University

Keegan, D. 1986. *The foundations of distance education*. Beckenham: Croom Helm.

Lewis, R. 1988. The open school? In *Open learning in transition: an agenda for action,* edited by Paine, N. Cambridge: National Extension College.

Manpower Services Commission. 1984. A New Training Initiative.

Moore, MG & Kearsley, G. 1996. *Distance education: a systems view*. Belmont: Wadsworth Publishing.

Moore, M. 1973. Towards a theory of independent learning and teaching. *Journal of Higher Education* 44:661-679.

NCHE 1996. National Comission on Higher Education (South Africa). A framework for transformation: Deport. Pretoria: NCHE.

Rowntree, D. 1990. *Teaching Through Self-Instruction: How to Develop Open Learning Materials*. London: Kogan Page.

Rumble 1991. 'Open Learning,' 'Distance Learning,' and the misuse of language, in Course 2 – *The Development of distance education: A Reader.* Cambridge: University of London and International Extension College.

Wedemeyer, CA. 1977. Independent study. In *The international encyclopaedia of higher education*, edited by AS Knowles, Boston: CINED.

20

Monitoring for quality in a mass literacy programme

Elijah Sekgobela

The mass literacy program referred to here is the South African National Literacy Initiative (SANLI), a literacy initiative of the national Department of Education (DoE) in South Africa. The literacy initiative was conceived as a campaign the aim of which is to reduce the rate of illiteracy in the country, or, in the words of the Minister of Education, to 'break the back of illiteracy amongst adults and youth in five years'. It is estimated that over four million adults are currently functionally illiterate in South Africa. These adults are the target of the SANLI campaign.

The Adult Basic Education and Training (ABET) Institute at the University of South Africa (Unisa) has joined with the DoE to put into operation the South African National Literacy Initiative. Through the deployment of its ex-students, who have completed either the one-year certificate or the three-year diploma course in ABET offered by the Institute, the latter has enabled the DoE to take the delivery of SANLI to scale, as is shown later in this paper. In addition, the countrywide network of tutors that the ABET Institute has established for its formal courses has provided the basis for a monitoring system for the execution of SANLI.

The fact that SANLI is a non-formal programme and that it aims at mass delivery does not mean that the approach is so permissive that educational quality is compromised. It is therefore fully recognised that the learning process needs to be structured in such a way that it is purposeful and the learners are active participants in their own learning. Hence the ABET Institute's decision to enlist its cadre of trained adult educators as volunteer educators and its tutor network for the monitoring role, focusing specifically on issues of quality in the delivery of the SANLI programme.

The discussion that follows starts with a statement of the purposes of the monitoring role. This is followed by a description of the organisation of the monitoring role, the key areas in the monitoring process and the monitoring instrument.

Purpose

Three key reasons were identified for the monitoring role. These were to (1) ensure that the outcomes of the literacy campaign were attained; (2) ensure coherence in the rollout and operation of the literacy programme; and (3) gather information from the literacy units and feed this information back to the units with a view to improving operations on the ground.

Organisation of the monitoring role

This section describes the monitoring structure and indicates the scale of the monitoring enterprise over the two-year period that the ABET Institute has been involved with the SANLI campaign.

The monitoring structure

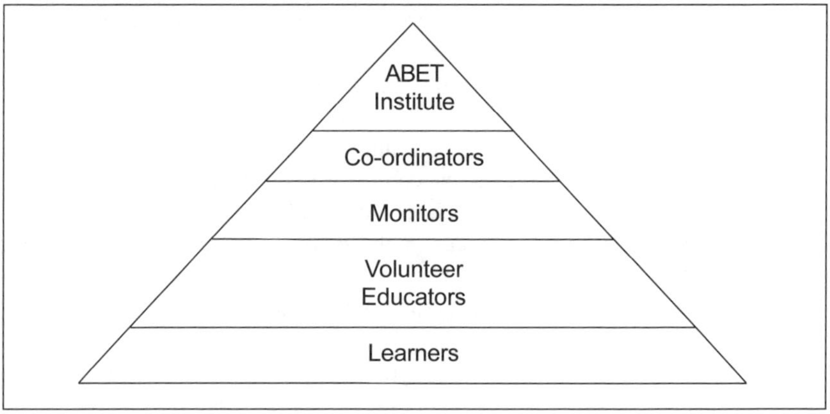

Figure 1 SANLI monitoring structure

As shown in the figure above, the monitoring structure involves learners, volunteer educators, monitors, co-ordinators and the ABET Institute staff.

Since the literacy campaign targets adult learners, the monitoring system is geared towards meeting their learning needs. Although the structure above gives the impression of a top-down system, in fact the functioning of the monitoring system is bottom-up. Through the different levels of the monitoring structure, information about operations on the ground is gathered with a view to solving problems or facilitating operations. The information is collected using the following mechanisms: (1) queries conveyed to the ABET Institute by all the levels of the monitoring structure, including outsiders who take interest in the literacy classes; (2) class attendance registers; (3) monthly reports submitted by monitors and co-ordinators;

(4) field visits to the learning sites by the ABET Institute staff in order to gain first-hand knowledge of the situation on the ground; (5) review and evaluation studies commissioned from time to time which enable the learners (in particular) to voice their experiences and feelings about the state of the literacy classes; (6) monthly meetings amongst co-ordinators, monitors and volunteer educators at the different learning sites; (7) national co-ordinator meetings which take place at the ABET Institute's offices in Pretoria; (8) biannual national tutor/co-ordinator workshops.

Scale of the monitoring function

Table 1 Scale of operations

Participants	Year	
	2002	2003
Co-ordinators	35	54
Monitors	765	1072
Volunteer Educators	4820	7673
Adult Learners	91987	192375

The figures provided in Table 1 give an indication the scale of operations of the SANLI programme for the years 2002 and 2003.

The volunteer educator/learner ratio is set at 1:15. Volunteer educators may give a maximum of five classes in a month. The monitor/volunteer educator ratio is 1:8, with monitors visiting each class at least once a month. Co-ordinators are in charge of geographical regions and act as the field managers responsible for the entire operation in the regions allocated to them.

Key areas in the monitoring process

The three reasons cited under the section headed 'Purpose' also point to the key areas in the monitoring process. The outcomes of the literacy campaign are the ultimate 'products' that the campaign seeks to realise. The other two, viz. ensuring coherence in the operations of the campaign and information gathering, describe the 'process' issues in the field.

Products

The outcomes of the campaign may be classified in three categories, namely quantitative, qualitative and developmental benefits, as listed in Table 2.

Table 2 Campaign outcomes

Quantitative Outcomes	Qualitative Outcomes
To ensure that: • two million adult learners complete the SANLI programme by 2004 • 166 668 volunteer educators are trained to deliver literacy programmes to the above-mentioned learners • national awareness is increased, and that there is participation in and contribution to SANLI=s literacy campaign by a broad section of society • there is clarity about functions and that effective institutional arrangements are in place to drive this campaign	To help people develop: • the capacity to cope in a literate world • the ability to express their thoughts more effectively • the ability to understand, without assistance, information in simple print and in the language of the local economy • an understanding of different perspectives and approaches to the same situation (critical thinking and problem-solving skills)
Developmental benefits	
• improved community participation in the education of children • improved enrolment, retention and performance at primary and secondary school levels, due to parents = increased commitment to education • improved success rates on campaigns on issues such as sanitation, environmental awareness, family planning, HIV/AIDS and tourism generation • increased participation by communities in government community development initiatives • increased social and economic interaction leading to a mushrooming of local co-operatives • empowerment of the dispossessed • reduction in infant mortality rates • creation of an enabling environment for entrepreneurial initiatives • increased workforce productivity	

Source: Extracted from SANLI documents.

Like other mass literacy campaigns in other parts of the world, the outcomes that are set for the SANLI campaign are not confined to reading, writing and counting. They extend to other fields pertaining to issues such as health, income generation and civic education.

The outcomes of the SANLI campaign are essential to the monitoring task because they help to focus and give meaning to the monitoring activities.

Process

Process is concerned with the actual activities that take place on the ground. Based on the experiences gathered in the pilot phase of the SANLI programme, process has manifested itself in terms of three phases which are outlined below.

First phase – setting up the literacy units: This phase is concerned with logistical aspects that pertain to setting up the literacy classes. It focuses on recruiting co-ordinators and monitors; recruiting the volunteer educators (the cadre of students who have completed the Unisa ABET programmes, targeting specifically the unemployed); training and orientating the volunteer educators; recruitment and registration of learners; placement of learners; and supply of learner and educator packages.

Second phase – teaching-learning: The first phase lays the foundation for the second one, which is the teaching and learning phase. This deals with aspects such as classroom management (of course, where the educator has access to such facilities); compiling lesson plans; facilitation inside the classroom; and assessment of learners.

***Third phase – momentum building and maintenance*:** The third phase is not a stand-alone phase. It has been isolated from the other two simply to emphasise its importance in the literacy campaign. The main emphasis in this phase is to build up momentum in the campaign as a whole, that is to create momentum in the classroom in order to improve attendance and raise awareness of the literacy campaign.

The three phases discussed above are crucial in the monitoring process for a number of reasons. These assist monitors to identify the areas in which the volunteer educators and the adult learners need to be supported. Indeed, this is the key function of monitoring, namely that monitors deal with the barriers to learning that may occur, which may also obstruct the attainment of the outcomes of the campaign as a whole. Another reason is that, during these phases, the items that can be included in the monitoring instrument or questionnaire are identified. Different weights are given to items included in the monitoring instrument at any particular point in time. In the first phase logistical matters carry more weight. Once the literacy units are established and running, the teaching-learning aspects need more attention. When classes are running smoothly, momentum building becomes more essential, bearing in mind the challenge of maintaining high attendance in the literacy classes.

Conclusion

The monitoring function described above is not regarded as an add-on function, but as an integral part of the whole programme. It is a support function which is intended to assist in the attainment of the outcomes of the literacy programme by improving the operations on the ground and empowering the volunteer educators.

By engaging learners through interviews and group discussions, it endeavours to give them a voice and a sense of belonging in the literacy campaign.

Index

Subject index

Adult Basic Education (ABE),
case studies, 11-18, 21-22, 31, 51-59, 67, 73, 81-84, 86-96, 115-119, 125-126, 152-158, 170, 174, 179-180, 204-206, 236-238, 282-291, 357-359
definitions, 3, 107-108, 117-118
funding and resources, 13, 24-25, 37, 67-68, 76-77, 94, 101, 113, 115, 141, 147, 151, 158, 173, 187, 190-191, 199, 219, 228, 232, 239, 240-241, 247, 266, 273, 282, 292, 294, 296-297, 300-302, 304, 306-309, 315, 318, 326, 329, 333, 341, 358-359, 363
see also Donor organizations
policy and planning, 3, 5-9, 11, 25, 29, 60, 76, 101, 103, 109-113, 139, 143-144, 155, 169-170, 198-199, 219, 221, 225-232, 288, 326, 353, 361
quality assurance and measures, 24-25, 187-188, 190-196, 201, 209, 212, 341-342, 371-375
research, reports and surveys, 3-4, 25, 29, 46, 67-68, 70-71, 101, 137-143, 162, 164, 188, 194-196, 199, 201, 207, 221, 257, 263, 266, 326
Adult education programmes
see Programmes and projects
Adult educators, 1, 4-6, 8-12, 14-26, 29-31, 34, 36, 38-41, 50-55, 58, 61, 67-72, 74, 78-81, 86, 91-92, 95, 101, 103, 106, 112, 114-119, 122, 125-127, 129-133, 137-146, 148-152, 155-159, 161, 165-183, 193, 205-206, 222, 225-226, 231-232, 236, 238, 244-247, 252, 258, 260-264, 269-274, 278-281, 294, 296-297, 299, 301-302, 305, 309, 311-312, 315, 326, 345, 347, 372-375
competencies, 14-16, 19-20, 44, 101, 115, 122, 131-132, 140, 167, 181, 243-245, 278, 280-283, 288, 303, 307-308, 310, 318
professional status, 226
remuneration, 130-131, 169, 208, 238, 276, 305
responsibilities, 138, 140, 144, 168, 175, 178-179, 222, 270-273, 279, 303, 306
selection, 3, 237, 243-244, 246, 252, 278-279, 281, 302,305
see also Skills development, Training of adult educators
African Institute for Economic and Social Development, 192
Agricultural extension
see Skills development
Asia Pacific Programme of Education for All (APPEAL), 175
Asian South Pacific Bureau of Adult Education, 32
Bridges to the Future (BFI), 189-190, 322
Broadcasting
see radio and television under Media by type
BUNYAD, 196
Collaboration
see Partnerships
Commonwealth Local Government Forum (CLGF), 282
Commonwealth of Learning (Canada), 318, 348
Community Based Organizations (CBOs), 196
Community Centres
see Learners and learning
Computers
see Media by type
Conferences and forums,
5th International Conference on Adult Education (CONFINTEA V), 5-7, 220, 228-229

International Conference on Adult Basic and Literacy Education in the Southern African Development Community (Pietermaritzburg, South Africa, 2002), 299, 315
Mid-Decade Review (Amman, 1995), 228
Pan-Commonwealth Forum on Open and Distance Learning (Durban, South Africa, 2002), 256, 266-267
World Conference on Education for All (Jomtien, Thailand, 1990), 8, 137, 164, 199, 227-229, 242-243
World Education Forum (Dakar, Senegal, 2000), 1, 6, 8, 202, 220, 229, 242, 299
Continuing education, 12, 22, 31, 34, 38-40, 60, 144, 165, 242, 246, 256, 260, 345-346
Continuing Education: Libraries and the Internet (CELI), 350, 352
see also Libraries, Lifelong learning, Media by type
Correspondence education
see Distance Education (DE)
Declarations, goals and slogans
Agenda for the future, 5, 228-229
Convention of the rights of the child, 221, 229
Each one teach one, 162
Hamburg declaration, 5, 7, 219, 222, 225, 229, 299
Jomtien declaration, 228
Let's teach ourselves, 179-180, 182
Millenium development goals, 202, 229
Pietermaritzburg declaration, 299
Teaching with computers, not about computers, 335
Universal declaration of human rights, 220
World Declaration on Education for All (EFA), 6, 8, 68, 137-139, 164, 197-199, 201, 221, 227-230, 232, 308, 315-316
Distance Education (DE), 7-10, 12, 16-17, 23-25, 50-51, 54, 67-69, 72, 7477, 79, 107, 115-116, 134, 138, 141-143, 152, 161, 173, 180, 187-190, 192-194, 205, 215, 222-224, 231-232, 247, 256-259, 261, 264, 268, 274, 278-279, 281, 283, 285, 288, 291, 293-297, 316, 318, 332-333, 346, 350-351, 357-376
Accrediting Commission of the Distance Education and Training Council (DETC), 367-368
definitions, 259, 361-363
methodology, 68, 69, 73, 75-76, 81, 123-124, 151, 187-188, 190-191, 278
see also Learners and learning centres, Open and Distance Learning (ODL)
Donor organizations
Anglo American Corporation, 359
Carnegie Fund, 282
Department of International Development (DFID), 13, 133, 318, 348
European Union (EU), 282, 290, 315, 332
German Technical Corporation (GTZ), 13, 332, 336, 340
Global Fund, 315
International Monetary Fund (IMF), 332
SIDA, 350
USAID, 334
World Bank, 195, 197-199, 228, 330-331, 334
see also funding and resources, under Adult Basic Education (ABE)
Educational technology
see Media in education
Field workers
see Adult educators
Formal education, 6, 8, 10-11, 46, 77, 142-143, 152, 195, 221, 225-226, 228-230, 256, 263-264, 345
see also Non-formal education, Tertiary Education

Gandhi Foundation, 163
Gender
see Women and gender
German Adult Education Association (DVV/IIZ), 13, 21, 116, 293-296, 299-301, 305-308, 310-312, 315
Globalization and effects, 19, 195, 197-198, 200-201, 221
Grassroots facilitators/ functionaries
see Adult educators
Health and HIV/ Aids
see under Skills development
Illiteracy/ illiterates
see Literacy
INADES-formation (IF), 192-194, 212
Informal education
see Non-formal education
Institute for International Cooperation (IIZ), 293, 310
International Extension College (IEC), 93, 204-205
Language and languages, 199-201, 204, 214, 224, 242-246, 252, 285, 334-335, 253
indigenous/ local languages, 19, 48, 112, 191, 194, 201, 253, 285, 334
language death/ decline, 199-201
national/ official languages, 2, 102, 111-112, 131, 252-253, 285-286, 293
Arabic, 200, 206
English, 19, 39, 112, 121, 131, 194, 200, 270, 275, 302, 333, 353
French, 200
IsiXhosa, 302, 369
IsiZulu, 369
Kiswahili, 285-286
Mayan languages, 334
Portuguese, 242, 252-253, 255
Spanish, 200, 293, 334, 339
Translation, 19, 39, 58, 339
see also **Country index**
Learners and learning centres,
community learning/ literacy centres, 13, 20, 70, 129, 165, 167-168, 170, 173-174, 181-182, 220, 295, 320, 325-327, 334, 348, 366, 369
community learning and technology centres (CLTCs), 190
distance learning centers (DLCs), 334
learning societies, 5, 200, 219-221, 230, 312-314
self-study/ self-help groups (SHG), 55, 179, 195, 205, 261-263, 278, 290, 320, 324
technology/ telecentres, 334-335
see also Media in education
Libraries and library services, 347, 350-352, 364, 366
Life skills
see Skills development
Lifelong learning, 1, 5-7, 23-24, 29, 38, 51, 73, 134, 138, 141, 219-222, 225, 227, 229-230, 232, 293, 309, 312-314, 316, 321, 329-330
definitions, 225, 313
see also Continuing education
Life-wide learning, 7
Literacy, 1, 6, 8, 11, 13, 20, 23, 29-30, 46-49, 68-69, 71-72, 103, 108, 116-118, 131, 138, 144-145, 149, 156, 161, 163-164, 167, 173, 176, 180, 183, 187, 190-191, 195, 197-202, 204-205, 224, 236, 238, 241, 245-246, 251, 253, 259-260, 270, 293-294, 299-300, 315-316, 318-321, 324-325, 327, 345, 348, 371-376
definitions, 2, 17-18, 199-201, 241
International Literacy Day, 313
International Literacy Institute, 322
'literacy second' or REFLECT approach, 299-301
Literacy by type,
computer, 20, 318, 323-325
digital, 10, 248
functional, 85
information, 190, 325

mathematical / numeracy, 30, 116-117, 131, 201, 242-243, 300, 325
multiple literacies, 7, 24, 199, 213
post-literacy, 85, 205-206, 258-260
reading and writing, 200, 325
social, 199-200
technological, 190, 325
three 'R's', 71, 241
see also Skills development
Literacy levels by continent/ region
Africa, 1-2, 203-204
Arab, 2, 203
Asia, 1, 203
Caribbean, 2
China, 202
Global, 1-2, 6, 202-203
Lao, 201
Latin America, 2
see also **Country index**
Literacy workers
see Adult educators
Media in education, 1, 11, 46, 52, 59-60, 68, 76, 102, 123-124, 134, 148, 184, 188-189, 229, 258-265, 281, 290, 313, 329, 331, 345-354, 361-362
digital divide, 326
Media by type,
audio-cassette, 9, 47, 51, 54, 67-68, 75, 81, 94, 148, 191, 207-208, 214, 261-265, 319, 322, 324, 361
audio-visual, 350
computers, 20, 68, 148, 190, 214, 319, 322, 325, 333-334, 349, 361
CD-ROM, 323, 338-339, 342, 349, 352, 364, 369
electronic, 259, 261
email, 347, 349
film, 50
information and communication technology (ICT), 1, 7, 10-12, 19, 21-22, 25, 30, 123, 142, 184, 188-190, 220, 222-223, 225-229, 231, 261, 265, 313, 318-327, 329-330, 332-335, 346-350, 352-353, 369
internet, 142, 324-326, 330-339, 347-350, 352-353, 369
adult learning listserve (APAL), 311
subject gateways, 349-350
websites, 325, 335-338, 340, 342-343, 346-350, 353, 361, 370
mass media, 10, 191-192, 214, 259
multi-media, 68, 142, 214, 322-323, 334, 346, 354, 369
print, 10, 22, 54-55, 58, 67, 76, 94, 123, 188, 214, 259, 261-262, 265, 321, 323, 349, 351, 354, 361-363
radio, 9-10, 14, 18, 22, 46-48, 55, 59, 67-68, 73-77, 81, 94, 96, 102, 124, 148, 152-157, 187-195, 206-208, 213-214, 247, 256, 258, 261-262, 265, 290, 324, 350351, 364
instructional radio, 224
interactive radio instruction (IRI), 223-224
radio farm/ rural forum movement, 262
television, 48-50, 55-59, 96, 124, 148, 189, 214, 323-324, 332, 350, 364, 366
video and video conferencing, 25, 49, 53, 55, 59-60, 68, 123, 194, 261, 261, 264-265, 319, 322, 334, 348, 352, 361, 364, 366
Networks and networking, 21-22, 25, 257, 265-266, 296, 299-301, 311-312, 315-3-6, 318, 330, 335-343, 345-346, 349, 352, 366
Adult Learning Network (ALN), 311-312
definitions, 346-347
Global Development Learning Network (GDLN), 334
networking technology, 22, 324, 330, 335-343, 345-347, 369
see also Media by type
Non-formal education, 6, 8-9, 11, 22, 24-25, 46, 73, 77, 142-143, 165, 227-228, 256-264, 266, 294, 318, 324, 326, 330
see also Formal education
Non-governmental organizations (NGOs), 8, 12-13, 16-17, 24, 30-31, 34,

44, 51, 53-55, 59, 67, 70, 74-79, 83-86, 103, 138-139, 143-144, 147-148, 158, 163-166, 169-171, 175-176, 180-181, 183-184, 196-198, 204-205, 232, 236, 269-274, 278-281, 294-295, 299, 304, 308-314, 319, 322
Action Aid, 32, 196-197, 300
OXFAM, 163, 197, 273
see also Partnerships, Programmes and projects, and **Country index**
OECD, 190
Open and Distance Learning (ODL), 1, 8-12, 16-17, 22-24, 29-32, 46-50, 51-54, 57-61, 67-70, 73-81, 84, 86, 96-97, 102-103, 137, 139, 141-143, 148, 152, 155-159, 161, 167, 176-177, 180-184, 187, 189, 204, 209, 215, 219, 222-232, 236, 256-266, 268-269, 281, 291, 329-330, 332, 357, 362-365
definition, 8, 222, 259, 361-363
dis/advantages, 141, 224, 263-264
methodologies, 7-9, 34, 46, 57, 262-264
see also Distance Education (DE)
Partnerships, 12-13, 15, 24, 49, 75, 86, 93, 127, 127-129, 133-134, 176, 189-190, 198, 205, 219, 231-232, 236-245, 247-254, 257, 266, 268, 270, 277, 293-297, 299, 305-306, 312-314, 318-321, 330, 366
see also Donor organizations
Pearson Education, 310
Policies
see policy and planning under Adult Basic Education (ABE)
Popular education
see Adult Basic Education (ABE)
Poverty and poverty reduction, 3, 7, 14, 18, 47, 106-107, 164, 167, 221, 228, 294, 300, 315, 329-332
poverty reduction strategy plans (PRSPs), 197
Preraks
see Adult educators,
Primary education, 6, 8, 71, 106, 152, 198-199, 220-230, 285, 293-294
universal primary education, 71, 74, 143
see also Tertiary education, Youth education
Programmes and projects, 6, 9, 12-14, 16-18, 21, 29-32, 46-48, 101-102, 126, 145-158, 162-173, 175, 181-183, 187-189, 192-194, 204, 219, 223-236, 256-260, 262-265, 268-279, 286, 296, 301-305, 333-334
accreditation/ certification, 22-23, 50, 54-55, 74, 93, 126, 142, 146, 152-153, 163, 184, 257-259, 265-266, 268-269, 272, 274, 276-279, 293-296, 301-308, 315, 367-369, 371
approaches/ models, 18, 24, 29, 31, 46-47, 83, 129, 131-132, 147, 153, 162, 189, 194, 196-197, 205-207, 212-213, 236-238, 241-247, 249, 259, 265, 275, 279, 283-288, 295-297, 300-304, 308, 313-315, 318, 320-321, 327, 362-263, 372, 374-375
curriculum design and content, 15, 19-25, 31, 34-36, 39, 44-45, 51, 53-58, 61-62, 73-74, 91-92, 94, 97-102, 119-122, 131, 166, 169-173, 176-177, 180-181, 184, 193-196, 200, 211-214, 242-245, 258-259, 265-266, 270-271, 275-279, 285-286, 294-295, 301-303, 322, 363-369
delivery/ implementation, 46-49, 51-53, 74-77, 91-96, 113, 130, 161-163, 167, 171, 183, 190, 194-195, 236, 238-239, 250, 252-254, 280-281, 289-290, 320, 322, 325, 363, 374
enrolment, 74, 76, 143, 149, 159, 173, 236, 239, 249, 269-270, 275, 289, 297, 301-304, 363, 374
evaluation/ assessment, 29, 36-37, 47-49, 52, 58, 74, 77, 92-93, 95-96, 127, 130, 132-133, 140, 150-151, 156-157, 167, 173, 188, 195, 198, 206-210, 237-239, 244, 262, 270-272, 280-283, 289-291, 300, 305,

309-310, 315, 318, 320-323, 327, 342, 273
kits/ manuals, 31, 34, 36-37, 51-52, 54, 58, 75, 95, 155-156, 163-164, 172, 174-175, 180-183, 188, 240, 260-261, 265, 278, 294-295, 310-311, 315-316, 321, 323, 363-364
mass delivery campaigns, 20, 23-24, 46-48, 51, 58, 124, 145, 159, 161, 187-189, 191-192, 196, 215, 224, 256, 262-263, 352, 363, 371-376
see also **Country index**
Quality assurance
see quality assurance and measures under Adult Basic Education (ABE)
Radio
see Media by type
Research
see research, reports and surveys under Adult Basic Education (ABE)
Self-help/ self-study
see under Learners and learning
Skills development, 2-3, 7-8, 11, 14-15, 21, 26, 30, 32, 44, 46, 49, 53-54, 69, 85, 95-96, 108, 110, 114-119, 131-132, 134, 138, 144, 152, 154, 180-182, 190, 196, 201, 205-206, 220, 230, 242-246, 260, 264, 271-274, 280, 282-284, 293, 321-322, 349
agricultural extension/ environmental/ rural development, 3, 8, 11, 14, 26, 32, 46, 49, 54, 75, 116-117, 164, 180-181, 190, 192, 260, 262, 268, 271, 274, 300, 308-309, 345
business/ economics, 2-3, 30, 116, 132, 207-208, 260, 300, 313-314, 325
critical thinking, 243
democratic/ social/ political, 2-3, 11, 15, 75, 117, 242-244, 25o, 260, 345
health and HIV/ Aids, 7-8, 11-12, 14, 21, 26, 32, 49, 116-117, 132, 164, 181, 190, 207-208, 221, 260-261, 299-300, 308, 313-315, 345, 348
logical/ mathematical, 242, 244
problem-solving, 325
Slogans,
see Declarations, goals and slogans
Tertiary education, 12, 24, 29-30, 34, 41, 48, 53, 76, 115-116, 142-143, 146, 151, 187-189, 223, 237-239, 241, 244-248, 253-257, 262-263, 285, 293-295, 301-305, 314, 329, 340, 347, 357-358, 366
Mega-universities, 116, 363
see also **Country index**
Theatre for development, 18, 207
Training of adult educators, 1, 4-6, 9-25, 29-53, 59, 67-70, 74, 92-96, 106-107, 115-122, 127, 137-140, 143, 152, 161, 165-172, 174-175, 219, 223, 225, 231, 237-238, 240-245, 251, 254, 256-258, 263-264, 269, 278-281, 293-295, 301, 318-319, 321-322, 329, 332, 345
approaches and methodologies, 5, 31, 34, 39, 53-55, 58, 67-68, 70, 117, 120, 147, 155-157, 161-164, 167-176, 179-182, 187, 193, 196, 209, 211, 263-266, 291, 295, 301
bottom-up/ inter-active/ learner centred/ participatory, 5, 13, 25, 34, 39, 44-45, 49, 55, 68, 68, 72, 72, 75-76, 130, 134, 168, 187-189, 196, 209, 211-215, 300, 319-321, 363
conventional/ traditional, 139, 167, 223, 259, 264, 319, 323, 325
direct/ face-to-face, 9, 22-23, 34, 41-43, 49, 51, 54, 67-68, 75-76, 81, 85, 124-126, 134, 147, 161, 167-168, 180, 188, 191-192, 204, 214, 222-223, 258-259, 263-265, 270, 279, 287, 307, 333, 364-365
Education, training and development (EDT) practice, 302-304, 306-307
Freirian pedagogy, 163-164

Learning by doing, 266
ODL methodologies, 34, 46-50, 53-59, 139, 161, 187, 215, 291, 307
Participatory research approach (PRA), 320
study-group model, 187, 212, 215
top-down/ trickle-down/ cascade/ pyramid, 5, 13, 34-40, 68, 124-125, 134, 170, 178, 188, 272, 321
tutors and tutorial groups, 9, 188, 207, 259-260, 265-266, 296, 363-366
centres, 165-170, 173
see also Learners and learning
delivery, 36-41, 44, 53, 57-58, 76, 92, 94, 124, 127-130, 158, 227, 249
evaluation/ measurement, 29, 36-39, 41, 51, 54, 58-59, 72, 96-97, 150, 156-157, 278-281, 286-287, 300-301, 303
needs, 12, 14-15, 19-24, 79-81, 113-114, 139-140, 148-151, 154-158, 173, 220, 227, 245-246, 271-275, 282-287, 302, 307, 318, 322-323
trainees'expectations, 149-150, 156-157
Training of Trainers (TOT)
see Training of adult educators
UNESCO, 1, 5-6, 32, 182, 184, 190, 196-197, 199, 201, 228, 243, 332, 369
Experimental World Literacy Programme, 197
Institute of Education (UIE), 1, 6, 11, 31-311
UNDP, 32, 145,147, 151, 159, 332
UNHCR programme, 204
UNICEF, 145, 147, 190
V-AID, 162-163
WHO, 32
Universities
see Tertiary education
Women and gender, 2-3, 15, 18, 31-32, 36, 47, 53-58, 67, 69, 74-76, 102-104, 106, 109, 126, 130-132, 138, 145, 164, 166-167, 173, 181, 202, 204, 206-208, 228, 278-279, 285, 293, 297, 300, 302, 313, 319, 323-325
Youth education, 6, 8, 36, 47-48, 54, 109, 126, 190, 202, 220-224, 227, 230, 236-237, 241-245, 248-249, 254, 268-269, 293-296, 323-324

Country index

BANGLADESH, 1, 15-16, 161-184
background, 161-167, 176, 182-183
case studies, 170-171, 174, 179-180, 182
educational/ training institutions
Bangladesh Open University, 183-184
Grassroot training centres (GTCs), 169-170
Institute for Non-formal Education, 184
Saturia Area Development Centre (ADC), 174
government, 162-165
Bangladesh Academy for Rural Development (BARD), 162-163
Department of Adult Education, 162
Department of Rural Development, 162
Mass Education Department, 162
Ministry of Education, 162, 164-165
National Co-operative Union of Bangladesh, 163
policies, 169-170
literacy rates, 161-162, 183
non-governmental organizations (NGOs), 163-166, 169-172, 175-176, 180-181, 183
Bangladesh Rural Advancement Committee (BRAC), 163-164, 166

Campaign for Popular Education (CAMPE), 176
Christian Commission for Development in Bangladesh (CCDB), 171
Dhaka Ahsania Mission (DAM), 171
Friends in Village Development Bangladesh (FIVDB), 164, 166, 170-171, 175
Jagarani Chakra, 171
Village Education Resource Centre (VERC), 171
PROSHIKA, 164, 166, 171-175
programmes and projects,
Asia Pacific Programme of Education for All (APPEAL), 175-176
BARD/Comilla project, 162-164, 166
Directorate of Non-formal Education (DNFE), 165, 169-171, 184
Integrated Non-formal Education Programme (INFEP), 165
Mass Education Programme (MEP), 164-165
PROSHIKA project, 164, 166, 171-175
Total Literacy Movement (TLM), 165-166
Universal Education Workers (UEWs), 172-173

BOLIVIA,
12, 18, 293-297
background, 293
educational institutions,
Bolivian University (CEUB), 294-296
Spanish University (UNED), 295-296
government, 293-294, 297
Ministry of Education, 294-296
literacy rates, 293
programmes and projects,
Alternative Education programme, 294
Proyecto Formacion de Educadores de Jovenes y Adultos a Distancia (FEJAD), 12, 18, 293, 295-297

BOTSWANA,
191, 310, 350, 353
educational institutions
Botswana Open School, 192
University of Botswana, 310

BRAZIL,
10, 12, 17, 19, 236-255
background, 236-237, 250
educational institutions, 238-239, 241, 244-248, 250-251, 254
Council of Higher Education Institutions, 239
government, 236-238, 240-241, 247, 249, 251-252
Brazilian Institute for Geography and Statistics, 237, 248-249
Brazilian National Education Plan, 242
Law for Guidelines and Bases of Education in Brazil (1996), 242
Ministry of Education, 13, 236, 238, 240-241, 247, 249, 251
National Institute for Education Studies and Research, 249
policies, 242
Secretariat of Distance Education, 247
languages, 242, 252
literacy rates, 236-238, 240, 242, 248-249, 254
non-governmental organizations (NGOs), 236, 240
Association for the Support of the Solidarity Literacy Programme, 236
Brazilian Co-operation Agency, 252
Private Sector and Civil Society, 240, 250
programmes and projects,
Digital literacy project, 248
Large Urban Centres project, 240
National Literacy programme, 19
Programa de Alfabetizacion Solidaria, 10, 12, 17, 19, 236-255
Radio School project, 247-248

CENTRAL AMERICA and the CARIBBEAN,
21, 329-343
background, 329-331
countries,
Caribbean, 329-330, 332, 335-336
Costa Rica, 329, 331-334
Dominican Republic, 333, 336-337
El Salvador, 329-331, 333, 336-337, 340
Guatemala, 329-330, 333-334, 336-337
Haiti, 330
Honduras, 329-330, 336-337
Nicaragua, 329-331, 333-337
educational/ training institutions, 329, 332-333
National Technical Institute (INATEC), 333, 340
National Training Institutions, 12, 333
National University of Distance Education (UNED), 333
government/s, 329, 333-335
policies, 329, 332
languages, 334
literacy rates, 329, 331-332
programmes and projects,
Better Educated Rural Society, 334
Micro, Small and Medium-sized Enterprises (MSMEs), 330, 332, 335-338, 340-341
Spanish Foreign Aid programme, 333
Toolbox Network, 22, 330, 335-343

DOMINICAN REPUBLIC,
see Central America and the Caribbean

EAST TIMOR,
252-254
literacy, 252-253
programmes and projects,
Community Literacy Training project, 252-253
Solidarity in Literacy programme, 252-253

EGYPT,
13, 278-281
non-governmental organizations (NGOs),
NGO Service Centre, 13, 278
Office of Civil Society Strengthening and Promotion (OLSSP), 278
Training of Trainers (TOT) for Adult Educators programme, 278-281

EL SALVADOR,
see Central America and the Caribbean

ETHIOPIA,
192

GHANA,
191, 214, 262-263, 351
Community Services Foundation, 189
literacy campaigns, 261

GUATEMALA, and HAITI,
see Central America and the Caribbean

INDIA,
1, 15-16, 29-58, 318-324
background, 29-34, 46, 48-50
case studies,
Paripurna Mahila Course, 53-54
Training of Preraks in Madhya Pradesh, 51-53
educational/ training institutions, 30-32, 34
BR Ambedkar Open University, 32, 34
Indira Gandhi National Open University (IGNOU), 32, 34, 50, 55-56, 58, 60, 319
Madras University, 48-49

M.S. Swaminathan Research Foundation (MSSRF), 319-320, 322, 324, 326
National Open School (NOS), 32, 50, 53, 60
Shivaji University, 50
University Grants Commission (UEC), 34, 41-43
government,
agencies, 30-32, 38, 48, 51
All India Radio (AIR), 46-48, 56
Central Health Education Bureau, 48
Department of Women and Child Welfare, 55
Directorate of Adult Education, 31
Directorate of Agricultural Extension and Co-operative Education, 48
District Institute of Education and Training (DIET), 31
District Resource Units (DRUs), 31
Indian Satellite Research Organization, 55
Indian Space Research Organization, 49
Institutes of People's Education, 31, 51-52
National Council of Educational Research Training (NCERT), 50, 58
National Institute of Education, Planning and Administration (NIEPA), 31
National Institute of Public Co-operation and Child Development, 50, 58
National Institute of Rural Development, 31, 58
National Literacy Mission (NLM), 31, 34, 38, 47-52, 55
policies, 29-31, 58, 60
State Resource Centres (SRCs), 31-32, 34, 37, 39, 50-52, 319-326
Worker's Education, 48
languages, 53
literacy rates, 29-30
non-governmental organizations (NGOs), 31-32
Asian Centre for Organization Research and Development (ACORD), 53-54, 59-60
Astha, 31
Bharat Gyan Vigyan Samithi, 31, 34
Bhartiya Grameen Mahila Sangh, 51, 60
Indian Adult Education Association, 31-32
Nirantar, 31
Pria, 31
programmes and projects, 2, 29-31
Centre Based Adult Education programmes, 34, 41
Commonwealth of Learning Literacy project (COLLIT), 348
Continuing Education programme, 31, 34, 38-40, 60
Farm Forums and Radio Rural, 46-47
Indore State Resource Centre Training programme, 38
INSAT programme, 49
Integrated Child Development Services (ICDS), 47-48
Mahila Samakhya, 31
Mass Programme of Functional Literacy, 31, 34, 41
National Adult Education programme, 31
Panchayat ODL Training programme, 58
Project Radio Education for Adult Literacy (PREAL), 47
Rural Functional Literacy project, 31, 46
Satellite Instructional Television Experiment (SITE), 48-49
Total Literacy Campaigns (TLCs), 31, 35-36, 38, 48

KENYA,
9, 192, 204, 206-207, 366
Women in Fishing Industry project (WIFIP), 206-211
Tropical Institute for Community Health and Development (TICH), 207, 210

MOZAMBIQUE,
252, 260
educational institutions, 253
government, 258
languages, 253
literacy rates, 253, 258
programmes and projects
Solidarity in Literacy programme, 252
Working Group on Radio and Other Media, 258

NAMIBIA,
10, 125-126, 192, 258, 262, 268-174, 367
background, 125-126, 268-269
certificate/ diploma courses
Diploma in Adult Education and Community Development, 258, 274
Higher Diploma in Adult Basic Education and Training, 277
Junior Secondary Certificate, 268
educational institutions,
Centre for External Studies, 262
Namibian College for Open Learning (NAMCOL), 10, 23, 125-126, 192, 268-269, 275-277
University of Namibia (UNAM), 22-23, 258, 262, 274-276
government, 262, 268-274
Directorate of Adult Basic Education (DABE), 271
Directorate of Habitat, Community and Early Childhood Development, 273
Directorate of Rural Water Supply, 271
Ministry of Agriculture, 262, 272-273
Ministry for Basic Education, Sport and Culture (MBESC), 268-269
Ministry of Regional and Local Government and Housing, 273
programmes and projects,
Alternative Secondary Education programme, 268
Certificate in Education for Development programme (CED), 23, 268-277
National Literacy Evaluation Report, 270-271
National Literacy Programme in Namibia (NPLN), 269, 271

NICARAGUA,
see Central America and the Caribbean

NIGERIA,
1, 11-12, 14-16, 137-159, 367
background, 137, 142-144, 147
case studies, 11, 152-158
certificate/ diploma courses
General Certificate of Education (GCE), 151
educational institutions, 142, 146-147, 151, 158
National Open Polytechnic, 142
National Open School, 142
National Open University, 142, 151
National Teacher's Institute (NTI), 142, 152
University of Abuja, 142, 151
University of Ibadan, 142, 146, 151
University of Lagos, 142, 146, 151
government, 137-140, 142-143, 146, 150-153
agencies, 137-138, 143
Bauchi State Adult and Non-Formal Education Institute, 146-147
Federal Constitution, 144
National Adult Education Centre (KANO), 146
National Centre for Adult Education (NCAE), 140-141, 145

National Commission for Nomadic Education (NCNE), 137, 151-158
policies, 11, 137, 139-140, 143-144, 155, 158
non-governmental organizations (NGOs), 138-139, 144-145, 147-148, 158
programmes and projects,
Interactive Radio Distance Learning Scheme (IRI), 14, 137, 152-157, 159
Radio for Adult Education among Pastoral Nomads, 14

PAKISTAN,
162, 204, 262
educational/ training institutions,
Alama Iqbal Open University, 262
East Pakistan Adult Education Co-operative Union, 162
East Pakistan Adult Education Guild, 163

SOUTH AFRICA,
1, 11, 13-15, 21, 106-134, 142, 223, 268, 299-314, 360
background, 106-107, 109, 111
case studies,
NAMCOL, 125-126
student encounter, 357-359
educational institutions,
Peninsula Technicon, 310, 305-306
University of Cape Town, 301-305
University of Natal, 301, 307-308
University of Pretoria, 358-359
University of South Africa (UNISA), 9-10, 16, 21, 23, 115-134, 189, 268, 270, 277, 358-376
Adult Basic Education and Training Institute (ABET), 9, 15-16, 23, 106-108, 115-134, 268, 270, 277, 371-376
government,
Adult Basic Education and Training Act (2000), 111
Department of Education, 107, 126, 301, 371
Education White Paper No.4, 107, 109
Employment of Educators Act, 109
Human Rights Commission, 15
Human Sciences Research Council (HSRC), 112-113
Independent Electoral Commission, 15, 133
National Commission for Higher Education (NCHE), 360, 362
National Education Policy Act (1996), 107, 109
National Qualifications Framework (NQF), 107-108, 110-111, 114, 301, 306, 315
policies, 106-114, 116, 306
Policy for Adult Basic Education and Training, 107
Sectoral Education and Training Authority (SETA), 304, 312, 314
Skills Development Act, 110
South African Constitution, 107-108, 112
South African Qualifications Act (1995), 107, 110
South African Qualifications Authority (SAQA), 110, 301, 306
languages, 111-112, 115, 131
literacy rates, 108, 112-114, 126, 206, 371
non-governmental organizations (NGOs), 115, 299, 304, 308-309, 313-314
Fair Share, 300
IDASA, 18, 300
programmes and projects, 111, 124
Fair Share, 300
Kruger to Canyons, 300
Learning Cape Festival (LCF), 312-315
Learning for Development, 18, 300

South African Literacy Campaign, 16, 124
South African National Literacy Initiative (SANLI), 126-131, 133-134, 371-376
UNISAABET programme, 115-117
SchoolNet South Africa, 190
Women for Peace, 300
Southern African Development Community (SADC),
see Botswana, Mozambique, Namibia, South Africa, Zambia

SUDAN,
203-204
Building Literacy with SOLO Press Project (BLSP), 18, 204-206, 208-212
Sudan Open Learning Organization (SOLO), 204-205, 210-211

TANZANIA,
1, 9, 15, 17, 67-104, 191-193, 212, 261, 282-291
background, 67, 70-72, 74, 77, 282-283, 286, 290
case studies, 81-84, 86-91
South African exiles, 91-93
Training of Local Government Councillors, 94-96, 282-291
educational/ training institutions,
Co-operative College Moshi, 70, 73, 75-77
Correspondence Education Centre (CEC), 76
Field Extension Department (FED), 76
Institute for Adult Education (IAE), 70-72, 77, 192
National Correspondence Institution (NCI), 74, 76-77, 192
Open University of Tanzania (OUT), 74, 76, 96
University of Dar es Salaam, 76
government,
agencies, 67, 70-72, 75-80, 83, 86, 282-289
Basic Education Master Plan (BCMP), 72
Civil Service Reform programme, 282
Education Act No.17 (1992), 74
Education and Training Policy (1995), 73
Ministry of Education and Culture (MOEC), 77, 103
Ministry of Natural Resources and Tourism (MNRT), 96
National Examinations Council of Tanzania (NECTA), 104
policies, 67, 70, 72-73, 76-79, 101, 103, 282-284, 288-289
Regional Local Government Officers (RLGOs), 288
languages, 102
literacy rates, 71, 285, 290
non-governmental organizations (NGOs), 70, 74-79, 97
Centre for Educational Development in Health (CEDHA), 75
INADES-Formation Tanzania (IFTZ), 74-75
Southern African Extension Unit (SAEU), 75, 91-96, 282-284, 288, 290-291
programmes and projects, 83-84
Action Research Training (ART), 193
Adult Education/ Literacy Expansion programme, 91-93
Health through Sanitation and Water (HESAWA), 75
Local Government Councillors Distance Education project, 23, 94-96, 282-285
Radio Study Group Campaigns on Health Education, 261
South African Exiles programme, 91-93

Training Integrated in Peasants' Actions, Challenges and Organizations (TIPALO), 193

ZAMBIA,
191-192, 262, 318, 345-347, 350-351
educational institutions,
University of Zambia, 348
government,
policies, 195
Zambia National Broadcasting Corporation (ZNBC), 194-195, 351
languages, 194
programmes and projects,
Commonwealth of Learning Literacy project (COLLIT), 21, 348-349, 351
Community-based Non-formal Education for Rural People (CERP), 21, 348-349, 351
Radio Farm Forums (RFF) 192, 194-195, 212-213, 262